One Blood

One

Spencie Love

with a Foreword by John Hope Franklin

The

University

of North

Carolina

Press

Chapel Hill

&

London

Blood

- The Death and
- Resurrection of
- Charles R. Drew

The publication of this volume was aided by a generous grant
from the Z. Smith Reynolds Foundation.
The paper in this book meets the guidelines for permanence and
durability of the Committee on Production Guidelines for Book
Longevity of the Council on Library Resources.

Library of Congress Cataloging-in-Publication Data
Love, Spencie, 1949–
One blood : the death and resurrection of Charles R. Drew / by
Spencie Love, with a foreword by John Hope Franklin.
p.   cm.
Includes bibliographical references and index.
ISBN 0-8078-2250-7 (cloth : alk. paper)
1. Drew, Charles Richard, 1904–1950 — Death and burial.   2. Drew,
Charles Richard, 1904–1950 — Legends.   3. Discrimination in medical
care — United States — History — 20th century.   4. Race relations —
Folklore.   5. United States — Race relations — History — 20th century.
I. Title.
RD27.35.D74L68   1996
617'.092 — dc20   95-35720
[B]   CIP

00 99 98 97 96   5 4 3 2 1

FOR GARRETT, DANIEL, & MARGARET

Love

made seasonless

above all change, betrayals of falling suns

and in memory of

James Spencer Love (1896–1962)

Herman Hunter Murchison (1904–1985)

Joseph Linwood Drew (1909–1991)

Waddell Avery (1928–1993)

now that the dark earth

enfolds your body

and the bright sky

has swallowed your spirit

I take you to my heart for all time

God that made the world, and all things therein,

seeing that he is Lord of heaven and earth, dwelleth

not in temples made with hands; Neither is worshipped

with men's hands, as though he needed any thing, seeing

he giveth to all life, and breath, and all things; And hath

made of one blood all nations of men for to dwell on all

the face of the earth, and hath determined the times

before appointed, and the bounds of their habitation;

That they should seek the Lord, if haply they might feel

after him, and find him, though he be not far from every

one of us: For in him we live, and move, and have our

being; as certain also of your own poets have said, For

we are also his offspring.

—Acts 17:24–28

As you know, there is no scientific basis for the

separation of the bloods of different races except on

the basis of the individual blood types or groups.

—Charles R. Drew, 1942

Contents

Illustrations can be found on pages xxii–xxiii, 127–38, and 233–44.

Acknowledgments

The families of Charles R. Drew and Maltheus R. Avery were essential to this work, and they remain its most inspiring source. I am deeply grateful to them for the time they spent with me and for the warmth and practical support they extended to me throughout this undertaking. When Joseph ("Joe") Drew drove me around his and his brother's childhood haunts in Washington, D.C., one hot summer day, he not only brought to life a bygone era, but his quiet dignity, kindliness, and gentle humor also made me feel that I had gotten to know a bit just what "Charlie" was like in person. Although Lenore Drew was suffering from Alzheimer's disease when I interviewed her, she retained the poise and graciousness that Drew was so drawn to, and her memories of him were vivid and intact. Nora Drew Gregory and Eva Drew Pennington each gave me a sister's perspective on Drew, and they both extended such genuine, enthusiastic welcomes to me and my efforts that I felt a true connection to the whole Drew clan. As I struggled to pull photographs together before publication, Nora Gregory stepped in to help and made all the difference. Her extra work, her determination, and her love meant a great deal to me. It has also been a great pleasure to begin to get to know each of Charles Drew's children — Bebe, Sylvia, Charlene, and Charles Jr. I have had the opportunity to share with the Drew family a number of special occasions honoring Drew, and both the events themselves and this extended contact with family members deepened my appreciation for the fine man Drew was.

I first met Waddell and Hilda Avery on another summer day at their home in Alexandria, Virginia, and then Parnell Avery a few weeks later, at an Avery family wedding in Monroe, North Carolina. Little did I imagine before those meetings the depth of the bond we would forge. Waddell and Parnell not only told me their brother Sonny's story; they also taught me a great deal about the whole world of segregation and segregated medical care. Over a period of several years, they also showed me just what it meant to be adopted into the Avery clan. We have now shared funerals, graduations, memorial services, history seminars, historical conferences, barbecues, dinner parties, and a number of other celebrations: I have gotten to know not only Waddell, Parnell, and Hilda but also many other family members, including Sonny's two beautiful daughters, Malthaus and Regina, and Waddell and Hilda's children, Pamela, Bryan Waddell, and Paula. To my great regret, Waddell Avery died unexpectedly in the fall of 1993; nonetheless, I feel sure he is watching over the completion of this project.

I am also very grateful to the many other people whom I interviewed, who so openly shared with me the pains, perplexities, and pleasures embedded in their personal history.

I owe a special debt to John Hope Franklin. He strengthened my conviction at the beginning of the project that it was possible. He supported, inspired, and cheered me throughout its long labor. At the end of the project, he made me know at a deep level that it was worthwhile. I also owe a special debt to Gilberta Mitchell, another true friend and an inspiration. By inviting me to be a member of the Charles Drew Memorial Marker Steering Committee in Alamance County, she demonstrated to me over a period of years just how one creates and sustains, through cooperative effort, a lasting memorial to carefully chosen ideals. My fellow committee members became important and valued companions on the journey this book launched me on: they were John W. Patterson, David Maynard, Hilliard Parker, Roy D. Moore, and Robert Earl — all Omega brothers, as Drew was — and also Pat Bailey, Marvin E. Yount Jr., and Charles E. Kernodle Jr. Working together as a team on the Drew Memorial Marker and the ceremony for its unveiling, we felt Drew's legacy live on.

Larry Goodwyn, my adviser, deserves special mention. He consistently encouraged me to think big and thereby kept before me the larger implications of this project. I am especially grateful to him for his steady support of me as an individual with an approach and timetable of my own. This required a certain irreverence toward academia's more petty demands, and a great deal of courage, vision, and understanding on his part, all qualities I continue to associate with him.

I wish to give special thanks to the staff of the Moorland-Spingarn Research Center at Howard University, whose expert and friendly assistance helped make my sojourn there, working with the Charles R. Drew Papers, enjoyable and fulfilling. In particular I want to thank Esme Bhan, Paul Coates, Karen Jefferson, and Donna Wells. The staff members at Duke University's Perkins Library deserve mention as well: over a period of years, I made use of every department of the library for this project, and I unfailingly received enthusiastic and highly competent help. At the revision stage, I found the staff at the University of Oregon Library both kind and efficient, as they helped me locate and pull together critical sources from around the country. I also want to thank the staff at the American Red Cross National Headquarters for sharing with me their large active file on Charles Drew.

A number of fellow historians read the manuscript at critical stages and gave valuable advice. Bill Chafe helped launch me on the project in his Oral History Research Seminar at Duke University. George Tindall anchored me firmly in the southern historical tradition with his well-known course on southern history. Jacquelyn Hall, a pioneer in oral history methodology, gave me good advice at several important junctures. Another important early reader of the manuscript was John Richards, who, by introducing me to a number of classic works of historical literature, gave me a glimpse of what was possible. Ray Gavins pushed me to refine my thinking at an important early stage. At a later point, Jack Cell read the entire manuscript and gave excellent advice. At a still later stage, Iris Tillman Hill, director of Duke University's Center for Documentary Studies, gave the manuscript a very careful reading and offered expert editorial commentary. Elizabeth Sifton, an editor at Knopf, also gave the book a thorough reading and encouraged me greatly with her enthusiastic response to it. Fellow historians Barbara Steinson and Sara Wilkerson cheered me on.

A number of individuals offered timely assistance that expedited completion of various stages of the manuscript. Dee Reid read an early rough draft and helped me see it as a structural whole. Henry Christner, whose editorial judgment I have valued for many years, read the manuscript in its entirety at a critical juncture and helped me realized that it was indeed done. Ron Maner provided expert advice on the handling of footnotes. Duke University medical historian Jim Gifford kindly helped me locate critical Duke medical records. Tom Clark provided special computer expertise to speed the preparation of the bibliography. Mary Ellen O'Shields supplied highly skilled computer assistance and unfailing good humor.

When I met Barbara Hanrahan at the University of North Carolina Press and discussed the book with her, I knew I had found the editor I had been looking for. I appreciated not only her highly professional, prompt, and insightful responses throughout the publication process but also her confidence in the book. I owe a great deal to both Todd

Savitt and Charles Wynes, my two academic readers. They both were unusually generous and supportive in their responses to *One Blood*; the many suggestions they offered were invaluable. Christi Stanforth, my copyeditor, was a true pleasure to work with, as was Rich Hendel, the book designer.

An important episode in this decade-long project was when Alfred A. Moss Jr. read the manuscript and soon afterward agreed to introduce me as the Letitia Woods Brown Memorial Lecturer at the annual Washington, D.C., Historical Studies Conference. A man who excels at forging connections, Al has been a wonderful friend. Katherine Fulton, a journalist friend with a striking dedication to social justice, helped me on a number of occasions. Allister and Sue Sparks, who are now enjoying the results of many years of resisting South Africa's oppressive white supremacist government, were important spiritual companions through much of this journey.

Other important readers and companions, who offered meaningful friendship and wise counsel in the final stages of publication, were Sharon Schuman, Marci Gordon, Quintard Taylor, Sandi Morgen, Alexis Halmy, Robin Morris Collin, and Dennis Greene. All of them helped immeasurably in bridging the gap between my old life and my new life after a cross-country move.

I feel an especially deep gratitude toward Cathy Abernathy, who shared much of this journey with me as only a true friend and historian possibly could. Her commitment to seeing the complexity of the truth was and still is an inspiration. Her loving support and her continuing involvement in the project have meant a great deal to me. Jane Levey, another dear friend and dedicated fellow historian, supported me in both profound and practical ways throughout the project, enormously assisting my research efforts in Washington, D.C., enabling me to make an important public presentation of my work there, locating valuable photographs, asking tough and useful questions about my work along the way and generally being an understanding ally because of her own struggle to balance the two jobs of being a historian and mother. Julia McLaughlin, a gifted psychologist friend, gave me her wonderfully sensitive feedback and encouragement at various stages of the writing. Laura Murphy, a fine artist and friend, always supported the quest for inner truth, coherence, and wholeness that this project ultimately came to represent to me. My beloved friend Butler-Brayne Thornton Robinson Franklin, who is now ninety-seven years old, first showed me that the particular world that surrounds each of us largely embodies what each of us has the power to imagine. She and her world, Fall Hill, nurtured and sustained me throughout this project, as did Bess and Fred Turk.

One Blood would have been unthinkable without the involvement of my family. I feel a special gratitude toward my husband, Garrett, whose powerful, creative spirit sets off sparks and ignites ideas wherever he goes. An avid newspaper reader, he happened upon the first Charles Drew story and brought it to my attention, thereby unwittingly launching me on *One Blood*. He regretted this discovery from time to time, when he felt the book consumed too much of my energy and attention. Nonetheless, throughout, he understood and affirmed the importance of what I was doing; he listened to me as I struggled with the project, and he unfailingly offered extremely insightful suggestions. A. C. Epps's and Rozanne Epps's support, which has been expressed in so many ways, was also crucial, and I am deeply grateful to them for their perseverance, faith, general exuberance, and unfailing love. A. C.'s deep interest in history and Rozanne's enthusiasm and talent for writing and editing made them wonderful intellectual companions. Essential in a different way were my children, Maggie and Dan, who have grown quite a bit older in the years of this project and who now sometimes like to be called Margaret and Daniel. They are both remarkable individuals who sustained and cheered me on a daily basis. Maggie inspired me with her sunny, playful imagination, her endless inventiveness, her unique sense of humor, her deep caring and creativity, her courage, and her determination to make things happen in the world. Daniel's unusual thirst for and appreciation of knowledge quietly supported me throughout this project, as did his wit, his mischievous ideas, his hugs, and his generous, wise spirit; he has also become an expert computer consultant whom I count on for assistance.

Finally, I owe a debt of gratitude to a certain small circle whose love has long sustained me: my parents, James Spencer Love and Martha Eskridge Love; my brothers, Charles Eskridge Love and Martin Eskridge Love; and my sister, Lela Porter Love. As no one else, my siblings share my longing to resurrect the magic and power of the past. In the circle also are my friends Clarence Tyson, Mamie Tyson, and Ethel Pauline Earnhardt, and, last but not least, my buddy Herman Hunter Murchison. It was Hunter who told me the essential stories and who listened with his whole heart. Although he died soon after I started this project, he accompanied and guided me through every step of it, and he is very much alive in it.

Foreword

I was well acquainted with Charles Drew and admired him for his numerous achievements as a physician and surgeon. When he died in April 1950, I mourned his death with countless others. I had no reason to question the circumstances of his tragic death in an automobile accident when it was reported in the press. The account seemed sufficiently normal. Nor did I have reason to question the subsequent account that he died because he was refused treatment at the Alamance County Hospital, in Burlington, North Carolina. By 1950 I had learned of so many unhappy experiences of African Americans in railroad cars, hotels, parks, and, yes, hospitals that it never occurred to me that Drew's alleged mistreatment during his final hours was out of the ordinary. When I was a freshman at Fisk University in 1931, our dean of women, Juliette Derricotte, was injured in an auto accident along with several students and subsequently died after being refused treatment at a small hospital in Dalton, Georgia. One of my friends, T. Edward Davis, had been traveling with Miss Derricotte, and the whole student body and faculty heard of the tragedy within hours after it happened.

In retrospect, I cannot determine why I did not write the legendary account of Drew's death in the 1956 revision of my general history of the African Americans, *From Slavery to Freedom.* Perhaps it was because there were so many other aspects of the record of the African American experience to set straight. Perhaps it was because I was not absolutely certain in my own mind whether or not the "facts" surrounding Drew's death were indisputable. Perhaps it was because I simply did not get around to giving this relatively recent event the attention that it deserved. In any case, it was not until Stan Swofford of the *Greensboro Daily News* interviewed me in 1982 and told me that a reliable witness had a quite different version of the tragedy that I confronted the fact that for more than thirty years the true circumstances of Drew's death had been distorted beyond recognition.

Subsequent to the appearance of Swofford's story about Drew's death, Spencie Love, a Duke University graduate student in my colloquium on the history of the South, came to my office and said that she wanted to dig more deeply into what we began to call "the Drew legend." It was obvious by this time that the legend had developed and spread to the point that it had a life of its own. Ironies as well as distortions abounded in the legend: first, the man who was responsible for developing the blood bank was denied access to it. Second, a great physician was turned away from a hospital that was the beneficiary of his work. Third, a man whose skin was as light as most white men's was turned away because he was black! I encouraged Spencie to explore the problem in all of its dimensions and, particularly, to examine the reasons why such a legend could thrive as it did in the years since Drew's death.

With energy, enthusiasm, and remarkable creativity and insight, Spencie Love has written a work that goes far beyond examining in detail how Drew died and how the legend grew. She has tried to penetrate through the many layers of mistrust, fear, anger, and confusion that have evolved between the races in American history and elucidate the larger human truths in that history. In the process, she has written an important commentary on race relations in the closing years of the twentieth century. She has not only applied the coup de grace to a legend; she has also provided excellent and credible reasons why that legend has flourished for such a long time. She has demonstrated that the legend has meaning and should not be ignored. Drew was not denied hospital care, but numerous other African Americans were. That is what nurtured the legend and underscored the way in which a mindless racism stood at the hospital door and barred the entry of American Americans who desperately needed hospital care.

In pursuing the Drew legend, and in describing a number of white supremacist myths that affected Drew's life, Spencie Love has demonstrated the pernicious effect that racially inspired mythology has long had in obscuring truth and reality. Her pursuit has done much, moreover, to emphasize the general value of working in historical legend and folklore, where so many of the misunderstandings and misconceptions regarding race in America lie buried. In her study, oral interviews, however, not only reveal popular conceptions of history, some of them erroneous; combined with traditional written documentation, they prove invaluable in uncovering the truth. Oral history thus is shown to be a vitally useful methodology. Similar research efforts may or may not be as rewarding or successful as this one, but they are important in the ongoing attempt to understand the vexatious problem of race in America, a problem as pivotal to America's future now as it has been at any other time in our history.

John Hope Franklin
Durham, North Carolina

One Blood

Charles Richard Drew
(Courtesy of the Moorland-Spingarn Research Center, Howard University)

Maltheus Reeves Avery
(Courtesy of Waddell Avery and Malthaus Avery Blake)

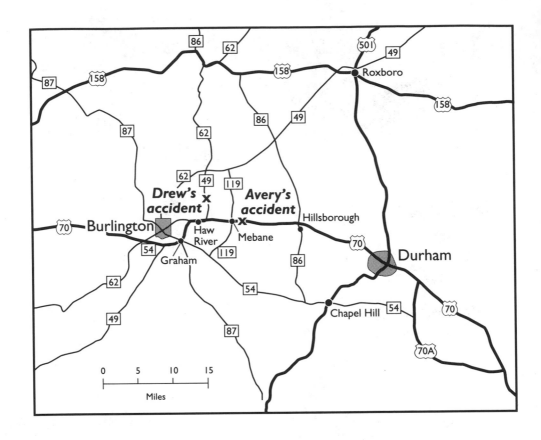

Introduction:
A Tragedy
Compounded
by a Myth

On 1 April 1950, Charles Richard Drew, a forty-five-year-old surgeon and medical professor from Howard University, died after an auto accident in rural Alamance County, North Carolina. Drew, a highly respected member of Washington, D.C.'s middle-class black community, was widely known in medical circles, nationally and internationally, for his pioneering scientific research in blood plasma and blood banking at the beginning of World War II. He had been driving all night from Washington with three other black doctors to a medical conference in Tuskegee, Alabama.

Within hours, a rumor about the accident began to travel: Drew had bled to death after a local hospital refused to treat him because he was black. Over a period of years, the story became a full-fledged historical legend, dramatizing the bitter irony embedded in black history. In 1964, at the height of the civil rights movement, Whitney Young wrote a column about segregated medical care that employed the Drew legend as a dramatic example of mistreatment.[1] Soon the legend was printed in other newspapers, in magazines, and in history books. It was featured on television shows: the man who had "discovered" blood plasma and had saved countless lives by helping set up the World War II blood collection program had been refused blood. The story is still widely believed today. Drew has become a popular black folk hero, known best in black schools, churches, and communities and through black-owned media but also known in mainstream popular culture.

A number of juvenile and popular biographies have been written about Drew;[2] newspaper and magazine articles about him surface regularly; and the first scholarly biography, Charles E. Wynes's *Charles Richard Drew: The Man and the Myth*, was published in 1988. Wynes's book offers an accurate, concise, highly readable account of Drew's life. While *One Blood* is in part another biographical study of Drew, it is also something different. Drew's character and life story have proven to be unusually susceptible to legends, myths, and misunderstandings. In fact, there is not one Drew legend; there are several. *One Blood* seeks to illuminate what is behind the profound legend-making impulse in those who are confronted with the "facts" of Drew's story. In the process, the book offers an exploration of the relation between myth, legend, and history, and especially of the ways these elements are intertwined in the American, southern, and African American historical traditions. By focusing on a specific set of historical incidents, the book attempts to provide a small circle of lighted terrain in which one can usefully contemplate such large — and at times overwhelming — issues as: to what extent is all history, whether scholarly or "popular," an exercise in myth and legend-making? How much have America's cultural and historical traditions been shaped by white supremacist myths and revisionist black legends, both often masquerading as hidden but nonetheless powerful assumptions? What would it mean to write a history of America that is truly interracial in spirit, substance, and scope? Finally, how can each of us best communicate across the gulfs of history, culture, and daily experience that divide us? This book offers no conclusive answers, but I hope its findings will jolt a few minds from simplistic or narrowly academic views about "truth," as they did mine. It was humbling to realize the extent of the darkness we all share, inhabit, and struggle so hard to see each other clearly in.

I first came across a story about Charles Drew in 1982 when I encountered it in a North Carolina newspaper. This story described the Drew saga as a "tragedy compounded by a myth" and said the legend that he had bled to death was not true.[3] Another black doctor who had been an eyewitness at Drew's death in 1950 had just come forth, thirty-two years later, to set the record straight. This doctor — C. Mason Quick of Fayetteville, North Carolina — said he had been trying to debunk the Drew legend ever since he had first heard it, some five years after Drew's death. Despite his efforts, the rumor kept cropping up at black social gatherings, at medical conferences, even among Drew's family members. Drew's own daughter, Charlene Drew Jarvis, who had been a child at the time of his death, still had doubts about the care her father had received, the story reported.[4]

I was intrigued. I had long been aware of the importance of stories as the shapers of my own and other people's sense of history. I had encountered the institution of segregation personally as a child and lived within its constraints and taboos. Although I had grown up during the civil rights movement and had lived and worked with many white and black people caught in the turmoil of social change, there was still a great deal I didn't understand about the South's interracial heritage.

I went to graduate school with the desire to understand American and southern history in a more rigorous way, hoping I would thus anchor the stories I had heard all my life in a larger framework. I was not disappointed. Not only did Duke have an excellent history department and a great library; in addition, Larry Goodwyn and Bill Chafe had launched the Duke Oral History Program there in the 1970s, encouraging research into minority history and the reinvigoration of American history with the stories of the many individuals and groups who had been neglected in traditional texts. The Drew story fit well into this whole approach. It not only opened a window onto the historical, structural underpinnings of segregation; it also allowed insight into ordinary people's versions of history, their memories, and the whole process of passing down a usable past.

I was drawn to the Drew saga, then, in a multitude of ways. Charles Drew himself, his intense face staring out from a black-and-white photograph in the newspaper story, seemed an unusual and intriguing man. He projected an idealism and a seriousness of purpose that transcended his society's somewhat stereotypical labeling of him as a "success." The stories that surrounded him made up a puzzle with missing pieces, and I was attracted to the elusiveness of the challenge it posed. There was conflicting evidence about the ultimate shape of the puzzle and, consequently, considerable anger and misunderstanding between those who held different views about it.

All of these circumstances should have indicated to me the daunting nature of the assignment I was taking on. Nonetheless, I ventured blithely into the grand hall of mirrors surrounding Charles Drew's life and death. My experience as an investigative reporter lent me an ill-founded confidence that I could solve the mystery in a relatively straightforward manner. I at first believed that I could discern "the truth" by simply gathering "the facts." I speculated that although Drew might have been treated at the hospital, he also might have been subjected to some form of inappropriate treatment there on the day he died.

Thus my journey took me first to the people who had been on the scene at Charles Drew's accident and death. My first interview, which took place on a crisp autumn day, was with the photographer from Durham's black newspaper who had taken a picture of Drew's wrecked car, C. R. "Chip" Stanback.[5] I seemed to have struck evidential gold. This man confirmed my original hypothesis by telling me that although he knew Drew had been treated at Alamance General Hospital in Burlington, he suspected that Drew had been taken to another hospital first and been refused treatment there.

But my belief that I had discovered the missing piece of the puzzle on my very first interview proved to be wrong. After more interviews with the black doctors who had been traveling with Drew and the white doctors who had treated him, I slowly came to the conclusion that the Drew legend had no basis in the facts of his death. It became clear that Drew had been promptly taken to one hospital and appropriately treated there by three white surgeons. He had died in the emergency room.

This conclusion might have been the end of my journey had I been solely interested in debunking the Drew legend. But that was not my aim. As this study demonstrates, there are different kinds of historical truth, and the history that people pass on orally—a group's legends—is an important clue not only to how they feel and think about their past but also to the very substance of that past. As Allan Nevins elegantly stated, "On the granite of hard fact grows the moss of legend, and even pure myth contains its grains of stony reality. . . . Not even American historians can ignore legends."[6]

The Drew legend is not literally true, but it reveals a large truth at the heart of black culture: it demonstrates the continuing psychological trauma of segregation and racism in American life. The legend's existence highlights the fact that the history many people live is not what they have learned in history books but what they have experienced themselves and what they thus pass down as folklore, art, music, and other forms of cultural expression. This "other history" that shapes ordinary people's lives — and that to a great degree has yet to be recorded — forms the core of this study.

I came to this work as a journalist, knowing the value of personal interviews mainly as sources of factual information that could not be found in written documents. I completed this book as a professionally trained historian with a far deeper and more complex understanding of the historical raw material that emerges from talking with individual people about their lives and delving into their historical memories. I came to know what I only intuited at the outset — that people's memories and beliefs about the past, even when incomplete and inaccurate in terms of details, are not only personally meaningful but also of vital historical importance.[7] As its research unfolded, *One Blood* revealed several kinds of importance indelibly embedded in common memories, shared within a group of people. First and most obvious is the fact that people's beliefs constitute a powerful force in history.[8] A second, related importance is that people's beliefs — even when judged faulty and inaccurate by objective standards — often point the way to aspects of their history that have been overlooked by traditional historians. Finally, most pertinent to this work was my gradual discovery of a third kind of importance, potentially more radical in its impact than the previous two: a group's shared memories, frequently expressed in the form of historical legends, may often be inaccurate as to surface details, but within them are important truths about that group's historical experiences. Almost as a secret coded language does, such legends offer the hidden clues to long-buried and traumatic historical experiences.[9]

Out of necessity, minority groups in America, as in other cultures,[10] have long passed their history down through oral traditions. As English historian Paul Thompson notes, "The strongest communal memories are those of beleaguered out-groups."[11] For much of the twentieth century the custom of many professional historians has been to dismiss oral lore as a collection of insignificant falsehoods — a kind of child's play; however, this custom is changing as historians come to understand better the great degree to which American history, like other national histories, has largely been shaped — and severely limited in its scope — by the elite groups who wield the most power in American society.[12]

A bracing corrective to traditional American history, elucidating issues of power and powerlessness tied to class, gender, race, ethnicity, and age, has been the "new social history" of recent years, inspired primarily by the civil rights movement and the women's movement of the late 1960s and 1970s. Historians' use of new research methods has constituted an integral part of this process. Since the powerless leave behind few written documents, historians seeking to be more inclusive have turned to the use of oral interviews and to the examination of cultural heritage — including folklore, music, and material objects — to bring the past to light.[13] As a result, our historical heritage is becoming more democratic, more egalitarian, and, finally, more human. New groups of people are becoming visible. Aspects of life that were formerly considered nonhistorical or inaccessible — family life, sexuality, and women's domestic sphere, to name a few — are now coming into view, along with the rich experiences of minority group members. It is an exciting time.

As an oral historian, I am aware that anyone concerned with recording the "truth" must proceed with great caution when using oral materials as valid historical evidence — especially when no corroborating written documents are available. But I come away from this project with a deep conviction of the importance of recording oral stories as a means of recovering lost, deeply buried pieces of our collective past. Recorders of this past will greatly expand the house of American history, opening new doors onto our increasingly complex and interrelated human story, by listening carefully to the tales, beliefs, and memories of all of America's peoples. Whole new wings will be constructed, new levels added on.

I believe that *One Blood*, in relation to this metaphor, represents a new wing that is soundly constructed and well illuminated, fashioned as it is by African American storytellers from the foundation of their own personal experiences. Through them the Drew legend is revealed as a different kind of historical truth, one of truly mythic proportions. The legend bears witness to the historical reality of white racism and to its brutal results. The legend's message is that even if you are a Charles Drew, a great man by any standard, you will not be treated appropriately if you are black in twentieth-century America. The legend speaks for the many undocumented experiences of black Americans whose medical treatment was delayed or denied because of white racism. With succinct elegance the Drew legend reveals the impact of segregated medical care and the hypocrisy of "separate but equal."

This study both traces the origin and evolution of the Drew legend and maps out the historical terrain that accounts for its genesis and growth. The work is divided into three parts. Part 1 lays out both the circumstances surrounding Drew's death and the almost fifty-year history of the legend. The first chapter documents what actually happened the day Drew died. The second chapter traces the Drew story from its early appearance as a rumor within hours after Drew died to its evolution during the 1950s and early 1960s as a persistent story with a definite shape. The third chapter shows how the rumor ultimately became part of the intricate fabric of black folklore, evolving into a full-fledged historical legend during the era of the civil rights movement. The chapter documents the further transformation of the Drew legend as it appeared in a variety of guises in newspaper and magazine stories, history and reference books, television shows, and memorials and rites honoring Charles Drew. The chapter also delineates the attempts to debunk the legend from the mid-1970s on. The Drew legend has persisted despite these attempts and is embedded in a rich cultural matrix indeed, shaped by nearly four hundred years of black historical experience.

Part 2 explores aspects of Drew's life as well as specific events of the segregation era that laid the historical foundation for the Drew legend. Drew in many ways epitomized Joseph Campbell's definition of a hero, thus making him a fitting protagonist of a legendary story. The specific circumstances and archetypal patterns in Drew's life that laid the foundation for the "refusal of treatment" part of the legend gained their power from the conjunction of Drew's pioneering work with blood plasma and the American Red Cross's subsequent World War II policies of excluding black donors from the blood program and later of segregating the blood of black and white donors. Since Drew was a black man, his own blood would have been refused (or later segregated). Aware that these policies were based on race prejudice, Drew protested them and thus entered the public limelight. Black newspapers, especially, reported his ironic fate throughout the 1940s, thereby laying the foundation for the later legend.

Drew himself withdrew from the national scene in 1941 and returned to the Howard University Medical School. There, in his role as chief of the department of surgery and head surgeon at Freedmen's Hospital, he emerged as a distinct kind of black leader — dimensions of his life that were crucial to his later enshrinement as an African American cultural icon. A final chapter in this part of the book explores in greater depth the complex mythology surrounding blood and race in American society that was at play during the war years — focusing on the white racist mythology, constructed in part by white doctors and scientists, behind the Red Cross blood policies. It describes further legends that sprang up around Drew as a result of his work with blood and of his stance against segregated blood, and the "counter-legends" that developed in response to them.

Part 3 points to the traumatic impact of racism and racist medical care on black Americans as the critical bedrock on which the Drew legend was built. A long chapter details the grim saga of a young man, Maltheus Reeves Avery, who actually suffered the fate that the legend attributes to Charles Drew, and the impact of Avery's death on his family over the ensuing years. The circumstances surrounding Avery's death illuminate the precise function of the legend in keeping a long-buried historical event alive.

As this outline suggests, my journey was long, convoluted, and full of surprises. The pieces of the puzzle slowly appeared, but they were bigger and more jagged than I expected, and they fit together in ways I could not have imagined when I began. History, I discovered, is not an impersonal body of scientific fact; it is not something "out there" that any of us can, in the manner of good investigative reporters, go "dig up" and display as "the truth." History is inescapably personal and culture-bound. I inevitably came to appreciate on a deeper level the power of stories and their mythic content. I encountered many individuals' different versions of American history, and in the process, I discovered the gulf that remains between the traditions of southern white history and southern African American history, long after the region's lunch counters and water fountains have been integrated.

There is no history, no matter how scholarly or seemingly "factual," that is not in the end simply someone's story. Robert Penn Warren captured the essence of this reality when he wrote, "Historical sense and poetic sense should not, in the end, be contradictory, for if poetry is the little myth we make, history is the big myth we live, and in our living constantly remake."[14]

The assertion that history is always "myth" might seem to be an undermining statement at the beginning of a work of history. Yet it need not be. In this study myth is shown to be not a kind of untruth but rather a sign of how a given group of people survive culturally. Mythmaking is the most profoundly human activity, for the capacity for story-telling is almost the definition of what it is to be human. If history is more than a body of mere "facts," its possibilities are much greater.

The lives we live are shaped by myths, legends, and stories of compelling power. Many were fashioned or came into being long before we were born, and some, transmitted to us as history, are crippling. From these we must free ourselves.

Ultimately, history is not a trap from which there is no exit. We are not only the recipients of myths; we are also mythmakers. History, though in one sense dead, always waits to be reborn. This circumstance does not diminish the essential seriousness of history as a pursuit. On the contrary, it contains the very essence of what makes us human, for at stake is no less a thing than human freedom.

I

Death and Resurrection

When our days become dreary with low-hovering

clouds of despair, and when our nights become darker

than a thousand midnights, let us remember that there

is a creative force in this universe, working to pull down

the gigantic mountains of evil, a power that is able to make

a way out of no way and transform dark yesterdays into

bright tomorrows. Let us realize the arc of the moral

universe is long but it bends toward justice.

— Martin Luther King, Jr.

Charlie Drew Is Dead

It was Friday, 31 March 1950. The three-day Cherry Blossom Festival had started that morning in Washington, D.C. At a gaudy ceremony at the Shoreham Hotel, the wheel of fortune had been spun, and one of fifty-one white maidens was selected to be the Cherry Blossom Queen. Although the trees had put forth buds in January, they were not blooming yet. It had been a cool spring.[1]

That same day, in a Washington courtroom, the practice of segregating black Americans was under siege. As a crowd of two hundred listened, two lawyers debated the validity of the District of Columbia's 1872 and 1873 laws against discrimination and segregation.[2] A restaurant on Fourteenth Street, Thompson's, had refused to serve three prominent "well-behaved Negroes" earlier that year; the most distinguished of these three was Mary Church Terrell, then eighty-six years old and an international leader in the women's rights movement.[3] The three black citizens — along with one white citizen — had gone to the segregated restaurant as members of a group that was determined to get the district to reexamine and reinstate the "lost" laws against discrimination, which had never been removed from the books but were never enforced. The group, called the Coordinating Committee for the Enforcement of the D.C. Anti-Discrimination Laws, had been formed in 1949, with Terrell as its chairman.

On that March day in court the city prosecutor argued that the laws forbidding segregation of the races still stood and that the district had the same power as any state to enact its own laws. The restaurant's attorney countered that the laws were obsolete because they had been in disuse for seventy-eight years. The prosecutor, who had been arguing in calm, legalistic terms, exploded when the other attorney suggested that rioting could occur if segregation were ended. He retorted angrily, Was it reasonable to expect Negro lawyers to travel to Union Station or National Airport for lunch when they had cases to argue?[4]

In the nation's capital and in the South as a whole, segregation was largely intact in 1950, as it had been for over half a century. In Washington, in all the former Confederate states, and in most communities throughout the country, black and white Americans lived in mostly separate — and unequal — worlds. The major assaults on the system of legal segregation — prevalent throughout the southern states — were soon to be launched, but in 1950, few people, black or white, could imagine that the system would be largely dismantled in the next fifteen years as a result of the civil rights movement.

Charles Drew had grown up and lived his whole life in a segregated society. In 1950, as the forty-five-year-old chairman of Howard University Medical School's surgery department and the chief surgeon at Freedmen's Hospital, the district's only black hospital, Drew lived and worked in a mostly black world.[5] This week, typically busy and intense, ended for Drew well after midnight, when he left a student council banquet at which he was a featured speaker. But his day was not over even then. Drew and another Howard medical professor, Samuel Bullock, along with two young surgery interns, Walter R. Johnson and John R. Ford, were planning to drive south that night, through Richmond, Virginia, and Greensboro, North Carolina, to Atlanta, on one leg of their journey to an annual, mostly black medical conference in Tuskegee, Alabama.[6]

Drew's wife, Lenore, aware of how hard he pushed himself, had urged him to fly down the next morning instead.[7] His sister, Nora Drew Gregory, an elementary school teacher in Washington and the last family member to speak with him before he set off, also asked, "Aren't you tired?" Drew said no.[8]

Drew ran by an inner clock: as a trained athlete who had spent his youth ignoring physical pain, he habitually disregarded his own exhaustion. Jack White, a surgeon who trained under Drew in the 1940s and remained a close friend, said, "He walked on his toes; he never gave in to physical discomfort, or the need for sleep. It was probably the reason for his death."[9] Still possessed with an athlete's sense of competitive sport, Drew felt himself to be involved in a much bigger game now. For almost a decade, since his completion of a surgical residency at Columbia University Medical School, he had been concerned with the training of young black surgeons for a rigidly segregated society in which there were not enough black doctors, much less black surgeons, to go around.[10] The two interns could not afford to fly, and Drew wanted them to be able to participate. Also, they were both to be residents at John A. Andrew Hospital the following year and needed to look for housing in Tuskegee. And Drew himself preferred the cheaper means of transportation, given that he had only a modest teaching salary, not the lucrative income that private practice would have assured him.[11]

Drew went to the hospital to make his rounds one last time,[12] and the group set off from Washington at some point between midnight and 2 A.M. in Samuel Bullock's 1949 Buick Roadmaster. Charles Watts, another of Drew's students at Howard, drove to Tuskegee in another car and had been assigned to find accommodations for the group in Atlanta for the following night. Their plan to "drive in one pop without stopping," said Watts, was natural: "During those times it was not easy to find places for black people [to spend the night]. We were going to stay at the Y in Atlanta."[13]

Despite the late hour and the constraints under which the trip had to be made, the four doctors were in a relaxed, festive mood. "It was a beautiful, starry, moon-lit night," Johnson recalled thirty-two years later. "We drove uneventfully through the Virginia countryside discussing a few personal-medical problems and anecdotes."[14]

Drew had made this trip south many times. Each year, free medical clinics were held at the John A. Andrew Hospital at Tuskegee for the rural black inhabitants of the surrounding region — from Alabama, Florida, Georgia, Louisiana, and Mississippi. Doctors traveled down from urban medical centers all over the East Coast; the majority were black doctors and professors of medicine from Meharry and Howard, the only two black medical schools then in existence.

It was the kind of setting that Drew thrived in; it offered "an opportunity to teach and inspire, to make contact with young physicians."[15] In 1938, Drew had stopped over in Atlanta on his way down and had met a young Spelman College professor, Lenore Robbins, at a party given by his friend Mercer Cook. On the way back from the clinics, a week later, he roused Lenore from her dormitory in the middle of the night and proposed to her. They married six months later. When Drew decided on a course of action, he wasted no time in pursuing it.[16]

The four travelers had many topics to discuss, for they shared career ambitions and problems. In Washington, Freedmen's was the only hospital where any of them could receive training or practice, because all of the district's other hospitals denied hospital privileges to black doctors. None of them belonged to the city's officially sanctioned medical organization, the American Medical Association, for it had an exclusively white membership. Black doctors in Washington consequently had their own medical society, the Medico-Chirurgical Society of the District of Columbia, and Drew belonged to this group.[17] However, for several years he had been waging a quiet but persistent campaign, through white medical contacts and friends at the highest levels, to win membership to the American Medical Association and the American College of Surgeons.[18]

Drew had experienced and witnessed the politics of the segregated medical professions from top to bottom: few were more aware of the limits set on black aspirations and needs. Few had tried harder to break down some of the barriers. In 1940, Drew had been the first black American to receive a doctor of science degree in medicine. Having submitted an impressive dissertation on "banked blood" at Columbia University, Drew had been chosen in the fall of 1940 to serve as medical director for the Blood for Britain project, a hastily organized emergency operation to send liquid plasma to British soldiers on battlefields in France. Drew had orchestrated this effort so well that he was called upon the following spring to set up the American Red Cross's first blood bank, a New York City pilot program that became the model for blood banks all over the country during the wartime national blood collection program instituted in late 1941. Few black doctors had achieved such national prominence. When the armed forces decided that black Americans would be excluded as donors, and then, after an outcry, that black people's blood would be used but rigidly segregated from white people's blood, Drew's conspicuous role in the program seemed bitterly ironic to many blacks and to white sympathizers.[19]

Drew was not driving during the first hours of the trip. About 5:30 A.M., the group neared the Virginia–North Carolina state line and spotted a neon sign for a roadside snack shop. They all got out and stretched and had some doughnuts and coffee before changing drivers and continuing on toward Greensboro. Drew now took the wheel, with Bullock beside him. Ford sat behind Drew, Johnson behind Bullock. Traffic was light. Johnson said the four exchanged more anecdotes and jokes after the stop, for it refreshed them all, but he and the others remember little else that took place between the 5:30 stop and 7:50 A.M., when tragedy struck.[20]

All the other doctors had dozed off as Drew, no doubt drowsy himself, drove along a dull stretch of NC 49 just north of the tiny mill village known as Haw River. The Buick had been passing through the Alamance County rural community of Pleasant Grove, known to local people as the home of the county's lightest-skinned black residents — those who were part-Indian and part-white — and a place where the women were noted for their beauty.[21] If the men had traveled a mile or two farther, they would have entered the rural all-black community of Green Level, where the small wood frame and cinderblock houses were more dilapidated, yet were sometimes painted brighter colors. Alamance County, like the rest of North Carolina and the South, was a segregated society. Some blacks and whites lived side by side there, but rigid segregation was the norm.

Apparently Drew fell asleep at the wheel while the car was moving at a high speed. In accounts of the accident written in 1982, Ford, Johnson, and Bullock later reconstructed what happened in the moments after Drew dozed off. Ford said he recalled the wreck "as clear . . . as if it happened today." He said that

> the wheels on the right side of the car hit the shoulder [and] Sam Bullock yelled out, "Hey Charlie." Charlie immediately took the wheel and turned left sharply so that the car rolled over as it was traveling over seventy miles per hour. It rolled over away from the driver's side with the doors on the driver's side, both front and back, opening up. Dr. Drew was half thrown out of the car so that when the car turned over a second time it slammed against his body and the car ended up

many feet perpendicular to the road but on four wheels with Dr. Drew still hanging out of the car.[22]

Ford said that he was catapulted through the air and landed some forty feet from the car. When he regained consciousness, he was sitting in a cornfield. His left arm was broken. He looked back and saw Drew lying near the car. He told his friends he had an overcoat in the car that they could use to cover Drew.

Johnson did not recall the car swerving off the road and flipping over. After the accident, he said,

> I awoke, sitting in the same position [I had been in before the accident], with our car facing south, the direction we were driving, about thirty yards in a cornfield on the left side of the highway. The car was right side up and only the left doors were open. I was terribly confused and had no idea what had happened actually, and I appeared to be alone in the car. Dr. Ford and Dr. Drew were missing. Dr. Bullock was wedged under the dashboard of the front seat . . . I got out and opened the door to help Dr. Bullock become unwedged. He then asked me what had happened, a question which I was unable to answer. He asked where Dr. Drew was, another question which I could not answer.

A few moments later, Bullock and Johnson found Drew lying on his back on the ground, next to the left front wheel of the car. Johnson said, "He was alive; his breathing was irregular and his face was pale and contorted as if in pain. . . . He was obviously in shock." An examination by both doctors revealed a deep wound in his left leg, an "avulsion of the quadrucept muscle," but Drew was not visibly bleeding from the wound or from the mouth, nose, or ears, as might be expected in a case of shock and internal injury. The two uninjured doctors then turned their attention to Ford, who was "quietly sitting on the ground about ten yards away, holding his arm." They examined him and confirmed that his arm — his left humerus — was broken, as he had already guessed. Johnson suggested that he put his left hand between the buttons of his shirt, using them as an improvised sling.[23]

By this time, on that mild sunny April morning, several motorists driving by had stopped to offer help. A highway patrol officer arrived within minutes of the accident. People who lived nearby called an ambulance. "A white fellow came to the scene and said, 'It looks like you boys are in trouble," Bullock remembered. "It all happened before anybody knew Dr. Drew or we were doctors."[24] At that time, a white farmer named Isley and his family lived in a small white frame house near the site of the accident. It is no longer standing. Farther off the road was black farmer Ed Farmville's home, the only other house visible amid fields of newly planted tobacco, soybeans, corn, and wheat.[25]

Farmville apparently also called an ambulance, and he telephoned neighbors Washington Irving Morris and Viola Covington Morris as well, telling them, " 'You need to come down here. Some Negro doctors have been killed. There's been a terrible wreck.' " Washington Morris, principal of Pleasant Grove Elementary School, and his wife, a teacher at the school, were recognized leaders in the black community. Farmville "thought we might offer some assistance," Viola Morris recalled fifty years later. By the time the Morrises arrived at the scene, the four doctors were already gone. A crowd had gathered, however; people were looking at the wrecked car and talking about the incident. Several people, sensing the importance of the doctors, picked up pieces of the shattered windshield and took them home as mementos.[26]

Several ambulances arrived at the scene. But an ambulance operated by a local white funeral home, McClure's, arrived there first, within about fifteen minutes.[27] Its driver stopped on the shoulder of the road and brought a stretcher out to where Drew was lying. After Drew was lifted into the ambulance, Johnson also climbed in, wanting to accompany Drew to the hospital. Ford was taken to the same hospital by a motorist, and Bullock, after staying with his wrecked car long enough to collect some of the baggage that had spilled out, was carried to the hospital by the patrolman.

Drew was brought into the emergency room of Alamance General Hospital at 8:30 A.M., forty minutes after the accident.[28] This forty-eight-bed facility, which in 1950 was the only hospital in Alamance County, stood about five miles from where the accident occurred, making it by far the closest place for emergency treatment. Located at 1308 Rainey Street on the east side of Burlington, the hospital was a three-story brick building constructed along classical lines, with steps leading up to its front portico and four white columns supporting its Parthenon-style corrugated tin roof. The one emergency room was located in the basement (actually the ground floor), down a ramp under the hospital's front portico. Duke Hospital, a larger, more sophisticated teaching facility, was thirty-two miles from the site of the accident. At that time it was routine to take a person injured in Alamance County to Alamance General Hospital first; if the person could be stabilized at this local facility and was judged to be strong enough to survive the trip, he or she would frequently would be taken on to Duke. The larger facility's doctors could offer more specialized treatment, particularly for brain injuries requiring the attention of neurosurgeons. There were no neurosurgeons at Alamance General Hospital.[29]

In 1950 Alamance General Hospital was a private hospital, and it had been owned by several different white doctors since 1916, when it had been opened as Rainey Hospital by Rainey Parker. The doctors who owned the hospital exercised virtually complete control over hospital staff through the board of trustees; the board determined which county doctors had privileges there, or, in other words, which doctors could admit and treat patients. In 1950, Ralph Brooks, a urologist, and George Carrington, a surgeon, owned and ran the hospital. Brooks had joined Parker in 1922, and Parker had left shortly afterward. Carrington practiced at the hospital part-time at first but became a permanent full-time doctor there in 1927. Although there were three black doctors in the county in 1950, they could not practice there. In fact, none had ever set foot in the hospital in 1950. The hospital primarily served white patients: like almost all of the county's other facilities, public or private, it operated on a segregated basis: only five of its forty-eight beds could be occupied by black patients, and these five beds were all in two small rooms in the basement. Black doctors could not practice in the hospital, even if one of their patients was admitted there. However, both black and white patients were regularly treated in the hospital's emergency room.[30]

Johnson assisted the ambulance attendants in rolling Drew into the emergency room. "He was still alive, periodically gasping," Johnson recalled. He stood by as the attendants attempted to determine the extent of Drew's injuries, checking his pulse and his respiration. Hospital staff members questioned Johnson as to what had happened, and he explained that they had had an automobile accident. As the routine examination continued, Johnson said, "a tall, ruddy, brown-haired man in a long, white coat [Carrington] came in the emergency room and observed the patient. He asked in astonishment, 'Is that Dr. Drew?' "[31] Johnson answered, " 'Yes, we had an accident on the highway.' " Later Johnson recalled Carrington's reaction: "In a commanding voice, he ordered emergency measures. At his request, fluids were assembled and attempts were made to place a tourniquet around . . . [Drew's] right arm. Concurrently, I was escorted from the emergency room to the waiting room."

Harold Kernodle Sr., a young orthopedic surgeon who had joined the hospital staff in 1946, was on call in the emergency room that morning, along with his younger brother, Charles Kernodle, a general surgeon who had joined the staff in 1949. Carrington and the hospital's other older surgeon, Ralph Brooks, intermittently joined the Kernodles in the emergency room during Drew's treatment.[32]

None of the three black doctors accompanying Drew witnessed what happened in the emergency room in the next hour or so. But they undoubtedly took comfort from the fact that the white doctors working to save Drew's life knew who he was. Ford, like Johnson, recalled telling the hospital doctors Drew's identity soon after their arrival. "I informed the physicians on duty as to who Dr. Drew was. They went to him immediately."[33]

Both Harold and Charles Kernodle confirmed that they knew who Drew was as they struggled to save him. In fact, both had heard of him before that morning. Harold Kernodle recalled that John Ford told them the unconscious man's identity. As a surgeon in the service in World War II, Kernodle had heard of Drew as "the instigator and founder of plasma. We knew what we were dealing with," said Kernodle more than thirty years later.[34] Charles Kernodle said he did not immediately realize who Drew was when he was wheeled into the emergency room, but he recognized Drew's name as soon as it was spoken, because he had heard it from a hematologist colleague, Ivan Brown, during his work as a resident at Duke University's blood bank in the late 1940s.[35]

Drew's identity may not have been obvious to all who were present. A black orderly, Otris J. A. Dixon, said he knew who Drew was,[36] but the anesthetist, a white nurse named Lucille Crabtree, remembered noticing only the severity of Drew's wounds:

We just knew they were victims. I didn't know they were doctors till later in the day. . . . It was early in the morning. We were in surgery, getting ready to operate, with a patient on the table. The emergency room called; they wanted me to come immediately. I didn't wait for the elevator. I ran down the steps. . . . Dr. Drew was on the main operating table. Right away I tried to get an open airway. Another attendant tried to get an IV going. It wasn't even an hour till he was dead. His chest was crushed; his head was crushed and broken. There was nothing anyone could do — even Duke. He was torn up too bad. . . . His brains were coming out of his ears. . . . In my opinion he could not have been saved.[37]

Lenore Drew, Drew's wife, wrote to Brooks thanking him and his staff for the care Drew had received and indicating her belief that the doctors had had no idea who he was as they worked to save his life. "It is our understanding that at the time of treatment and care you were completely unaware of identification. Such kindness cannot go unmentioned. Though all efforts were futile, there is much comfort derived in knowing that everything was done in his fight for life."[38]

If the medical personnel had not heard of Drew, they might have believed he was white. Drew looked like a white man. Many of his friends and colleagues observed that no one meeting him for the first time would have guessed he was black.[39] His wife, too, noted that "his skin was so white, people assumed he was white. Instead of waiting for them to find out [he was black]," she recalled, "he would say, 'When those of us who are Negroes' or some other phrase. He'd let people know right away."[40]

Harold Kernodle confirmed that Drew looked white. "He was a real good, sharp-looking man; he was what I call high yellow. He looked like a white man practically. Here in Burlington we have an area [Pleasant Grove] where the people look like this—they can pass for white people."[41] As I noted earlier, this was the very community in which Drew had his accident.

From these different memories, a coherent scenario emerges: the doctors accompanying Drew no doubt did inform the hospital staff who he was. The doctors who had heard of Drew before—the Kernodle brothers and Carrington—did register Drew's identity, perhaps not immediately but at some point during the morning. Other members of the Alamance General Hospital staff did not recognize Drew's name and worked on him as they would have on any other victim of an auto accident, their attention focused on the severity of his wounds. At the same time, they probably grasped that he was a person of some distinction, by the way Drew himself looked and by the appearance and manner of the doctors accompanying him. It was an extraordinary group to stumble into this small rural hospital. The hospital administrator, Marvin Yount, was not present when Drew was wheeled into the emergency room, and he had not heard of Drew before, but he recalled being informed in another part of the hospital early that morning that a "couple of prominent Negro physicians from Washington had been in a wreck and were there [in the emergency room]."[42]

Both of Drew's doctors and the other hospital staff members realized from the beginning that Drew probably could not be saved. Charles Kernodle recalled, "We realized he had a fatal injury when we first saw him. . . . I looked at his pupils. . . . They were dilated and fixed, not reacting to light. When someone is like that, he's unconscious and in shock, and he never recovers. . . . We started fluids on him, plasma probably. There was no time to give him whole blood. It took too long to cross-match."[43]

Charles Kernodle also remembered that while Drew was still alive, they called Duke Hospital to see whether doctors there could suggest any other emergency measures. He said they would have transferred Drew to Duke if they had believed he could survive the forty-five-minute to hour-long trip. But it seemed a bad idea, given Drew's condition. Also, Kernodle noted, he was aware at the time that if Drew died on the way, the Alamance General doctors would be criticized for poor medical judgment.

In the meantime, all three doctors who had accompanied Drew were waiting in the hall outside for news of his condition. Dr. Johnson recalled the "sad communion" that prevailed and how the wait seemed "endless." After more than an hour, Johnson said, "A doctor came and reported to us that Dr. Drew had expired. He said, 'We tried. We did the best we could. We started fluids but our efforts were unrewarding.' "

Another black doctor who was a close friend of Drew's, C. Mason Quick, arrived at the hospital within moments after he died, having driven from Winston-Salem after hearing about the accident. Quick recalled many years later, "As soon as they got to the hospital, Dr. Bullock called me. . . . Within five or ten minutes, I got in my car and went speeding over there. It took me a good hour. I arrived just as they were unhooking the tubes. A boy was standing in the hall. 'There he is,' he said. 'He just died.' "[44]

According to Drew's death certificate (signed by Harold Kernodle Sr. one month later), Drew died at 10:10 A.M., some two hours after the accident. The conditions leading to his death were listed as: "Automobile accident. 1. Brain injury 2. Internal hemorrhage lungs 3. Multiple extremities injuries."[45] Summarizing information about Drew's death some twenty years later, Marvin Yount wrote, "He was unconscious and in deep shock and was given fluids, plasma and other supportive measures. He was constantly attended by a physician who was a surgeon and other hospital personnel in the emergency room."[46]

Drew was just shy of his forty-sixth birthday, still youthful and vital in appearance and at the peak of his powers. His traveling companions were "grief-stricken," yet they derived some solace from their belief that everything possible had been done to save his life.[47] Bullock reported later, "Dr. Drew was . . . treated with all the current modalities known to medicine, at that time, (1950), intravenous fluids and plasma."[48] Johnson wrote, "The treatment at the hospital, routine for accidental injuries and specific for that period of time, suggests that a conscientious effort was made to revive Dr. Drew. It may be argued that given the same circumstances and the same period of time in other major medical centers, other results might have been obtained. But this would be pure speculation. . . . There was no evidence to suggest that Dr. Drew received less than acceptable emergency treatment."

Drew was never admitted to Alamance General Hospital, because he died in the emergency room. Thus, no official record of his admission to the hospital ever existed or could have survived. Clinical cards with brief notes on treatment were kept on patients admitted to the emergency room, and apparently such a card existed for Drew. Marvin Yount recalled that he had a card for Drew when Ada Dorsett of the local American Red Cross contacted him for information about Drew's treatment, possibly in the late 1950s. But the hospital was renamed and moved to a new location in 1961, and the card on Drew did not survive this move.[49]

The treatment Drew would have received at the hospital had he survived is easy to surmise: John Ford was admitted and stayed for two nights; he flew back to Washington on Monday, 3 April. Complete records of Ford's hospital stay survive, including a clinical card; a statistical record or clinical fact sheet; a physical examination report; an X-ray report; a graphic chart showing temperature, pulse, and respiration levels; a laboratory record; and a letter detailing his treatment, signed by Harold Kernodle Sr. and dated 3 April 1950.[50]

Soon after being brought to the hospital emergency room, Ford was taken to the X-ray department, where the physicians discovered that he had a "fracture of the left humerus completely through the surgical neck . . . [and] a fracture of the scapula"[51] as well as a concussion and severe injuries to his right knee. White patients waiting for X-rays apparently were shuffled aside when he was brought in because he was more seriously injured. Also, because the doctors decided it would be dangerous to move him before doing surgery on his knee, the patients outside had to wait a while longer. "[They] assured me that everything was fine and that they would take care of me there and the people there who were waiting for X-rays would just have to wait as my care came first," Ford recalled.[52]

While he was still in X-ray, Ford's knee wound was sewn up with catgut and silk, and a hanging cast was placed on his left arm. He was given tetanus antitoxin and Durocillin.[53] After being treated, Ford was assigned to one of the two basement rooms reserved for black patients. No white patients were placed in the basement, as it was occupied by these two small segregated wards, which accommodated a total of five black patients, and by the emergency room, the hospital kitchen, and two hospital staff dining rooms — one for whites and one for blacks. Harold Kernodle, who attended Ford, noted that in 1950 black patients were never put anywhere but in the basement. He added, however, that he was sure Drew would have been put on the first floor if no beds had been available in the two black wards. He said he believed no one would have objected, because "times were changing" in 1950.[54] Ford was also attended by a black nurse, Esther Pennix, the only black professional on the hospital staff.[55]

Ford's postoperative course at the hospital was "uneventful," according to Harold Kernodle.[56] Ford himself later wrote that he received "excellent care," though he noted that he "was treated in the basement . . . because in that day and time they did not allow people of color to be in any of the rooms upstairs." Ford added, "However, each day the administrator as well as the director of nurses came to me apologizing for the location of my room."[57] Yount, the administrator that Ford was referring to, obviously established rapport with the patient. He recalled that Ford told him "the care was good but the accommodations were crummy." Yount agreed that the accommodations were not ideal.[58]

While Ford got situated in his basement room, Quick took Bullock and Johnson back to the site of the accident. They looked at the car once more and at "the things that had spilled out of the trunk all up and down the highway," making sure there was nothing else to gather up and take back to Washington. In the meantime, Drew's body was transported to Sharpe Memorial Chapel, a black funeral home in one of Burlington's downtown black neighborhoods — obviously a poorer part of town, where small homes were interspersed with an occasional pool hall, short-order grill, or juke joint. The three black doctors stopped by the funeral home to make sure all the arrangements had been handled properly. By this time, another black doctor from Winston-Salem, J. C. Jordan, had joined them. At this point, no one else was there but the doctors and the undertakers. After conferring for a short while, Quick drove Bullock and Johnson to Winston-Salem. From there, they soon got a plane back to Washington.[59]

Drew's body stayed at Sharpe Memorial Chapel in Burlington most of Saturday, waiting for an ambulance from Washington's McGuire Funeral Home, another black mortuary, to come pick it up. John Sharpe, John Pennix, and Willis Gray, three black men, owned the funeral home in Burlington at the time, and both Pennix and Gray remember that Saturday well. Pennix recalled, "There was a lot of excitement about who he was." Both were at the funeral home at different times during the day, and together they recalled the scene: "When the news got out, there were a lot of people coming in here, from Alamance County and beyond, practically all over the state. There were about 150 people in and out of here that day, mostly black people, a lot of black doctors, and reporters too. They came here because they thought they could see him, but they couldn't. There was no time to prepare him. People kept calling. The phone was ringing all day long."[60]

C. R. "Chip" Stanback, a professional photographer who was working as a freelancer for the *Carolina Times*, Durham's widely read black newspaper, remembered going to the funeral home that day with the paper's editor, Louis Austin. " 'Let's go. Dr. Drew is dead,' he said to me. I had to wrack my mind to know who Dr. Drew was," Stanback recalled years later. Austin, however, did know, and he made Drew's accident his major front-page story in the next issue. A banner across the top read "DR. DREW KILLED IN WRECK." In the center of the page was a photograph of Drew wearing a doctor's white coat, seated next to a microscope. The story headline read "Noted Physician Fatally Injured in Auto Wreck near Burlington."[61] At the bottom of the page was Stanback's photograph of the wrecked car, shot through a fence at the dealer's where it had been towed. The caption read "WHEN DEATH RODE THE HIGHWAY FOR DR. CHARLES DREW." Stanback recalled that Drew's body had not been processed and the undertakers would not let them see it.[62] Apparently no one saw the body but the two drivers from McGuire Funeral Home, who arrived late that afternoon and carried it back to Washington.

Even after the excitement of the day died down, John Pennix, one of the undertakers, recalled one way in which the event lingered. Some three or four weeks after the accident, the State Highway Commission painted a large red circle with an X inside it at the spot on NC 49 where the accident had occurred. Located near where Pennix's grandparents lived, the mark was "as large as an automobile wheel," and it "lasted until they resurfaced the road," Pennix said. Pennix believed that markers of this kind were "not done in every case—a lot of people were killed on the highway in Alamance County." In the undertaker's view, "It was done to show a noble person had passed away."[63]

Viola Covington Morris, one of the Pleasant Grove residents who had come to the scene of the accident early Saturday morning, was one of those who picked up a piece of the shattered windshield from the car that Drew had been driving. On the morning of 1 April, she only knew that the person who died had been a "prominent black doctor." Later that day, she learned that the doctor's name was Charles Drew. As the years passed and stories about Drew proliferated, the large chunk of glass came to mean more and more to her. Morris said she kept the glass in her classroom for some fifteen years and showed it to her students. One day in the 1960s, she was disappointed to find that "someone had taken it—it had disappeared."[64]

News of Drew's death reached Washington long before his body did. Nora Drew Gregory, Drew's sister, remembered that a "woman doctor" called her from Freedmen's Hospital early Saturday morning, saying she had bad news and asking whether she could bring Charles Drew's four children, ages nine, eight, six, and four, to Gregory's house. Nora Gregory told her husband to "go to Mama"—to comfort Charles Drew's mother, who lived in Arlington, Virginia.[65]

Drew's younger brother, Joseph "Joe" Drew, remembered getting a telephone call from Bus Rector, a friend who worked at the Georgia Avenue gas station closest to Howard University. "He told me Charlie had been killed in an auto accident. I wanted to verify it, so I called Mickey's office [Dr. Burke Syphax, a colleague of Drew's at Howard University]. Dr. [Clarence] Greene answered, and he confirmed it." Joseph Drew immediately went to his brother's house on College Street on the Howard University campus. By the time he arrived, a couple of doctors, Frank Jones and others, were already upstairs with Drew's wife. Joe Drew saw her after about an hour.[66]

Lenore Drew remembered Lillian Wiggins, a Howard physician, coming to the house with the news. "Everything went cold," she recalled. "But there was no real recognition of what had happened. When you have children, the first thing you think about is them, if you're a mother. If somebody throws you in the water, you try hard to swim." Other Howard doctors arrived soon and went upstairs to Lenore Drew to explain what had happened and comfort her.[67]

Bebe Drew Price, Drew's oldest daughter, remembered seeing her mother seated on the bed between two men. One of them had his arm around her. "They were all looking at their shoes. Dr. Wiggins said to me, 'Get your clothes on. Your father's gone away and he's not coming back.' "[68]

For most people who knew Drew, not just his family, his death was shocking, because he was young and vital and because it came so unexpectedly. One friend remembered someone stopping at a traffic light in Washington, blowing his horn, flashing his lights, and then making a U-turn to tell her: "Did you hear? — Charlie Drew was killed." This friend went to Drew's house and offered to help in some way. She spent the day in the basement folding the children's clean clothes, Lenore Drew recalled.[69]

Nora Gregory, Joseph Drew, and Burke Syphax went together to Lincoln Cemetery in Suitland, Maryland, near southeast Washington, to pick out a burial plot. Gregory recalled her brother "walking and walking, saying, 'I want it to be the highest spot.' "[70] After being prepared by McGuire Funeral Home, Drew's body lay in state for public viewing at Howard University's Andrew Rankin Chapel for most of Tuesday, 4 April, and for several hours on Wednesday morning, 5 April. W. Montague Cobb, an eminent black Howard University anatomist, historian, and civil rights activist who had grown up with Drew, commented on the scene in the chapel in a detailed obituary about his friend and colleague: "The endless procession which passed through Rankin Chapel from noon to midnight [on Tuesday] as he lay-in-state in an atmosphere of moving beauty and dignity were a token of the extent to which his character and achievements had gripped the public imagination. The many distinguished figures in medicine and public life from near and far who attended his magnificent funeral were a measure of the esteem in which he was held by the informed and responsible."[71]

Drew's funeral was held at the Nineteenth Street Baptist Church at 1 P.M. on Wednesday, 5 April. This black church, which dated back more than a hundred years, was the church Drew and his parents had gone to all their lives. Hundreds came, filling the church to overflowing. Joseph Drew remembered that when the funeral procession stopped at Nineteenth and E Streets, near where he and his brother had lived and played as boys, the cars stretched back three blocks, all the way to Pennsylvania Avenue. Policemen were posted at every corner.[72]

Nora Gregory remembered being overwhelmed by all the people, first at the house, then at the chapel, and finally at the funeral. "There will always be people, lots of people," Burke Syphax told her.[73] Drew's other sister, Eva Drew Pennington, was also impressed with the magnitude of the funeral. "It seemed to me that only Franklin Roosevelt's funeral was bigger in D.C. . . . The florists in Washington were sold out of flowers," she recalled. Pennington also remembered walking by the open casket and seeing that her brother's hands had been "mangled" by the accident.[74]

Among Drew's pallbearers were his oldest friends, the people he had grown up with in Washington, and those he had worked with at Howard. Among them were his distinguished Dunbar High School and Amherst College classmates W. Montague Cobb; Howard University French professor Mercer Cook; and Judge William H. Hastie, a former dean of Howard Law School and the first black governor of the Virgin Islands, who was then serving on the Third Circuit Court of Appeals as the nation's first black federal judge.[75] Also included were fellow surgeons Clarence Greene, Burke Syphax, and R. Frank Jones, along with another old friend, Leonard Hill. Mercer Cook recalled "tears streaming down [Leonard Hill's] . . . face." Drew had operated on Hill the year before, and Cook remembered hearing Hill say, through the tears, " 'Who would think I would be his pallbearer, only a year later?' "[76]

Among the distinguished guests who came to the funeral were administrator Oscar R. Ewing, head of the Federal Security Administration, which had jurisdiction over Howard University, a federal institution; two doctors from New York, Allen Whipple of Memorial Hospital and John Scudder of Presbyterian Hospital, both of whom Drew had worked with during his years doing research on blood plasma as a doctoral candidate; and another New York physician, Edward Howes, who had paved the way for Drew's fellowship to Columbia University. A delegation from Harlem Hospital included Ira McCown, Irving Carrington, Marshall Ross, Peter M. Murray, and Cecil Markez.[77]

Meanwhile, at the medical conference in Tuskegee there was also mourning of Drew's death. Joe Gordon, a participant, recalled, "His death completely clouded the conference. Dr. Drew practically was the conference: he was going to give the main talks. . . . We were flabbergasted."[78]

In Tuskegee on Wednesday, at the exact moment Drew's funeral started, the doctors who were gathered for the annual clinics stood for a moment of silence at John A. Andrew Hospital, paying tribute to Drew.

Officials had considered calling off the clinic when news of Drew's accident first reached them, but they decided that Drew would not have wished them to do so. An article about Drew's accident written during the clinics expressed the sense of loss the group felt: "Charley Drew is dead. It is almost impossible for us assembled here . . . to believe it. Everything we say, every thing we propose, every reference to what has been accomplished is so permeated with his ideas, his vigorous spirit, his sound wisdom, his clear vision."[79] The article further noted, "Dr. Drew and Dr. Ford, seriously injured, were taken to the hospital in Burlington. Every facility of the hospital was made available; the entire staff of physicians and nurses worked tirelessly."

The *New York Times*, the *Washington Star*, the *Washington Post*, *Time* magazine, and the *Journal of the American Medical Association* all carried stories of Drew's auto accident and death, as did the *Washington Afro-American*, the *Washington Times-Herald*, the *Journal of the National Medical Association*, and other major black newspapers around the country.

Eleanor Roosevelt was among those who wrote letters of sympathy to Drew's widow.[80] John Hope Franklin, a prominent historian; Mary McLeod Bethune, former president of the National Council of Negro Women; and Pearl Buck, Pulitzer Prize–winning author of *The Good Earth*, also wrote letters of condolence, as did many others.[81] Hubert Humphrey, then a young congressman from Minnesota, requested that Drew's newspaper obituaries and a *Washington Post* editorial about Drew be entered into the *Congressional Record*.[82] The editorial read as follows:

> Dr. Charles R. Drew, whose life was snuffed out in its early maturity by an automobile accident on Saturday, was among the most gifted of American surgeons. He chose to devote his gifts to the advancement of medicine rather than to the advancement of a personal career or to winning the monetary rewards that were easily within his reach. In particular, he devoted his gifts to the training of young Negro surgeons desperately needed for the medical care of their race. . . . He will be missed, however, not alone by his own race but by his whole profession and by men everywhere who value scientific devotion and integrity.[83]

2

They Wouldn't Treat Him

•
•
•
•
The story of Drew's mistreatment started as a rumor in
1950, grew into a widely circulated historical legend in the
1960s, and has been reported as historical fact in newspapers, magazines, and history and reference books for
more than thirty years, ever since National Urban League
director Whitney Young wrote a column repeating the legend in 1964.[1] Many have tried to eradicate it—colleagues
of Drew at public meetings, Drew family members and
friends, newspaper and magazine writers, even institutions
such as the Howard University Medical School and the
American Red Cross—but in vain. Despite repeated public
debunkings, the story about Charles Drew's death is still
being told. Today, for many Americans, Charles Drew is the
man who pioneered the use of blood plasma, who saved

soldiers' lives in World War II, and who ironically bled to death after being refused treatment at a whites-only hospital in the South.

Over the years, many versions of the story have circulated. Some tellers of the legend have said that Drew died because the hospital would not give him blood or plasma. Still others have reported that delayed treatment caused his death. Yet others have said that having been turned away at a white hospital, Drew died on his way to a black hospital. Yet the basic message has been the same: Charles Drew was treated inappropriately because he was a black man.

The legend is not true in a literal sense. But truth has many levels. For the people who tell the story and believe it, the story is true because it makes a meaningful statement about the world Drew lived in and the world they live in today.

The legend's growth illuminates life in multiracial American society. The ironies are powerful. For just as Charles Drew used his talent and courage to bring faint rays of light into that realm of dark conformity that constituted the world of segregated American medicine, so the legend of his death casts a different kind of light on the underside of American race relations during the segregation era. C. Vann Woodward probed this obscure terrain and described it as "the twilight zone that lies between living memory and written history, . . . one of the favorite breeding places of mythology." As Woodward noted, "This particular twilight zone has been especially prolific in the breeding of legend. The process has been aided by the old prejudices, the deeply stirred emotions, and the sectional animosities that always distort history, however well illuminated by memory or research."[2]

Woodward's passage points to both the difficulty and the significance of this elusive conjunction of fact and memory and suggests the inherent subjectivity of the historical data itself. This study anchors itself in that very difficulty, illuminating in the process the fact that all history is subjective. For some this intention may sound like an illegitimate aim, if not one that subverts the very craft of historical writing. Certainly, the ready acceptance of subjectivity in the creation of history is an intellectual mouthful that is hard to swallow: when one turns to a history book, one looks for and is nourished by hard nuggets of fact that one accepts as pieces of social reality. Without this hunger and its apparent nourishment, history books would not exist.

Yet we must recognize that a reader of history books really enters into an illusion created and sustained by historians — the illusion that he or she is experiencing life at some point in the past. For illusion it is, no matter how fully historians themselves imaginatively step into other eras. No one can go back in time and relive events that are gone. Historians, then, are like magicians: they put vanished sand back atop the hourglass and then pretend to describe its descent. As an astute observer noted, "Historians live by the myth of realism."[3]

How much more elusive, then, is a mere legend, the story of an event that never happened. Yet its very elusiveness points to the subjective nature of all historical writing. A legend focuses our attention on the hidden elements of history—the psychic and cultural realities that lie beneath the ephemeral surface of events. In the end, it is to our advantage that the precise history of the Drew legend can never be told fully, because that fact reminds us how much is invisible to historians looking for hard evidence.

One begins, then, directly confronting the difficulty: while a historian can (at least theoretically) trace something like the precise route fugitive slaves followed when escaping north, it is clearly impossible to trace the diffuse route by which the Drew story spread from person to person before it appeared in print, or in the years after.[4] Yet we know that it did spread and that much more passed invisibly along the same chain of memory and popular experience. In fact, even when the story was repeated after 1964 in newspapers, magazines, documentaries, television shows, and history books, these appearances should be understood as markers of a subterranean process. Like buoys floating on the rippling surface of social life, they mark deep underwater currents of culturally transmitted historical memory.

To understand the origins and spread of the Drew legend, we must not only use the techniques of social history but also borrow concepts from psychology, anthropology, and folklore. We will begin by looking at how the Drew story started as a rumor and at the individual and group psychology this rumor expressed. As we observe how the story spread farther, especially among black Americans, our understanding of the role of African American folklore must come into play, for the Drew story became a folk legend that was part of a larger body of black folklore going back to slavery and beyond. At this stage, the Drew legend materialized as a single thread in the intricate fabric of African American culture, both coloring it and colored by it. The distinction between a rumor and a legend is a subtle but important one. As Patricia Turner pointed out in a recent study of rumors in black folk culture, rumors have generally been studied by social scientists, while legends have been viewed as a specialty of folklorists. Like Turner, I see the boundaries between rumor and legend as somewhat blurred. The distinction between the Drew rumor and the Drew legend is primarily one of solidity and durability. If the rumors about Drew's death had faded quickly, they would have remained mere rumors. They persisted, though, and over time formed themselves into a coherent, stable narrative echoing deeply rooted themes in African American history and culture: thus the Drew story ultimately constituted a legend.[5]

As the legend's oral tradition found its way into print during the civil rights movement, and then afterward into a printed dialectic of ferment—with regular debunkings and reaffirmations of its truth—it became more actively historical, with power to influence actual events of the late twentieth century. At each stage, the legend served as a lens into the complexity of social history, demonstrating how historical experience shapes historical memory and, concurrently, how individual and cultural consciousness shape history. The legend, and individual reactions to it, reveal much about white and black culture in America, showing how group history and culture shape perceptions of reality.

As we follow the path of the legend, however, it is important not to force a reductive equation between black culture and white culture. Each has its own history and its own internal complexities: the truths relevant to one culture often have less relevance to the other. White culture is dominant in America; black culture is fighting for its life. That distinction makes for profound differences in the mythologies the two have spawned.

Probably within hours and certainly within days after Drew died, rumors about the circumstances surrounding his accident started to fly. His family and his colleagues knew the real story, but others, touched by his loss and not privy to the same reliable sources of information, began to speculate about how and why he had died and to supply explanations that fit their own personal experience. In Washington, D.C., where Drew was most widely known, and particularly on the Howard University campus, his death was big news; it shocked and dismayed the many people for whom he was already a legendary figure.

Betty Quander, a black nurse who was working at Freedmen's Hospital in April 1950, said she first heard the rumor at the hospital "a week or two after it happened." As a nursing assistant in Freedmen's male surgery ward since 1947, she "remembered seeing Dr. Drew come in with all the medical students. He was a handsome, energetic, very capable person—very genial." She recalled in 1985, "I heard he was refused treatment. It happened in the South. Soon after it happened, I heard it being discussed by some doctors. It seems to me it had something to do with blood, something to do with his care that involved blood after the accident—that perhaps his life could have been saved. Everyone was so shocked and upset. . . . It was a crushing blow because he was such a fine doctor. . . . I remember all types of rumors . . . going around the hospital, maybe a week or two after it happened."[6]

Delyour Johnson, another nurse who worked in Freedmen's Tuberculosis Annex in 1950 and who later was the nurse supervisor there, similarly recalled that rumors surfaced soon after Drew's death: "People were very shocked at his death. Everybody was talking about it. He was a young man . . . with such promise. His life was snuffed out. Because he was black he was not treated at the white hospital . . . in the South. [I heard the story] . . . right after his death, within days."[7]

Drew was not as well known at Howard University's School of Dentistry, but the rumors developed there as well. Stephen Thomas, a man from Burlington, North Carolina, who was a dentistry student in April 1950 and who subsequently practiced as a dentist in Burlington, recalled in 1985, "I heard when he got killed . . . in the spring of the year. Friends said to me, 'Steve, a guy got killed down there in your town.' It was the talk of the campus for weeks. They said he was killed in an accident. They sort of condemned the hospital for not paying more attention to him than they did. Segregation was in its heyday. They were mad over it. They thought he had not received adequate care quick enough. You know the way segregated hospitals were back then. They put him in a ward and left him unattended."[8]

Another man who had been a student at Howard's School of Dentistry in 1950 also recalled the rumor. Chester Redhead, a dentist with a well-established private practice in Harlem, New York, told the story he heard then and, in 1985, still believed to be true: "He had a car accident down South, Georgia, I think. They wouldn't give him any blood. I believe he died from loss of blood. I heard it right around the time Drew died—everybody was talking about it on campus."[9]

Old friends of Drew from Washington, D.C., knew the rumors were not true, but they too heard them in the weeks after Drew died. Beatrice Mair said that "immediately after his death" she heard the story that he was refused treatment. "Somebody reported they didn't get immediate attention and this is what caused his death," she recalled in 1985. She felt that the rumor was inevitable. "This was the natural reaction because of the terrific segregation system we had at that time. I had my own question. What kind of treatment would he have received if he had been recognized as a Negro? Because the hospital was segregated, would he have gotten immediate care? Would he have gotten the best care?" Mair knew Drew could have passed for white. In her mind, then, "history" and "legend" were not far apart. She knew the facts, but she had her "own question."[10]

Meanwhile, the rumor began to acquire detail. Another of Drew's childhood friends — Mercer Cook, a professor at Howard University, said he remembered hearing the story of refusal "right at the time" Drew died. According to Cook, people told a slightly different version: "They said, 'Well, you know, at Duke, they wouldn't treat him. Duke refused to take him in.'" Cook, too, believed such a story to be inevitable — "prejudice being what it was, race relations being what they were. A story like that you can't really squelch because too many want to believe it. It's too tender."[11]

John Hope Franklin, an eminent historian noted for many classic works on race in America,[12] attended Drew's funeral in Washington. In 1982 he told a reporter, "I have heard that story almost since the day Charlie died. I never questioned it. Thank God I didn't put it in my books."[13] Franklin later explained, "I thought Drew died because he was not admitted to a white hospital."[14] He added, "I revised *From Slavery to Freedom*[15] in 1956, and I'm lucky I didn't put it in. It's not not in there because I didn't believe it."[16]

The story went around not only in Washington's black community, where Drew was relatively well known, but in segregated black communities all over the country. Thelma Vine, a black woman who served in 1950 as a nurse at North Carolina A&T State University's infirmary in Greensboro, said she remembered the day of the accident: "Let's face it. In the 1950s, before the civil rights movement, segregation was in effect. . . . Because of Drew's being black he was not given the service he could have had."[17]

Another black Greensboro resident, Warmoth Gibbs, dean of A&T's School of Education and General Studies in 1950, also recalled hearing the story the weekend Drew died, at a conference in Atlanta, Georgia: "I was in a meeting of the Association of Collegiate Deans and Registrars in Atlanta, Georgia, when it occurred. It was discussed at the meeting —

how he'd had an accident and wasn't admitted to the hospital. . . . He went to one or two hospitals. He'd been injured but he didn't get the treatment he needed."[18]

Even in Alamance County, where Drew was treated at the local hospital, the Drew legend has been widely believed in the black community from the early 1950s to the present day. Otris J. A. Dixon, the orderly on duty at Alamance General Hospital when Drew died there, said he had heard a version of the legend "through the grapevine." Dixon recalled hearing it "right after it happened — maybe just a year later. They said because it [Drew's death] happened in the South, he didn't get the right attention." Dixon, of course, knew the legend was not literally true, but he made sense of it in his own way: "Dr. Kernodle could not get his type of blood — he couldn't match it. And he couldn't send him on to Duke for a transfusion."[19] Viola Covington Morris, the Pleasant Grove schoolteacher who came to the scene of the accident on 1 April with her husband, Washington Irving Morris, to see if they could offer assistance, heard rumors of mistreatment from that day on. "We heard everything in the world after that; for years, I've had to tell people who hurled insults at Alamance General Hospital that it's not true Drew was treated badly," Morris said in 1990. Morris recalled that she called the hospital that morning and, by talking with a nurse, satisfied herself that Drew had actually been treated as well as possible. But Morris added that she understood why people continued to believe Drew had been mistreated. "People talk that way because it [mistreatment] has happened to us all our lives," she said.[20] Other Alamance County residents also heard the legend repeated in the early 1950s, and they believed it, too. Gilberta Mitchell, a schoolteacher and community leader in Alamance County, said she first heard the Drew legend "within two years after . . . [Drew's] death or earlier than that," although she never believed it because she knew he had been treated at the local hospital. She said she has heard Alamance County schoolteachers, especially black teachers, repeat the legend ever since the 1950s.[21]

In cities where black newspapers gave the story of Drew's death front-page prominence, the rumors were especially likely to proliferate. Ira McCown, a black surgeon in New York City who was a friend of Drew's, said he heard "a day after the accident" that Drew bled to death. McCown knew it was not true but understood why the rumor grew: "Blacks couldn't be admitted to many hospitals in the South. When rumors [that people have reason to believe] start, they grow like pineapples," he said.[22]

Over the years many people troubled by the legend have blamed black newspapers and magazines for creating it.[23] C. Mason Quick, Drew's friend who has tried to debunk the legend, has always held the black press responsible for starting it. He commented that the legend's persistence "makes you doubt whether George Washington ever cut down a cherry tree or whether Abe Lincoln ever lived in a log cabin."[24]

Newspapers did play a role in turning Drew into a public figure in the 1940s and 1950s. They spread the legend in later years. But they did not "create" the legend. Many newspapers did report Drew's death, and black-owned newspapers dramatized the event in a way white-owned newspapers did not. But none suggested that Drew had been mistreated. In fact, several black-owned newspapers—unlike the white-owned papers—made a point of reporting that Drew had received excellent care from white doctors. Most notably, next to its major story about Drew's death, the *Baltimore Afro-American* ran a sidebar headlined "Drew's Death Stuns Bullock: Changed Flying Plan to Take 2 Others." The story focused mainly on Samuel Bullock's shock over the accident and on his wife's hysteria because she at first thought Bullock had been killed. Under the subheading "Hospital Services Creditable," however, the story reported, "Asked about hospital service given them in Burlington, Dr. Bullock said that they were shown the utmost respect and courtesy. 'They seemed shocked' by the fact that it was Dr. Drew.' He said further that hospital authorities had already made plans to transfer Dr. Drew to Duke Hospital, one of the nation's richest."[25]

North Carolina's oldest black newspaper, the *Carolina Times* of Durham, reported, "Drs. Bullock and Johnson escaped with minor injuries and left for Winston-Salem after being treated at Alamance General Hospital. Dr. Ford, who was more seriously injured, was confined in the hospital with a fractured arm and several other injuries about the body."[26]

The first newspaper article in which the Drew legend appeared in print was the Whitney Young column, published in the fall of 1964. During the same year Young also published a book that repeated his version of the legend; it too marked a first. Other books repeating the legend followed in the late 1960s. Thus, it was in the 1960s that the essential components of the historical puzzle that the legend was to create fell completely into place. Though each would take on additional texture in ensuing years, the jagged outlines of fact, rumor, and printed legend became clearly visible in the era of the civil rights movement. But how does one begin to approach the evidential contradictions here? At first glance, the puzzle seems to make no sense. But after study, the pattern reveals a striking, if buried, inner logic.

We can begin by understanding the circumstances that contribute to the growth of rumors. In periods of crisis and social upheaval, rumors are especially common, and they sometimes shape groups' actions in important ways. The well-known southern sociologist Howard W. Odum witnessed the rapid escalation of racial rumors and fears among southern whites at the onset of World War II. In 1943 Odum wrote a book titled *Race and Rumors of Race: Challenge to American Crisis* exploring the southern white folk consciousness that he believed lay at the root of the phenomenon. The war threatened the South's segregated social order, Odum pointed out, and whites expressed their uneasiness about black social mobility through rumors. During the war, rumors spread among black Americans as well. Walter White, then executive secretary of the NAACP, made a trip to Europe to investigate the reality behind a variety of rumors about relations between black and white American troops — including a number of stories about black servicemen being assaulted by white servicemen. He subsequently published a book, *A Rising Wind*, about the widespread racial discrimination he encountered.[27] Sociologist Tamotsu Shibutani, after noting the similar growth of rumors in the San Francisco Bay area among Japanese Americans at the start of World War II, went on to study rumor in depth in a 1966 book called *Improvised News: A Sociological Study of Rumor.* Shibutani argued that "crises are the crucibles out of which . . . innovations emerge; . . . new modes of action often get their initial direction in attempts to cope with emergencies."[28] He stressed that rumors represent plausible constructions of events that grow out of people's attempts to make sense of events when they lack critical information.

In *I Heard It through the Grapevine*, Patricia A. Turner explores contemporary black rumors and traces their prevalence and themes to the earliest encounters between Euro-Americans and African Americans. Black Americans have long passed around rumors that reflect their often well founded fears that white Americans are attempting to hurt, violate, contaminate, or appropriate black bodies or parts of black bodies, Turner says. She documents the pervasiveness of "metaphors linking the fate of the black race to the fates of black bodies" — an idea that would suggest that the spread of rumors about Drew's death was part of a larger phenomenon. Turner echoes the observation that rumors abound in times of social conflict, especially in stressful encounters between groups of people who view each other as threatening. She notes that racial rumors were rampant not only in the 1940s but also in the 1960s, during the civil rights movement, and that to a large degree they have been a phenomenon of American history from its earliest interracial beginnings. Indeed, the "stressful encounter" between black and white Americans has now lasted almost four hundred years, with rumors and legends repeatedly cropping up on both sides of the racial divide.[29]

Two psychologists, Gordon W. Allport and Leo Postman, were intrigued by the widespread World War II–era phenomenon of rumor-mongering and were concerned about the dangers it posed. In 1947 they published a useful book, *The Psychology of Rumor*, on exactly how and why rumors circulate. During World War II, many rumors were motivated by white Americans' cultural and racial antipathies. In particular, there were a variety of antiblack rumors that made blacks the scapegoats for white fears about whites' changing economic and social status and sexual morality. There were rumors about black soldiers lacking loyalty or being lazy, rumors about black men sexually molesting white women back home, and rumors about black women in the South forming "Eleanor Clubs" — treating their white mistresses like their servants and reversing the social roles.

Allport and Postman's focus on the individual psychology of rumor transmission is especially helpful in shedding light on the origins of the Drew rumor. They point out that rumors are most likely to develop when their theme has special importance to the people who hear them and when the facts are "shrouded in some kind of ambiguity." In each rumor that arises, they note, "there is often some residual particle of news, a 'kernel of truth.' " Another useful concept they discuss, relevant to the Drew story, is the "rumor public: . . . Physicians, clergymen, aviators, or stag parties will launch into tales that reflect the common interests of the group. . . . A rumor public exists wherever there is a community of interest."[30]

Middle-class blacks striving to break down the barriers of segregation, as Drew had before them, were especially susceptible to the Drew story. Plese Corbett, an Alamance County extension agent who lived within a mile of the site of Drew's accident, heard the rumor in the 1950s and still believed it thirty years later. Like Drew, who had gone from Washington, D.C., to Amherst College, this man had gone to Massachusetts for a college education. He had heard of Drew's work with blood plasma then and had been impressed by Drew's opposition to segregated blood when Corbett was serving in the army during World War II. And, like Drew, Corbett had returned to a southern community where segregation was still intact. In 1985 he told the story about Drew's death that he had always believed: "If they'd accepted him at the hospital he wouldn't have died. They didn't accept him because he was a Negro. . . . In this area here, Pleasant Grove, everyone talked about it. It moved from one to another because of the position he [Drew] held and what he had done . . . [and because of] . . . what he stood for [with the blood bank]. He didn't believe in segregation, in separating people. He was for helping all people."[31]

People pass on a rumor because it conveys an experiential truth that has a deep meaning for them. If the right conditions—importance of theme and factual ambiguity—are present when news is passed around, a rumor reflecting the psychic reality of the people in a common group is likely to emerge, especially in a period of social upheaval, when people feel a greater need to account for their situation. From the early forties on, black Americans—along with southern whites—experienced constant social upheaval. During the war years, the democratic rhetoric combined with the flagrant discrimination toward blacks dramatically heightened black awareness of the American government's hypocrisy and made blacks as a group far more militant.[32] White Americans, too, were in turmoil. Describing the onset of this tumultuous era, C. Vann Woodward noted, "Quite abruptly and unaccountably—or so it seemed to many Southern white people—an avalanche of denunciation, criticism and opprobrium descended upon the South from above the Mason and Dixon line. Militant and organized demands from both Negro and white sources of pressure were raised for immediate abolition of segregation. . . . [The demands] . . . coincided with the war crisis that had already frayed people's nerves."[33]

Southern whites reacted to outside criticism as they had many times in the past: by attempting to justify black oppression. As Lillian Smith wrote, "tolerance faded. . . . Negroes in the Air Force were 'flying over white heads.' This made folks uneasy. 'They were down in the field. Now they're up in the sky.' It shook the Southern mind. And Negroes were murmuring, *If we fight for you, how about letting us vote?* Much of the unease was subliminal. But some of it came out in squawks and yapping. Southern Congressmen made shocking speeches spilling over into race hatred. There was a revival of the Klan. And fresh panic about 'intermarriage.' "[34] When old fears of black equality were thus stirred up, mob violence erupted against blacks from the war years through the 1960s.

When people experience disturbing social change, they unconsciously "project" their emotional state onto the environment. Allport and Postman point to dreams, including daydreams, as an example of how the process works: "The child asleep dreams of finding mountains of candy; the inferior youth asleep triumphs on the athletic field; the apprehensive mother dreams of the death of her child. . . . Rumor is akin to the daydream at second hand. If the story we hear gives a fancied interpretation of reality that conforms to our secret lives, we tend to believe and transmit it."[35] The psychologists sum up their rumor formula as follows: "Rumor is set in motion and continues to travel in a homogeneous social medium by virtue of the strong interests of the individuals involved in the transmission. The powerful influence of these interests requires the rumor to serve largely as a rationalizing agent: explaining, justifying, and providing meaning for the emotional interest at work."[36]

Black Americans in the 1950s and even more in the 1960s had reason to find the theme of Drew's story compelling. World War II marked a watershed in black history and set in motion profound changes in race relations. One historian called the war years the "forgotten years" of the black revolution, a period that culminated in the 1960s; he noted James Baldwin's comment that the treatment of blacks during the war represented "a turning point in the Negro's relation to America: . . . a certain respect for white Americans faded." Black sociologist E. Franklin Frazier said that World War II was a watershed after which blacks were no longer willing to accept discrimination without protest.[37]

While the lives of most African Americans did not change dramatically during the 1950s, segregation was on the defensive, its basic premises crumbling. Black hopes were raised dramatically in 1954 when the Supreme Court ruled segregation unconstitutional. Years of setbacks followed, including the lynching in 1955 of Emmett Till, a fourteen-year-old black boy who dared to joke with a white woman; the temporizing *Brown v. Board of Education* implementation decision that same year; a riot that broke out at the University of Alabama when Autherine Lucy, a young black woman, sought admittance in 1956; and the actions of the angry white mobs, incited by Governor Orval Faubus, that threatened black children trying to integrate Central High School in Little Rock, Arkansas, in 1957. Other developments that dismayed blacks and their white allies were the spread of white racist Citizen's Councils in response to school integration and the many forms massive resistance took in the years after the *Brown* implementation decision. There were new sources of hope as well, including President Eisenhower's reluctant but decisive enforcement of Little Rock's integration with federal troops, and, above all, the worldwide impact of the Montgomery bus boycott in 1955 and 1956 and the emergence of Martin Luther King Jr. as an inspiring black leader. But this hope was buffeted as the forces of white reaction grew. As the 1950s came to a close, desegregation had ground to an almost complete halt.[38]

Drew had been, as King was in the process of becoming, an accomplished black leader with humanitarian values. He was a black hero who had been taken away in his prime, in a senseless fashion, at an obscure place in the rural South. In the terminology of psychiatric theorist Carl Jung, Drew's death evoked an "archetype" — a victim archetype deeply ingrained in African American culture as a logical function of a history of enslavement and oppression. Historically, many blacks had suffered and were still suffering Drew's general fate — an early, violent death and the waste of their talents, and white mistreatment was often the cause. Distress and anger were natural reactions to the loss of so valuable a member of the community. It was a small mental leap to the conclusion that Drew had in some way been mistreated just as the community had. This leap was all the more likely because the facts of Drew's death were ambiguous — inevitably so, given the site and manner of his death. Such "facts" would remain ambiguous to many even after they were told, for they contradicted the reality of everyday life.

The *Pittsburgh Courier*, one of the nation's oldest black newspapers and one with a very large circulation, ran a sensational front-page story on Drew's death, with a banner headline. It is easy to imagine how it and stories like it stirred black readers' familiar feelings of loss and outrage. The story began, "Death — horrible and certainly unexpected — has taken the man who gave the world the blood plasma which, during World War II, saved the lives of hundreds of thousands of American and British soldiers and civilians. Dr. Charles Richard Drew was killed in an automobile crash near Burlington, N.C. last Saturday morning."[39]

The *Carolina Times* in Durham similarly gave the Drew story big play and dramatized its meaning. On its front page the paper ran a banner headline more than an inch high: "DR. DREW KILLED IN WRECK."[40] The cutline under a photograph of Drew, dressed in a white coat and posing with a microscope, commented, "Dr. Charles Drew, noted blood plasma expert, whose untimely death in an auto wreck near Burlington early Saturday morning, rocked the nation." Drew's death did rock black America, which was already fighting its long war against segregation and discrimination. Indeed, Drew was a man who by his very existence demonstrated the absurdity of segregation. Not only had he passed the important tests of the white world with flying colors; he had done so in a field of science, a discipline in which (at least theoretically) impersonal, objective standards reigned. Finally, he had served humanity at large through his work on preserving human blood components in order to save lives.

Both of Drew's sisters believe that the Drew legend evolved because of black people's feelings about his death. Nora Drew Gregory said people felt "one of our heroes has been badly treated."[41] The deeper truth the legend transmitted was quite similar: We have been badly treated by the bad luck of unnecessarily losing this hero. Eva Drew Pennington commented, "There was anger and frustration on the part of black people in general. It's still going on. Also, people thought Charlie's contribution a great thing. They thought he'd been abused and they were angry about it."[42]

But it was not only people's feelings that gave rise to the rumor and then the legend. Such an explanation would underestimate the historical significance of the legend. The reality of what was still going on and what had happened historically created the climate of belief among black people in which the rumor took root. The rumor grew because it expressed not only a psychic truth but also a larger social and historical truth: black people had died and were continuing to die throughout the country, and especially in the South, because they had been refused appropriate, prompt medical treatment in situations where it could have been made available. Blacks had suffered and continued to suffer from discriminatory medical care. Charles Drew himself, during the war years, had encountered racial discrimination in the form of the American Red Cross segregated blood polices, and as we shall see, this encounter had laid a crucial piece of the foundation for the legend. The larger truth in all these instances was the murderous impact of institutional racism, reflected consistently in inferior medical care and higher mortality rates for black Americans than for white Americans.

Many aspects of the history of black medical care in America give credence to the stark archetype of black mistreatment at white hands that the Drew legend represents. Tragic incidents and shocking statistics from each era of black history have been documented by medical historians.[43] Although there were always white doctors who did not conform to prevailing practices, the systemic norm was a callous neglect of black medical needs, a tendency to blame black people for their own medical problems, and a willingness to exploit poor African Americans for the purposes of medical experimentation. The results of this discriminatory health-care system have been documented in black medical publications, especially the *Journal of the National Medical Association*, throughout the twentieth century. Blacks have suffered dramatically higher disease and mortality rates than whites, at least since the Civil War and Emancipation, when comparative studies were first begun. During the post-Reconstruction era, freed slaves died at such alarming rates that white observers predicted that African Americans were headed for extinction. Many concluded that black people were "not fit" for freedom. The prevailing belief in this period of Darwinian logic, which celebrated the "survival of the fittest," was that blacks were genetically inferior and would hence die out as a race. American Indians were similarly thought to be "vanishing Americans." Medical science was a crucial component in support of this belief, just as it had been a bulwark to moral complacency about slavery.[44]

The specific era in which the Drew legend took root, and which it reflected, was characterized quite dramatically by two important facts. First, by the mid–twentieth century, access to a modern hospital had become the preeminent symbol of decent medical care.[45] Second, there was a significantly inadequate number of doctors, hospital, and hospital beds for black people throughout the first seven decades of the twentieth century.[46] Writing in 1957, W. Montague Cobb summed up the historical roots of this situation and termed it the black "medical ghetto."[47] He pointed out that there were only two black medical schools, Howard[48] and Meharry;[49] only about ten black hospitals where black doctors could obtain approved internships; and just over a hundred additional black hospitals around the country, the majority of them in the South. During this same era, only a handful of blacks were admitted to white medical schools, and virtually all southern white-owned hospitals excluded black physicians from their staffs and denied young black doctors internships or residencies. Black doctors were also excluded from the American Medical Association and its local chapters and from virtually all other white-run medical organizations.[50]

Throughout this period, the health-care needs of blacks were known

to be significantly greater than those of whites, as evidenced by comparative mortality and disease rates. Although black mortality rates decreased
steadily throughout the era of segregation, they remained significantly
higher than white rates. Throughout the first half of the twentieth century, blacks suffered disproportionately from tuberculosis, infant and
maternal mortality, pneumonia, influenza, syphilis, nephritis, and cere-
bral hemorrhage. In 1948, blacks still died from syphilis at five times the
rate whites did, from tuberculosis at three times the rate whites did, and
from pneumonia at twice the rate whites did.[51]

In his 1987 book about twentieth-century black health care, medical
historian Edward Beardsley summed this situation up as follows: blacks
are "victims of a society built on economic exploitation and on class and
racial hierarchies." They "have borne for far too long a disproportionately heavy burden of illness, physical pain, and emotional despair."[52]

Throughout the twentieth century, black health professionals have
been alarmed by the disproportionately high black mortality and disease
rates. They have periodically conducted major health and mortality studies, the most comprehensive of which were the reports of the Atlanta
University conferences in 1896, 1937, and 1949. The U.S. Census Bureau also issued volumes of social and economic statistics on blacks;
published in 1918 and 1932, these numbers revealed the persisting
inequities. Paul Cornely, a professor of public health at Howard University, researched and wrote a massive report on black health and mortality
for the Rosenwald Fund that appeared in 1940 and was the first such report to have an impact on a large white audience.[53] A book on the Rosenwald Fund's history concluded that by 1948, when the fund terminated,
"Negroes, denied full employment and educational opportunities, still
died in larger numbers than whites of illnesses bred in poverty and
ignorance. Their life expectancy at birth was almost ten years shorter
than that of their white fellows. They made up ten percent of the population, but they had access to only one percent of the hospital beds in the
country. Even in extreme emergency, many general hospitals refused
them admittance. . . . Only recently, three Negro students, injured in a
collision, were denied admission to hospitals."[54]

The Atlanta University conference report on the health and health
education of blacks, published in 1949, reiterated this point: "The practice of providing services for Negroes in separate facilities or in an inadequate portion of available facilities makes it even more difficult for the
Negro to obtain indispensable care. Often, this practice has resulted

directly in tragedy; lives have been lost, which might well have been saved, had the Negroes been admitted to accessible hospitals."[55]

Paul Cornely, the Rosenwald Fund researcher cited above, conducted numerous studies from 1934 on demonstrating the limited medical care available to southern blacks and the severity of their health-care problems. In 1956 he reported, "Hospital services for Negroes in 1930–39 were at the lowest possible level. The availability of hospital beds for them, particularly in the South, was minimal. . . . The first seven or eight years of the decade of 1940–1949 were not too different."[56]

It is, of course, difficult to measure precisely the quality of health care a group receives, but most people who attempt to do so agree that the basic indices of health care in the twentieth century include the ratios of available hospital beds, trained physicians, and, increasingly, trained specialists to the number of individuals in the populations under study.[57]

At midcentury, around the time Charles Drew died, many studies concluded that there was an appalling shortage of beds for blacks in most of the South. In 1947, W. Montague Cobb wrote, "It is the current accepted standard that there should be 4.5 general hospital beds per 1,000 of the population. In 'some areas where the population is heavily Negro there are as few as 75 beds set aside for over one million of this group.' "[58] A Commission on Hospital Care published a report surveying these conditions in 1947 and concluded, "Negroes in the United States form one of the largest minority groups. . . . In general, there is not now available to them the same quality or quantity of medical and hospital care as there is for the white population. This is due, in part, to inadequate facilities, to the inferior quality of those which are available, and to the inadequate number and quality of Negro physicians and nurses."[59] In 1950, the ratio of all physicians to all persons in the United States was 1:755; of all black physicians to all black persons, 1:3,681. In the thirteen southern states, the ratio of all black physicians to all black persons was 1:6,204.[60]

There is no way to know how often what allegedly happened to Drew did actually happen to other black people. But there is no question that the Drew legend sprang not only from the whole nature of the segregated system but also from real incidents of refusal that resulted in death.[61] Undoubtedly, many such hospital refusals went unreported throughout this period, especially in such Deep South states as Mississippi, where the racial climate was more polarized, where black lives were viewed by some as more expendable, and where humane and progressive voices were totally silenced. When neglect, brutality, illness, and early death were the norm for a group of people who were poor and voiceless in prosperous American society, a hospital refusal was not necessarily an extraordinary event: to many, it was simply the way life was.

In the late 1940s, a black doctor in Clarksdale, Mississippi, P. W. Hill, lost his wife and newborn baby because she needed a caesarean section and couldn't be admitted at the local white hospital. Hill had not even tried to get her admitted at the white hospital; instead, he had put his wife in an ambulance and begun a desperate drive north to Memphis and its black hospital, some eighty miles away, only to have her and the baby die en route. When a reporter asked him why, he answered, "In the South, when you're black, you don't try to fight the pattern. White people do not admit black folk to their hospitals. Black folk do not even ask for admission. They just die."[62] In this climate, ordinary people repeated stories of hospital refusals not because they were unusual but because they were emblematic — because they summed up the whole oppressive situation.

Herbert Morais began his book *The History of the Afro-American in Medicine* with a story about a "critically ill" black person being taken to a hospital in a southern city in 1963 and being told that there was "no room" — even though there were empty white beds — because the black beds were full.[63] An *Ebony* magazine article published in 1967 opens with the story of a mother calling a black doctor to treat her teenage son, who is suffering from acute appendicitis. The doctor phones the hospital where he is on staff and is told that no beds are available. The doctor then refers the mother to a white physician, who is able to secure a bed at the same hospital.[64]

The trauma of segregation is embedded in memories of refused, delayed, or discriminatory medical attention. The testimony of many black people, in interviews, magazine articles, and literary works, amply reveals this. And it is not hard to understand why. People are most vulnerable — desperately dependent on others who are trained to help — when they are ill or injured. At no other juncture does the "system" reveal its fundamental humanity, or lack of it, more graphically.[65] And at no other point does being treated as less than human have more serious consequences. Martin Luther King Jr. expressed an awareness of this truth when he commented at a 1966 medical convention in Chicago, "Of all the forms of inequality, injustice in health is the most shocking and the most inhuman."[66]

Explaining why he had always believed the Drew legend, John Hope Franklin commented in 1983, "Stories like that [Drew's refusal of treatment] abounded at that time."[67] Indeed, Franklin himself vividly recalled a specific instance of hospital refusal that resulted in the deaths of two people he personally knew. The incident was quite thoroughly documented at the time it occurred.[68] In 1931, Franklin was an undergraduate at Fisk University in Nashville, Tennessee, when Juliette Derricotte, the university's dean of women, and three undergraduates had the misfortune to have an automobile accident in the small white cotton-mill town of Dalton, Georgia. Derricotte and one of the undergraduates, Nina Johnson, died several hours after being refused care at Dalton's segregated hospital. Not surprisingly, another of the undergraduates on that trip—Edward Davis, a friend of Franklin's—also believed the Charles Drew legend.[69]

Derricotte's tragedy was well documented because she was a prominent black woman and because, as an international YWCA leader, she had significant contacts in the white world. Many incidents of black people being refused treatment at white hospitals undoubtedly went unreported when they occurred, especially in areas where no black newspapers existed.

Certain key events in Drew's own life add a further crucial dimension to an understanding of the Drew legend's origins. In 1941, after Drew had successfully established the first American Red Cross blood bank in New York City, the U.S. Armed Forces announced that black donors would be excluded from the American Red Cross blood banks then being set up across the country. Thus Drew's own blood would have been refused had he wished to donate it to the cause. Later on in the war, after many individuals and civil rights groups had protested the policy of exclusion, the American Red Cross adopted a new policy of accepting black donors but segregating black and white blood.[70] This subtle shift in racism was officially followed as a nationwide policy until 1950. Drew protested the new policy of blood segregation; he made a speech about it as early as 1942, and again in 1944, when he received the Spingarn Medal.[71] Throughout the 1940s, newspaper articles referring to Drew and his work in pioneering the use of blood plasma made mention of the ironic fact that Drew's own blood would have been refused or segregated by American Red Cross blood banks. In 1943, the *New York Daily Worker*, a Communist paper, made an argument against the continuing segregation of blood by using Drew's story to show the absurdity of the practice:

"An official of the American Red Cross the other day told *The Worker*—in answer to a direct question — that the blood of Negro and white donors is still segregated. . . . Dr. Drew, therefore, being a Negro — in spite of the fact that he has done more than any other person in the development of the blood bank—would be considered unfit to have his blood mingled in the bank with that of the men with whom he worked."[72]

In 1944, a *Coronet* magazine article about Drew that was picked up by newspapers around the country began thus:

> When the Red Cross began to collect blood for plasma, that of Negroes was not accepted. Later it was received but segregated, although eminent scientists say there is no known means of distinguishing between plasma made from the blood of persons of different races.
>
> It is therefore ironic that the man who more than any other is responsible for the medical miracle which has saved the lives of tens of thousands of soldiers and civilians throughout the world is a Negro.
>
> He is Charles Richard Drew.[73]

Similarly, the entry for Drew in *Current Biography 1944* noted, "Ironically enough, at the time he set up the bank his own blood would have been rejected by the Red Cross if he had offered it. Even today it would be segregated."[74]

Also in 1944, a well-known New York columnist, Albert Deutsch, focused on the irony of Drew's story in a column he published in the *New York PM Daily* as a biting "memorandum" to congressional representatives John Rankin and Andrew J. May about race, blood, and white supremacy:

> You'll appreciate, I'm sure, the juicy irony in the story of Dr. Charles R. Drew. . . . [Drew was just] awarded the Spingarn Medal for "the highest and noblest achievement" by an American Negro. . . . Dr. Drew rates the award for his outstanding work in blood plasma. And thereby hangs an instructive tale, gentlemen. . . . At the very time Drew was setting up . . . [the] Red Cross blood bank, helping save thousands of American lives through his brilliant scientific and administrative work, his blood would have been rejected by the American Red Cross had he offered to donate it. Later, when the Red Cross modified its policy and accepted Negro blood on a Jim Crow basis, his blood would have been segregated with that of other Negroes.

All because of the blind, baseless prejudices of gentlemen like your-
selves.[75]

In the early 1950s, when they heard of Drew's death, black Americans
effortlessly blended that piece of news with similar stories of traumatic
deaths and with what they had previously heard about Drew. As Allport
and Postman note,

> Our memories are too unstable to retain each particular event
> inviolate in identity, filed away, as it were, for future reference. The
> "storehouse" theory of memory has long since been discarded.
>
> What usually happens is that an event once experienced becomes
> blended with previous related events, so that they form a generalized
> memory. Everyone has had the shock of discovering that he has con-
> fused two different people in memory, or that a single recollection of
> childhood turns out to be a fusion of entirely distinct episodes.[76]

Depending on one's point of view, one may view this phenomenon as
the product of either a faulty, irrational memory or a highly selective
memory with an inner logic of its own. Yet herein lie the origins of the
Drew legend. It may be plausibly argued that black Americans retained
about Drew a memory that something had been refused him, something
related to blood. As in a dream, all the actual events — the events of
Drew's life as well as his death, along with events involving other "victims" — were transposed, rearranged, and blended together until they
made a suitably coherent and powerful story that expressed these people's own experiences. It was not difficult to transform the concepts "his
own blood would have been refused" and "so many have died this way"
into the single concept "he died because he was refused blood."

When people pass on rumors or have dreams, what matters is less the
details — the so-called facts — than the underlying message. Even after
people pass on different details and incorporate new elements into a
story, what emerges is a common tale that meets the psychic needs of the
group. Each person who repeated the Drew rumor told a slightly different version, drawing from an individual reservoir of memory, experience, and imagination. At the same time, in an almost uncanny fashion
that reflects the creative logic of ingrained traditions of story-telling,
different people wove different elements into a common theme so that
the story, in whatever form it was told, remained essentially the same.

It is the importance of the message that keeps a story alive, not the
details or "facts." Even people exposed to the "facts" of Drew's death

and treatment do not uniformly change their convictions about his fate and its meaning. If they have reason to take its basic message to heart, people demonstrate great cleverness in cooking up new versions of the legend to incorporate known facts. Stephen Thomas, a black dentist in Alamance County who began practice in Burlington in June 1950, learned that the Kernodle brothers operated on Drew and gave him excellent care. Yet in 1985 he still believed that Drew had been mistreated and had died unnecessarily. Not surprisingly, he told a unique version of the legend: "You know the way segregated hospitals operated back then. They put him in a ward and left him unattended until they recognized who he was—then he got all the attention in the world. When I came back to Burlington in June, they were talking about it. They said a little time passed before they recognized who he was. One of the Kernodles recognized him. Then he got all the attention he could get."[77]

Very often, as in this black dentist's story, a fact is incorporated into a legend but is given an emphasis and a meaning at odds with the actual historical event it describes. It is true that the Kernodles did not recognize Drew immediately; they probably would not have recognized *any* car wreck victim immediately. But in Drew's case, this did not matter. The surgeons treated Drew right away, and Ford as well.

Allport and Postman conclude that individuals use three mental processes common to rumor transmission, dreaming, and memory retention to transform a true story into a fiction: leveling, sharpening, and assimilation. These processes explain why "as a rumor travels, it tends to grow shorter, more concise, more easily grasped and told." With leveling, the number of details in a story declines sharply as it is passed on until it stabilizes into a brief, concise statement. Sharpening—a reciprocal process defined as the "selective perception, retention, and reporting of a limited number of details from a larger context"—occurs simultaneously with leveling. The two processes always go hand in hand, but the psychologists point out that although "sharpening occurs in every protocol, the same items are not always emphasized. What is sharpened in one protocol may be leveled in another." The multiple versions of the Drew legend verify this finding. The dentist's story is a good example of the process of selective sharpening and also of the final process, assimilation—the "powerful attractive force exerted upon rumor by the intellectual and emotional context arising in the listener's mind."[78]

In the earliest years of the Drew story, we can reasonably assume, it was passed around primarily by black people who were most likely to have heard of Drew — black doctors and other black people in the health professions, as well as those who traveled in circles Drew's life had touched: for example, students and employees of Howard University, American Red Cross blood bank workers, and Amherst or McGill alumni. For those people, the story expressed a personal sense of loss and a long-felt frustration with segregation and segregated medical care.

Throughout the 1950s and 1960s, when groups of black people discussed themes related to the Drew legend — the dangers of the road, painful and humiliating encounters with white medical authorities, the hypocrisy of segregation, the lie of America as a meritocracy, or the futility of higher education and achievement given the persistence of white racism — the Drew legend often came up. Groups of black doctors, individuals most closely identified with Drew, were perhaps the most likely to repeat the story. Many black physicians have reported that the Drew legend almost invariably surfaced at medical meetings from the early- or mid-1950s on. C. Mason Quick, the young black doctor trained by Drew who was on the scene at the time of his death, has encountered the story repeatedly over the years and has tried to correct it many times: "Whenever there is a gathering of black medical people with the same lifestyle the question [about Drew's treatment] comes up. 'Are you from North Carolina?' they ask me. 'Oh, that's where Drew died. . . . Aw, it's a shame — the way he died.' They make North Carolina sound worse than anyplace. You wouldn't believe the bitterness some of these young black doctors feel. It's happened over and over again."[79] Samuel Bullock, another of the doctors accompanying Drew on his fatal trip, said he first encountered the story two or three years after Drew died. To his great frustration, he has been hearing it ever since: "Frankly, I've been trying to bury Charlie Drew for thirty-two years," he commented in 1982. "I don't know how often I have to say what happened to get it right."[80]

Burke Syphax and Jack White, surgeons and professors at Howard University Medical School and former students of Drew, both reported that they heard the story at Freedmen's Hospital from the late 1950s on.[81] Syphax heard the story more and more frequently in the 1960s. In the late 1960s, he and other doctors at Howard got involved in attempting to refute it.

Joe Gordon, another of Drew's students, was in Tuskegee, Alabama, on 1 April 1950, waiting for Drew to arrive at the medical conference. He did not hear any rumor about Drew's mistreatment then; he first heard it in 1952 when he went back to Meharry Medical College after serving in the Korean War. "I heard the story from other black doctors—how he was treated very poorly. He couldn't get blood. That was the thing that broke the camel's back."[82] Gordon moved to Winston-Salem in 1955 and got to know another black physician, Rembert Malloy, who had been on the scene at Drew's death. Malloy told him that Drew "had been excellently cared for" and that "he was never admitted to the hospital because he died in the emergency room."[83] Gordon had believed the legend until Malloy told him the full story.

The black doctor who has unquestionably taken the most heat from other doctors concerned about Drew's fate is W. C. Shanks Jr., the younger of Burlington's two black general practitioners from 1946 until 1986, when the older doctor died. "I first heard the story [about Drew's mistreatment] at a black medical meeting in a big city a few months after the incident. 'He was denied admission to the only hospital in town, a white hospital. He bled to death.' I've had to get on the floor at public meetings—I've tried to dispel it everywhere I've been. It has really hurt me in trying to get young [black] doctors to come to town. Most have heard the story."[84]

As the 1950s gave way to the 1960s, the Drew legend was told in ever-widening circles of people, and increasingly among people who had no connection to Drew. The "rumor" continued to spread, rather than die out, because it took on greater meaning as the civil rights movement grew into a force that both changed individual lives and transformed American society. With the unfolding of the civil rights movement, those who heard or told the Drew legend undoubtedly felt greater urgency and meaning in the story. The consciousness of southern black people and of blacks all over the country was transformed by the historical events of the era and by the psychic pain, anger, and loving solidarity the movement elicited as a powerful group experience. Thousands of blacks and whites participated in the movement. During those years there were more reasons and opportunities for black Americans and their white allies to reflect on the bitter injustices and ironies of the past, to share useful stories, and to expect that the telling of those stories would help usher in a new world. As the years passed and the toll of the movement itself grew—as young black men struggling for justice were killed or abused in the South—the Drew story grew in significance.[85]

Understanding the role of individual psychology in rumor transmission is vitally necessary. But since the creation of a legend is a complex cultural phenomenon, we need to expand our conceptual framework to trace the path of the Drew legend. Innumerable rumors rise from the sea of social exchanges among a particular group of people in a given period of history, but only a few reach the status of legend — what Allport and Postman define as a "solidified rumor, . . . an unusually persistent bit of hearsay which, after a prior history of distortion and transformation, ceases to change as it is transmitted from generation to generation."

Thus, in the next chapter we must turn from the disciplines of psychology and sociology to that of anthropology, and especially one of its subfields — folklore — to follow the path of the Drew story as it solidified into a true historical legend. The Drew legend is above all a powerful African American cultural phenomenon, not a chance individual delusion born of private fantasy and fear. It can only be understood in the context of African American culture, a culture with a history going back almost four hundred years, and one as rich, meaningful, and complete as the Anglo-American culture that spawned a devastating racial mythology about black people.[86]

3

That Black Man Who Bled to Death

On 5 December 1955, at the beginning of the Montgomery bus boycott, Martin Luther King Jr. spoke to an overflowing crowd gathered at the Holt Street Baptist Church. He proclaimed, "Right here in Montgomery when the history books are written in the future, somebody will have to say 'There lived a race of people, black people, fleecy locks and black complexion, of people who had the moral courage to stand up for their rights.' And thereby they injected a new meaning into the veins of history and of civilization."[1]

This prophetic statement was borne out as the civil rights movement grew into the largest social movement America has yet witnessed, with its images flashed worldwide on television screens and its freedom songs sung by groups trying to overthrow oppression in all parts of the globe—from China to East Germany, to Eastern Europe and to South Africa.[2] The movement, along with King's articulation of its meaning, brought the deeply rooted black religious perspective into mainstream American history and world culture. While this perspective drew inspiration and tactics from Gandhian nonviolence, its roots went back to a nineteenth-century folk faith that God was watching America, witnessing black people's suffering, and working to bring about a day of reckoning.[3] This faith was expressed in many ways, perhaps most of all by countless individual acts of resistance to oppression. But its enduring legacy resides most powerfully in the black church and in the many cultural expressions the church has generated, from haunting spirituals to rousing gospel music to powerful sermons to a long tradition of preacher-prophets whose words and lives have functioned as a moral force in America.[4]

In the changed environment the movement created, the Drew rumor was transformed into a deeply rooted African American historical legend and was for a time incorporated into mainstream American history. Dick Gregory, the black comedian who was active in the civil rights movement, believed the Drew legend and told it to audiences throughout the 1960s, the period Gregory later called the "adolescent stage of black expectation" that saw "the destruction of those promises and persons black folks had treasured and admired most."[5] In his anguished book about this period, *The Shadow That Scares Me*, Gregory told the Drew story to express his own bitter awareness that black people could not expect a good education to earn them respect or even the most minimum humane treatment in America, as he had formerly believed it would. In telling the story, Gregory sought to shatter the Horatio Alger myth as one that applied to black Americans. "Human dignity and respect are not based on education," Gregory asserted, pointing out that education obviously did not save Drew:

> Just stop to think how many people the world over would have died if there were no such thing as blood plasma. The research and education of an American Negro, Dr. Charles Drew, made blood plasma possible. His brilliant mind used his education for the benefit of the entire human family. And yet Charles Drew bled to death in the waiting room of a Georgia hospital, following an automobile accident, because that hospital did not accept "niggers." Dr. Drew made blood plasma possible for mankind and died from the lack of it—because his skin was black.[6]

During an interview in 1987 Gregory did not recall when or where he had first heard the story of Drew's mistreatment, but he still believed it. He told a version somewhat different from the one he had committed to print almost twenty years before, but its import was unchanged: "He had an auto accident. . . . [It was] in North Carolina I believe. They took him to a segregated hospital and they wouldn't admit him. They were taking him to a black hospital and he bled to death." Gregory most likely heard the Drew story by word of mouth, probably during the 1950s. "I've known that story for as long as I can remember," he commented.[7]

Gregory offered a window onto the African American folk perspective at a critical moment in the life of the Drew legend. It is not possible, of course, to trace all the oral tellings of the legend during the 1960s, but through Gregory's version of it, and the wider transmission that his version indicates, we can easily imagine how Whitney Young might have heard the Drew legend through the grapevine, believed it, and then written about it in a column that subsequently spread the legend more widely. But to understand more fully the Drew legend's power and persistence, it is necessary first to observe the deeper roots of the legend in African American folk culture.

Black Americans, like other ethnic groups in the United States, most notably Native Americans, have out of necessity transmitted their history orally. Over time they have created a rich body of folklore that serves them as "folk history" — a necessary counterpoint to mainstream "white" American history, which has rendered their struggles invisible. As folklorist Gladys-Marie Fry pointed out, "In the absence of literacy, the traditions of a people are transmitted by word of mouth from one generation to another. . . . Orally transmitted folk legends form the hard core through which the Black tells of his historical experiences. . . . [They reveal] . . . a tough, vital personality whose inner core of stability endured in spite of overwhelming odds."[8] As one can learn through the works of Fry and other scholars who have collected and studied black folklore — Zora Neale Hurston, Langston Hughes, Richard Dorson, Robert Thompson, Sterling Stuckey, Daryl Cumber Dance, Patricia Turner, Charles Joyner, William Montell, and Lawrence Levine,[9] among others — black people have used stories not only to preserve their history and beliefs but also to instruct the young in the ways of the world to ensure their survival.

Levine summed up the historical scope of this black cultural heritage as follows: "Upon the hard rock of racial, social and economic exploitation and injustice black Americans forged and nurtured a culture: they formed and maintained kinship networks, made love, raised and socialized children, built a religion, and created a rich expressive culture in which they articulated their feelings and hopes and dreams."[10] In his pathbreaking book on black culture, Levine demonstrated that blacks were telling their own versions of American history more than one hundred years ago. Out of a deeply felt need to make sense of their past, blacks frequently debunked many of America's mainstream myths.

In the 1880s, for example, folklorists uncovered a story embedded in the local black oral tradition of Washington, D.C., which was accepted as true by a majority of the black citizens in that area. The story went that George Washington, "during his final moments on earth, turned to the friends and relatives gathered around his death bed, 'rolled his eyes' and pleaded, 'Forever keep the Negroes down.' "[11] Another African American folk legend Levine reports is one that tells of Andrew Jackson vowing he will build a house nine miles long and put all the black people in it and burn them before he will set them free.[12]

Historian Raymond Gavins, in an article published in 1989, brought into focus the continuing significance of black folklore in the era of segregation: "Afro-American history, from periods of slavery and emancipation to those of segregation and desegregation, is an incredible human odyssey. It . . . is a story of survival, and the survivors—slaves, free Negroes, freedpeople, propertyless and segregated workers, civil rights activists, students in formerly all-white schools, and community leaders—boldly demonstrate the adage of 'holding out and winning through.' . . . [A] 'rich expressive culture' has reinforced blacks' collective will to survive."[13]

Robert Hemenway, writing about Zora Neale Hurston's achievement in celebrating black folklore during the segregation era, evoked the value she found in it:

Zora Hurston . . . exhibited the knowledge that the black masses had triumphed over their racist environment, not by becoming white and emulating bourgeois values, not by engaging in a sophisticated program of political propaganda, but by turning inward to create the blues, the folktale, the spiritual, the hyperbolic lie, the ironic joke. These forms of expression revealed a uniqueness of race spirit because they were a code of communication — interracial propaganda — that would protect the race from the psychological encroachments of racism and the physical oppression of society. Hurston knew that folklore did not arise from a psychologically destroyed people, that in fact it was proof of psychic health.[14]

In her recent study of contemporary African American rumors, Patricia Turner drew a similar conclusion: "rumors themselves do not cause the wounds from which African-Americans suffer — racism, inequality, and prejudice do. Like a scab that forms over a sore, the rumors are an unattractive but vital mechanism by which the cultural body attempts to protect itself from subsequent infection."[15]

Just as blacks' stories about national white leaders' racism made sense of their world, the Drew victim legend served a valuable function during the racial tension of the 1960s. It did more than warn about the dangers of travel in the rural South and the realities of segregated medical care. By illustrating the larger social reality and by channeling black anger, outrage, and despair, it served a purpose that black folklore had long served in America. Inevitably, it thrived and grew, illustrating Frantz Fanon's observation that "when a story flourishes in the heart of a folklore, it is because in one way or another it expresses an aspect of the spirit of the group."[16] Indeed, stories vividly expressing blacks' fears of bodily mistreatment at white hands have circulated widely among African Americans since their first encounters with whites, during the slavery era. Turner's detailed account of these rumors and legends is a compendium of feared abuses chronicling the depth and range of blacks' psychological trauma throughout American history: American blacks, she notes, have passed around stories of white people as the perpetrators of everything from cannibalism, castration, mutilation, burning, drowning, and mysterious kidnapping to the large-scale murder of innocent black victims and genocidal conspiracies against blacks, in the form of food contamination, leading to sterilization; blood contamination, in the form of the planting of the AIDS virus among blacks by government authorities; or social contamination, in the form of the distribution of addictive drugs in black communities, also by government authorities.

The Drew legend indeed not only referred to a specific twentieth-century dilemma — medical care shaped by institutional racism — but also, like the many rumors and legends Turner discusses, expressed a number of powerful and important themes in black history and culture. Once all its elements were in place, the story evoked memories and awarenesses that reached back from segregation to slavery and beyond. It sprang to new life during the civil rights movement, especially from 1960 to 1968, because the movement itself activated historical memories among African Americans and underscored their deep meaning. Further, the movement, and the extensive media coverage it elicited, provided the nation with a rare moment in which black people's heroism, suffering, and perceptions of the American past were transmitted to white audiences for the first time. Thus, through a conjunction of historical and cultural forces the Drew legend became a part of mainstream American history and popular culture during the 1960s. The legend endures because it continues to express, in a multifaceted way, much about what it has meant historically to be black in America.

The multiple antecedents for the Drew legend can best be understood as themes, rooted in large part in black Christianity, that weave through the saga of African Americans from its earliest beginnings. First is the theme of bleeding to death. Second is the theme of blood shed or freely given as payment for and entitlement to full, equal participation in American society. Third is the theme of apocalyptic resurrection, the redemption of America's soul through black suffering and the emergence through historical processes of transcendent spiritual values. Fourth is the theme of a common humanity blacks share with whites, a theme also essentially Christian and expressed in a well-known biblical passage that is often cited by African Americans; it begins, "For God has made one blood all nations of the earth" (Acts 17:24–28, King James translation). The Drew legend reflects all these cultural themes. Through the lens of the legend, Drew, as a humanitarian blood plasma pioneer, is seen as a black leader who gave blood sacrificially, who was mistreated and consequently bled to death. Those who mourn Drew's death and honor him pay homage not only to the African American heritage but also to humanitarian values — to Drew's faith in the oneness of mankind, in "one blood." White or black, they thereby experience some relief and redemption from narrowly racial or racist values.

It is hard to overstate the archetypal familiarity of the theme of a black man bleeding to death at white hands. Even the most cursory investigation of black history or literature summons up such images,[17] and each era has offered its twists on the theme. The theme of the shedding of blood runs like a dark stream through the history of blacks in America. One of the first major African American historians, George Washington Williams, described his lifework in 1882: "I have tracked my bleeding countrymen through the widely scattered documents of American history; I have listened to their groans, their clanking chains, and melting prayers, until the woes of a race and the agonies of centuries seem to crowd upon my soul as a bitter reality."[18]

W. E. B. Du Bois wrote in a similar yet more hopeful vein, "This is a beautiful world; this is a wonderful America, which the founding fathers dreamed until their sons drowned it in the blood of slavery and devoured it in greed."[19] Vincent Harding closed his history of African Americans, *There Is a River*, in a similar way: "Always the blood, blood of life, blood of death. Knowing that more would be shed, they were remembering the blood streaking the waves of the Atlantic, . . . remembering the blood in the tracks of the Underground Railroad, remembering the blood on a thousand thousand white hands, remembering the blood crying out from the battlegrounds of the Freedom War [the Civil War], blood so freely shed in that year of jubilee, blood for the remission of sins. Many thousands gone."[20]

The black church provided an overarching meaning to this consciousness of blood shed by allowing African Americans a group identification with a bleeding Christ and a faith in resurrection and ultimate transcendence, sometimes with an otherworldly emphasis and sometimes with a more secular, political one. This basic Christian myth entailing suffering, blood sacrifice, death, and resurrection is a cornerstone of the strain of black culture that gave rise to the civil rights movement. During the slavery era, African Americans expressed these themes through unique cultural expressions in the black church, especially through spirituals. These spirituals' powerful impact in uniting protestors during the movement and their subtle transformation into radical new meanings demonstrated the continuity and versatility of black culture.[21]

But Christian mythology alone did not supply the theme of bleeding to death in black history and culture. Just as the Drew legend has a basis in historical fact, real historical conditions reinforced the theme of bleeding to death. The theme flows from African American history at its roots: in Africa folklorists have long said that their continent was bled of its best people as a result of the slave trade.[22] Slave narratives repeated the theme of "bleeding to death." In one of the most famous of these, Frederick Douglass, the great nineteenth-century black abolitionist leader, wrote about how he was once badly beaten by an especially vicious slaveholder and how this beating led to his resolve to resist: "For a time I thought I should bleed to death. . . . [I] presented an appearance enough to affect but a heart of iron. From the crown of my head to my feet, I was covered with blood. My hair was all clotted with dust and blood; my shirt was stiff was blood. My legs and feet were torn in sundry places with briers and thorns, and were also covered with blood."[23]

Slave narratives rest on a bedrock of historical experiences, among which is the haunting fact that countless Africans who died on their way to America on slave ships died of dysentery, a disease that seemed to cause a person quite literally to bleed to death. At the time, dysentery was called the "bloody flux" and was the most common cause of mortality on the Middle Passage.[24] Many other black people "bled to death" as slaves on southern plantations, some from overwork, whipping, and medical neglect,[25] others from medical mistreatment or from nineteenth-century white doctors' improper experimentation on black patients[26] or overeager application of heroic methods as cures. For some unknown reason, blacks did not seem to southern physicians to survive bloodletting as well as whites did. Thomas Jefferson went so far as to advise his overseer, "Never bleed a Negro."[27] During the whole era of slavery, blacks relied primarily on African American folk healers to cure their ills, physical and spiritual, and viewed white medicine with suspicion.[28] During the Civil War, black blood was spilled in the cause of Emancipation: many blacks served as soldiers, and they suffered proportionally higher mortality rates than white soldiers.[29]

After the war, as black people fled the rural South and crowded into cities seeking new opportunities, black mortality rates soared. Most died from diseases that resulted from poverty, inadequate diets, and unhealthy living environments.[30] But the widespread practice of lynching — almost an epidemic between 1890 and 1910 — also took many black lives through the whole post–Civil War era and well into the twentieth century, providing a new set of horrific images of blacks bleeding to death at white hands.[31] Many other black people ended up destitute and dying in hospitals for the poor, giving rise to a whole body of folklore about "night doctors."[32] According to folk belief, night doctors were sinister characters, often robed in white like Ku Klux Klan members, and sometimes called "Ku Klux doctors." It was said that they came in the night, often with a wagon, and kidnapped black people off the streets to take them to hospitals to be experimented on and killed: "victims of the notorious night doctors . . . [allegedly] suffered bizarre and terrifying deaths." Blacks commonly believed that night doctors "bled their victims to death, usually by making an incision at the bottom of the foot."[33] Another crucial part of night doctor lore was the belief that the unfortunates who were kidnapped were also dismembered and mutilated after being drained of their blood. Night doctor lore had real events behind it: poor blacks were frequently exploited as experimental material in charity hospitals, during both the slavery era and the period that followed.[34]

Given the uncertain state of medical science in the eighteenth century and most of the nineteenth too, and given their captive status, blacks were often the guinea pigs of some new method — a surgical intervention, a potion or drug designed to cure them, a previously untried inoculation, or even purely a medical experiment.[35] Whether it was at the hands of a slaveowner using trial-and-error cures on his bondsmen, a medical student learning on a patient at a hospital that served the poor, or an established physician trying to gain fame through a new surgical technique, blacks frequently were the victims. Some antebellum physicians even believed that blacks "did not experience pain to the same degree as whites . . . because of their (different) nervous systems"; such a belief served as a useful rationalization for their excessive experimentation on black patients.[36]

Although poor whites suffered abuse as well, blacks probably suffered disproportionately. Many of the purely medical experiments that physicians conducted relied on the captive status of slaves: even when the experimentation ultimately led to benign life-preserving results, it is clear that white subjects would not have been put at risk in the same way.[37] Usually these experiments were life-threatening,[38] and sometimes they were forms of torture for the participants.[39] In addition, blacks were unquestionably used for public display of medical procedures or abnormalities and were treated with a kind of disrespectful humor in a way that whites were not.[40]

In 1854 a newspaper editor in Richmond, Virginia, commented on blacks' attitude toward the local hospital: "Among them there prevails a superstition that when they enter the [medical college] Infirmary they never come out alive. . . . [T]herefore they will not complain, but will often conceal their real condition until too late to do good."[41] Throughout the nineteenth century, most people viewed hospitals as disreputable places that only the poor and dying frequented. Blacks were not alone in fearing them as experimentation houses that one entered reluctantly, if at all, uncertain if one would come out alive. However, there is evidence that blacks probably had more deeply rooted fears about hospitals, which usually were white-owned and run, than most whites did, and that their fears were often justified.[42]

Another element behind the night doctor lore was the widespread practice of robbing black cemeteries for bodies to be used for anatomical dissection. As David C. Humphrey, a writer on this subject, noted, "The safest way to [procure cadavers without provoking constant outrage] was to steal the dead of groups who could offer little resistance and whose distress did not arouse the rest of the community. . . . [B]lacks lacked the power to protect their dead. . . . Dissecting a black was largely a matter of finding a body."[43]

In northern cities, blacks protested the desecration of their burial grounds when they could, but they were rarely able to stop it. In 1788, when rumors indicated that few blacks were "permitted to remain in the grave" in New York City, the free and enslaved blacks petitioned the New York City Common Council to end the grave robbers' horrible practice: under " 'cover of the Night, and in the most wanton sallies of excess,' they dig up the bodies of blacks, 'mangle their flesh out of a wanton curiousity, and then expose it to the Beasts and Birds,' " the blacks protested. The common council did nothing, however, and one white New Yorker commented that the " 'only subjects procured for dissection are the productions of Africa' " and executed criminals; hc added, " '[S]urely no person can object.' " In 1882, Philadelphia's black community protested the regular, organized plundering of its cemetery for Jefferson Medical College so angrily that the state legislature passed an anatomy law requiring state officials to turn over all unclaimed bodies to an anatomy board. When such laws were passed in a number of other northern states in the late nineteenth century, body-snatching continued under a new guise: it quickly evolved into a "farflung interstate business. Southern body snatchers . . . regularly shipped the bodies of Southern blacks to Northern medical schools." As Humphrey points out, the bodies increasingly came not only from cemeteries but also from southern hospitals, prisons, almshouses, mental institutions, tuberculosis clinics, and morgues — in short, from any place where poor blacks, who had no means of stopping the practice, were likely to die. In the South, this corrupt body traffic persisted well into the twentieth century — longer than in the North, because fewer laws were passed in the South and because southern blacks had less political power than northern blacks.[44]

Another reason for black mistrust of white medicine lies in the fact that southern white doctors, as a group, were among the major architects and propagators of myths of black inferiority during both the slavery and segregation eras.[45] Whether blacks had greater susceptibilities or immunities to particular diseases, both situations were used as rationales for enslavement of them and/or discrimination against them.[46] As slavery increasingly came under attack in the nineteenth century, a number of southern doctors and some northern ones maintained that blacks were so physiologically different from whites that special medical knowledge was needed to treat them. All writing in this vein agreed that on a civilization scale, blacks were hopelessly inferior to whites and, because of their inherited physiology, incapable of improving or progressing in any way. Not all southern doctors succumbed to the nonsense that passed as "medical truth" in this era, but a majority of southern physicians did believe that there were significant biological racial differences and that these differences justified slavery.[47] Very often, doctors took the position that "black blood" was fundamentally different from white blood. Not surprisingly, medical care in the post–Civil War and segregation eras failed to meet the most basic human needs of black people.[48] White doctors, anthropologists, and sociologists subsequently blamed black people themselves for their high mortality and disease rates, attributing such numbers to biological inferiority.[49] Thus, the encounter between white caretakers and black victims has a multilayered history of betrayal and mistrust behind it, a history reflected in a large body of oral and written lore preceding the Drew legend. From slave narratives to modern fiction, black storytellers reenact many versions of this harmful encounter.[50]

In Ralph Ellison's *Invisible Man*, a pivotal scene shows the black protagonist trapped in a white-run hospital suffering medical "care" that is in fact a kind of medical experimentation designed to render him impotent as a human personality:

I listened with growing uneasiness to the conversation fuzzing away to a whisper. Their simplest words seemed to refer to something else. . . . Some of it sounded like a discussion of history. . . .

"The machine will produce the results of a prefrontal lobotomy without the negative effects of the knife," the voice said. "You see, instead of severing the prefrontal lobe, a single lobe, that is, we apply pressure in the proper degrees to the major centers of nerve control — our concept is Gestalt — and the result is as complete a change of personality as you'll find in your fairy-tale cases of criminals transformed into amiable fellows. . . . what's more," the voice went on triumphantly, "the patient is both physically and neurally whole."

"But what of his psychology?"

"Absolutely of no importance!" the voice said. . . .

"Why not castration, doctor?" a voice asked waggishly, causing me to start, a pain tearing through me. . . .

They laughed.

"It's not so funny. It would be more scientific to try to define the case. It has been developing some three hundred years — " . . .

When I emerged, the lights were still there. . . . My eyes were swimming with tears. Why, I didn't know. . . . Where did my body end and the crystal and white world begin? Thoughts evaded me. . . . No sounds beyond the sluggish inner roar of the blood. . . . Suddenly my bewilderment suspended and I wanted to be angry, murderously angry. But somehow the pulse of current smashing through my body prevented me. Something had been disconnected; . . . I was beyond anger.[51]

Ellison's hero is the Black Man writ large, and all of his experiences are charged with symbolic meaning designed to express a transcendent truth. This particular scene, in which white nurses and doctors hover and joke over the prone, helpless protagonist, who is attached to a machine that administers electric shocks, dramatizes several truths lodged deep in black consciousness. First is the awareness that a black person is not viewed as fully human, and the searing pain this knowledge generates. Second is the realization that white medicine, though it seems to offer respite, is in fact part of the system — indeed, a special instrument of the system. Innocent trust quickly gives way to abiding mistrust toward the dispensers of white medicine, who wound the soul while ministering to the body. Finally, there is the awareness that survival of a kind lies in black culture and in black healers. It is as if, time and again, white medical professionals drain away the lifeblood — the vital essence — of their black patient-victims, while black healers offer comfort, relief, and some essential restoration. It is no accident that when the white doctors ask Ellison's victim what his name is, he cannot remember it. Sorrowfully he recalls, "It was as though a vein had been opened and my energy siphoned away. . . . Maybe I was just this blackness and bewilderment and pain."[52] Yet when the doctors insist on an answer, he finds some solace in identifying himself with figures from black folklore: Buckeye and Brer Rabbit. "I laughed, deep, deep inside me, giddy with the delight of self-discovery and the desire to hide it. Somehow I was Buckeye the Rabbit . . . or had been, when as children we danced and sang barefoot in the dusty streets:

> Buckeye the Rabbit
> Shake it shake it
> Buckeye the Rabbit
> Break it break it."[53]

Both the Drew legend and Ellison's tale draw their inspiration from a deep stratum of experience, codified in folklore. The fate of both men evokes the same archetype of the black man as the helpless victim of white racism, whose vital forces are allowed to drain away. In the post-Reconstruction era, black folklore supplied the image of night doctors draining victims of their blood. During and after the segregation era, it was the hospital's refusal to treat black patients — to let them enter — that caused them to lose all their blood, and thus die. This transformation from one kind of legend to another is related to the transformation of medical care that began in the late nineteenth century and dramatically accelerated during the early decades of the twentieth century. Fry's informants, interviewed in the mid-1960s, no longer believed in night doctor lore but instead tied it to an earlier time, pointing out that hospitals "now" had enough bodies on which to experiment. But one informant noted, "Hospitals is night doctors now."[54]

Especially from about 1920 on, the hospital became the critical institution for the provision of up-to-date medical care.[55] Until the early twentieth century, medical science had relatively little to offer the sick. As one writer put it, before about 1915 the "average person had little more than a fifty-fifty chance of benefiting from an encounter with the average doctor." But the late nineteenth and early twentieth centuries witnessed the major scientific breakthroughs that turned medicine into not only a real healing art but also a powerful and prestigious profession in American society.[56] Just as medical science was undergoing this transformation, the same medical science was judging black Americans unworthy to benefit from its progress.

A powerful indication of black attitudes toward white medicine is a widespread phenomenon that doctors and Red Cross blood bank workers have observed over a period of many years. African Americans have long been reluctant to donate blood, and they volunteer their blood in proportionally smaller numbers than other Americans do. This reluctance originally was thought to stem from deep-rooted folk superstitions about blood loss,[57] but more recent observers of the phenomenon have realized that racial discrimination and persisting inequality have been important causal factors: the reluctance reflects a pervasive and profound distrust of white medicine.[58]

The Tuskegee syphilis experiment, a classic example of twentieth-century white racist attitudes, illustrates the kind of historical encounters that shaped black perceptions of white medicine. James Jones's

1981 book, *Bad Blood: The Tuskegee Syphilis Experiment — A Tragedy of Race and Medicine*, describes a forty-year medical experiment in which the United States Public Health Service allowed 399 poor black men in rural Alabama to suffer the ravaging and often fatal effects of untreated syphilis. The researchers claimed that the experiment was justified by the scientific knowledge to be gained from it, but even its research design was flawed. White doctors lied to their black patients, failing to inform them that they were suffering from a fatal disease. Subjects of the study were only told that they had "bad blood." They were not treated even after penicillin, a known cure of syphilis, was discovered in the 1940s. These doctors led their patients to believe that they were receiving treatment for their condition (a "blood tonic"); then they conducted autopsies on the patients' disease-ridden bodies.[59] The black men in the Tuskegee syphilis experiment were, in a metaphoric sense, allowed to "bleed to death" as a result of medical neglect and hypocrisy.

Thus, when viewed through the lens of black culture, the Drew legend was not a new story but a very old one: it rested on several layers of earlier black medical folklore. Predating the Drew legend and often told in the same breath with it is another "bleeding to death" story that is well known among black Americans — the Bessie Smith legend.[60] Smith, a famed blues singer, died on 26 September 1937 after a late-night auto accident near Clarksdale, Mississippi. Smith actually died in Clarksdale's small black hospital, the G. T. Thomas Hospital, and probably was not even taken to the better-equipped white hospital. Rigid segregation prevailed in Mississippi in the 1930s. But the rumor that she had been refused treatment at Clarksdale's white hospital and had thus bled to death began circulating within days after she died. Like the Drew rumor, the Bessie Smith rumor was unstoppable once it got underway, and it too remains an often-repeated bit of African American folk history.[61] In 1960, Edward Albee ensured the Bessie Smith story historical permanency by publishing *The Death of Bessie Smith*, a play that dramatized her legendary demise.[62] Later one of her biographers aptly commented, "Bessie Smith became better known for the way in which she allegedly died than for what she had done in life."[63] The precise circumstances surrounding Smith's death, like those surrounding Drew's death, are still being debated today, and even her biographers do not agree on how she died.[64] In one sense, though, the Bessie Smith legend is true: she literally could not be and was not treated at Clarksdale's white hospital.

The theme of black people's blood — their suffering and sacrifice — as the price of full citizenship, and the related theme of redemption and justice for the whole community, white as well as black, also reach far back into African American history, reflecting a unique prophetic aspect of black Christianity. Martin Luther King Jr. believed that black freedom would make white freedom possible and, further, that white freedom was conditioned on black freedom.[65] In this belief, he followed a long line of black prophets who held a similar view. A number of African American leaders and spokesmen — David Walker, Nat Turner, Henry Highland Garnet, Frederick Douglass, and W. E. B. Du Bois, to name a few — used blood imagery to express these allied themes. Each conveyed a vision of black Americans as a people destined to spill their blood so that America can become what it professes to be.

Walker, a free black born in the South in 1785, traveled widely and lectured on the abolition of slavery. His *Appeal*, published in 1829, was an impassioned call for slave rebellion. In it, Walker attacked white Christians for their hypocrisy and prophesied that a just God would destroy America if it did not end slavery: "I tell you Americans! that unless you speedily alter your course, you and your Country are gone!!!!!! For God Almighty will tear up the very face of the earth!!! . . . Do you think that our blood is hidden from the Lord, because you can hide it from the rest of the world. . . . Will he not publish your secret crimes on the house top?"[66]

In 1831, Nat Turner led a bloody slave revolt in Virginia in which some fifty-five whites were killed. He was inspired by visions: one showed white and black spirits in battle and blood flowing in streams, and another showed the crucified Christ laying down his yoke so that Turner could take it up and bring on the "great day of judgment." Turner saw "drops of blood on corn as though it were dew from heaven" and regarded this as a sign that the time was fast approaching for what he viewed as his act of Christlike redemption.[67]

Henry Highland Garnet, a black minister and abolitionist leader, despaired of appeals to white Christian morality as a means of ending slavery, and in 1843 he called for its violent overthrow by the slaves themselves: "Think how many tears you have poured out upon the soil which you cultivated with your unrequited toil and enriched with your blood . . . there is not much hope of redemption without the shedding of blood. If you must bleed, let it come all at once — rather die freemen, than live to be slaves. . . . In the name of God, we ask, are you men? Where is the blood of your fathers? Has it all run out of your veins?"[68]

Frederick Douglass eloquently called for black emancipation. He argued that emigration or colonization was no solution, since America could become its best self only with the presence of African Americans:

> the destiny of the colored American, however this mighty war shall terminate, is the destiny of America. We shall never leave you. The allotments of Providence seem to make the black man of America the open book out of which the American people are to learn lessons of wisdom, power, and goodness — more sublime and glorious than any yet attained by the nations of the old or the new world. Over the bleeding back of the American bondmen we shall learn mercy. In the very extreme difference of color and features of the Negro and the Anglo Saxon, shall be learned the highest ideas of the sacredness of man and the fullness and perfection of human brotherhood.[69]

W. E. B. Du Bois closed his 1903 book, *The Souls of Black Folk*, with a similar message: "Your country? How came it yours? Before the Pilgrims landed we were here. . . . Actively we have woven ourselves with the very warp and woof of this nation, — we fought their battles, shared their sorrow, mingled our blood with theirs, and generation after generation have pleaded with a headstrong, careless people to despise not Justice, Mercy, and Truth, lest the nation be smitten with a curse. Our song, our toil, our cheer, and warning have been given to this nation in blood-brotherhood? Are not these gifts worth the giving? . . . Would America have been America without her Negro people?"[70]

Martin Luther King Jr., a product of this long tradition of preacher-prophets, expanded the powerful theme of redemption through suffering, adding to it the tactics and commitment of Gandhian nonviolence. He quoted Gandhi to describe the nonviolent resistance necessary for the movement: "'Rivers of blood may have to flow before we gain our freedom, but it must be our blood. . . . Things of fundamental importance to people are not secured by reason alone, but have to be purchased with their suffering.' "[71] In his eulogy for the four black girls who were killed in the bombing of the Sixteenth Street Baptist Church in Birmingham, Alabama, on 15 September 1963, King said, "The innocent blood of these little girls may well serve as the redemptive force that will bring new light to this dark city. . . . The death of these little children may lead our whole Southland from the low road of man's inhumanity to man to the high road of peace and brotherhood. . . . The spilt blood of these innocent girls may cause the whole citizenry of Birmingham to transform the negative extremes of a dark past into the positive extremes of a bright future."[72]

The whole concept of "one blood" — though it has a modern scientific, secular meaning that Drew himself articulated — also has deep roots in African American history and black Christian culture. The phrase comes from a passage in the Book of Acts that ironically has been interpreted both by racists, to justify segregation, and by integrationists, to inspire the cessation of oppression:

> God that made the world, and all things therein, seeing that he is Lord of heaven and earth, dwelleth not in temples made with hands; Neither is worshipped with men's hands, as though he needed any thing, seeing he giveth to all life, and breath, and all things; And hath made of one blood all nations of men for to dwell on all the face of the earth, and hath determined the times before appointed, and the bounds of their habitation; That they should seek the Lord, if haply they might feel after him, and find him, though he be not far from every one of us: For in him we live, and move, and have our being; as certain also of your own poets have said, For we are also his offspring. (Acts 17:24–28 (King James translation)

In 1947, Theodore G. Bilbo, a U.S. senator from Mississippi, wrote in his violently segregationist book *Take Your Choice: Separation or Mongrelization,* "Probably the most frequently used religious plea for the social equality of the races is that 'God hath made of one blood all nations.'" Bilbo then proceeded to attack the concept: "Nothing is more sacred than racial integrity. Purity of race is a gift of God, but it is a gift which man can destroy. . . . Everyone knows that the white person who marries a Negro becomes the parent not of a white child but of a colored one. . . . When the blood of the races mix, the white blood . . . is forever lost."[73] In 1956, Robert Penn Warren quoted a white Southern Baptist minister who similarly insisted that segregation was ordained by God: "'It is simple. . . . It is a matter of God's will and revelation. I refer you to Acts 17. . . . This is the passage the integrationists are always quoting to prove that integration is Christian. But they won't quote it all. It's the end that counts.' . . . '*And hath made of one blood all nations of men for to dwell on all the face of the earth, and hath determined the times before appointed, and the bounds of their habitation.*'"[74]

In the nineteenth century, before Emancipation, slaves who knew the Bible referred to this same passage as evidence that God himself intended their freedom and affirmed the common humanity of black and white people. In her well-known narrative *Incidents in the Life of a Slave Girl*, for example, Harriet Jacobs wrote, "[Slaveowners] seem to satisfy their consciences with the doctrine that God created the Africans to be slaves. What a libel upon the heavenly Father, who 'made of one blood all nations of men'!" She further noted, "And then who *are* Africans? Who can measure the amount of Anglo-Saxon blood coursing in the veins of American slaves?"[75] In another famous slave narrative, *Running a Thousand Miles for Freedom*, William Craft prefaced his saga with the comment, "Having heard while in slavery that 'God hath made of one blood all nations of men,' . . . we could not understand by what right we were held as 'chattels.' "[76]

Martin Luther King Jr. resurrected the biblical "one blood" concept. In a passage that reflects Drew's scientific perspective, King clothed the idea in more modern garb, while reaffirming its moral imperative: "Integration seems almost inevitably desirable and practical because basically we are all one. Paul's declaration that God 'hath made of one blood' all nations of the world is more anthropological fact than religious poetry. . . . The world's foremost anthropologists all agree that there is no basic difference in the racial groups of our world. Most deny the actual existence of what we have known as 'race.' There are four major blood types and all four are found in every racial group."[77]

The Drew legend was catapulted into African American folk history in the civil rights era as the deaths of black people of yet another generation reminded the black community of its history of suffering as the price of Americanization. Leading as it did to bloody encounters between protestors and white racists and to the violent deaths of many black people, the movement conjured up still more images of black people as bleeding victims. But the protestors were more than victims. Through their commitment to Christian love and nonviolence, ordinary people, both black and white, became spiritual brothers and sisters, leaders who displayed remarkable courage and took a stand for transcendent values. Though the early idealism of the movement was eclipsed by bitterness, interracial conflict, and violence, the movement did for a time reawaken faith in the oneness of humanity and the reality of shared ideals. In a number of ways, the movement provided the fertile ground in which the Drew legend grew.[78]

As the 1960s witnessed the increasingly tumultuous events of the civil rights movement, the Drew legend gained further credibility. Whitney

Young, then executive director of the National Urban League, was the first person to commit the Drew legend to print. There had never been a written version of it until the summer of 1964, when he told the story in his book *To Be Equal* to illustrate how serious the black health-care problem was.[79] Young had only recently begun his term as the league's director, and the book was designed to serve as his blueprint for a newly energized, more activist organization. Young was significantly "more outspoken than his predecessors"; he took the unequivocal position that civil rights were no longer negotiable.[80] In April 1964, the *Amsterdam News* in New York began publishing a biweekly newspaper column called "To Be Equal" under Young's byline. It soon became weekly, and by the fall of 1964 it was carried in thirty-seven newspapers around the country, both black and white. Young's speechwriter, Dan Davis, and several other writers on the staff of the National Urban League actually wrote most of the columns after consulting with Young.[81] In an October 1964 column, Young told the Drew story as he believed it had happened, just as he had in the book. This column helped to launch the wider circulation of the legend throughout the 1960s. Young made the story more detailed, more elegant, and more polished than it typically was in a simple person-to-person telling. From 1964 on, for many who heard it, the story assumed the aura of authority, of ineradicable historical truth.

Few Americans have ever heard of the great surgeon, Dr. Charles Drew.

Unlike Salk, Pasteur or Lister, his name is not a household word, even though his contributions were great.

Perhaps, if tragedy had not struck him down one April day 14 years ago, he might have done even more for humanity than he did.

It happened one April day while he and three other doctors were driving to attend a medical conference at a southern university. Near Burlington, N.C. their automobile swerved to avoid an object in the road. Drew was critically injured and began to lose blood rapidly.

His colleagues flagged down a passing car and rushed him to the nearest hospital. At the door, he was turned away. It was a "whites-only" institution.

By the time he was taken to a nearby "colored hospital," Dr. Charles Drew, the man who developed the theory of blood plasma and pioneered the blood bank, had bled to death.

His death highlighted the racial segregation which then existed in most southern hospitals, and still clings to many today.[82]

Many people, especially whites, encountered the Drew legend first in Young's column. For many others, the column probably only confirmed what they had already heard in a less polished form through the grapevine. Young confessed to Drew's sister, Eva Drew Pennington, one of his close friends, that "he hadn't really researched it. . . . So many said it [happened], he believed it. He was annoyed with himself for having done it. . . . He was going to write another book about his fight for black people and correct the story about Charlie, but he died in Africa before he could write it."[83] Young's researcher and ghostwriter for the book in which the legend first appeared in print, a white man named Lester Brooks, essentially confirmed Pennington's explanation, although he believed there had also been some news clippings on which to base the story: "As we related it, he was in a crash and tried to seek help at the hospital and was turned away. It seemed to be well known. This was the prevailing story."[84]

Young used Drew's story to dramatize the state of black health care and to argue for immediate action to remedy the situation. In the column he reported that southern hospitals still housed blacks in separate wards or in the basement, while northern hospitals segregated patients by rooms; he then reviewed the Civil Rights Act provisions that barred hospital discrimination, and he pronounced that American health institutions were operating on "borrowed time."[85] Young's story was carefully timed. Not only did the Civil Rights Act generally bar the kind of discrimination southern hospitals had been practicing, but that same year, on 3 March, the Supreme Court had acted favorably toward black plaintiffs in a medical case that was to hospitals what *Brown v. Board of Education* had been to public schools: the Cone Hospital lawsuit, which originated in Greensboro, North Carolina, and was handled by the NAACP Legal Defense Fund.[86]

Though Young told the Drew story to serve a specific political purpose, it undoubtedly resonated on a deeper level for the many readers who were encountering it for the first time. The social and political climate of the time was so charged that the story rippled out like a deftly thrown stone in a pond, touching a wider and more receptive audience as many Americans began to look at American history in a new light. Historian William Chafe summed this period up as "America's crisis of the soul"; he explained, "Americans witnessed and participated in confrontations that challenged the very viability of their collective identity. It was a time of horror, embitterment, despair and agony."[87]

As historian Harvard Sitkoff noted, "The nature of the struggle [had] changed after Birmingham" in 1963 — after Police Chief Bull Connor set loose attack dogs and turned firehoses on masses of civil rights demonstrators there; and in the months that followed, black anger and militancy spread, erupting into almost eight hundred boycotts, marches, and sit-ins in some two hundred cities and towns across the South. Blacks protesting and suffering brutal attacks by police and white mobs became the number-one feature of the news media during this intense period. Sitkoff concluded that more racial change came in several months of 1963 than had transpired in the previous three-quarters of a century.

In June 1963, thirty-seven-year-old Medgar Evers, field secretary for the NAACP, was shot down by segregationists at his home in Jackson, Mississippi. In November, President John F. Kennedy was assassinated, just months after he had called for a new civil rights bill and after King had articulated his dream to a crowd of 250,000 at the March on Washington. And early that fall, four young black girls were killed in a church bombing in Birmingham. Although the momentum for change that had been unleashed allowed Congress to pass the Civil Rights Act — President Lyndon Johnson signed it into law on 2 July 1964[88] — interracial violence persisted: southern black churches continued to be burned by white bigots, and the toll of deaths kept growing. On 4 August 1964, the bodies of three missing civil rights workers were found by federal agents in an earth dam near Philadelphia, Mississippi; all of them had been shot. Movement activists, embittered by their losses and exhausted by threats, were losing faith in governmental authorities and in America. Speaking at the funeral of James Chaney, one of the three murdered civil rights workers, SNCC member David Dennis cried out, "I'm sick and tired of going to the funerals of black men who have been murdered by white men. . . . We've defended our country. To do what? To live like slaves?"[89]

Between 1964 and 1968, a number of writers and reporters repeated the Drew legend in print. Some obviously relied on the Whitney Young version; others invented their own versions of the story, elaborating new details and heightening the dramatic effect, untroubled about exercising artistic license as long as they adhered to the basic message. From 1964 to 1974, the legend was never questioned in print. This decade marked one of the most traumatic, divisive periods in American history, one that witnessed the expansion of United States' military involvement in the Vietnam War and the broad-based movement against it; Malcolm

X's assassination in 1965; and the bloody Watts, Newark, and Detroit riots. Between 1965 and 1968, some three hundred race riots erupted, resulting in the deaths of at least 250 African Americans, the wounding of 8,000 others, and the arrests of some 50,000.[90] The Black Power movement and the women's movement were born. The period culminated in Nixon's resignation in August 1974.

The year 1968 further engraved the Drew legend into African American folk memory. After King was assassinated in early April 1968 in Memphis, the legend gained new vigor. A legend—even one that has almost died out—often begins to circulate more widely after some new episode expresses its theme. King, like Drew, was cut down in early April in the South; he was a black hero who was taken away suddenly and unnecessarily in his prime. King's death, the riots that followed it, and Robert Kennedy's death the same summer reiterated old, bitter themes that by 1968 were painfully etched in the forefront of many people's consciousness: violence and injustice woven into the very fabric of American society, the waste of those who espoused humanitarian values, and the death of hopes for a more democratic, peaceful society. At this historic moment, Malcolm X's bitter words echoed what many felt: "I don't see any American dream; I see an American nightmare."[91]

King's loss was incalculable. It "robbed the nation of its last best hope for fundamental change, without violence, without hatred," Harvard Sitkoff noted. In the years afterward, King's character was subject to intense mythologizing. Viewed through the lens of Christian mythology, King was seen as a Christlike martyr for a higher cause, a martyr whose blood was shed for many, because he had tried to " 'redeem the soul of America.' "[92] In his speeches and writings, King elicited this reading of his life; when he declared that he had "been to the mountaintop," he aligned himself as well with the Old Testament Jewish leader Moses. He concluded his final speech in Memphis, the night before he died, on a characteristically apocalyptic note: "I want you to know tonight, that we, as a people will get to the promised land. And I'm happy tonight. I'm not fearing any man. Mine eyes have seen the glory of the coming of the Lord."[93] The mythologizing of Drew was shaped by the spiritual themes that were visible in King's life.

The events of the period had a lasting impact on American historical writing, as well as on popular American consciousness about the nation's past and its future. In 1967, for the first time, a historian included the Drew story in an American history book. William Loren Katz, a white historian, used this description of Drew's death in his book *Eyewitness: The Negro in American History*: "On April 1, 1950 Dr. Drew was injured in an auto accident near Burlington, North Carolina. Although he was bleeding profusely, he was turned away from the nearest 'white' hospital. By the time he was taken to another hospital, the scientist had bled to death."[94] The story had now graduated into historical fact. Young's column was certainly crucial in that process, but so was the political climate. When Katz learned, four years after publishing the book, that the story was not true, he commented that although Alamance General Hospital "was free of discriminatory practices, few others in the South were at this time." He noted, "This explains why Dr. Whitney Young, myself, and other authors were willing to accept this version of the story without more thorough checking."[95]

One reason the Drew legend was elevated to the status of historical fact was that the American history profession itself underwent a revolution in the late 1960s and early 1970s. Moderate "Negro history," which had focused primarily on black "contributions," was replaced almost overnight by "black history" and "black studies," radically revisionist interpretations of the American past that focused on America's tragedies and the emptiness of the American dream.[96] The impact of the civil rights, women's, and antiwar movements combined with forces within the profession to create a commitment to a "new social history" — a history about ordinary people, written from the bottom up and incorporating analyses of class, race, and gender. During this period, many basic American history textbooks were rewritten to incorporate the heroes and victims, the triumphs and suffering, of black America.[97] New books were published, including celebratory biographies of black heroes and texts documenting black oppression. The Drew legend was carried along on this rolling tide of change.

In 1968, two more history books told Drew's story: Dick Gregory's *The Shadow That Scares Me* and Dorothy Sterling's *Tear Down the Walls: A History of the Civil Rights Movement* both essentially repeated Whitney Young's version of the legend.[98] In late March 1968, *Time* magazine ran a short piece about the dearth of black heroes in American history writing. One passage read, "Dr. Charles Drew pioneered in new techniques to store blood plasma. Drew, ironically, bled to death after he was injured in a car crash — and was turned away by an all-white hospital."[99]

Sepia, a black magazine, ran one of the most dramatic literary versions of the legend in December 1968. The article explicitly connected the deaths of Drew and King as exemplary of a "sick society." The article's headline and deck read, "Dr. Charles Drew: Blood Bank Pioneer Who Bled To Death — While his life blood bubbled away, the man who gave the nation so much died when refused service in a North Carolina hospital." It began with this dramatization:

"I am sorry, but we do not admit Negroes to this hospital. You will have to take him to your hospital across town."

Sickened, the tall Negro turned away. Back in the car the victim of the automobile accident slumped in the back seat, his life blood bubbling away in a bright stream. He turned anguished, questioning eyes to the driver.

But he knew the answer before it was spoken.

The sight of the blood did not repel the dying man. He had worked with blood for long years, stanching it, testing it, typing it, making plasma from it, discovering new ways to preserve the life-giving fluid.

He had saved many lives. His own he could not save.

By the time they reached the hospital for Negroes, Dr. Charles Drew was dead.

Thus ended the life of the man who was eulogized after his death as one who had "a burning passion to make a better world." In two days and one month he would have been 46 years old.[100]

And the 1974 edition of *Webster's Biographical Dictionary* closed its otherwise accurate entry on Drew with this statement: "On April 1, 1950, he was injured in an automobile accident near Burlington, North Carolina. In dire need of a blood transfusion, he was turned away from a nearby hospital because of his race, and, as a result, he died on the way to a hospital for Negroes."[101]

As the legend spread in the late 1960s, it began to generate increasing conflict and confusion. In 1970, the *Miami Herald* carried two stories about Lenore Drew visiting and speaking at three public schools (two in Miami, one in Pompano Beach) that were named after her husband. The stories were written by two different reporters for different editions of the paper. One story commented that when she was "[a]sked about the commonly held belief by many that the blood bank founder died from the denial of blood plasma, because of his race, . . . [she] said she did not know."[102] The other story reported that when the children were asked to tell what they knew about Drew, one "added a story frequently told: 'He died because he couldn't get blood.'" The reporter neither affirmed nor denied the story but gave it in greater detail: "The story is that Dr. Drew, bleeding to death in a segregated hospital, was denied the blood plasma he helped develop because the hospital had only plasma labeled 'white.' "[103]

The media was not the only entity that registered Drew's ascent into the role of an increasingly relevant but controversial black folk hero-victim. The American Red Cross increasingly became a battleground where conflicts about Drew's role in blood plasma work and his manner of death were played out. In the mid-1960s, the Red Cross received such a torrent of requests for information about Drew, many of them reflecting concern about his alleged mistreatment, that in 1967 the national organization's executive vice president asked its official historian to complete a monograph on Drew to correct the myths about him. Clyde E. Buckingham, the organization's longtime historian, completed the monograph in April 1968.[104] The monograph was intended only for in-house use and was classified as confidential, apparently because it was not considered politically wise at the time to "attempt to demythologize any black national hero."[105] From 1968 well into the 1980s, but especially in the late 1960s and early 1970s, American Red Cross officials repeatedly prepared fact sheets on Charles Drew, sending them to individuals and organizations in order to debunk the Drew legend and monitoring the media's presentation of Drew and his role in the American Red Cross. Typical of this period was an incident in 1967: a community group in Willingboro, New Jersey, sought to foster national recognition of Drew by having Congress declare 3 June "Dr. Charles Drew Day."[106] The local chapter of the Red Cross wrote to its regional office to clarify Drew's role in the organization.[107] The letter was forwarded to the Red Cross's national headquarters, and one of the group's national officials wrote back asserting that Drew had not been "national director" of the Red Cross, as the community group claimed, nor had he "died because 'blood was not available for him because he was a negro.' "[108]

Also typical of this era of heightened interest in and competing myths about Drew was a letter from an individual to the American Red Cross that began:

> One of the most dramatic illustrations of the evil consequences of prejudice and segregation was (is) that Charles Drew who did so much to provide blood for thousands of people, was turned away from a "whites only" hospital and died enroute to a hospital for blacks.
>
> I was shocked to see that you, whose programs owe so much to him,

omitted this little detail in the biographical pamphlet you distribute. You have here an opportunity to quietly teach many people a powerful lesson. Why don't you use it?[109]

A Red Cross official who was either ignorant of the facts or frustrated with the growing controversy wrote back to this inquirer that Drew was " 'dead on arrival at the hospital,' " generating yet another falsehood. He noted that the organization's official historian — presumably Clyde Buckingham — had first heard the erroneous story of Drew being refused treatment in 1968.[110] The official obviously had access to Buckingham's monograph. Either he didn't read it carefully or he was attempting in an ingenious way to quell the whole controversy. If Drew were already dead when he arrived at the hospital, the hospital's policies and actions would have been of little consequence.

A textbook publisher also opted for the "dead on arrival" theory out of his confusion and frustration with the controversy. When his theory was directly challenged, this man simply gave up. Alamance County hospital administrator Marvin E. Yount Jr. attempted to broadcast the facts of the true story after he encountered the legend in 1971 in Katz's book. Yount, the administrator of Alamance General Hospital in 1950, was still on the job in 1971 — the hospital was the same corporation, although its name had been changed and a new building built. He had first heard the erroneous story one day in the operating room from one of his surgeons, twenty-one years after Drew's death: George Smedberg, a white surgeon, exclaimed to him, "Marvin, I didn't know you ran such a racist hospital in the old days!" Smedberg explained to Yount that his son had brought home a history textbook, *Eyewitness*, that said the old hospital had turned Dr. Drew away and let him bleed to death. Smedberg brought Yount the book the next day, and Yount read the false story with amazement and indignation.[111] Beginning a crusade to eradicate the legend — a crusade that would continue for almost twenty years — Yount immediately wrote the publisher to correct the story, which he termed a "highly inflammatory statement": "Dr. Drew was brought immediately after the accident to the only available facility within 30 miles which was a relatively small and old hospital known as Alamance General Hospital," wrote Yount. "He received immediate attention from a Board man in surgery but because of the extreme severity of his injuries, it was impossible to bring him out of deep shock and he died within an hour and a half."[112]

The publisher wrote back that the company had corrected the story in a revised edition of the book. The new version, which was enclosed, read,

"On April 1, 1950 Dr. Drew was injured in an auto accident near Burlington, North Carolina. He was bleeding profusely and was rushed to a hospital for emergency treatment. By the time he arrived at the hospital, the scientist had bled to death."[113]

Not surprisingly, Yount was not satisfied. He wrote back enclosing Drew's wife's letter of thanks to the surgeon, Ralph Brooks, and a more detailed account of Drew's treatment. He included his own suggested revision of the book: "On April 1, 1950, Dr. Drew was injured in an auto accident near Burlington, North Carolina. He was taken to the Alamance General Hospital — now Memorial Hospital of Alamance County — where despite every effort to save his life he died in approximately an hour and a half. Another negro physician, Dr. John Ford, was admitted to the hospital and treated for several days."[114] A few days later, the executive vice president of Pitman Publishing Corporation wrote Yount, "Due to the amount of conflicting information which Pitman has received in reference to this situation, we have decided to delete from the book references to Dr. Drew's death."[115] This episode vividly illustrates the legend's power — and the consequent difficulty of getting at the real story once the legend had spread.

The late 1960s and early 1970s witnessed the death of the civil rights movement. It was a period of alienation, fragmentation, and extreme polarization within almost all segments of American society — between young and old; between conservatives, liberals, and radicals; and between black moderates and black extremists. The history of the Drew victim legend can be viewed not only in terms of its growth over time but also as a story whose message had different meanings at different times, depending on what social group was passing it around. For the black doctors who told it in the 1950s, its message was different than for black radicals of the late 1960s. For the doctors, the story was primarily a tale about inequities in the medical profession; for Black Power advocates and their sympathizers, it became a story about black genocide.

A surviving newsletter from a Black Political and Cultural Enrichment Conference held at SUNYA in Washington, D.C., in 1972 allows a glimpse at what the Black Power movement was making of Drew's life and death in this period of extreme polarization and heightened black consciousness. A science symposium called "Black Power Thru Black Science" was an important part of the conference and was dedicated to Drew. Lenore Drew was an honored guest; a blood drive was held in Drew's honor, and a Charles Drew Scholarship Fund was set up as a permanent memorial to Drew. In discussing Drew's achievements, the newsletter betrayed its author's paranoia about the lack of appreciation of Drew in the wider world and at the same time displayed an almost touchingly naive inflation of Drew's contributions and status:

> [H]e never received the nobel prize "*maybe because no black person is supposed to receive the nobel prize in science*" even though his contribution to medical science has more value to mankind than the contributions of any of the medical nobel laureates of his era, except, perhaps the discovery of penicillin.
>
> There was no surgeon better than Dr. Charles Drew in the United States or anywhere else on the surface of earth at the time of his death.[116]

The newsletter also repeated the legend:

> Yes, his work has saved more than 70 million lives! Yet—
>
> Do you know? Do you know that he died because the HOSPITAL to which he was taken after an auto accident REFUSED TO GIVE HIM BLOOD TRANSFUSION?—BECAUSE HE WAS BLACK—they refused even to allow the creation of his OWN BRAIN to save HIS OWN LIFE!!!![117]

One can see that each phase of this tumultuous period of American history, from 1950 through the mid-1970s, was reflected in the career of the Drew legend—in the actual form in which it was told and in the context of belief that surrounded it. By studying the steady series of newspaper and magazine articles, poems, books, and documentaries, we witness Drew's evolution from a fairly traditional black American achiever in the 1950s to a martyr-victim in the late 1960s and early 1970s. Drew slowly became a fallen god in the pantheon of black culture, an archetypal hero-martyr-victim figure similar to Martin Luther King, President John F. Kennedy, or Jesus Christ.

Three poems about Drew written at different times by different people demonstrate Drew's evolution from an ordinary hero into a demigod. Only the poem written at the latest point in time shows awareness of the legend; however, the visions of Drew invoked by the three suggest the direction in which the legend itself deepened in significance over time.

Ernestine Fleming, a resident of Washington, D.C., wrote a poem called "Blood Not Race" within days after Drew's death and sent it to his mother. This poem focuses mainly on Drew's role as a surgeon and his work with blood. Its message is twofold: that Drew will continue to live as an inspiration to others, and that the meaning of Drew's life — that what matters is not race but love and human connection — will also live. This poem exalts Drew in an understandable, down-to-earth way:

> You took the blood of mankind,
> And proved that God above
> Intended that men should together live
> Governed by the power of love.
>
> .   .   .   .
>
> All men shall bow at your shrine
> A lasting monumental tower,
> For you have proved that race is none,
> But blood the living power.[118]

In the mid-1950s another Washington resident named Georgia Douglas Johnson, a well-known poet-activist in the black community and a friend of the Drew family, wrote a second poem to Drew. She too focused on Drew as a hero-model, but in her poem Drew is presented as a Christ figure from whom victimized young black men can draw strength and whom they can emulate. In this poem Drew's meaning has become more religious and universal:

> He was a prince!
> Undaunted by the galling rasp
> Of prejudice.
> He strode ahead!
> No suppliant on bended knee
> But level-eyed, urbane, of fair address
> He faced the world.
> Nor dallying
> As though he knew
> The time was short
> With night at hand . . .
> And yet,
> With years enough
> (Even as Christ)
> To end his task.
> He had a charge to keep,
> A truth to prove,
> A cause to win!

O sable youth!
Dethroned and garroted,
Regard him!
Drink deeply of his spirit's wine
And then-arise
Elixored, strong,
Strike through the webbed-iron of despair
Unleashed and free,
Then prove yourself
Like him —
A man.[119]

In 1972, Howard Wright, editor of the Black Power movement news-letter at SUNYA, wrote a poem to Drew in celebration of the Black Weekend Science Symposium that honored Drew. In Wright's poem, the legend is not told explicitly but is instead assumed. Drew is no longer only a Christ figure offering sustenance to blacks as individuals; his sacrifice, his death, has given birth to a black nation, and he comes across as more of a Malcolm X figure:

ON THE DAY THAT CHARLIE DIED
MY GRANDMOTHER GAVE UP MATZOHS AND
NEVER THOUGHT OF WEARING GREEN PANTS
WHEN CHARLIE DIED AND TOOK HIS LAST
BREATH THE SUN AS IF BY MAGIC DECIDED
NOT TO SHINE
AND THE MOON SAID FUCK THE SKY AND
WEPT THE SILENT TEARS THAT BLACK
FOLKS SHOULD HAVE BEEN SHEDDING
THE BLOOD THAT RAN FROM HIS VEINS
SEEPED THROUGH THE GROUND GIVING
NEW LIGHT TO A NEW ORDER OF THINGS
ON THE DAY THAT CHARLIE DIED THE
WHOLE WORLD TREMBLED BECAUSE
THEY DIDN'T REALIZE THAT HIS BLOOD
WAS ON THEIR HANDS,
AND THAT THIS WAS GIVING AWAY [sic] TO A NEW
NATION . . .[120]

This poem reflected a new aesthetic, a way of seeing that grew out of the anguished politicization many black Americans experienced in this period. It was a cultural outlook that would transform black culture as a whole, but not all blacks shared it in the early 1970s. Disunity and class conflict that had been briefly buried during the movement reemerged in full force in the 1970s as conservative thinking chipped away at the victories of the 1960s. As historian David Chalmers noted, "By the early seventies [after the United States' military withdrawal from Vietnam], the fire had gone out."[121] What followed was a decade of transition and confusion — a "microcosm of the unresolved conflicts within American society."[122] The course of the Drew legend continued to reflect the changing social climate: from the mid-1970s on, repetitions of the legend alternated with emphatic debunkings of it.

Just as the dramatic spread of the Drew legend was fueled by larger forces, so were different people's attempts since the mid-1970s to debunk the legend. This is not to say that individuals who have labeled the Drew story a "myth" have necessarily been consciously serving a political purpose; in most cases their conscious goal has been to set the record straight. Nonetheless, what people are capable of believing is affected enormously by the prevailing political and social climate. For certain groups far more than others, the civil rights movement had a transformative impact. During the 1970s, many blacks moved out of the ghetto and attained middle-class status. Their move left those unable to exit more deeply locked into poverty and hopelessness than before and resulted in the "bifurcation of black America into a two-class society."[123]

In the more conservative political climate of the mid-1970s, a number of these middle-class blacks were concerned that the larger truth of this new historical reality be affirmed in the publications they read. This shift was illustrated in 1974 when, for the first time, a writer labeled the Drew story a myth. In an *Ebony* magazine article called "Charles Drew's 'Other' Medical Revolution,"[124] Hamilton Bims essentially began a revisionist history of Drew's career when he discussed the fact that a false story about Drew's death had been in circulation for some time. In attempting to account for the myth's existence, Bims made factual errors of his own:

> The dying Drew was sped to a hospital where doctors discovered serious injuries to his chest. His right leg had been severed to the bone. A good deal of rumor has surrounded his treatment, as he was transferred at once to neighboring Duke University. A myth has developed that he was denied transfusion by local attendants at the all-white hospital — ironical, of course, in light of his research. Yet the myth is just that — an intriguing misconception. "They gave that man all the

help they could," says Dr. Bullock. "The only reason they sent him to Duke was that the university hospital had much better facilities. But no one could save him. He was hurt too bad."[125]

Bims challenged the legend and focused on Drew's achievements as a surgeon and teacher rather than as a plasma pioneer. By 1974 a growing number of black people were beginning to see a more complex historical truth in Drew's story.

White southern commentators were also ready for what they undoubtedly viewed as a more balanced historical record. In 1975 a newspaper columnist in North Carolina wrote "One Myth We Can Do Without," an article directly refuting the Afro-American Bicentennial Commission's official biography of Drew.[126] In 1980, on the anniversary of Drew's death, a reporter in Burlington also tried to set the record straight: "A great scientist dies — History books a lie," ran the subheadlines.[127] And in 1982, Stan Swofford, an experienced civil rights reporter on a Greensboro newspaper, wrote a story that was carried on the Associated Press wire and published in newspapers all over the country, titled "Witness Dispels Myth in Black Doctor's Death."[128]

Soon afterward, the *National Medical Association Journal,* the major journal of the black medical world, carried a story attempting to explain the myth and at the same time refute it.[129] In 1984 the *National Medical Association Journal* carried a second story, which decisively refuted the myth by providing the eyewitness account of Walter Johnson, one of Drew's traveling companions. In it, Johnson described Drew's accident and subsequent treatment.[130] A year later, the *Nation* carried a story about race relations in North Carolina and referred to the persistence of the Drew myth as evidence of the power the past still exerted over racial attitudes.[131]

People rarely repeat stories in a social-political vacuum. Those who debunked the Drew legend were likely to come from one of two social groups. The first was black middle-class professionals who identified with Drew and took comfort in knowing that he was recognized for who he was — that he did not suffer the fate of some nameless black man on the road. Such an outcome affirmed their own real progress, made possible by the civil rights movement. Typical of this group were such people as Ira McCown, a black surgeon who was a friend of Drew's, who vehemently termed the legend "a damn lie." McCown believed not only that Drew had been treated but also that he had been treated at Duke Hospital, a more prestigious institution than Alamance General Hospital.

Drew would have been taken to Duke had he been deemed capable of surviving the trip. "They knew Drew at Duke and so the legend couldn't happen," McCown explained.[132]

Like McCown, C. Mason Quick, in his efforts to spread the truth about Drew, had a special interest in the meaning of Drew's fate as a friend and fellow doctor. Although he was aware that many ordinary black people had died and suffered in circumstances similar to those the legend described, it troubled him to think people believed a falsehood about Drew. In an interview, Quick told how in the early 1950s, the town of Fayetteville, North Carolina, where he lived and worked, had only one hospital. Regardless of what their illnesses were, black patients at this facility — Highsmith Hospital — were all put together in a single basement ward. "Space was a problem. I'm sure people were turned away. Many times there were no available beds because black patients couldn't be moved upstairs," Quick said.[133] Quick was a witness to Drew's death, however, and he felt that this gave him a special responsibility to get the truth about it out.

The second group was southern whites, people with their own interests in exploring black history and attempting to foster interracial racial understanding. The Greensboro newspaper's 1982 debunking set off a chain reaction of articles that illustrated how different social groups and individuals increasingly drew very different meanings from the legend. It also demonstrated that individuals will go on believing the legend regardless of what facts are presented to them — in short, that "debunkings" have very little force when the legend points to deep-seated historical truths.

The Greensboro article ran in daily newspapers all over North Carolina, and in many other parts of the country as well. Editorial writers across the state were quick to comment on it and accept it as the truth. The *Greensboro Daily News* editorial read,

> There are reasons why North Carolina was the target of the Drew myth. Like the rest of the South, it was a rigidly segregated society before the civil rights reforms of the '60s. . . .
>
> Yet Dr. Quick of Fayetteville eloquently put the state and the Drew myth in proper perspective. "I'm a black man and this is my state. I know you can indict North Carolina for a number of things. But you can't indict her for this."[134]

Many black people who read the debunking story questioned its veracity and still had doubts about the treatment Drew received. For example, one man who was apparently a member of the same black fraternity Drew belonged to, Omega Psi Phi, wrote this letter to the editor of the Burlington newspaper:

> The recent front page articles . . . are unacceptable in my opinion. Dr. Drew . . . is a well-respected man in the "Black diaspora" but his tragic death in Burlington in 1950 I believe was caused by racial prejudice. . . . I can recall the hospital I was born in, Homer G. Phillips, named after a black physician and a noted community leader in St. Louis, Mo., who was also a member of Omega Psi Phi Fraternity, [and who] bled to death because a "white only" hospital at the time didn't want to treat him after he was shot.[135] I recently went to a dentist here in the Burlington area, an office near the Memorial Hospital complex. After entering the office (I had an appointment) the doctor refused to introduce himself to me — he told me to look on the door for his name — and he wouldn't even shake my hand after I extended it. . . . I immediately . . . left his office. . . . Yes, . . . people in the "medical field" are still like this in the 1980's.[136]

In this same era of debunkings, the legend undoubtedly continued to spread as folklore within the black community, sometimes, as in the example above, in response to a debunking. It also spread farther into mainstream culture through appearances in popular magazines, newspapers, and even television shows. In the 1970s, the popular sitcom *M*A*S*H* aired an episode that introduced many white as well as black Americans to the Drew legend. This episode played on white people's irrational fears about getting a transfusion of "black" or "mixed" blood during an operation and waking up marred in an irrevocable way, no longer racially "pure." A white patient, about to be put to sleep, says, "Hey, make sure I get the right color of blood, Doc." Hawkeye and his medical team decide to play a trick on the man: while he is under anesthesia, they paint his skin a darker hue. When he wakes up, the black nurse congratulates him on successfully "passing": "They got you down as white. Good work, baby!" One of the doctors then brings him a lunch of fried chicken and watermelon. He grows distraught and demands, "Did you give me the wrong color of blood?" Hawkeye answers, "All blood is the same. . . . Have you ever heard of Dr. Charles Drew, soldier? . . . Dr. Drew invented the process for separating blood, so it can be stored. . . . He died last April after a car accident in North Carolina. He bled to death. The hospital wouldn't let him in. It was for whites only."[137]

In 1980, an assistant professor of history at the University of North Carolina at Wilmington wrote a short piece about black history achievements that included this statement: "a black doctor, Dr. Charles Drew, researched and invented the process for blood plasma that saves millions of lives. Ironically, Dr. Drew was allowed to bleed to death when he was denied emergency treatment at a white-only hospital."[138] And in 1981, when the U.S. Postal Service issued a stamp honoring Drew, the Sunday *New York Times* carried a feature article titled "He Pioneered the Preservation of Blood Plasma." This article told a somewhat muted version of the legend: "He was traveling by car to avoid segregated public transportation when he was fatally injured in an accident in the South. The segregated hospital to which he was taken had no blood plasma that might have saved his life."[139] Later in 1981, a freelance writer published in several newspapers an article called "What Color Blood," which wildly dramatized Drew's alleged mistreatment and unnecessary death:

Drew, age 45, was hemorrhaging profusely, and nothing the ambulance attendants could do would staunch the flow of bright red arterial blood. Unless he could receive a blood transfusion, he would die.

The ambulance screeched to a halt at a hospital, and the ambulance attendants prepared to wheel Drew into the emergency room for the urgently needed transfusion.

But Drew was denied admission to the hospital.

You see, Drew was black, and in 1950, North Carolina hospitals — as well as most other public facilities — were rigidly segregated.

"I'm sorry," the hospital official said, in response to the ambulance attendants' pleas, "but I have no choice. It's the law."

The emergency room personnel directed them to another hospital that treated "colored" patients. The ambulance rushed off, siren screaming, red lights flashing, but it was all in vain. Charles Drew bled to death on the way. For want of a transfusion, a black man had died.[140]

Keenly aware that the legend had not died and was being repeated in Alamance County classrooms in the mid-1980s, one of the county's widely respected black community leaders, Gilberta Mitchell, attempted to get the North Carolina Highway Commission to set up a marker at the site of Drew's accident. This effort failed, because Drew was not a North Carolina native or inhabitant. So Mitchell and a group of Omega Psi Phi brothers then set up an ad hoc committee of local citizens, including Charles Kernodle, one of the doctors who had treated Drew, and Marvin Yount Jr., the Alamance hospital administrator. This group spent a year raising money for an impressive granite marker and in the spring of 1986 organized a memorial service for its unveiling in order both to honor Drew and to refute the legend. More than three hundred people, black and white, including most of Drew's family from Washington, D.C., participated in the event.

Once again, it was an early April Saturday morning in North Carolina, as it had been thirty-six years before, when Drew died: the trees on Highway 49 wore a haze of green; redbuds and dogwoods were in bloom. The large group sat under a blazing hot sun on folding metal chairs on an expanse of cracked red clay located across the road from the site of Drew's accident. They listened in silence as a white choral group sang the "Battle Hymn of the Republic" and as a black board member of the American Red Cross spoke about Drew's legacy: "There is no such animal as black blood and white blood. . . . The puncturing of the myth of racial blood differences may have been Charles Drew's greatest contribution, for it helped us understand our common heritage and our common humanity." Later they came and stood in a circle around the tall granite and bronze marker sheathed in white silk, with "In Honor of Charles Richard Drew" engraved on it, while a band of Omega Psi Phi brothers sang and swayed in unison to their fraternity hymn, for which Drew had penned the lyrics. The cornfield where Drew's car had flipped over was overgrown with pine trees, but little else had visibly changed in this rural community of Pleasant Grove since 1950.[141] Even in 1986, despite this event, local residents continued to repeat the Drew legend.

In the spring of 1989, Onye E. Akwari, a black professor of surgery and physiology at Duke University, coordinated an unprecedented educational conference at Duke for sixty black academic surgeons from around the country.[142] The group — many of whom were members of the Society of Black Academic Surgeons, an organization formed in 1987 — held their closing meeting at the Charles Drew Memorial in rural Alamance County. There, on a rainy April morning, they heard Charles Kernodle, one of the surgeons who treated Drew, speak and testify to the hospital care Drew had received. Yet even after this event, arranged by Akwari because he knew that many of the surgeons believed Drew had bled to death, a number of the participants still firmly believed the Drew legend.[143]

Drew has become an American folk hero. Each April, while cherry and azalea festivals take place in the South, some group in the South is participating in a Charles Drew memorial service, inevitably a ritual invoking high ideals such as the pursuit of truth and human brotherhood. Elementary schools around the country, as well as bridges, buildings, and dormitories, have been named after Drew. Scholarship funds have been set up in his name. There is a park named after Drew in New York City, where he did his blood plasma research. There is a Charles R. Drew Postgraduate Medical Center in the Watts area of Los Angeles, affiliated with the University of Southern California and the University of California at Los Angeles medical schools. A Drew postage stamp was issued in 1981 on Drew's birthday, 3 June. Portraits of Drew hang at the Clinical Center of the National Institute for Health in Bethesda, Maryland, and at what in 1977 was named the Charles R. Drew Blood Center at the American Red Cross Building in Washington.[144] Yet even today, if one picks up a newspaper or magazine article about Charles Drew, the odds on whether one will encounter the legend or the literal truth are about even. Though the Drew legend has been identified, labeled, and called a "myth" in a pejorative sense in print and over airwaves for more than twenty years, it still lives, unstoppable, as a refined slice of African American folk history.

In classrooms around the country, at all levels, teachers still repeat the Charles Drew legend to instruct the young about segregation and its injustice to black Americans.[145] In 1985, when asked if he had heard of Drew, a Washington cabdriver gave a typical response: "He was that fellow who worked with blood and they wouldn't give him any blood, down South."[146] In the same year, Fred Young, the white president of Elon College, the only small liberal arts college in Alamance County, was questioned about Drew. He quickly responded, "Wasn't he that black man who bled to death?"[147] Also in 1985, the director of Harlem Hospital's blood bank in New York City related a version of the Drew legend: "Drew advocated the use of plasma. When he met with his accident, there was no plasma for his use. They had a shortage and they didn't have enough for him."[148]

American Red Cross officials say that many black Washingtonians still refuse to give blood because they still believe Charles Drew died after he was refused a transfusion.[149] "All these things [about Drew] keep coming out every year in Black History Month. . . . Blacks won't give blood in Washington. . . . [T]hey 'know' one of their people died because he couldn't get blood, so they won't give blood," commented the organization's top research specialist in 1985.[150] Almost ten years later, in 1993 and 1994, Drew's daughter, District of Columbia councilwoman Charlene Drew Jarvis, traveled around the country attempting to dispel the Drew legend because she was aware that African Americans continued to be reluctant to donate blood, bone marrow, or organs needed by other African Americans. Many still believed that their donations might be refused to black patients, just as they believe that Drew was refused treatment when he needed it.[151]

The Drew legend has grown since 1950 and persists today as an archetypal story because it expresses the truth conveyed in a 1969 book called *Black Rage*: "For white America to understand the life of the black man, it must recognize that so much time has passed and so little has changed."[152] As a vehicle of communication, the legend merges psychic and cultural-historical realities in a short, ironic message. That message is a statement about the psychic trauma associated with being a black American and about the African American historical experience. Behind the Drew legend are countless individual stories reflecting real incidents from the "middle passage" until the present.

II

The Life
and Times
of Charles
R. Drew

We know that ghosts cannot speak until they have drunk

blood; and the spirits which we evoke demand the blood

of our hearts. We give it to them gladly; but if they then

abide our questions, something from us has entered into

them; something alien that must be cast out, cast out in

the name of truth.

—U. V. Wilamowitz-Moellendorf,

   Greek Historical Writing and Apollo

4

Bright
New
Steel

White racism and its legacy form the subject of the Charles Drew legend. But a legend needs a hero. Drew's character was the frame on which the threads of the legend were woven into the fabric of African American folklore. He evoked admiration and even awe in those who knew him long before he died, for he exuded a heroic aura. Interviews with Drew's family members and friends dramatically attest to this fact and provide a special angle of vision that is further supported by Drew's self-revelation in his writings. His character literally inspired legend-making. Popular and juvenile biographers, filmmakers, and playwriters have been naturally drawn to Charles Drew as a subject and have done their own share of mythologizing about him. There have in fact been a number of legends about Drew, not just the well-known victim legend.

Joseph Campbell's definition of the archetypal hero describes Drew and his life's trajectory: "The hero is the man of self-achieved submission[,] . . . the man or woman who has been able to battle past his personal and local historical limitations to generally valid, normally human forms. Such a one's visions, ideas, and inspirations come pristine from the primary springs of human life and thought. Hence they are eloquent, not of the present disintegrating society and psyche, but of the unquenched source through which society is reborn."[1]

Drew was a special kind of hero. To the racially fraught environment of America he brought an unusually idealistic humanitarianism and a driving passion for scientific truth. Even before Drew's work with blood plasma, there was an underlying tension between who Drew was and what America was. A man unbounded by the normal configurations of race, class, or cultural provincialism, he found that his own nation was a prison shaped by racist myths and structures. The tension grew during his life as he gained a larger arena in which to act — and as his environment clamped down on him. The fact that he did not swerve from his original convictions and managed to articulate them more clearly when life threw a major hurdle in his path — namely, the American Red Cross policy of segregating blood plasma — transported him irrevocably into the public limelight. By dying traumatically in his prime, he completed the pattern that ultimately transformed him into a legendary historical figure.

Drew's beginnings were not those of Ralph Ellison's protagonist — the confused black Everyman of the postwar generation, relatively unaware of his own history until knocked on the head with it. Nor were they those of the legendary poor boy who makes good in the classic Horatio Alger myth, even though some of Drew's biographers have painted his youth this way.[2] Rather, Drew started life as a prince, if a relatively obscure one. He grew up well-supported and secure, with every expectation of success and happiness that an intelligent, athletic, enterprising, and handsome young man can have. Drew's brother Joseph said, "[People have] tried to make us into a poor family — [and Charlie] a Horatio Alger, risen from the ranks. We had no money, but we had enough. We lived well."[3]

Drew was born on 3 June 1904, the eldest of five children, in a rambling sixteen-room house that belonged to his maternal grandparents, Joseph and Emma Burrell, at 1806 E Street NW in Washington, D.C. Drew's parents, Richard Thomas Drew and Nora Rosella Burrell Drew, had been living with his father's kin at 821 Twenty-first Street NW, but they came to the big house on E Street to await his arrival and his home delivery by the family doctor, Charles Marshall of Freedmen's Hospital. They moved to the house somewhat more permanently in 1908, after three years at another Drew home at 1149 Twenty-first Street NW (1905–8). And in 1914, when four children had been born, they moved down the street from the big family house to Number 1826. All of these childhood homes were in a mixed though predominantly black neighborhood: there were Irish, Italian, French, and Jewish stores, and white neighbors as well. Called "Foggy Bottom" because of the "heavy mists from the Potomac,"[4] it was a tough but respectable part of the city, with many single-family brick dwellings.

Segregation was a daily reality: "if you crossed certain lines, you usually had a fight and would throw a few bricks."[5] One of the neighborhood swimming pools and the nearby movie theater on Ninth Street were for whites only, as were virtually all of the district's restaurants, places of entertainment, sporting events, hotels, and department stores. Washington was a city with a distinctly southern ambiance, and its school system was rigidly segregated. Black Washingtonians did, however, have their own swimming pool at the foot of the Washington Monument, and the Sylvan Theatre there was open to both races, as were four baseball diamonds and a skating rink on the Ellipse. "We were aware of discrimination, yet we lived in our own little world," Joseph Drew noted in 1985. "Of course, there could be some prejudice, but it never touched us. The whites [near us] weren't any better off, and they were not as well off educationally."[6]

The Drews lived modestly, and the two boys worked at afternoon and summer jobs — mostly newspaper routes and construction work. Drew's father had attended the famous M Street High School,[7] the predecessor to Dunbar High School. He earned a steady income as a carpetlayer, at least until the Great Depression hit. The elder Drew was a gentle, family-oriented man, red-haired and freckled, whose skills included boxing,[8] swimming, baseball, barbering, and singing. He belonged to a barbershop quartet called The Highwarden Quartet, which performed on riverboat excursions down the Potomac River past Mount Vernon.[9] He had the distinction of being the only black member of an all-white American Federation of Labor union — the Carpet, Linoleum, and Soft Tile–Layers Union accepted him because his "work was so good"[10] — and the additional boon of serving as the financial secretary of this union's Washington local (Local 85). Drew's mother, an outgoing, strong-willed woman, was highly respected by her eight younger siblings[11] and by her own children. She was among a handful of black women of her generation to graduate from college. After completing a degree in pedagogy at Howard University in 1901, she married Richard Drew in 1903 and, except for steady volunteer work in the community, became a full-time wife and mother. Her husband felt his wife "belonged in the home."[12]

The years of Drew's childhood were terrible ones for American blacks as a group: it was the period known as the nadir of American race relations.[13] Lynching was at its height;[14] the disfranchisement of all southern blacks — and Washington's blacks as well — was a recently accomplished fact;[15] the massive legal system of segregation was being erected through the multitude of state laws that were passed following the Supreme Court's decision in *Plessy v. Ferguson* (1896).[16]

In Washington itself, after a brief period of greater opportunity for blacks during Reconstruction, conditions steadily worsened from 1883 on into the 1920s, after the Supreme Court ruled in 1883 that discrimination against individuals was not prohibited by the Thirteenth and Fourteenth Amendments. One writer commented, "By the end of the [nineteenth] century, if it was not quite a hell, Washington was surely a black man's purgatory."[17] After Woodrow Wilson, a southerner by birth, became president in 1913, Washington became much more strictly segregated, and "piece by piece colored Washington fell apart."[18] Educated Washington residents like the Drew family had every reason to be aware of what was happening on both a local and a national scale. The editor of the local black paper, the *Washington Bee*, "shelled the citadel of race prejudice . . . [with] criticism of white American civilization [that] was relentless and often bitter."[19]

The Drews, however, like many middle-class Washington blacks of their generation, had much to be proud of in their own large family and immediate culture. They were clannish and closely knit. Washington in this period was described as having "the most distinguished and brilliant assembly of Negroes in the world";[20] in fact, during this period the city was "the center of the black aristocracy in the United States."[21] Washington's sizable free black community dated back to the late eighteenth century, and a number of black families traced their fair-skinned lineage, and their prosperity, back several generations. Such families "refused to admit to being much ruffled by loss of political influence and the fastening on of segregation. . . . [They] paced their lives to equable and cultured cadences."[22] Washington historian Constance Green divides the black community of this era into three distinct social groups: "the blue-veined aristocrats, of antique lineage and affluence . . . numbering no more than a hundred families; the middle class, 'derived mainly from the District's 18,000 mulattoes,' . . . gaining its livelihood from government jobs and service occupations; and the rest, the lower classes, darker and poor."[23]

Some rigid caste lines within Washington black society were not crossed, and there were also many subtle gradations within these groups.[24] The Drew family at the turn of the century did not yet belong to the elite, since they were relatively new to the city and were middle-class rather than wealthy; but there was nothing to stop their upward ascent in black society. The parents of both Richard Drew and Nora Drew had migrated from Virginia to Washington in their youth and found better lives there, as had thousands of southern blacks of the generation that grew up after the Civil War.[25] Both Drews were so fair-skinned they could pass as white; they belonged to the growing group of Washington mulattos that increasingly dominated the segregated world of the city's social, cultural, and intellectual affairs.

During Drew's lifetime, white ancestry was not something a black person of good breeding discussed; however, Drew obviously had white forebears, probably English and Scottish or Irish, as well as black and Indian ones. His maternal great-grandmother was known to be a white woman, Margaret Freeman, born in Upperville, Virginia, in 1839. There were probably other white ancestors as well: all the Drews looked white.[26]

By the early twentieth century, Washington's black community had developed meaningful social institutions that shaped a distinctive black culture. Most important were Howard University, started in 1867, with its medical school and law school;[27] the Bethel Literary and Historical Association, the "principal forum for enlightened discussion of race problems," where "the most notable Negroes in the country" spoke and newcomers sometimes tried out new ideas and gained fame;[28] the Association for the Study of Negro Life and History, started by Carter Woodson in 1915; and within months after Woodrow Wilson became president, the Washington branch of the National Association for the Advancement of Colored People (NAACP), which for a time became one of the largest in the country, with 143 dues-paying members.[29] Government employment made Washington's black professional class somewhat different than that of any other city. Also important were Washington's black churches, a variety of cultural and musical groups, and its distinctive black social clubs, including the Washington chapter of Sigma Pi Phi (the Boule), black America's most prestigious professional fraternity.[30] The Twelfth Street Branch YMCA, the nation's first black YMCA, opened in 1912. It made available to black youths their first gymnasium and swimming pool and also served as a meeting place for the NAACP and other community groups.[31]

The Drews belonged to the stable, prospering Nineteenth Street Baptist Church, whose history extended back more than half a century and whose pastor, Walter Brooks,[32] was a highly respected black community leader. Within the church and outside it, they enjoyed meaningful social and leadership roles. Richard Drew was the music director. Nora Drew was on the church's board of trustees; a born organizer, she started the first black YMCA in Arlington, Virginia, through her Jenny Dean Club. In 1920, the Drew family had moved to a two-story white frame house at 2505 First Street in Arlington, then a rural, all-black neighborhood, after Elsie, Drew's oldest sister, died during the 1918–19 influenza epidemic (and after a five-day race riot erupted in the district in July 1919).[33]

The Drew children attended segregated schools, which received less money than their white counterparts but were excellent nonetheless. Charles Drew attended Stevens Elementary School and, in the fall of 1918, started high school at the now legendary Paul Laurence Dunbar High School, which had opened only two years before. "A magnificent five-story brick building of Tudor architecture, with 110 rooms," for the next six decades Dunbar maintained a reputation as the best black college preparatory school in the country. Many of its graduates went on to careers in law, government, academia, and medicine.[34] Black historian Rayford W. Logan, born in Washington in 1897, was a graduate of the M Street High School (Dunbar's predecessor) and a member of the Nineteenth Street Baptist Church. In 1977, he delivered a speech praising the segregated world he and Drew grew up in. We were the "lucky generation," Logan said. "Colored boys and girls of my generation were lucky in . . . having been born and educated in Washington, D.C." Logan went on to describe his high school's excellent teachers, small classes, and classical curriculum, as well as his generation's relative innocence and insulation from drugs, alcohol, pornography, and "the vast wasteland of television."[35] The Drews had every reason to look to the future with optimism. "We were gently protected [and] very much taken care of, as God's gifts to mankind. They taught us to do the best you can . . . and that you are superior to those creating problems," Drew's oldest sister recalled in 1985.[36]

Though there was no family favorite among the children, Charles Drew had a special place as the first child; he was without question the shining star in his mother's firmament. There was an unusually tight bond between mother and son from his infancy (when Drew cried so loudly that his mother feared the neighbors would think she was beating him[37]) well into his mature manhood. Drew wrote his mother a long poem when he was a medical student at McGill. Its essence is captured by these lines:

It is the sweet hour — when I dream — make plans — sing — or just sit
And wonder how my little plans, full of hope, into the great plan will fit
Today I have spent this dream hour with you, Mother mine, as many, many before
For me you are still the best sweetheart of all — the one whom I most adore.
You're smiling now — that sweet bright smile — that warms my heart clear through
Sounds like a kid writing his girl — but I know that you know it's true.[38]

Drew's drive to achieve may well have been inspired at least in part, by his devotion to his ambitious and well-educated mother. In 1939, soon after Drew fell in love with his wife-to-be, Lenore Robbins, he wrote her, "On my mother's birthday you wrote me the loveliest letter I've ever received. . . . It is symbolic for me, joining you in my mind and heart, you about whom all my future revolves, to all that is finest, dearest, loveliest in the years that have passed, that part which has clung to at least a few ideals, has striven to be decent and achieve simply because it would please one of earth's sweetest souls, my mother. I should like to do things to make you proud."[39]

As the oldest son, Drew was also his father's right-hand man and the stand-in when his father was absent. Drew's relationship with his father was more low-key than that with his mother, but it was a warm and mutually supportive one. The younger Drew had shown himself to be unusually enterprising and self-reliant, organizing ten boys into a paper delivery business in 1917–19; one summer during high school, he stayed on at a grueling glass factory job in New Jersey long after his classmates had departed, even though the heat burned his hair off, in order to save money. He took over as head of the Drew clan when his father died in 1935, after being laid off from work. Drew loved and admired both his parents, and they loved and admired him. Even at his farthest reaches from home, during his years in medical training in Montreal and later New York, Drew's parents remained the central people in his heart and life.[40]

To his siblings, Drew was a cheerful, energetic, yet always hard-driving presence. They respected him, even adored him, and perhaps sometimes resented him for his paternal strictness with them. His oldest surviving sister, Nora, recalled in 1985, "Charlie was a happy person, popular . . . outgoing . . . with definite charm. Girls loved Charlie. He played the saxophone badly, the piano loudly; he whistled alto and soprano parts at the same time and he sang — we called them 'Charlie's shouts.' " Reflecting on his fame, she added, "He commanded respect by his presence. He stood very straight, a big, powerful man. If I was reading a magazine, he'd say, 'Aren't you going to school in September?' He adored Mom and Pop; he thought Pop was the quintessence of all that was wonderful. . . . I don't think Charlie knew it, but he was always something of a legend, as the first child."[41]

Drew's youngest sister, Eva, commented, "Charlie was very handsome. . . . Girls really loved him. But Charlie was [also] the reliable one. . . . He worked hard and was very conscientious. He was totally organized down to the last tee. . . . I adored him and I was a little bit afraid of him. He had very strict ideas about the way he wanted me to grow up and dress. He became the father of the family after our father died."[42]

From an early age Drew was an eager competitor. At the age of eight, he won all the medals in the "small boys class" at a local swim meet. From there he went on to become a four-letter man at Dunbar and to win the school's James E. Walker Memorial medal for all-round athletic performance in both his junior and senior years. He was also captain of Company E in the Third Regiment of the High School Cadet Corps. During his years at Dunbar, Drew undoubtedly got his first exhilarating taste of what it was to be a leader and a hero, both as a cadet corps leader and as a gifted athlete.[43]

Rayford Logan, speaking about his own experiences as a Dunbar cadet corps leader during President Woodrow Wilson's inaugural parade in 1913, described a kind of incident Drew probably was familiar with:

The colored cadets were, of course, behind the white cadets. On a street behind the Capitol was the staging area for the cadets from the [white] Culver Military Academy. They stood up when the white cadets came by, looked down the street, saw the Negro cadets and sat down. I was Captain of Company A, the lead company. According to instructions, we were to form columns of platoons; we had been marching in columns of fours. I barked out the command: "Platoons right front into line, March!" They performed so well that some of the cadets from Culver stood up. . . . I learned then, this lesson: a lot of people don't believe we can do it, but when we do it, they recognize that when we are given equal opportunity we can compete on equal terms with anyone.[44]

Drew's most important experiences as a youth, however, were undoubtedly on the playing field, as an athlete and team member. In 1940, when he was completing his medical education, he wrote his old Dunbar coach, Edwin B. Henderson, "I owe you and a few other men like you for setting most of the standards that I have felt were worthwhile, the things I have lived by and for, and whenever possible, have attempted to pass on. . . . Some few always have to set the pace and give the others courage to go on into places which have not been explored."[45]

Drew's brother commented most aptly on his personality: "He was always very ambitious and restless. . . . He had a tremendous will to win, to get ahead. It devastated him if he didn't win; Mother would get upset too."[46] Another companion of Drew's youth, W. Montague Cobb, in summing up Charles Drew's personality years after his death, reiterated Joseph Drew's description: "[He was] intense, . . . always sticking to anything that needed to be done and not sparing his own energy; . . . he would spend unconscionable hours to get things finished."[47]

In the Dunbar High School yearbook for 1922, his senior year, Drew is described as "Ambitious, popular, athletic, sturdy." The quotation under his photograph reads, "You can do anything you think you can."[48] Drew emerged from his youth with a more-than-ordinary desire to compete and win; even as a very young man he understood both the cost and the glory of being a victor in the game of life. Possessed with self-confidence and a strong inner drive toward excellence, he had every reason to want to keep playing, especially when the stakes were high.

Charles Drew himself was, like most heroes when viewed close-up, an extraordinary ordinary man. As with most historical figures that reach legendary status, it is difficult to separate out the critical elements that led to his evolution into heroic stature. One could puzzle forever over whether his character attracted to him the events that made him memorable or whether those events transformed his character. But events in themselves do not explain the phenomenon of heroism. An indefinable something within a given individual goes forth to meet events — and possibly even attracts them to itself and to the individual. That inner passion is ignited by events and transforms the individual. In the evolution of a hero, one inevitably witnesses a complex and sometimes long, drawn-out interplay between this inner quality and a set of events. Events at first appear to rain down upon the individual by pure chance. As the individual becomes more self-aware, the events seem less and less arbitrary. In the ultimate test that elicits the individual's heroic behavior, the critical event has an almost-preordained quality about it. Certainly, a close examination of Charles Drew's life and of his ultimate fate as the hero-victim of the Drew legend provides this compelling impression.

After Dunbar, Drew spent a full eighteen years completing his formal education. He was at Amherst College from 1922 to 1926; he was a coach and science instructor at Morgan State College in Baltimore, Maryland, from 1926 to 1928; he attended McGill Medical School in Montreal, Canada, from 1928 to 1933; he spent two years of internship and residency in Montreal from 1933 to 1935; he taught at the Howard University Medical School from 1935 to 1938; and, finally, he completed his formal education at Columbia University Medical School from 1938 to 1940. From the time he went off to Amherst in 1922 to the time he completed his doctor of science degree in medicine at Columbia in 1940 marks a distinct period in his life. When Drew went off to Amherst, McGill, and Columbia, he was primarily hoping, like many others pursuing higher education, to expand his worldly opportunities. But more transpired in this period of his life: being a black student in elite, predominantly white institutions strengthened Drew's character and his sense of mission, making him aware of himself as a pioneer and an outsider in ways he had probably not been aware before. In 1939, he wrote his wife-to-be, "I'm the prodigal, the wanderer, the black sheep of the family — Yet strange enough I fear a bit of the pet because I'm never there [at home in Arlington]."[49]

Patiently and zealously, during this long period, Drew acquired the knowledge and courage to confront those who questioned his worth with the force of his own character and life and with scientific facts. He possessed a forthright, confident manner, a "strength of personality" that drew people to him and made them "instinctively look up to him," Lenore Drew said. Because he looked white, he made it a habit to let people know right away that he was black when he introduced himself. "He was a presence" to be reckoned with[50] and was at ease in any company, humble or powerful, poor or rich. The process by which Drew came to be who he was is highly instructive. It not only allows a more intimate look at American racism; it also shows more precisely the nature of Charles Drew's heroism.

At Amherst, Drew hit his zenith as an athlete. During his freshman year he threw himself wholeheartedly into every sport he could. That year and throughout college, he let his academic studies take a back seat, which led him at one point to a conference in the dean's office and a lecture warning him to shape up: "Mr. Drew, Negro athletes are a dime a dozen," he was told.[51] W. Montague Cobb, who was at Amherst with Drew, said Drew was so versatile as an athlete that he could as easily have played baseball or basketball as track and football. "The track and the baseball coach fell out with each other [over Drew]," said Cobb, adding, "He never got a mark better than C in college."[52] On the playing field, in both football and track, Drew quickly turned himself into a legendary figure, not only piling up awards and trophies but also providing moments of glory that lived for years in the memories of many who watched him play. During his freshman year he lettered in track; he was the school's only freshman that year to earn a major letter. And because he was the track team's consistent high scorer for three years, he became team captain his senior year and also won the Junior National American Association of Universities (AAU) high hurdles championship that year. As the most valuable member of the football team, he was awarded the Thomas W. Ashley Memorial Trophy his junior year; he was also chosen for honorable mention as an All-American halfback in the eastern division in 1925. His senior year he was awarded the Howard Hill Mossman Trophy for bringing "the greatest honor in athletics to his Alma Mater" during his four years at Amherst.[53] When Drew died in 1950, an article about him in the *Amherst Alumni News* noted, "Each college generation treasures its recollection of some particular pinnacle of athletic achievement. The men of Drew's time will never admit that any other high moment could approach his forty-yard touchdown pass to John McBride, which, in the last minute of play, defeated Wesleyan in 1923."[54]

Amherst coach D. O. "Tuss" McLaughry affirmed the same sentiment about Drew and went on to analyze his athletic prowess in a 1952 article in the *Saturday Evening Post* titled "The Best Player I Have Ever Coached." There he wrote, "In all of Amherst College's long history, no campus generation treasures a more glorious football memory than the graduates of 1923–26. Easily their most memorable thrill while I coached there was given them by a tall, well-built Negro halfback from Washington, D.C. named Charlie Drew."[55]

For Drew, in his youth, athletics provided an experience that could not be matched by any other endeavor. The grueling physical effort required, the emotional intensity of being under pressure in a win-or-lose situation, the sense of unity that teamwork demanded and that was elicited in the crowd by a rousing game, and the pageantry of the whole affair — all these matched Drew's temperament and values. In one of his few surviving writings from the period before he went to medical school, Drew wrote eloquently about what being a college athlete had meant to him. He was twenty-two years old and had just graduated from college and left his own stellar career as a college athlete behind, but now he was training other young men to do as he had done. Right after college, during the two school years from 1926 to 1928, Drew worked as the athletics director and as a biology and chemistry instructor at Morgan, an all-black college in Baltimore, Maryland, because he needed to earn money for medical school. He was as successful a coach as he had been an athlete: he brought the school's teams, "especially football and basketball, from little better than high school caliber, into collegiate championship class."[56] The following excerpt comes from an essay by Drew on college athletics that was published in the Morgan College newspaper during football season. In it Drew reveals himself with striking candor and completeness:

> College athletics are to me a means, not an end in itself. . . .
>
> Here early in life, in play, [the athlete] becomes accustomed to meeting all kinds of odds, and overcoming them, if he is made of the right stuff. Here he has to subordinate self for the good of the whole team. Here he learns to keep plugging away, to give more than he has, when his body is worn out and every move is pain. In the throes of impending defeat in agony of a losing battle he learns to fight and fight till the end, with nothing to drive him but his own indomitable will that says, fight on, and the knowledge that others have fought the same battles and won. Such a test tries a man's mettle, and if he survives the battle and comes out "bloody but unbowed" a new world of confidence will be born for that man and this confidence will give

him faith enough in himself to face the problems in the battle of life with the firm belief that he has got the stuff to see it through. . . . On the other hand the man who is physically and mentally fit to play at games, yet fails to make good when put under fire, knows himself for the coward and laggard that he is. Some hope lies in this knowledge. Maybe the yellow streak can be purged in time by real red blood. I do not say that the fellow who does not engage in this killing competitive life lacks any of the finer qualities of manhood or possibilities of heroic action in the case of emergencies; what I do say is that we cannot guarantee these untested goods. We can put our stamp on a man whom we have seen go through the fire and come out more glorious for his having gone through, strong and clean and true like bright new steel.[57]

What Drew had experienced on the football field — and at track meets as well — he was irresistibly drawn to throughout his life. He believed that life itself was serious sport. The team and what one had to give to it to help it win was a metaphor he clung to and redefined as he grew older. But athletics gave Drew not only some of his best moments in college but some of his worst as well. During his junior year he injured his leg while playing football. He developed a serious infection and had to be hospitalized and operated on. His decision to be a doctor dates from this episode.[58]

Drew had arrived at college planning to be an engineer, despite the fact that there were practically no black engineers. He switched to a career in medicine partly because, as he told one magazine interviewer, he "got banged up in football and wanted to know how the body works."[59] When he applied to medical school, he wrote, "My first real urgent desire to study medicine came when my sister died with an attack of influenza in the great epidemic here in 1920. No one seemed to be able to stop it and people died by the hundreds every week. I have studied the sciences diligently since that time."[60]

College athletics also brought Drew face to face, in a way he had probably not experienced before, with the reality of racism. In an obituary for Drew, Montague Cobb, one of Drew's Amherst classmates, reported an "unforgettable" incident of discrimination that he, Drew, and two other black members of the track team had experienced. It occurred during Drew's junior year, early in 1925, when Drew was just recovering from his leg injury.

There were four colored boys on that team. . . . The meet was close but Brown won by a few points. Collectively, the four colored boys had won a substantial number of the points of the Amherst team.

After the meet we found ourselves last to leave the dressing room. As we emerged the rest of the team was standing unusually quietly over by the convoy of limousines in which we travelled. The head coach, the coach of field events, and the student manager, were in a huddle, but still we did not catch on. Then the manager came over and said he was very sorry but that during the meet the Narragansett Hotel had heard there were colored boys on the Amherst team and had sent word that they would not serve them with the team although they would serve "Doc" Newport, the colored trainer. . . . The four of us went to the Brown commons, but it was a silent, spare meal. The convoy picked us up and we each rode in different cars, but the night ride back to Amherst was painfully silent in those four cars. That was such a bad one that it was seldom mentioned afterward even among ourselves.[61]

In football, too, Drew faced racial slights. According to Cobb, "Princeton had been famous for breaking up any colored player" at football games. Amherst's coach contacted Princeton's coach before the game and was assured that there would be no rough behavior. But when Cobb's and Drew's classmate Ben Davis, a six-foot-two tackle who was darker-skinned than Drew, appeared, Princeton fans began to yell, "Get that chocolate bar!" By the second half of the game, the Princeton audience had learned that Drew was black too. "When he was spilled upside down, a cheer went up on the Princeton side."[62]

At college, Drew was forced to realize that no amount of effort or excellence could win certain contests. According to Amherst tradition, he should have been the football team's captain his senior year. But because he was black, and because football was the important sport on campus, he was denied the honor. Drew himself ended the growing controversy over his denial of the captainship by quietly refusing to dispute his right to the position and accepting the choice of a white player.[63] As one of a handful of outstanding men in his senior class, he should also have been tapped to join a special small club called the Scarab. When he was not, again for racial reasons, it split the club in two; some members resigned in protest.[64]

These were not isolated instances of racism at Amherst; many other more casual occurrences forced Drew, as one of "an all-time high of 13 blacks in a school body of 600,"[65] to be aware of his race and the limits it imposed on him. The college fraternities did not accept blacks; neither did the glee club, because glee club members sometimes stayed in Amherst alumni's homes. Another black Amherst classmate, Mercer Cook, recalled, "Everybody was supposed to say hello on campus. But there were certain people who would not reply [to us]."[66]

For any ambitious, idealistic black person, growing up in America in the early twentieth century posed an almost insoluble problem. Drew was not alone in being faced with ironic double messages whichever way he turned. The group of black men at Amherst in the 1920s was exceptional: each one had to find his own way to contain his anger and frustration, fulfill his ambitions, and hold onto his dignity and larger humanity despite the corrosive impact of American racism.

A young black Amherst graduate of the 1960s wrote, "The blacks attending Amherst in the 1920s were indeed a rare breed of people. Coming mainly from the Washington, D.C. middle class and Dunbar High School, virtually all of them went on to become important men in the quest for racial equality."[67] But Drew, as one of his classmates put it, was alone in being "probably the only immortal in the class." This classmate traces Drew's immortality to his developing "techniques to package blood plasma which saved countless lives."[68] Drew's work with blood was crucial in elevating Drew's life to the status of myth. But the work with blood alone did not make him a hero.[69] A significant part of the reason Drew was an immortal, a legendary figure, can be traced to the unique way he attempted to "solve" the racial dilemma that all the other ambitious young black men of his generation faced. In many ways, Drew's football years at Amherst set the pattern for what he would do later on a larger scale. Drew's pattern was to drive himself to excel in an arena where race was no impediment to success and, in succeeding, to scale racial barriers that none before had scaled—and thus open new doors for others. Success in objective arenas, Drew believed, would ensure that his worth was recognized, and in the process, racial prejudice would inevitably crumble. Tragedy was an inevitable price of this "solution."

Choosing medicine as his arena, Drew pieced together an identity during his years at the McGill and Columbia medical schools. Unfortunately, relatively few primary sources survive from Drew's McGill years. Nonetheless, from his writings both before and after this period, we find significant evidence to suggest the impact of these years on the way he ultimately chose to "solve" the dilemma of race.

Even before he went to medical school, Drew knew he wanted to be a surgeon. A woman friend writing to congratulate him on getting into medical school evoked what a formidably determined, idealistic, and mature young man he was at this juncture: "I am so glad to know that you can realize your ambition — Five years from now I can acknowledge the great surgeon — Dr. Drew — as one of my friends — For you will succeed — You are such a splendid type of manhood — Charlie — I envy you."[70] Drew's early desire to be a surgeon reflected his characteristic determination not to settle for the ordinary — in this case, the ordinary path of the black physician.[71]

At the time Drew went to medical school, only a handful of black doctors had ever received specialty training.[72] Black scientists attempting to climb the higher reaches of their professions faced difficulties that were dramatically illustrated by the tragic life of marine biologist Ernest Everett Just, who was then working at Howard University.[73] Because of inadequate funding for black health institutions, black scientists encountered significant obstacles to their work, and black physicians were essentially forced to resign themselves to second-rate medical educations and careers. As I noted earlier, Howard and Meharry were the country's only all-black medical schools.[74] The majority of white medical schools refused black students; the few that accepted them took only one or two each year. The result was that proportionally there were many fewer entering slots for black medical students than for white students. Furthermore, even if one managed to get through medical school, which was a very expensive undertaking, opportunities for black graduates were severely limited. There were very few openings for black interns in white hospitals: for the most part, internships could only be had at black-owned hospitals, of which there was, again, a limited number. Residencies were also extremely hard to come by and were largely limited to black hospitals. The majority of black physicians had segregated practices that were relatively lucrative and secure, but that option limited them to a daily grind with few opportunities for professional growth and little chance to keep up with medical knowledge.[75]

Drew could not have realized all the racial and class barriers he was facing when he decided he wanted to be a surgeon. Young and relatively protected, he simply focused on finding enough money to go to medical school. He was shocked when he learned what it cost even to go to Howard University Medical School. Nonetheless, while Drew was at Morgan he applied to both Howard University and Harvard University medical schools—seemingly the best America's black and white medical professions had to offer. Howard's medical school refused him entry, on the grounds that he had not taken enough English courses to meet their requirements, and instead offered him a position as assistant football coach with faculty status. Harvard accepted him but deferred his entry until the following year because the class was full.[76] Drew was angry at being turned away from Howard; "he told the university officials that if his English was not adequate to permit him to become a student in their medical school, he was sure it would not qualify him for a faculty post in the Department of Physical Education."[77] Drew then applied to McGill University in Montreal, Canada, not only because it had a good reputation but also because it had a decent record of enrolling black students and treating them fairly.

During his four years at McGill, Drew continued to set new athletic records, becoming captain of the track team in his second year and winning Canadian championships in the high and low hurdles, high jump, and broad jump.[78] But for the first time in his life Drew poured most of his energy into intellectual work. Upon arriving at McGill Drew wrote to his father, "I started classes this morning. My class is 125 strong and most of them look like students, very, very few of the typical college looking fellows and they all seem as though they are here on business and the professors talk that way too—still they haven't anything on me, if I ever meant business I mean it now."[79]

Drew had clearly decided to try to become as exceptional in the field of medicine as he had been on the playing fields at Amherst. The results were quickly forthcoming. He won the annual prize in neuroanatomy; he became vice president of Alpha Omega Alpha, the medical honor society; he worked on the society's official publication, the *McGill Medical Journal*; and in his senior year he won the J. Francis Williams Fellowship in Medicine on the basis of a competitive examination given annually to the top five students in the graduating class.[80] Drew completed medical school in 1933, after five years, graduating second in a class of 137 students.[81] The medical school's dean, C. F. Martin, wrote of Drew soon after he graduated, "He was one of our best students—a very charming man, popular with the students and still more so with his teachers."[82]

In spite of these achievements, it was a lonely time for Drew. He had barely enough money to cover his living expenses, and he constantly lived on the edge. Soon after arriving in the city and finding a room in an Irish family's home, he wrote his father, "Frankly speaking, the going's going to be a bit hard. The school is in the most aristocratic part of the city and there is simply nothing cheap to be had anywhere. I walked for two whole days trying to find a room for less than $20 a month, most of them are $25–$30. I pay $20. Board can be had for as low as $35 a month, but you see what that adds up to at a minimum $50 to $60 a month. Doesn't look so good does it?" But Drew's conclusion was more optimistic: "I've got enough to make this year and maybe by that time I will have learned to turn a few tricks here, I always luck out."[83]

The situation worsened after the onset of the depression. Drew's father was laid off from his job. Cut off from his family and from the world of his childhood and youth, and living in poverty, Drew was isolated as never before. On New Year's Day of 1930, he sat down and wrote a letter to himself, reflecting on his painful situation. He spoke of his physical hunger and his hunger for companionship and of his pride and "independence" — his determination not to accept gifts of money from his friends because he did not want to be "obligated" or "prejudiced by . . . obligations." He noted that his friends couldn't comprehend that he was broke even when he frankly told them that he was; he told about how he had once pawned and then recovered his suitcase and tuxedo, and how he did not doubt that he would steal if he got hungry enough. After almost three hours of writing, he concluded, "Here I am: a stranger among strangers in a strange land, broke, busted, almost disgusted, doing my family no good, myself little that is demonstrable. Yet I know I must go on somehow — I must finish what I have started. . . . This is one hell of a New Year's Day!"[84] This period obviously accentuated Drew's sense of being an outsider. By the spring of 1931, after completing three years of medical school, he did not have enough money to continue. If he had not received a Rosenwald Fellowship for $1,000, he would have had to quit and go home.[85]

Nonetheless, Drew made several lifelong friends during this period. One was Richard B. Dunn, who later became a gynecologist in Greensboro, North Carolina, and who recalled, many years later, a favorite student haunt that he and "Charlie" frequented — Kaufman's, where they consumed "pigs' knuckles and beer." Dunn remembered Drew as a "charming, cheerful, and delightful young man who, by sheer force of personality, stood out in whatever group he happened to be in at the moment."[86] Drew was also involved in a fairly prolonged and serious love relationship with a young white woman named Mary Maxwell, who later committed her life to the Baha'i faith.[87] A number of letters from Maxwell to Drew are preserved among Drew's papers. The handwriting is hard to read, but one can determine from them, and from two letters to Drew from Mary's mother, that Maxwell and Drew had an emotionally intense relationship and a real spiritual bond. The letters indicate that Maxwell may have wanted more from the relationship than Drew himself did. It is not clear that Drew was ever in love with Maxwell, even though he obviously cared about her deeply, and she about him. Mary's mother too was fond of the young medical student; in one letter to him she wrote, "Somehow, Charley, courage and gentleness seem the key-note of you to me, and aside from your splendid intellectual attainments, these are innate qualities which have a peculiar appeal to my way of thinking, and I always loved the words of Baha'u'llah in speaking of the higher paths of service in life, such as your own, 'Cowards have no place in these fields!' "[88] This brief comment suggests how forcefully Drew struck others with his seriousness of purpose.

Another important friend was John Beattie, a young English bacteriology professor who stimulated Drew's interest in blood research. Drew traced his earliest significant exposure to this type of scientific research to a biology paper called "Growth," dealing with fluid distribution in developing embryos, that he wrote under his Amherst biology teacher, Otto Glaser.[89] But it was Beattie who played the first major role in introducing Drew to medical research on fluid balance in the body and reactions to shock.[90] After graduating from McGill, Drew worked closely with Beattie, serving as an intern and then a resident in internal medicine at Montreal General Hospital. In order to try to save patients suffering from shock, Drew sometimes had to try to cross-match blood types in last-ditch rescue maneuvers so that person-to-person whole blood transfusions could be given. Occasionally, he probably served as a blood donor himself. The technology of blood-banking had not been developed yet, and it was not uncommon for patients' lives to be lost in urgent situations because no proper donor could be found.[91]

One night while Drew was on duty at the hospital, a fire swept through the building and critically injured a large number of patients.[92] Some people believe that the traumatic impact of this small disaster and the urgent need for Drew personally to play the role of rescuer to a number of patients in severe shock, along with all his other experiences with blood transfusions, deeply impressed on Drew the need for some better antidote than whole blood to the fluid loss that precipitated shock. Drew may well have been drawn to medical research into blood substitutes because he could appreciate the dramatic life-saving potential of such scientific work. Drew's brother Joseph noted that Drew's interest in blood work dated from an incident in which "a couple of people were burned very badly and he gave them plasma."[93] As a doctor, Drew obviously had an appetite for the heroic role that he had played on the football field. The year he died, he described his job as follows: "Each case marks the beginning or end of a life drama. It's in this mood of constant climax that a doctor lives."[94] Soon after completing medical school, Drew expressed his desire to do life-saving scientific work when he wrote the Rosenwald Fund a letter of thanks for his fellowship: "It is my constant hope that I shall be able at some time to add some new thought, discover some new process or create something which will prevent or cure disease, alleviate suffering or give men a chance to live. . . . and thereby in part [I can] repay the debt which I am happy to acknowledge."[95]

Due to the legendary aura that surrounded Drew once he took on a public role as a blood plasma pioneer, his biographers — newspaper and magazine writers as well as authors — find it irresistible to overdramatize any encounter Drew had with blood. One of Drew's more imaginative biographers presents Beattie's and Drew's collaboration at an old man's deathbed in a highly charged scene. They are having trouble finding the right type of blood, and when he discovers that his own blood matches, Drew heroically rolls up his own sleeve, refuses novocaine, and plays donor: "As his blood flowed through the tube into the old man's vein, Drew watched in awe at the miracle that was taking place before his very eyes. The cold, ashen face began to pinken; the life that had teetered precariously on the brink of the grave slowly moved back . . . back. Warm, rich, life-giving blood from a young man's body surged through his system. . . . Drew looked down at the needle in his arm. . . . His blood wasn't black. . . . It was red. . . . 'Take all you need,' said Drew. 'Beans make good blood.' "[96]

At the very end of Drew's sojourn in Montreal, when he had seemingly already cleared the toughest hurdles, he suffered the worst setback of his medical training. He had already obtained not only his M.D. degree but also a Master of Surgery (C.M.) degree, and he had completed a year of internship and a year of residency in internal medicine at Montreal General Hospital. But when he applied for residencies in surgery all over the United States, he was not accepted anywhere. After six and a half years of intense effort and high achievement, he was essentially told that he could go no farther. In December 1934 — his final year at Montreal General Hospital—he received a letter from the Mayo Clinic that apparently made a very deep impression on him. Only a water-stained envelope marked with reddish-brown spots survives; on it, Drew wrote what appear to be notes from a book or lecture or possibly his own private musings:

> Buddha Gautama
> 560 B.C. — the wis- [torn off]
> white elephant dream
> All existence involves suffering; suffering
> is roused by desire,
> especially the desire for
> continuance of existence;
> the suppression of desires
> will lead to extinction
> of suffering
> Whatever is subject to origination
> is subject also to cessation or destruction.[97]

Did Drew simply attend a lecture on Buddhist thought? Possibly, but this fragment of historical evidence probably means more than that. In the same month, December 1934, Drew wrote to Montague Cobb, his old friend from Dunbar and Amherst, and asked him about the "set-up at Howard (University Medical School)," where Cobb by this time was teaching: "No, I am not about to apply for the job of professor, at least not yet, but I should like to have an idea of the set up there, so I might bear it in mind in my further training."[98]

For Drew, the Mayo refusal may well have been a turning point. His letter to Cobb indicates that he was now considering the option of making his career at Howard, as he had not done before. Given that Howard's medical school had refused Drew some years earlier, it may have been somewhat painful for him to realize that Howard might be his only option. He did not know it in December 1934, but he indeed did not have an alternative to Howard. When Drew's father died in 1935, leaving the family with few financial resources to draw on, the need for Drew to come home and take over as a provider for the clan made Howard the inevitable choice. In later years, it was the Mayo refusal, among all the others, that he discussed with colleagues, perhaps because the Mayo Clinic was where he had really wanted to do his surgery residency. In a speech about Drew after his death, Robert Jason, who was then dean of the Howard medical school and had been Drew's chief in pathology during 1935 and 1936, revealed a few of the reasons that the Mayo refusal was so painful to Drew:

Charlie had proved himself to be one of the top three if not the best student of his class. With this background he had every reason to believe that he would have been accepted at the Mayo Clinics for a residency in surgery. He was turned down. In a very frank discussion of this very subject with Dr. Allen O. Whipple, Head of the Department of Surgery of Columbia University, Charlie learned the reasons why he had not found a place in any of the name institutions of this country in which he sought to be trained in surgery. . . . Dr. Whipple [told him], "I am certain that you could do well with the average patient. But could you, with your background[,] feel at ease and render competent service if one of your patients in surgery were a Morgan, an Astor, a Vanderbilt, or a Harkness? We have such patients here. In the selection of our residents we choose only from among superior students and we take into account their family and personal background."

It was in this way that Charlie learned what he had had occasion only to suspect before. In the competition for a place at the top in his chosen field, merit alone was not enough. In this land of equal opportunity for all, he found that the opportunity for him was not equal. He had against him his identification by race and by family income![99]

In 1935, Drew contacted Numa P. G. Adams, dean of Howard University Medical School, to ask whether there was an opening in surgery. Adams, who in 1929 had taken over as the medical school's first black dean, was committed to rebuilding the program so that it would be at least on a par with the better white institutions in the country.[100] Through the support of private philanthropy—particularly the generous backing of the General Education Board (GEB), which was funded by the Rockefeller Foundation—Adams was able to realize many of his goals. Between 1920 and 1942, the GEB contributed $634,000 to Howard University's medical school, affecting virtually every aspect of its activity and making it a far more viable institution than it was when Drew first taught there.[101] Part of Adams's plan was to develop and support black leadership at Howard's revamped medical school. He was supported in this goal by Mordecai Johnson, the university's first black president. Adams had been interested in Drew for some time and thus quickly hired him as an instructor in pathology for 1935–36.[102] In a personal evaluation of Drew during the year, Adams checked off all the stellar qualities that described Drew, then commented, "A very high type of man. Intelligent, forceful. Willing to work."[103]

At the time, a pathology appointment comprised the initial year of an education in surgery.[104] While the preclinical part of Howard's program had already been strengthened with the hiring of new professors and the addition of courses, the school's administrators had begun to recognize that even the best-trained black medical graduates were — as Drew had discovered — unable to get clinical appointments at white-run institutions around the country. It was thus decided that Howard needed its own residency programs in the fields of surgery and medicine. For this purpose a white surgeon, Edward Lee Howes, was hired in 1936 to set up a surgical residency program at Howard with the understanding that at the end of five years, a black successor trained under him would be chosen. In 1936–37 and again in 1937–38, Drew received training under Howes, first as an assistant in surgery on the medical faculty and a resident at Freedmen's Hospital, then as an instructor in surgery and an assistant surgeon in the hospital. Howes liked Drew. In a letter to Robert A. Lambert of the GEB, Howes characterized him as a "good man, who taught well, showed good judgment, and had practically no race prejudice."

There were a number of reasons that Adams so determinedly worked toward the transformation of Howard's medical school into a black-run institution with black heads of departments trained at the best institutions in the country. Before Adams's time, it was an "entrenched . . . cliché" in Washington that the medical school was "run from the [all-white] Cosmos Club. The implication was that although the School's faculty was mixed, the major decisions affecting operations were made informally by the ranking white members among themselves."[105] The result was that the white professors ran the medical school for their own convenience and the black professors failed to get enough clinical experience to move to positions of advanced responsibility. This situation undoubtedly produced low morale among the black faculty, and although there is no evidence to indicate Drew's response to Howard between 1935 and 1938, Drew himself clearly saw the need for the changes Adams was working toward, and he embraced Adams's vision as his own.

Through Adams's efforts, against much opposition, the GEB made available a number of two-year fellowships for the specialty training of black graduates in various medical fields. Adams insisted that his men seek training that would make them competitive with the best white medical graduates, so he encouraged all of them to pursue their doctor of science degrees.[106] Thus, through Dean Adams and a favorable set of historical circumstances, Drew won the opportunity to do what he had always wanted to do — receive top-notch surgical training in one of America's most prestigious medical institutions. Adams recommended Drew for one of these Rockefeller Fellowships.[107] In the fall of 1938, Drew went off to Columbia University's medical school for two years of graduate study under Allen O. Whipple, then regarded as one of the "great men" in American surgery. Drew was assigned to work under the immediate direction of John Scudder, assistant professor of clinical surgery, whose team of researchers was involved in studies relating to fluid balance, blood chemistry, and blood transfusion.

The period at Columbia offered Drew the opportunity of a lifetime, and he knew it. Soon after arriving he wrote his mother, "This place is so immense and has so many ramifications that I haven't even found my way around it yet. . . . What I get out of this year will depend to a large degree on the amount of work I do and the ability to get along with people and get them to give out what they know. I believe I'll do both without too much strain. There are some grand people here, it's good to feel the impact of new ideas and the surge of creative activity." Though Drew was at first bewildered in Scudder's laboratory — immediately after Drew arrived, Scudder apparently took a much-needed vacation and left Drew in charge — he threw himself into scientific research as never before.[108]

Under Whipple's leadership, in the seventeen-year period before Drew arrived, one of the finest surgical residency programs in the country had been developed at Columbia University and Presbyterian Hospital. Whipple, who had been made director of the surgical service in 1921, insisted on longer, more thorough training of surgeons than the usual one year of internship in surgery: under his leadership, the university required surgeons to have an additional three years of residency. As a result, Columbia was a pioneer in medical education.[109]

No black resident had ever been trained at Presbyterian Hospital when Drew arrived, and initially there was an assumption that Drew himself would work primarily in the laboratory and would not attend patients.[110] Presbyterian Hospital had been founded to serve "the Poor of New York without Regard to Race, Creed, or Color"; there was even a legend that James Lenox, its primary founder, had given the money for the hospital because one of his servants, who was black, had been denied admission to the existing hospitals in New York City.[111] The hospital did embrace the principle of nondiscrimination in its treatment of black patients, but the principle did not extend to black doctors. Like most white-run hospitals of the era, Presbyterian refused to offer them staff privileges.

But Drew was determined to get the full experience of being trained as a surgical resident. Through sheer charm and perseverance he won over Dr. Whipple, who by 1938 was at his peak as a leader in the field of surgical education. One of Drew's colleagues commented, "He persuaded Whipple to train him as a resident, to let him come on the wards and make the rounds. It was a bootleg residency—a backdoor thing. He was so irrepressible they just allowed it. Surgical residencies for blacks did not open up until the late 1940s and early 1950s. Most black surgeons who got training before that time got it through paternalistic means."[112]

Ira McCown, a surgeon at Harlem Hospital and a close friend of Drew's during this period, also said that Drew "operated with Whipple because Whipple liked him." He further commented that if Drew "had looked colored, the situation might have been different": he might not have had the opportunity to treat Whipple's patients, McCown believed. Drew was Columbia-Presbyterian Medical Center's first black resident in surgery, McCown said.[113] As a result of Drew's work there, Whipple came to be one of his greatest admirers.[114] In a 1940 report on the surgical residency program, Whipple mentioned Drew's and Scudder's valuable research as one of the justifications for an extended residency program.[115]

Drew clearly made many friends and won over many people in his two years at Columbia. A soft-spoken, sophisticated, and obviously brilliant man at this point in his life, Drew fit easily into the urbane, upper-class, and frequently snobbish ambience of Presbyterian Hospital. One well-known story is that since there had been no black residents before, and segregation was thus the norm, the other Presbyterian residents were asked whether they would allow Drew to eat with them in the hospital dining room. One southern resident, a man from Mississippi named Octo Lee, was "appalled that they would even ask him," because he and all the other residents thought Drew was "just great."[116]

This culminating period of Drew's formal education was an unusually intense time. Once again, there were financial problems. Due to Drew's father's death three years earlier and the continuing financial needs of his younger siblings, who were still trying to complete their educations, Drew was forced to live on a tighter budget than ever.[117] By this time, though, he was accustomed to privation and accepted it as his lot. During these two years he lived like a man possessed, working day and night to get as much as he could from one of the most intellectually stimulating medical environments in the country.

Another important development was the commencement of the relationship that marked the single most dramatic change Drew ever experienced in his personal life. In April 1939, during his first year at Columbia, Drew met Lenore Robbins, a young woman from Philadelphia who was working as a home economics professor at Spelman College in Atlanta, Georgia. On his way to the same annual medical conference at Tuskegee Institute that he was journeying to on his death trip, Drew stopped in Atlanta to visit one of his childhood friends, Mercer Cook, and his wife. When the Cooks learned that Drew had seen Robbins in a Spelman dining hall and wanted to meet her, they gave a party and invited her. At the party the two danced, and for Drew it was a compelling encounter. On his way back from the medical conference, he left his friends, took the train through Atlanta, and roused Lenore from her dormitory at one in the morning to propose to her. Later that spring he wrote her,

> I met you and for the first time mistress medicine met her match and went down almost without a fight. . . . I knew clearly just how lonely I had become, just how badly I needed someone rather than just something to cling to, someone to work for, rather than just a goal to aim at, someone to dream with, cherish from day to day, and share the little things with, the smiles and if need be the tears that will sometimes come. When I first kissed your hand it was almost reverently done for even then I felt an inward surge that was inexplicable. When you walked I felt lifted by the graciousness of your carriage, when you talked it was your gentleness that struck so deeply. When you smiled there was a sweetness that only a fortunate few can carry over from an unspoiled childhood to full glorious womanhood; poised but vibrant, there was something which responded in me and left a glow which still suffuses my whole being and warms my heart. It's a grand feeling, Lenore. The only rash, unplanned, unpremeditated thing I've done for years is already paying dividends in a thousand delightful ways.[118]

Lenore registered her first impression of Drew in an article she wrote about him after he died: "The moment I saw him I knew he was a man to be reckoned with. He seemed to be from another — a more old-fashioned and courtly — time and place."[119] It was a stormy and difficult courtship from the beginning, with Drew passionately pursuing and Lenore questioning whether a wife was what Drew really needed; in the process the two revealed much about their characters. Drew wrote Lenore in May, "I didn't know that I had put anything into my last letter which would make you say, 'Frankly, I'm not sure a wife would help you.' If I did, I take it back." Drew went on to tell Lenore about his many years of being strong for others and yet very lonely. He expressed the feeling that she, like no other woman, could relieve his loneliness by allowing him to be "weak" with her. He wrote, "I feel I could trust you always and heed you as the better part of my own conscience." In this letter and others, Drew revealed himself as a person with great passion and intensity. He obviously was attracted to Lenore not only for her beauty but also for her cool-headedness, her more pragmatic, relatively unemotional personality.[120] In another letter he traced the "unfuddled manner" of Lenore's thought process to her hormonal makeup.[121] As in so many love relationships, what attracted Drew to his wife later became a source of tension for the couple: it was hard for Drew to achieve the intimacy he sought with Lenore.

The two married on 23 September 1939, only five months after they met. Drew's financial situation became tighter than ever when they moved into a small $100-a-month New York apartment at 250 West 150th Street that they shared with another couple — even though Lenore for a time worked as a laboratory assistant at Columbia.[122] Lenore soon got pregnant, and in the summer of 1940 their first child, a daughter whom they named Bebe Roberta (after the Blood Bank), was born. From the spring of 1939 until the spring of 1941, Drew and Lenore rarely lived together for long, partly due to financial pressures and partly due to the changing demands of their two lives, Drew's shaped by ever-more-intense work in New York, Lenore's by motherhood. Lenore shuttled back and forth between Washington, New York, and Philadelphia, and Drew wrote many letters to her, baring his soul about his life goals and his hopes for their relationship. These letters are an important primary source disclosing Drew's heart and mind at a critical stage in his evolution. Increasingly, as Drew's training as a surgeon neared completion, he came to articulate his mission in life. The letters primarily chronicle

Drew's unceasing struggle to achieve, even while they reveal his un-usually tender, passionate, and at times playful nature. In one of his earliest letters to her, he spelled out his life quest: "For years I have done little but work, plan and dream of making myself a good doctor, an able surgeon, and in my wildest moments perhaps also playing some part in establishing a real school of thought among Negro physicians and guid-ing some of the younger fellows to levels of accomplishment not yet attained by any of us. I have known the cost of such desires and have been quite willing to do without many of the things that one usually regards as natural."[123]

A few months into the relationship with Lenore, Drew was trying hard to get her to share his driving vision of personal triumph over adver-sity and apply it to the relationship itself: "We're facing a difficult year Lenore but if our hearts keep right I'm sure we'll come out of it strong and shining like glimmering steel after the severe test of fire to go from there perhaps under less strain."[124]

By the fall of 1939, Drew's final goals at Columbia had taken shape: he and Scudder had applied for and received the backing to start an experi-mental blood bank. Through its operation Drew knew he would obtain the experience and the scientific data to complete a doctoral thesis on banked blood, which in turn would allow him to complete the require-ments for the doctor of science degree in medicine. Also, by this time Drew had won Whipple's crucial backing for his plan to take the exam-ination of the American Board of Surgery and thus receive board cer-tification. He wrote his wife, who was then in Washington, "So you see all the things I told you I wanted to do are at least going to be given a chance."[125] In the same letter Drew told Lenore of the obstacles he had had to face. At least one of his benefactors did not believe that he or any black should receive the doctor of science degree: "[Dr. Robert A.] Lam-bert of the Rockefeller Foundation [then associate medical director] is opposed to it, attempts have been made before by others to no avail."[126] Drew's response to this obstacle was clear: the doctor of science degree took on more meaning to him, and he began to consciously envision himself as a medical pioneer for his race. "There is more here than meets the eye. There are no such Negroes at present. . . . It's much more than a degree I'm after. There are those in high places who feel that Negroes have not yet reached intellectual levels which will permit their attempting the very highest reaches."[127]

Drew was determined to attempt the highest reaches himself. He steadily climbed upward during the next year. Through his research at the blood bank, he produced a mammoth doctoral thesis titled "Banked Blood: A Study in Blood Preservation." It was the size of a telephone directory and was recognized as bringing together all that was known in the field up to that time.

By the spring of 1940, as Drew finished his two years at Columbia, his career dream, which he had sketched out to Lenore in a hazier form a year before, had crystallized. He was more confident than ever in spelling out his desire to develop a team of stellar surgeons at Howard University's medical school. Many of Drew's prior experiences helped him forge his commitment to the creation of a "tradition" in black surgery, with himself as pioneer and his students as his disciples. Drew's athletic endeavors, both as a team member and as a coach, obviously fed his vision. Undoubtedly, Drew also hoped to create what he himself had witnessed at the highest levels of white medicine yet had not been able to experience fully, since he had at at times been treated as an "outsider." And the three years he spent at Howard before coming to Columbia had shown him that his dream of a black-led team of surgeons not only was sorely needed there but would indeed fit within the new black-leadership framework put forth by the medical school's dean, Numa Adams, and supported by the university's president, Mordecai Johnson. As he was completing his education in 1940, he wrote to Edwin Henderson, his old Dunbar coach, about his new goal:

> My next big meet is at Howard in the Department of Surgery. There the situation is comparable to the sport situation when I took over at Morgan College. They were playing high school teams and getting licked. . . . In medicine, we still are in the scholastic class. Whether I can do anything about that or not is a challenge that is well worth taking on. Seventy years there has been a Howard Med School but still there is no tradition; no able surgeon has ever been trained there; no school of thought has been born there; few of their stars have ever hit the headlines. In American Surgery, there are no Negro representatives; in so far as the men who count know, all Negro doctors are just country practitioners, capable of sitting with the poor and the sick of their race but not given to too much intellectual activity and not particularly interested in advancing medicine. This attitude I should like to change. It should be great sport.[128]

In June 1940 Drew returned to Howard University, this time as an assistant professor of surgery and a full-fledged surgeon at Freedmen's

Hospital. Drew could say of himself that he had gone through the fire and come out "bright new steel." In true heroic fashion, he had battled past many limitations and achieved the ambitious goals he had set for himself. He thought he was going home for good when he returned to Washington in the summer of 1940; having barely lived with his wife, Drew was eager to assume the role of husband and family man — to begin so-called normal life — after eighteen long years of lonely achievement. But fate was not yet finished with Drew.

Charles Drew at the age of approximately six months
(*Courtesy of the Moorland-Spingarn Research Center, Howard University*)

Richard Thomas Drew,
the father of Charles Drew
(Courtesy of Nora Drew Gregory)

Nora Burrell Drew,
the mother of Charles Drew
(Courtesy of Nora Drew Gregory)

Charles Drew with three of his four siblings, Washington, D.C., ca. 1915: from the left, Joseph L. Drew, Nora Drew, Charles R. Drew, and Elsie Drew
(Courtesy of the Moorland-Spingarn Research Center, Howard University)

Charles Drew, age eleven or twelve
(second row from the top, to the left of and
below the mustachioed man in the bowler hat),
with members of Washington's Twelfth Street
YMCA, ready to set off on a hike and picnic
(Courtesy of W. Montague Cobb)

Richard Thomas Drew
and his two sons, Joe (at left)
and Charlie (at right)
*(Courtesy of the Moorland-Spingarn
Research Center, Howard University)*

Charles Drew as a
lifeguard at the Francis Pool,
Washington, D.C., early 1920s
*(Courtesy of the Moorland-
Spingarn Research Center,
Howard University)*

Charles Drew (first row, first from left) and members of the
Alpha Omega Alpha medical fraternity, McGill University, 1933
(Courtesy of the Moorland-Spingarn Research Center, Howard University)

Charles Drew with the first mobile blood collection unit, New York, 1941
(Courtesy of the Moorland-Spingarn Research Center, Howard University)

Lenore Robbins Drew,
whom Charles Drew
married in 1939
(Courtesy of Bebe Drew Price)

Charles Drew,
his sister Nora,
his mother, his sister Eva,
and his brother Joe,
ca. 1941 *(Courtesy of the
Moorland-Spingarn Research
Center, Howard University)*

Portrait of Charles Drew in the laboratory, ca. 1941
(Courtesy of Scurlock Studio)

Charles and Lenore Drew
with their four children in the late 1940s:
from the left, Bebe, Rhea Sylvia, Charlene,
and Charles Jr. *(Courtesy of the Moorland-
Spingarn Research Center, Howard University)*

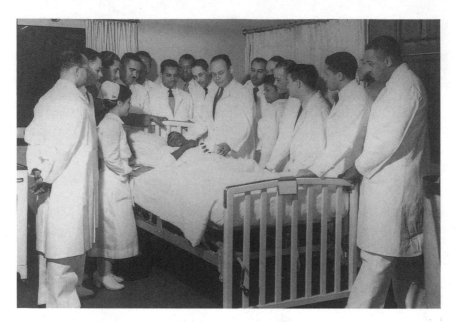

Charles Drew (center) on duty as chief of surgery at Freedmen's Hospital
(Courtesy of the Moorland-Spingarn Research Center, Howard University)

Charles Drew in a formal portrait taken shortly before his death
(Courtesy of Nora Drew Gregory)

Charles Drew giving a speech a couple of days before his death
(Courtesy of the Moorland-Spingarn Research Center, Howard University)

Structure that housed Alamance County General Hospital, where Drew died
on 1 April 1950 *(Courtesy of Nancy Scott Fuller and Gilberta Mitchell)*

Joseph Drew, Charles Drew Jr., and
Charlene Drew Jarvis in the spring of 1986
at the Charles Drew Memorial Marker,
which stands at the site of Drew's fatal
accident in Alamance County
(Photo by the author)

5

The
Bloods of
Different
Races

Had Drew not been called back to New York City to play an important and public role in blood plasma research in the fall of 1940 and the spring of 1941, he probably would not be the protagonist of a historical legend today. If he had simply resumed his teaching and medical duties at Howard, he would have placed himself in a setting in which few but his own circle of colleagues and friends would have noticed and remembered him. But Drew *was* called back to New York City. During and shortly after his six-month period there, the foundation of the victim legend and of a number of other legends surrounding Drew's life was laid.

The importance of Drew's work as a blood plasma pioneer and its conjunction with the subsequent World War II policy of blood segregation catapulted him into the realm of historical mythology. Drew had what we might term legendary potential — but the mythology we are investigating was ignited not simply by his character and circumstances but also by the complex symbolism inherent in blood and in white Americans' irrational beliefs about it. Consequently, Drew's life was shrouded in mythology from the World War II years on. The mythology consisted of multiple legends about Drew and his work with blood, which will be explored in depth in Chapter 7.

In returning to Howard to teach, Drew dedicated himself to passing on what he had learned about overcoming racial barriers in a place where he believed it could make the most difference. He believed his work at Howard to be his most significant contribution to the world, the essence of what his life was all about. But the world judged the matter differently. From September 1940 through January 1941, Drew served as medical director of the Blood for Britain project, a hastily organized humanitarian operation that required the preparation and shipment of large amounts of liquid plasma to British soldiers wounded on French battlefields. And from February to April 1941, Drew served as medical director of the first American Red Cross blood bank, a pilot dried-plasma program that served as the model for blood banks in the national blood plasma program, which would begin in May 1941. These were public roles of international as well as national consequence: Drew was on the cutting edge of one of the largest cooperative medical undertakings in world history.[1] Both these jobs, unlike his work at Howard, offered Drew the chance to demonstrate what he was capable of, not only as a scientist but also as a leader, in the brightly lit arena of the powerful, at a moment fraught with deep emotion and future consequence.

When Drew walked onto this world stage, he did so as a man who seemingly had transcended the color line. He had been called on not as a token or "race spokesman," as some outstanding black individuals were during World War II,[2] but because he was a scientist with specialized training for the job and he was a hard-driving, efficient worker of proven competence. John Bush, president of the Blood Transfusion Betterment Association, sent Drew a cable to offer him the position of medical supervisor: "I am requested to offer this position and all it involves to you as being the best qualified of anyone we know to act in this important development."[3]

But in Drew's moment of triumph, he was brought into a head-on conflict with American racism. This conflict affected him personally, but it also affected thousands of other black Americans: some months after

Drew had completed his work on the two major blood plasma projects, the American Red Cross announced that it would exclude black Americans as blood donors to its national blood collection program in November 1941.[4] In January 1942, the Red Cross — responding to a torrent of protest from both black citizens and open-minded white citizens — changed the policy of exclusion to one of segregation of black and white blood.[5] Black Americans were no less outraged, though, by this altered plan.[6]

Given that mythology has so often obscured the truth about Drew's actions during this time, it is necessary to explore what he actually accomplished in the jobs he held in late 1940 and early 1941 and, subsequently, what he actually said in the heated protest against blood segregation. The multiple legends that surround these events can then be seen more clearly for what they are. Not only popular writers attuned to Drew's larger historical significance have enshrined Drew in legend. Scholarly Red Cross and army historians also have depicted Drew's role in the blood program; in the process they have fostered what might be termed "counter-legends." The complex array of competing myths that have arisen from Drew's work with blood plasma offers a unique opportunity for witnessing firsthand the confusion, blindness, and bias that racism engenders.

In late September 1940, Drew was offered the medical directorship of the Blood for Britain project.[7] He was to develop standard technical procedures for separating liquid plasma from whole blood on a much larger scale than it had ever been done before and to arrange for a method of shipping large quantities of plasma overseas, all in a way that would ensure the stability and sterility of the final product. It was a rare opportunity indeed for a black scientist of Drew's day, when techniques of separating plasma from whole blood and the science of blood-banking itself were still in their infancy.[8]

An American doctor, O. H. Robertson, is credited with having established the first blood storage device in France during World War I, in 1917. It consisted of a refrigerator of slightly modified blood, situated near the front lines; from this device Robertson gave twenty-two transfusions.[9] Russian scientists, however, experimenting with transfusions of cadaver blood in the late 1920s, conducted most of the early research that led to blood-banking. It was not until 1937 that the first real "blood bank" in America was founded by Bernard Fantus at Cook County Hospital in Chicago — a "central depot in the hospital where donors could be sent to have blood drawn and stored for future use." Fantus coined the term "blood bank," and soon afterward "the words were like magic on the tongues of the populace."[10]

Also during World War I, a British medical officer named Gordon R. Ward reported on the effectiveness of plasma as a substitute for whole blood. Plasma is the pale, protein-rich fluid portion of the blood, in which the red corpuscles are suspended. Though it is not a true blood substitute — it does not contain oxygen — plasma is very useful in restoring fluid and proteins when a person has lost a great deal of blood. Unlike whole blood, it can safely be given without blood-typing, and it rarely transmits syphilis or malaria.[11] Again, though, not until the late 1930s did a number of scientists, scattered throughout the United States, begin to separate small amounts of plasma from whole blood and demonstrate its stability as a product that could be stored and shipped. Experience with blood banks had already shown that whole blood could not be stored for long, even when refrigerated. Plasma could be stored almost indefinitely; its advantages in wartime were thus increasingly obvious.

John Elliott and his associates in Salisbury, North Carolina, are most commonly viewed as the group that initially pioneered much of the work on plasma as a substitute for whole blood. In September 1936, Elliott read a paper titled "A Preliminary Report of a New Method of Blood Transfusion" at a North Carolina medical gathering; in December 1936, this paper was published in *Southern Medicine and Surgery*.[12] But as with most scientific breakthroughs, other scientists were achieving similar results with plasma almost simultaneously. In 1935, the year before Elliott read his paper, two Philadelphia doctors, Stuart Mudd and Eliot M. Flosdorf, had published an article announcing their discovery of a process for drying blood serum for transfusion. Not surprisingly, when Drew set up the American Red Cross dried plasma pilot program in the spring of 1941, he recommended the laboratory Mudd and Flosdorf were associated with, Sharp and Dohme, as the best one for the process of drying the plasma. Two other scientists at that laboratory, William J. Elser and John Reichel, were also involved with this breakthrough plasma experimentation. In 1938, another highly reputed doctor — Max Strumia, at Bryn Mawr Hospital — began to produce small amounts of dried plasma in a simplified drying unit he had invented. Yet another doctor, well-known physical chemist and hematologist Edwin Cohn, of Harvard University, had been conducting studies on blood and its components in cooperation with English scientists for some twenty years prior to World War II. Although his work was unpublished in 1940, his findings and expertise represented another valuable resource when this country launched its major blood collection programs.[13] Both blood-banking and plasma development, like many other scientific advances, were the achievement of many scientists, doctors, and laboratory technicians working together and separately over a period of almost fifty years, especially during the decade between 1935 and 1945.

Drew could be counted among these scientists before he took the Blood for Britain job. Drew had entered the field of blood research in 1938, when he began working in John Scudder's laboratory at Columbia University. Scudder and Drew were initially engaged in studying and measuring fluid loss and blood volume as it related to shock in critically ill patients. Scudder and Drew initiated the establishment of an experimental blood bank at Presbyterian Hospital on 9 August 1939, and Drew's research through this blood bank provided the primary source material for Drew's own massive study on banked blood, which became his doctoral dissertation in the spring of 1940. This dissertation and the scientific articles that Scudder and Drew published from 1939 through 1942 reveal that Drew (and to a lesser degree Scudder) became progressively more involved with research specifically related to blood preservation, as opposed to shock and fluid balance. Throughout 1939, in articles based on their research, Scudder's name preceded Drew's, but by early 1940, Drew was listed first or alone. Drew's dissertation and his published scientific articles attest that he not only was doing original research on blood preservation but had also surpassed his teacher in this field even before he returned to New York in the fall of 1940. At that point, Drew was probably as knowledgeable on the latest developments in blood-banking research as anyone in the world.

In an oft-quoted statement from this period, Scudder described Drew as a born scientist: "Drew was naturally great. A keen intelligence coupled with a retentive memory in a disciplined body, governed by a biological clock of untold energy; a personality altogether charming, flavored by mirth and wit, stamped him as my most brilliant pupil. His flare for organization with his attention to detail; a physician who insisted upon adequate controls in his experiments. . . . [He became] one of the great clinical scientists of the first half of the twentieth century."[14]

But Drew's achievement with the Blood for Britain project and the American Red Cross pilot blood program involved more than pure scientific research. Blood-banking and plasma research were in their infancy, and so were American blood donor programs. Both of Drew's undertakings in these fields required the synthesis of complicated and conflicting findings about blood plasma procurement and the organization of blood donor programs whose size and complexity were unprecedented. The two projects' different goals — to collect, store, and ship the necessary amount of liquid plasma for soldiers in England, and to stockpile dried plasma for wartime uses in the United States — also complicated Drew's task.

Although the British Red Cross had initiated a blood donor program as early as 1921, the American Red Cross did not approve its first small blood transfusion service until 1937, in Augusta, Georgia. Concerned with the organization's reputation, top officials of the American Red Cross were reluctant to take responsibility for a program in a field so new and fraught with medical and social uncertainties. Ironies reside in this first small blood donor program. It was initiated by local southern doctors and residents because doctors had observed that a number of indigent black women — obstetrical patients — had bled to death due to the university hospital's inability to procure whole blood for them for transfusion purposes. This first American Red Cross donor program was biracial and received enthusiastic support at its inception: 513 white and black donors immediately volunteered to give their blood. By 1938, there were six small American Red Cross blood donor programs, primarily in southern cities.[15] By 1940, the Red Cross had a handful of other small blood donor programs scattered throughout the country. All of these, however, were donor-to-donor blood transfusion programs; they did not involve the collection of blood or plasma to be stored and used later.

Around this same time, New York City was rare in having its own privately run blood service — the Blood Transfusion Betterment Association, which had been in operation for twelve years. Formed in 1929 by a group of leading New York City hematologists, the association was this country's first blood service. The hematologists had joined together in order to learn more about the science of blood transfusions and to prevent medical abuses that apparently were common when blood procurement was left entirely to hospitals. Unlike the British Red Cross's early blood donor program, this association paid its donors and did not primarily serve the indigent. The presence of this pioneer organization and of several blood researchers, including John Scudder and Charles

Drew, in the New York area ultimately led those who launched the Blood for Britain project to base it there.[16]

The U.S. army and navy began to get involved in blood research and procurement in the spring of 1940, when Axis victories made it clear that the United States would soon be involved in the war. In March 1940, the surgeons-general of the army and navy appointed medical officers in each service to undertake full-time study of blood transfusions for military use. Captain Douglas B. Kendrick was appointed as the chief of blood procurement for the army, and Lieutenant Commander Lloyd R. Newhouser was appointed to a similar position for the navy. In 1940 and 1941, the army and navy conducted their own blood transfusion research projects in preparation for U.S. military involvement.[17]

The real impetus for the Blood for Britain project came on 12 June 1940, when a special meeting was called at the New York Academy of Medicine. This meeting brought together top administrators of the Blood Transfusion Betterment Association; representatives of the army surgeon general's office; members of the National Research Council;[18] a number of scientists specializing in blood research, including Scudder and Drew; and scientists from various large commercial laboratories. Some weeks earlier, Scudder had recommended to John Bush, president of the Blood Transfusion Betterment Association, that a program be established to collect and ship blood to the United States' allies in Europe. Scudder had come up with the idea of shipping plasma overseas when Allen O. Whipple flew to Rome to attend United States presidential envoy Myron Taylor, at President Roosevelt's request, and carried liquid plasma that Scudder and Drew had prepared.[19] At the meeting, Scudder reported that plasma samples received from John Elliott had been tested by Drew and that subsequent studies at Presbyterian Hospital had shown that through refrigeration, plasma could be preserved safely for at least two months. Those at the meeting agreed that the Allies urgently needed help and that plasma, rather than whole blood, should be shipped in either liquid or dry form. In mid-July, Sir Edward Mellanby, secretary-general of the British Medical Research Council, cabled Norman Davis, chairman of the American National Red Cross, that England was willing to receive supplies of liquid plasma. Only then was the Blood for Britain project officially endorsed. During this same period, many other British scientists were unofficially cabling American scientists urging them to launch the project; John Beattie had cabled Drew as part of this effort.

The project actually began operations on 15 August 1940 at Presbyterian Hospital in New York City. Eight other New York hospitals soon joined the project as blood donor centers. The American Red Cross and the Blood Transfusion Betterment Association agreed to cooperate in this experimental project, and together these organizations provided the necessary funding. The New York chapter of the Red Cross took on the responsibility of enrolling the donors for the project, while the Blood Transfusion Betterment Association oversaw the actual taking of the blood and its technical preparation into plasma. The American National Red Cross then shipped the plasma to the British Red Cross to be delivered to military authorities. In an unprecedented effort, the New York Red Cross launched a dramatic publicity campaign for blood donors. By late September the number of donors grew to a weekly average of more than 1,300; it stayed at this level until the project ended in January 1941. The donor aspect of the project was an unqualified success; however, the early shipments of plasma to England had arrived with a cloudy appearance, raising the question of contamination. Stricter controls were thus adopted for donors, and in September the Blood Transfusion Betterment Association's Board of Medical Control decided that a full-time medical supervisor should be hired to provide greater technical supervision of the project.

Although John Scudder was considered for this job, he apparently was not available. So Bush cabled Drew in Washington, asking him to come fill the newly created position. Popular versions of the Drew saga paint the false scenario that the whole Blood for Britain project was initiated when John Beattie, Drew's former McGill professor, who was then an acting lieutenant colonel in the British army and involved with blood procurement, cabled Drew from England in September 1940 asking for "five thousand ampoules [of] dried plasma." Beattie did wire Drew this request.[20] Although it had no official backing, the wire's purpose was to expedite Drew's involvement with the project, which had been under discussion before he was officially offered the job. Drew himself believed that Beattie's cable played a role in getting him back to New York.[21] Letters between Drew and Beattie later in the fall of 1940 confirm that Beattie stayed involved with the project and was greatly concerned with its outcome.[22]

Within weeks after Drew took charge of the technical phases of the project, setting up even stricter controls for processing the blood into plasma, the plasma shipments were reported to have arrived in perfect condition. Drew reported to a Board of Trustees meeting on 6 November that techniques of collection had been uniformly standardized at all participating hospitals and that plasma shipments had subsequently tested sterile upon arrival. Red Cross historian Clyde Buckingham noted in a three-page monograph about Drew, "Six weeks after he began work as medical supervisor for the Plasma for Britain Project, Dr. Drew had become an acknowledged leader in the program."[23]

Both Drew and Scudder were keenly aware of the significance of their research months before the Blood for Britain program was launched, and they were thinking about how to use their expertise to help implement a national blood collection program.[24] Also, a couple of months before the conclusion of the British project, which focused exclusively on the collection of liquid plasma, Drew was already sending queries to scientists and commercial laboratories around the country to pool knowledge about dried plasma research, anticipating United States wartime needs.[25] All along, Drew had been working on putting together a system for the collection and processing of blood into plasma, based on his own research and on the findings of U.S. and foreign scientists. In late December 1940, Drew and Tracy Voorhees submitted to the Red Cross a proposal that a three-month pilot program for mass production of dried plasma be launched. This proposal spelled out some of the features of what ultimately would become the model program. In January 1941, Drew "made one of his more important contributions toward the future blood services in America" when he submitted a detailed "idealized system" to National Red Cross vice president DeWitt Smith.[26] A few weeks later, in his final report on the Blood for Britain project in January 1941, Drew conclusively demonstrated the importance of continuing plasma research in New York in the following months. The actual publication of Drew's report in late January 1941, as American Red Cross historian Clyde Buckingham noted, made Drew

> nationally known as an expert on methods and techniques of blood procurement and processing. He had brought together, for the benefit of hematologists everywhere, the latest knowledge acquired by scientists working in several different fields. Included were the results of research studies and clinical tests of academic and commercial laboratories on both sides of the Atlantic and the experience and practical knowhow gained in both English and American programs. . . . [His work constituted] a major step forward toward the goal of mass production of blood supplies in the large quantities and in the form

which could be used by the armed forces under conditions of modern warfare.[27]

Top Red Cross officials and scientists who had collaborated with Drew recommended that he be retained as medical director of the Red Cross's experimental pilot program and that his leave from Howard University be extended. By staying on in New York until 1 April 1941, Drew was able to complete what he had started: to establish and supervise a model blood collection program and the processing of the blood into dried plasma on a large scale. And when the national blood plasma program was expanded to other American cities after Drew left Red Cross employment, it became the model.

The Red Cross pilot program differed from the Blood for Britain project in several key ways: the final product was dried plasma instead of liquid plasma, because military authorities thought the dried form was easier to ship over long distances and store on battle fronts. The blood was collected and processed at one central laboratory rather than at several different hospitals, as in the British project. For the first time, mobile units were used to collect additional blood at industrial plants or large department stores; Drew himself supervised the first mobile unit run — a trip to Farmingdale, Long Island, on 10 March 1941. Finally, the National Research Council replaced the Blood Transfusion Betterment Association as the organization ultimately responsible for the technical aspects of the program, including the maintenance of standards. Donor response was much lower than with the British project; rumors of blood contamination and the absence of any war emergency apparently both played a role in reducing public enthusiasm. But Drew and his co-workers were able to learn what they needed to refine many of the technical procedures for a large-scale national program.

All the Red Cross historians who have completed monographs on the national program view this New York pilot program and the technical expertise it amassed as pivotal. Buckingham is careful to credit the other individuals who modified and improved technical procedures after Drew left the Red Cross, but he notes, "The importance of the earlier work by Doctors Rhoads, Drew, and others should not be underestimated."[28] William DeKleine, who as medical director of the American Red Cross in 1940 and 1941 was in charge of procuring donors for the critical New York projects, described the program Drew supervised from February to April 1941 and concluded, "Thus was set in motion the national project for the production of the No. 1 life-saving agent of the war, . . . dried plasma."[29] Robert Fletcher, although primarily interested in the internal functioning of the Red Cross, noted the importance of the strict medical and technical procedures that the whole Blood Donor Service rested on and stated that the New York pilot program that Drew supervised marked the "birth of the Blood Donor Service."[30] Brigadier General Douglas B. Kendrick, an army historian who wrote a massive book on all the World War II blood programs, also noted in passing the critical importance of the New York pilot program: "The experience of the New York chapter served as a pattern for the organization and operation of the Blood Donor Service."[31]

When one adds Drew's own version of events to the outline of the larger picture that Buckingham and the other Red Cross historians provide, one can recognize both the hazards and triumphs of Drew's undertaking — and the extraordinary excitement Drew felt about being a true pioneer. Drew probably deserves the titles of "blood plasma pioneer" and even "father of the blood bank" at least as much as, and perhaps more than, any of the other scientists involved in this massive undertaking. Drew would not, however, have claimed this role for himself. He was always modest in assessing his own contribution, whether insisting that Scudder share in the recognition he received[32] or in pointing out that the blood program was made possible through the efforts of many people working together.[33] It is simply that Drew was the man of the hour, and he more than lived up to the role. He commanded respect and proved himself a leader in a national emergency.

Drew did not write many letters between September 1940 and April 1941 — he was too busy — but the letters to his wife and mother that survive from this period are revealing. All were obviously written in great haste, and in them Drew indicated the great stress he was under due to his awareness of the importance of the undertaking. In October 1940, he wrote his mother, "The pace is so fast here . . . that there simply is no time for anything. . . . At this time it is difficult for the job here is big, hard and important. Mistakes will have international sequellae and must not be made."[34] In the same letter Drew discussed the "financial morass" he had been in, his concern over the fact that his wife had moved back to Philadelphia from Washington due to her mother's illness, and his anxiety about taking his American Board of Surgery written examination, for which he felt he was unprepared.

Other letters show that the pressure never let up but that Drew was a man joyfully in command of a task whose significance he fully understood. Drew never inflated his own role, but he did clearly note his achievements in the midst of both personal and job difficulties; he expressed his happiness when the shipments of plasma to England arrived uncontaminated;[35] his excitement in being asked to stay on to supervise the New York pilot program;[36] his pleasure when he successfully directed the first mobile unit blood collection run.[37] Most revealing, however, is a letter Drew wrote to his wife in February 1941 summing up his relationship with John Scudder. Drew and Scudder were personal friends, as other letters attest,[38] but deep tensions had inevitably developed between them, especially when Scudder learned he would not take over as Drew's successor as technical director of the national blood program:

> Scudder, of course, was very hurt when the job he has felt that he was creating for himself was not offered to him. I truthfully felt very badly for him. There is no doubt about his knowledge of the subject and his deep interest in it, but he has antagonized so many people that his nomination for the job became almost an impossibility. I tried to save some of his face by adding his name to my report to the Board of Medical Control [about the Plasma for Britain project]. I feel that I have now paid back in work and favors any debt I might have owed as a result of his early kindnesses to me here in New York. Our relationship will never be entirely cordial for there is enough of the Nietzschean about him to feel that "man is but to be surpassed" and he will not ever take kindly to the idea that I started under him and gradually took over.[39]

Scudder differed with Drew on the issue of the necessity for segregating the blood of different races. In 1959, Scudder "stirred broad controversy when he advocated a 'race to race' policy in blood transfusions," which he claimed might prevent the creation of blood disease. Whether Scudder believed in segregating blood along racial lines in 1940 and 1941 is not clear.[40]

Drew also faced obstacles closer to home — at Columbia itself — in the course of completing his work. One letter indicates that Drew was mistreated in some fashion; the letter is unclear, but it suggests that an older surgeon on the Presbyterian Hospital staff[41] may have tried to take some of the credit for the blood bank work Drew had done. In April 1940, in response to a letter from Drew, a resident who was a friend of Drew's wrote,

Your letter has burned me up so badly. . . . That son-of-a-bich [*sic*] . . . ought to be . . . hung up by his ears and weasels allowed to gnaw at his testicles. But what even makes me madder is that Whipple and Scudder will allow you to be exploited to such an extent. . . . I seriously think that either you or Scudder should talk to Whipple as eventually it will bring nothing but ridicule on . . . [him] and P.H. [Presbyterian Hospital] both as somebody is sure to ask him a lot of questions and get him all fogged up. If . . . [he] had had even the inkling of an idea to begin with or had even done any part of the work there might be some reason for what he is doing but . . . [he] was opposed to the blood bank at the start and only jumped on the band-wagon when he saw that you were getting someplace. Personally I wouldn't take it without a squawk and if you need any witnesses I am ready to testify on a stack of bibles two feet high as to the work you have done and the hours you have put in, however I realize that you have lots of witnesses and if its any consolation to you all of the younger fellows know where the brains and the work both in Scudder's lab and in the blood bank have come from for the past year and half.[42]

At any rate, Drew clearly felt at this point that he had outstripped his mentor and that his own personal achievement was solid. In the same letter in which he discussed Scudder, he stated his conviction that his section of the report on the Plasma for Britain project marked his "single greatest writing effort" and that it "will in years to come prove of greater value to all concerned than any thing . . . [I] might have done at Howard" during the same time span. In an obvious attempt to console his wife about his protracted absence, he wrote in an unusually intense way about what his own role in the plasma projects had meant to him:

Our separation has caused us to miss much that we may have shared together. For this I am sorry. Many of the days and nights have been lonely here for me. I know that they were much more lonely for you, but from times immemorial, men who have beat out new paths into unknown regions have had to strike out alone, leaving all that was dear behind. These have been new paths that I have been treading, Lenore, as new as the uncharted seas that the early sailors defied, as strange as the new lands early explorers mapped while good wives waited in fear and loneliness lest the wandering ones failed to return. Yet, it has always been true, that where one man dared to go, others would follow, and these, the ones who followed after, often brought their whole families along and knew more joy than those who first came that way, and some of those who came along later, were the children of those who had gone before, and their joys were a recompense to those who had gone on ahead, — the lonely ones. Maybe Bebe will some day live and laugh and work under conditions which will make you glad that during long, apparently useless days you pushed back the tears and lived alone while I — I found new places in which to grow.

I know that you think all of this is just a little bit heroic, sometimes I do too, and laugh at myself. But most of the time I am deadly serious about it, as though I had nothing to do with it but simply carried out commands given me by some inner force which never wants to play. I should play more, we should play more.[43]

Drew's clear sense of himself as a pioneer and a hero not only surfaced during this period but became part of his permanent identity as well. The stakes were high; in addition, the pressures on Drew were greater and came from more sources than ever before. He now had a wife and child to support, and his wife was not happy. He obviously felt that she was not supportive of him during this critical period, and he clearly was not able to be sufficiently supportive of her at long distance.[44] Drew no doubt internalized a heroic stance at least partially to compensate for and cope with the strain and loss inherent in this situation.

The conditions under which Drew left the New York Red Cross job are not entirely clear, largely because Drew himself was reserved on this subject in his letters. When Drew was about to leave New York, he wrote his mother, "These six months have been interesting and instructive in many ways."[45] Drew did resign from the New York job a month early — a month before his leave from Howard was up — on 1 April 1941. He wrote Lenore two weeks before leaving, "There are some things that I will leave unfinished here which I naturally would like to finish but I feel that the moment is propitious for pulling out."[46]

One legend asserts that Drew angrily left New York because of the blood segregation policy, but there is no evidence to support this scenario. Drew himself never refers to any awareness on his part of an emerging exclusion or segregation policy. In fact, in June 1941, when he traveled to a public meeting in New York in order to answer questions about the infant national blood program, he was asked about the racial designation of blood, and he responded that no distinction was being made regarding race.[47]

Another version of the legend above asserts that Drew left New York outraged because he was refused a national job with the Red Cross. But Drew never indicated that he expected to be asked to stay longer than April 1941. Drew himself consistently indicated that he expected to return to Washington in order to resume married life and teach at Howard University—to fulfill his long-range goal of creating a tradition in surgery there.[48] Apparently Drew and his New York colleagues considered it a personal triumph for him that he would return to a much higher position at Howard than the one he had left—as chairman of the department of surgery at Howard and chief surgeon at Freedmen's Hospital.[49] Drew was sufficiently mature at this point in his life to have few illusions about what would be offered him; he had already settled on what his special role in life was to be, and his additional year in New York apparently deepened his commitment to it, having armed him with a new level of personal power. In December 1940, when his job had been scheduled to end, he wrote Lenore, "I have made contacts that I may have waited a lifetime to make in the ordinary scheme of things. . . . Fate and chance have been very kind to me. I have gained insight into so many things that I did not clearly understand before I started this job."[50]

Drew's former Amherst classmate, W. Montague Cobb, always maintained that Drew would have been offered a wartime job had he been white.[51] Another of Drew's friends and colleagues, Ira McCown, a surgeon on the staff of Harlem Hospital during the time Drew was in New York, shared Cobb's conviction that Drew had not received a national Red Cross job because he was black.[52]

The fact that Drew consistently expected to return to Howard underscores one important piece of the scenario Cobb and McCown paint: because Drew was black he probably was not even considered for a national high-level job. However, Drew always bore personal racial affronts with silence and moved forward in the direction that was open to him.[53] As McCown himself noted, "Drew didn't have much to say" about not getting a national job. "He wasn't a fellow to brood over anything."[54]

Drew emerged from his experiences in late 1940 and early 1941 as a far more mature man than the one who graduated from Columbia in the spring of 1940. In a few fast-paced months, Drew had demonstrated his scientific and leadership skills. There was a dignity and poise, long in the making, in the way Drew silently accepted and embraced his fate: his return to Howard and the missionary role he knew he would need to play there. In his letters from this period, Drew showed himself to have not only an unshakeable confidence in his own abilities but also a more complete grasp of the world's reality, especially of individual human limitation. The job and its political ramifications had taught him a great deal, but it is highly significant that Drew had now been married for more than a year and was no longer caught up in the passionate idealism that characterized the early stages of his love affair with Lenore Robbins. Through his marriage—its frustrations and difficulties—he had been forced to come down to earth and adjust his thinking.[55]

In April 1941 Drew was certified as a diplomate of the American Board of Surgery. To Drew's medical colleagues, his stunning performance in the oral examination, in which he ended up confidently lecturing his examiners on the treatment of shock, exceeding the usual time limit, was as legendary as any of the more daring football maneuvers he ever performed.[56]

A magazine writer described the encounter thus:

When Dr. Charles Drew was taking an oral examination before the American Board of Surgery in 1941, one of Johns Hopkins' outstanding surgeons asked him a question. It happened to be on "water balance," . . . a subject in which Drew had done deep study. Without the least hesitation, Drew unreeled his vast knowledge of the subject. Taken by surprise, the examiner sent for help from other surgeons who were more acquainted with the subject than he. What had started as a routine question, ended up as a lecture by Dr. Drew to his examiners. Afterwards, the examiner wanted to know: "How many other colored fellows like you are they sending over to Johns Hopkins?"[57]

Charles Watts, a surgeon who was a student of Drew's, also recounted this well-known anecdote, identifying the examiner as Stuart Rodman. "Drew had the confidence," Watts commented. "He was just dynamic, a charmer. . . . He was six feet one, weighed 220, and he was a svelte man, all bone and muscle."[58] Drew's performance was all the more noteworthy in that he had not had the standard five years of residency that most examinees had had—only three and a half.[59]

In October 1941, Drew took over as head of the department of surgery at Howard and chief surgeon of Freedmen's Hospital, the role he filled until his death. In the same month, in recognition of his unusually commanding performance at his own oral examination, he was appointed an examiner for the American Board of Surgery. Without a backward glance, Drew threw himself into what he saw as his lifework:

the building up of Howard's surgical residency program, the creation of a team of black surgeons whose excellence, confidence, and opportunities would be as great as Drew's own.

In November 1941, soon after Drew had assumed his new leadership role at Howard, the American Red Cross announced its policy of excluding black blood donors. After the attack on Pearl Harbor in December 1941, America entered World II, and the national blood donor program quickly expanded, opening blood banks in major cities across the country and taking blood from a vast outpouring of patriotic donors, eager to help the Allies' cause. Blacks who went to enlist as soldiers or to donate blood, however, were turned away.

During the war's first weeks the black press gave front-page coverage to the Red Cross blood exclusion policy. In the meantime, the NAACP questioned Red Cross officials to determine who was responsible for the policy. In response to the outburst of protest, a meeting was held in Washington with Norman H. Davis, president of the Red Cross; Ross T. McIntyre, surgeon general of the navy; James Magee, surgeon general of the army; and F. D. Patterson, president of Tuskegee Institute and an official of the Red Cross. As a result of this meeting, the Red Cross officially announced on 21 January that it would accept blood from black donors but segregate it: "The facilities for processing blood plasma having now been expanded considerably . . . the American Red Cross, in agreement with the Army and Navy, is prepared to accept blood donations from colored as well as white persons. . . . In deference to the wishes of those for whom the plasma is being processed, the blood will be processed separately so that those receiving transfusions may be given plasma from the blood of their own race."[60] In the meantime the black press reported that Magee had refused to sign a statement allowing blacks to be donors until the Red Cross assured him that black blood would be stored separately.[61]

Drew was aware of the hurtful impact on black citizens in December, when they were turned away from blood centers, and after 21 January, when they were informed that their blood would be segregated. In 1942, Drew quietly and without fanfare spoke out against the policy of blood segregation. He made his views known to a variety of people, including his former colleagues in New York and reporters, but he did not take a dramatic public stand. According to *Current Biography 1944*, Drew said in 1942, "I feel that the recent ruling of the United States Army and Navy regarding the refusal of colored blood donors is an indefensible one from any point of view. As you know, there is no scientific basis for the separation of the bloods of different races except on the basis of the individual blood types or groups."[62] Undoubtedly, some blacks who were politically more outspoken felt that Drew could have done more. One of Drew's childhood friends, Mercer Cook, noted, "The whole issue of blood segregation was a difficult thing. Emotions were high. . . . There were blacks with Drew on it and there were blacks opposed to him. Some felt he didn't raise enough hell and say 'Down with Whitey.' "[63]

From his Howard University post, Drew spoke about his viewpoint in greater depth to a *Chicago Defender* journalist in the fall of 1942. His manner as revealed in this piece — which undoubtedly was one of the first to dramatize Drew's ironic encounter with racial mythology — characterized his whole style. With a manner that was calm, direct, and without rancor, he sought to explain why, from a scientific point of view, segregation of blood was not necessary. The journalist himself described Drew as a "quiet, unassuming man."

Is there a difference between the blood of different races?

Is it possible to transmit the traits and characteristics of one race to a member of another race by means of blood transfusion?

Is it possible to implant by blood transfusion potentialities in an individual of one race that will show up in succeeding generations?

. . . These are not humorous questions to some people. They are important not only for white people who fear that they or their offspring will get Negro characteristics but by good people who fear they may get the blood of bad people and thereby lose some of their virtue. Or by healthy people who may have the blood of less healthy people infused in their veins. . . .

But one can say without any hesitation that no difficulties have been shown to exist between the bloods of different races which would in any way counter-indicate the use of the blood from an individual of one race for the purpose of transfusion to an individual of another race providing bloods were of the same group.[64]

Drew also addressed white fears by acknowledging the social and historical reasons white people feared blood mixing, and he stated his own personal "solution" to the racial problem:

Like all other social problems where prejudice between races is concerned great difficulties face anyone who attempts to analyze the problems away. There are many white people who simply do not like

Negroes and their reason for not liking them is that their fathers did not like Negroes nor their fathers before them. They have been taught since infancy that Negroes are an inferior race. . . .

Only extensive education, continued wise government and an unceasing fight on our part to disseminate the scientific facts and raise our levels of achievement can overcome this prejudice which to a large extent is founded on ignorance.[65]

Drew quietly but consistently expressed his dismay and moral outrage toward the segregation policy. He wrote letters to friends and colleagues and, when he had the opportunity, took his stand against segregated blood with army officials. In a 1944 letter to a director of the Labor Standards Association who had asked for his views, he noted,

I think that the Army made a grievous mistake, a stupid error in first issuing an order to the effect that blood for the Army should not be received from Negroes. It was a bad mistake for three reasons: (1) No official department of the Federal Government should willfully humiliate its citizens; (2) There is no scientific basis for the order; (3) They need the blood. I would be heartily in favor of pressure of all types being brought on the Surgeon General of the U.S. Army to force him to rescind the instructions to the American Red Cross which demands the separation of the bloods of the donors. Such an order, I believe, would have a greater salutory effect upon the morale of Negroes than any other act which could be done at this time. I have had occasion to say this before both official and unofficial in Army circles and outside of it, but to date, with no avail.[66]

Drew was not an activist by nature, but in his new role at Howard in the midst of World War II he was fast becoming more aware of the need for strong black leadership: every day he confronted the many health difficulties poor black Americans faced. Also, their situation was exacerbated by the critical shortage of black doctors. In April 1943 Drew gave a radio broadcast calling for the stepped-up training of significantly more black doctors to help the war effort. On this occasion, he also took the opportunity to attack social segregation. Obviously identifying with the young men in the armed forces, Drew revealed much about his own evolving sense of the black cause:

As a teacher of many of the younger officers now serving, I know that all their loyalty will never waiver. Each will give a good account of himself in spite of the fact that the vast majority of Negro physicians enter the military service bitterly opposed to the Army's policy of segregation, unified in their distaste and dissatisfaction with the Navy's policy of exclusion and deeply conscious of the fact that while they serve those who go forth to rid the world of terror in far places emancipation is not yet complete at home. They fight the sincere fight of men who know disfranchisement and who long for freedom for themselves and all mankind. Freedom from want, freedom from fear, freedom from constant humiliation, freedom to rise by merit according to ability and freedom from the tyranny of small minds in high places.[67]

In the spring of 1944 Drew received the NAACP's 1943 Spingarn Medal for his work in blood plasma research.[68] It was then that he made his first public speech attacking the blood segregation policy. Drew began by recounting the history of blood transfusion research and of his own scientific work with blood in a low-key, anecdotal manner. But when he closed with his view on the segregation policy, he took a strong and emotional stand:

It is fundamentally wrong for any great nation to willfully discriminate against such a large group of its people. To the everlasting credit of the NAACP and many individuals, this first order [to exclude black donors] was fought bitterly. It finally was rescinded so that any citizen can give his blood if he so desires.

Then came the next step. It is with something of sorrow today that I cannot give any hope that the separation of the blood will be discontinued. . . . The same men who fight for this particular bit of discrimination are the gentlemen who fight all liberal policies. I recently was the subject for discussion by Bilbo in the Senate for daring to say that all blood is alike. . . .[69]

I think it is the unwillingness of the men now in charge of this program that they will not act to break up the segregation of the blood. One can say quite truthfully that on the battlefields nobody is very interested in where the plasma comes from when they are hurt. They get the first bottle they get their hands on.

The blood is being sent from all parts of the world. It is unfortunate that such a worthwhile and scientific bit of work should have been hampered by such stupidity.[70]

Drew himself believed that he had received the award at least in part because of the strong emotions surrounding the whole blood segregation issue.[71] The speech makes clear his feeling that because of the award and its impact on his life, he must begin to play a stronger, more visible role as an advocate of justice for black people than he ever had before:

The Spingarn Medal presentation has caused me to answer hundreds of people all over the world, asking about differences in race, color and blood. Many answers I do not know but I feel duty bound under such honors to become more aware of the great needs we have in all fields of activity when leadership is forced upon one in a manner quite comparable to this. As a task it has many good points and many which are trying. I am sure that people like Mr. Walter White are extraordinary. I think that is why the NAACP is so important because they have given leadership and I pledge you that in the future as I have tried in less degree in the past, I shall try to be worthy of this great honor. A great mass of people have been hurt sorely and unnecessarily by a form of discrimination which should never have come about. It is imperative therefore that we meet this new form and smash it as we must smash all the others.[72]

In August 1944 Drew did something he had never done before: he participated in a union-organized demonstration against segregation in Washington. In preparation for a Labor Day mass blood donation and protest rally at the District of Columbia Blood Donor Center, Drew spoke at a meeting of Local 10 of the United Federal Workers Association (CIO).[73] In his speech, titled "The Practice of Segregation in the Red Cross Blood Bank," Drew told the history of the blood program and the segregation policy and concluded by reiterating that there was no scientific basis for the segregation of plasma and that the policy was a "source of great damage to the morale of the Negro people, both civilian and military." According to an American Red Cross report filed on this meeting, the crowd of 150 responded most enthusiastically when Drew stated "that the source of plasma was disregarded by physicians and medical corps men actually on the fighting fronts."[74]

This meeting at which Drew spoke was prelude to a Labor Day program that included not only Federal Security Commission and War Manpower Commission members but also other CIO unions in Washington, some AFL unions, and the Labor Committee of the National Negro Congress. It brought Drew into public alliance with a new group of people. Clearly, the publicity that the Spingarn Medal had brought him — as well as the continued segregation of the armed forces during the war — was thrusting Drew into a new sense of himself. However, the war was soon to end. With this meeting, Drew's public role as a black blood plasma pioneer both peaked and ended. While a new role as a black leader was emerging for Drew, his image as a special kind of scientist and protest hero had already been stamped indelibly into the imagination of American blacks. And although Drew would move on to define his life in his own way, to train young black surgeons and wage a war on many fronts against segregated medical care, mythology had already claimed him for its own.

6

The
Group
as a
Whole

While Drew mythology was taking root, Drew himself, now back at Howard University, was trying to accomplish his chosen mission. His encounter with white racist mythology had had an impact on his life, just as it had touched other black Americans. Partly because of it, he had received the Spingarn Medal and had been called on to attack segregation publicly. Now, in devoting his energy to the Howard University Medical School, he was serving as a model for a new generation of black doctors. As a result Drew increasingly identified with the role of the sacrificial black leader. In 1944, the year he won the award, Drew wrote to a friend, Leslie Pinckney Hill,[1] and asked for a copy of a poem about Toussaint L'Ouverture, a poem whose opening lines evoked what Drew no doubt saw himself confronting:

To be a leader! What is that to be?
To stand between a people and their foes
And earn suspicion for a recompense;
To care for men more than they care for themselves;
To keep a clear discriminating mind
Between the better counsel and the best;
To be a judge of men, that no one may rank
In estimation higher than his worth,
Nor fail of scope to prove his quality . . .[2]

As chief of Howard's Department of Surgery and chief surgeon at Washington's only black hospital, Drew was now facing his real heroic task. As leader to a rising generation of black doctors, he now had to try to scale hurdles for his whole "team," not merely for himself alone. Segregation was intact in many parts of America, and it was as rigid as ever in postwar Washington.[3] Drew increasingly devoted his energy to breaking down barriers of race as he worked to find internships and residencies for his students in white institutions, challenged Washington's segregated hospital policies, and attacked racial restrictions in local and national medical associations. Although Drew was able to help his team clear some major obstacles in the 1940s, he found himself in a role whose burdens grew heavier rather than lighter with the years, as he became more aware of the cost of racial discrimination to himself and to his fellow black Americans.

Howard University Medical School was undergoing a painful transition. From being a second-rate school dominated by paternalistic white physicians, it was struggling toward first-rate status under the leadership of mostly black doctors and administrators. Mordecai Johnson, the university's president, was a man much like Drew in his missionary zeal and forceful personality,[4] and one of Drew's most important backers.[5] Johnson had termed Freedmen's Hospital in this era a "jim-crow shack."[6] Many of Freedmen's buildings dated from the early 1900s and needed significant renovation. Since Freedmen's depended on the federal government for its financial support, it was assured of survival, but its administrators never knew how much the annual appropriation would be, nor did they have significant control over it. Thus Freedmen's also often lacked up-to-date equipment. In addition, the hospital itself, which dated from 1863, was for more than a century the only full-scale hospital exclusively serving Washington's black population. It was chronically overcrowded. It had 520 general hospital beds; of these, only twenty were private, and none were semiprivate. Like his predecessors in the 1860s (when the hospital first opened its doors as an institution for the district's newly freed slaves), a Freedmen's patient slept in an open ward with thirty other people; his toilet and bathing facilities were inadequate. Sanitation was a chronic problem. Nonetheless, as one of black Washington's more important institutions, Freedmen's Hospital offered employment to black Washington's top professionals over a period of many years. Black doctors could practice at no other hospital in Washington, and Freedmen's was a source of great pride in the black community.[7]

Throughout Drew's medical career in Washington, black doctors were barred from Washington's white hospitals, from the local white medical society (the District of Columbia chapter of the American Medical Association), and from the American Medical Association itself. They were thus largely sealed off from the mainstream of the profession in their own segregated world, which centered around Freedmen's.[8] Inevitably, a number of black physicians were more intent on reaching "Cadillac" status and then resting on the financial security that segregation assured them than on putting in the long hours required to turn Howard's medical school and Freedmen's Hospital into top-notch medical institutions.[9] As in many environments where the rewards were limited, the competition was fierce and often petty.[10] Recalling this period at Howard, Cobb wrote, "The Negro medical world is a hard, narrow, self-triturating world. . . . It takes more blood and sweat and tears to build a medical school than most people realize."[11]

For a man of Drew's caliber and drive, it was an environment that called for greater sacrifice than ever. Drew did not relish bureaucratic politics, but he jumped in because he recognized the necessity. Feeling that he must carry his share of the burden of "enormous drudgery" work, Drew served as chief of staff at Freedmen's Hospital from 1944 to 1946 and as medical director of the hospital from 1946 to 1948, although the jobs did not appeal to him.[12]

Drew had his own style of operating as an administrator. When he saw something needed to be done, he moved quickly, avoiding red tape if he could. As Charles Watts, one of Drew's students and colleagues, noted, "He didn't always have time for politics. He did cut across corners to get a job done."[13] Watts explained further: "With a well-known name, and adept at promotion, he ran his department like a one-man show, drawing easily on contacts, whether here or abroad, for funding, equipment and other academic support. . . . 'If a group in New York wanted to do something for Howard, they didn't call the [university's] president — they telephoned Drew.' "[14]

Inevitably, Drew had his enemies. "Some were jealous of his success . . . and popularity," said Dr. Watts. "His biggest enemies were those who ran Freedmen's, the older physicians who were institutions there and who resented his rise. They thought he was a young buck."[15] Drew also had his differences with a doctor of his own generation — Joseph L. Johnson, interim dean in 1941 and full-fledged dean of the Howard Medical School from 1946 to 1955. Johnson was also a rising star at Howard, and he was envious of Drew. Drew did not take easily to Johnson's somewhat dictatorial style. As Jack White, another Drew student and colleague, explained,

> Johnson was not very democratic. He and Drew were temperamentally very different. Johnson was a tyrant type and everyone was afraid of him. He tried to control everybody but one he didn't control was Charles Drew. I don't think Charlie broke any rules but he was outspoken. Johnson angered him. He once said [to White] he was going to take Johnson over his knee and give him a spanking. Johnson was a little man who dressed impeccably, . . . a squirt. He wore little old-fashioned collars and diamond stickpin cufflinks. . . . Drew himself was very neat . . . but he was not fuddy-duddy or pompous like Johnson. He could have taken Johnson over his knee.[16]

Drew could have used his connections and accomplishments to achieve financial success; many of his peers found it noteworthy that he dedicated himself wholeheartedly to training his students and upgrading the surgical residency program. He lived on a modest teaching salary until his death.[17] He had unquestionably chosen a life of service.[18]

Drew did become a "family man" as he had wanted to. He and Lenore soon had four children. Their daughter, Bebe Roberta, had come first; Charlene Rosella, Rhea Sylvia, and Charles Richard Jr. followed in quick succession. Drew continued, though, to live the hard-driving relatively spartan life he had always lived. He worked twelve to sixteen hours a day; he did not take vacations or even go to church. He spent only Sunday afternoons with his children, having dinner with the whole Drew clan at his mother's home in Arlington, Virginia. He and his family lived decently and comfortably, but not luxuriously, in a roomy three-story house on the Howard campus, only minutes from the hospital and medical school. The property had a flower garden, fruit trees, and a grape arbor in back, but it was rented. Drew never owned a house. His one leisure activity was gardening: he had a large formal garden with canna flowers in a big circle: "the first thing he would do when he came home was go out and look at the flowers," his wife said. She also recalled that he was a "plain but immaculate" dresser. He had one or two "not expensive" suits, which he kept very clean, and one pair of special shoes, "great big cordovans with cracks and creases in them because he had damaged his feet as an athlete."[19]

Summing up her husband's character years after his death, she said, he was a "natural man, without 'pomp,' who brought the same energy and enthusiasm to great tasks and small, who liked to garden and cook and play the piano, who slept hard but not much. 'He once sewed the head on a rag doll for me, using a surgical needle.' "[20] She added, "He was a simple and uncomplicated person. . . . He didn't care much for complicated people. . . . He cared more for western movies where the good men came out the winners and the bad men were punished."[21] "It was an education just to live with him," she concluded.[22]

This relatively spartan and dedicated life centered around teaching, Drew's real love. Drew himself said in 1947, "The boys whom we are now helping to train, I believe, in time will constitute my greatest contribution to medicine."[23] Drew's wife commented, "He was a born teacher. Even when he would sit down with the children, he wanted them in possession of something when he got through with them. He had many other financial offers—he could have had his own lab and done research—but he wanted to train black surgeons. He felt he could do the most good that way."[24]

As Drew demonstrated, the struggle to help his students had to be waged on many different fronts. First and foremost in Drew's heart was serving as a friend, ally, and model to them, not only working with them daily while they were at Howard but also monitoring their progress after they had graduated. Drew was involved with every aspect of his students' education, from their academic achievement to their physical appearance, demeanor, self-image, and personal happiness.[25] Drew's students of this era affectionately dubbed him "Big Red" because of his tendency to flush a deep red when he was angry or upset. They paint a portrait of an extraordinarily disciplined man who retained the driving ambition of his early years and yet who displayed an unusual gentleness and fatherly concern.

Burke Syphax, one of Drew's students who later taught surgery at Howard, remembered when a student appeared with a hole in his sock. Drew told him to come to his house, where he would sew it up himself or give him one of his own pairs of socks. Syphax noted, "His forte—what made him different—was his knack of stimulating others. He went beyond being a teacher; he was a leader of men. Even every one of the poor little black boys on Drew's swim team became something—a coach or a school principal."[26] Another of Drew's students, Asa G. Yancey Sr., summed up Drew's special character as a teacher: "The unusual ability to make a sterile situation flower was a constant and thoroughly ingrained trait of Dr. Charles R. Drew. In preference to all else, there existed in him the desire to develop the undeveloped."[27]

Jack White, another of Drew' students, commented, "He was gentle, very gentle. . . . I heard him use the word 'Damn' once. . . . I never saw a man who used no confrontations the way he did but got respect without doing so. He had a burning desire to see excellence; he didn't want shoddy things happening. He took extra time with us if we were weak in some area. If anything ever happened to me, Drew was the first person I would call."[28] White recalled only one incident in which Drew spoke harshly to him. White had been joking with two residents in the operating room—a place where Drew did not tolerate levity. Later, when White was operating with Drew and asked him, "Why do you get all the best help?" Drew responded, "Well, if your manners improve, maybe you'll get some [better] help." Later, however, Drew apologized to White for his rough tone.[29]

White also recalled that when he was going to New York to be the first black resident at a white hospital, Drew instructed him that he should not be shy, that he must have a force of personality to deal with individuals who might run over him. " 'You may see a Mrs. Rockefeller,' " he told me. " 'You'll have to tell her, "Get in bed. I'll have to examine you." ' "[30]

Besides cultivating intense relationships with his students, Drew assisted them in climbing as high in the medical world as they could go. Drew alienated some of his colleagues at Howard by encouraging his better students to seek specialty training at white institutions, thereby draining Howard of some of its most talented graduates.[31] Drew traveled widely, keeping up his old contacts and making new ones, so that his students could break the color barrier at white medical institutions. While before Drew had had only to win opportunities for himself, in his new role he had to fight hard to create them for his students. There were almost no internships or residencies outside Howard when Drew started in 1941.[32] The bulk of them did not open up until after Drew died.[33]

Drew also tried to help his students win professional certification as specialists in their fields, another major hurdle they had to jump before practicing in the higher ranks of medicine. One of Drew's students, Frank Jones, later the medical director of Freedmen's, told of a humiliating incident that occurred in the late 1930s when he sought professional certification as a specialist and approached two white physicians for help. "One gentleman began pacing the floor muttering incredulously at this request: 'A nigger a member of the American Urological Society.' The other responded acidly, 'I would endorse you to the American Board of Urology, but I would never endorse you to the American Society, because I don't eat with niggers.' "[34]

Drew's sense of mission extended beyond the confines of Howard University. His commitment to the creation of a meaningful black tradition and a "team" of physicians grew with the years and transcended the limited goal of building some sort of power base for himself and his colleagues. In a letter to Jack White in 1946, Drew revealed his deep feeling for this "team" and his vision of its meaning:

> I know that you must feel that I have sent you off to the far, cold northland and left you to work out your destiny as best you could without further interest on our part. This is not true. We still love you and are extremely interested in what you do, what you think, and what you plan for the future. . . .
>
> Our horizons are being widened by the residents all the time and the things they write back, sharing with us as it were their daily experiences, enriches us all and at the same time forges the bands which unite us even more firmly so that each man is inspired to do more and more on his own in order to be worthy of the fine companionship of such a group. In the individual accomplishments of each man lies the success or failure of the group as a whole. The success of the group as a whole is the basis for any tradition which we many create. In such traditions lies the sense of discipleship and the inspiration which serves as a guide for those who come after, so that each man's job is not just his job alone but a part of a greater job whose horizons we at present can only dimly imagine for they are beyond our view.
>
> The thing which we have not had in the past is a group bound by similar training, aspirations and ideals to which we could feel that we

belonged. The sense of belonging is of extraordinary importance to man as individuals and as groups. The sense of continuously being an outsider requires the greatest type of moral courage to overcome before actual accomplishments can be begun. Our fellows are rapidly creating something which give[s] . . . them a sense of "belonging to." Within the protection of this feeling they should be able to accomplish more than the fellows who have gone before.[35]

Charles Watts explained that Drew "was a believer in the vanguard" and that he succeeded in creating one: "Between 1941 and 1950, more than half of the black surgeons receiving certification papers from the American Board of Surgery studied directly under Drew—eight to be exact. Another fourteen men, eventually earning their certificates, received part of their training in the Drew-run department. . . . The Drew-trained men were among the earliest pioneers in gynecology, neurosurgery, cardiovascular surgery, and other fields," and these men "were fashioning new images for blacks in surgery."[36]

Drew's wife said that the most satisfying moment in Drew's professional life came in December 1948:

He had sent his first graduate students up to Johns Hopkins, in Baltimore, to take their exams for certification by the American Board of Surgery (A.B.S.), and he had never been more anxious about anything.

Some people talk things out when they're worried. Not Charlie. He went down to the basement and, with a sledgehammer, began knocking to pieces an enormous old coal bin that had been cluttering up the place for years.

"Your boys will do all right," I tried to console him.

"All right won't be good enough," he said. "They're up there at Hopkins competing with graduates of the top medical schools, . . . with *rich* boys, Lenore, boys who've had every advantage."

. . . Finally the phone rang.

"That was President Mordecai Johnson . . . ," I told Charlie. "He . . . said to tell you one of your boys taking the examination came in second."

"Second!" Charlie threw down his hammer and let out a whoop.

"But that's not all," I went on. "He said to tell you another one of your boys came in *first!*"

Charlie dropped into a chair. "First," he said unbelievingly. . . .

Tears filled his eyes, . . . and his voice dropped to a whisper. "First and second. Well, what do you know about that?"[37]

There were larger professional and political battles for Drew to fight as well. Drew was very active within the black medical profession, generous with his time and counsel in maintaining regular contact with black medical societies around the country, speaking at conferences, and participating regularly in annual medical meetings such as those of the John A. Andrew Clinical Society at Tuskegee and the Homer G. Phillips Interns and Residents Alumni Association. As a member of a Dean's Committee, he made a lasting contribution to Tuskegee Veterans Administration Hospital, an important teaching facility for graduate medical education.[38] From 1944 until his death, Drew served as chairman of the surgical section of the National Medical Association. According to W. Montague Cobb, he "brought new vigor and standards to this group."[39]

Drew believed that affiliation with the nation's major medical associations was important for black physicians. It was not merely a matter of respect; as Drew knew, black physicians gained access to new medical information and important contacts through such affiliations. Between 1940 and 1945, Drew waged what he termed a "rather bitter battle" with the American College of Surgeons over their policy of excluding qualified black physicians. Drew himself did not apply for admission until early in 1945,[40] for he felt "time was needed for some of the bitterness of . . . [the] earlier discussions [between him and the group] to have died down."[41] Although a black surgeon was admitted to the college in 1945 for the first time, Drew was not. Drew believed bigotry was the reason. He wrote his old colleague John Scudder, "[The college's] . . . admission requirements are too ill-defined and its standards too low. . . . My contact with both the Canadians and the British has made it manifestly clear that they consider the American College of Surgeons to some degree a social organization whose scholastic and professional requirements, therefore, are purely secondary." Although Drew said he had been willing to be the "guinea pig" to test the college prior to 1945,[42] he apparently did not push hard to be accepted once he saw that the college was still willing to admit only a few token black surgeons and that its standards remained low. In early 1950, when he saw that conditions for qualified black surgeons were more favorable, he again began the process of applying and seeking the needed recommendations from colleagues.[43] Drew was not admitted as a fellow to the American College of Surgeons until after his death.[44]

In January 1947, Drew publicly attacked the American Medical Association on its hundredth birthday for its century-long policy of banning southern black doctors from membership. From 1870, when black membership was first discussed by the AMA, until 1968, the nation's largest medical association dodged the larger issue of black membership by giving local societies the prerogative to admit or bar whomever they wished. Only in 1968 did the AMA amend its constitution to forbid racial discrimination in membership at all levels and to authorize its House of Delegates to bar delegates from states where such practices existed.[45] Drew wrote a series of letters to the editor of the AMA *Journal*, Morris Fishbein, and then released them and Fishbein's responses to them to journalists and magazine editors. In his opening salvo Drew wrote with hard-earned pride and anger:

> At Howard University for many years no physician has been considered for a position of professorial or associate professor rank in the preclinical area who has not earned a Ph.D. in his special field. In Freedmen's Hospital, the teaching hospital for the clinical years, a man must have successfully passed his specialty board to be considered for the position of assistant professor. The chief of every department and subdivision in the departments is a certified specialist in name and practice. Match these standards with those of the great hospitals of the land and they will be found good, but it will not grant them the privilege of discussing common problems with fellow physicians in the learned councils of the American Medical Association now celebrating its one hundredth birthday. One hundred years of racial bigotry and fatuous pretense; one hundred years of gross disinterest in a large section of the American people whose medical voice it purports to be. . . . one hundred years with no progress to report. A sorry record.[46]

When Fishbein wrote back that since membership in the AMA could only be secured through entrance into a county medical society the national AMA could not be held responsible for barring southern black doctors, Drew attacked again:

> You know and I know that it is utterly impossible for a Negro physician to become a member of a county medical society in the South. The American Medical Association has stood behind the bylaws which

make this so as though God himself had written the bylaws. . . . [They] can and, I think, should be changed. . . .

I have had the pleasure of taking part in the annual meetings of [Negro medical] societies in Maryland, Virginia, West Virginia, North and South Carolina, Alabama, Georgia, Mississippi, and Louisiana. . . . [These groups] are a real and vital part of American medicine and should no longer have to explain on every application blank why they are not eligible for membership in the A.M.A. It is an unwarranted stigma. It is a cause of repeated humiliation. It is a constant indictment of the principles on which the American Medical Association is supposedly founded.[47]

Drew was never formally recognized as an American scientist or surgeon during his lifetime; he never became a member of the American Medical Association or a fellow of the American College of Surgeons. He was, however, recognized as an international scientist and physician. Drew for many years was a member of the American-Soviet Medical Society. Russian scientists had done some of the path-breaking research in blood preservation, experimenting primarily with blood from cadavers. As medical director of the two New York plasma projects, Drew had made contact with Russian physicians in the early 1940s. He attended the group's meetings and spoke at them after he returned to Howard.[48] In 1946, Drew was made a fellow of the International College of Surgeons,[49] which had been organized because some of its members had not been accepted in the American College of Surgeons for a variety of reasons.[50]

In Washington, Drew was also an active force.[51] Washington had two hundred licensed black physicians; it had more board-certified black specialists than any other American city — twenty-six out of the country's total of seventy-two.[52] Its medical institutions were rigidly segregated, in a characteristically southern pattern. When Drew returned to Washington in 1941, Freedmen's, with approximately 350 beds, was the only hospital at which black doctors could practice; it was also the only city hospital where black patients could obtain private rooms, and these were "tiny reconverted supply rooms."[53] Drew participated in efforts to open up the local white medical society — the District of Columbia chapter of the American Medical Association — to black members. No black doctor, however, was admitted to this society until 1952, two years after Drew's death. Working with other black physicians, Drew also sought to place black medical students in internships at Washington's other publicly funded hospital, Gallinger Municipal Hospital.[54] With 1,600 beds, Gallinger was much larger than Freedmen's, and at least 70 percent of its patients were black. Gallinger Municipal Hospital was the first Washington hospital other than Freedmen's to accept black interns, but it did not do so until 1948, under pressure from the federal government.[55] Drew also participated in efforts to create internships and residencies for black doctors at Washington's private hospitals.[56] There were twelve of these in all; three excluded black patients, and the remaining nine primarily served white patients, having only small segregated wards for black patients and turning blacks away if the beds in them were full. None of these private hospitals allowed black interns or doctors to practice at them until the mid-1950s.[57]

In 1947, Drew outlined the scope and nature of the struggle when he wrote to Asa Yancey, for whom he had helped secure the position of chief of surgery at the Tuskegee Veterans Administration Hospital. He first listed the goals he thought Yancey should pursue: they included the training of more black medical students, the training of more black interns and residents, better medical care for black patients, "the right for Negro patients to be treated by their own physicians," and finally "more opportunities for Negro physicians" to take part in the "larger medical life of the community." Drew added a note of caution: "Without some thought on our part, things will go on as they have gone on in the past. . . . Fellows like you are the ones who should give the most thought and in the early stages, put in the most labor. I can warn you in advance that the labor will not be appreciated nor the value of your work understood. Yet it must be done."[58]

Drew had had racial pride and a feeling for black history before this juncture.[59] But probably his sense of racial identification went deeper in these later years, as he was increasingly forced to witness and share the trauma of being black in America. His own work made him especially aware not only of the obstacles black medical professionals faced but also of the disproportionate health problems of black people. When Drew sent his correspondence with the American Medical Association editor to the press, he attached a statement about the health conditions of the nation's black population. He noted, "Approximately twice as many Negro mothers die in childbirth as the mothers of the nation as a whole. Approximately twice as many [black] children die in the early hours of life. The average Negro has a life span ten years less than the average American citizen of other racial origin."[60]

Despite the fact that Washington had an unusually large number of well-trained black physicians, the health conditions of Washington's black citizens were significantly worse than those of blacks in the nation as a whole. A special report published in 1948 by the National Committee on Segregation in the Nation's Capital pointed out the disproportionate disease and death rates of Washington's black citizens: the life expectancy of a black resident of Washington was ten to twelve years less than that of a white resident. In 1944 his chances of dying were 37 percent greater. Also, in 1944 a black person was more than four times as likely as a white person to die from tuberculosis — a disease, the report maintained, whose incidence could be correlated with unhealthy living conditions. In 1946, the black infant mortality rate was almost twice as high as the white infant mortality rate in Washington, and the black maternal mortality rate was six times as high as the white maternal mortality rate.

The report traced these statistics not only to the poorer living conditions Washington segregated black citizens endured but also to limited medical and hospital care. The hospital facilities available to black residents were inferior, the report noted, and were "far short of" black patients' "greater need" of them. The two hospitals that served the bulk of the black patients, Freedmen's and Gallinger's, operated on inadequate budgets, the report pointed out, and the segregated accommodations for black patients that the private hospitals offered were not only very limited in terms of number of beds but inferior as well. The report further noted that the color bar was rigidly maintained when the black beds were full, yet white beds were available. In 1945, a young black woman had been forced to deliver her baby on the sidewalk on a cold winter morning after being refused admission at one of the private, church-supported hospitals.[61]

As a resident of Washington and a surgeon at Freedmen's working under these conditions, Drew could not help being acutely aware of the plight of Washington's growing black underclass, whose problems were exacerbated by the city's rigid segregation. As the committee report noted, Washington had some of the worst slums in the nation, and although only 30 percent of Washington's population was black, 70 percent of its slum dwellers were black. Even though Drew himself was middle-class, living in relative comfort and security, he was not insulated from seeing the plight of his fellow citizens. In the wards at Freedmen's he saw Washington's poorest blacks as well as its more comfortable ones, and he was noted among his colleagues and students for showing the same empathy and gentleness of manner in dealing with all of them. "To see him examine a nice little old lady on a ward was like watching a giant with a feather. He was so gentle and tender with her," said Charles Watts. "He never lost the common touch."[62]

Drew's sister recalled that it was not uncommon for one of Drew's former childhood acquaintances to come in on a Saturday night cut up from a knife fight and say to the doctor in the emergency room, " 'Don't you touch me. You go get Charlie Drew and tell him so and so is down here.' " Drew would go and treat these people, she said; "it made people almost worship him."[63]

A physician who worked closely with Drew commented, "[Those] who search for the natural characteristics of Charlie Drew will find a wholesome, brilliant, warm, energetic, merciful, charismatic gentleman. . . . Everyone would light up, glowing with renewed energy, whenever Drew walked on the surgical ward, be it mid-day or 2:00 A.M."[64]

Drew had written Lenore Robbins in 1939 that being a physician forced him to face "daily the many defects in man, both physically and spiritually."[65] No doubt Drew found this ever truer as he gained more experience as a doctor in the years at Freedmen's and in hospitals up and down the East Coast. One can easily imagine that as Drew walked through ward after ward, seeing the many people whose bodies were ravaged by disease and by hard living, the words of the poem on Toussaint L'Ouverture that Drew had asked for spoke more and more to him:

> To walk with trouble with a heart that drips
> The blood of agony, yet with a face
> Of confidence and bright encouragement;
> To do and do and die to raise a tribe
> So robbed and bound and ignorantly weak
> That God himself conceals their destiny —
> To be a leader! God, that is the cost![66]

When Drew was called on in 1946 to give a speech to a Jewish group in Boston that had given a medical scholarship in his honor to a black student accepted at Tufts, Boston University, or Harvard, his address echoed the words of his poet friend: "It is fitting that such a program should be initiated here, for out of the heart and mind and blood of New England was forged the hammer which broke the chains of slavery. Out of its towns and hills and valleys went forth the fearless, Godlike, lonely men and women to teach these lowly and despised people — so robbed and bound and ignorantly weak that God himself concealed their destiny."[67]

In some deep sense, Drew was forced by America's racial history and by his own values and temperament to walk a tightrope over an abyss. Although proud of his own race, he was fundamentally a person who did not believe that racial identity was of primary importance. Drew was a humanitarian. Yet, like many other black leaders both before and after him, Drew was increasingly forced to build his life around the fact of his race. Given his values, his ultimate "solution" to the race problem was, first, to prove that he could personally transcend race, and second, to teach his "boys," his team, and all others to do the same. Ultimately, he hoped to create a world in which racial affiliation was of no consequence in what opportunities one was offered or in what one chose to do with one's life. Drew most fully articulated this approach in a 1947 letter to a Texas high school biology teacher who was organizing a program about Drew's achievements:

> To your students I would say this: There are so many things still unknown in almost every realm of knowledge, and the need for this knowledge is so great, that in the very vast majority of instances any new addition not only is accepted without very much regard to race, color or creed. There are many difficulties to overcome it is true, but our greatest difficulty still remains in the fact that we do not have very much to offer which anyone wants. So much of our energy is spent in overcoming the constricting environment in which we live that little energy is left for creating new ideas or things. Whenever, however, one breaks out of this rather high-walled prison of the "Negro problem" by virtue of some worthwhile contribution, not only is he himself allowed more freedom, but a part of the wall crumbles. And so it should be the aim of every student in science to knock down at least one or two bricks by virtue of his own accomplishments.[68]

One of Drew's students, Asa Yancey, summed up Drew's "solution" thus: "Dr. Drew had strong faith in the concept that if an individual performed exceedingly well in life's endeavor . . . that the excellence of performance would transcend the barriers of racial segregation and discrimination." But Yancey perceived an inherent problem with this approach. "Such was a lofty, excellent attitude. . . . The difficulty with this concept is the biologic truism that every uterus that contracts does not deliver an Ernest E. Just; a Samuel Kountz; a Martin Luther King, Jr.; a George W. Carver; a Marian Anderson; a Booker T. Washington; a Thurgood Marshall; or a Charles R. Drew."[69]

Drew himself intimated in his letter that there were inherent difficulties in such a solution. If one was forced to dedicate one's life to breaking down barriers by proving one's worth through humane contributions, one paid a tremendous physical and psychic cost. Writing in 1903, the year before Drew was born, W. E. B. Du Bois had reflected on this cost:

> [T]he Negro is a sort of seventh son, born with a veil, and gifted with second-sight in this American world, — a world which yields him no true self-consciousness, but only lets him see himself through the revelation of the other world. It is a peculiar sensation, this double-consciousness, this sense of always looking at one's self through the eyes of others, of measuring one's soul by the tape of a world that looks on in amused contempt and pity. One ever feels his twoness, — an American, a Negro; two souls, two thoughts, two unreconciled strivings; two warring ideals in one dark body, whose dogged strength alone keeps it from being torn asunder.
>
> The history of the American Negro is the history of this strife, — this longing to attain self-conscious manhood, to merge his double self into a better and truer self. In this merging he wishes neither of the older selves to be lost. He would not Africanize America, for America has much to teach the world and Africa. He would not bleach his Negro soul in a flood of white Americanism, for he knows that Negro blood has a message for the world.[70]

Richard Wright described the cost of this same struggle in 1937: "As I had lived in the South I had not had the chance to learn who I was. . . . I had been what my surroundings had demanded. . . . Never being fully able to be myself, I had slowly learned that the South could recognize but a part of a man, could accept but a fragment of his personality, and all the rest — the best and deepest things of heart and mind — were tossed away in blind ignorance and hate."[71]

J. Saunders Redding, a twentieth-century black writer of Drew's generation who was an "integrationist" like Drew, eloquently described his own cost in his book *On Being Negro in America*, published in 1951. Redding wrote,

I am tired of trying . . . to feel my way into the particularities of response and reaction that are supposed to be exclusively "negro." I am tired of the unnatural obligation of converting such talent and learning as I have into specialized instruments for the promotion of a false concept called "race."

. . . What I wanted . . . was to loose and shake off the confining coils of race and the racial experience so that the integration — my personal integration and commitment — can be made to be something bigger than race, and more enduring, and truer. For race is a myth: it is artificial; and it is, I hope, at last a dying concept. Meantime, while it lives, it is also a barrier and a terrible terrible burden. It is a barrier to nearly everyone, white and black, in America . . . but it is a personal burden to the Negro — a burden of shame and outrage imposed on him at the earliest moment of consciousness and never lifted till death, and all his energies, mental, emotional, spiritual, must be held in reserve for carrying it.[72]

Drew obviously felt the painful cost in some degree the way Redding did. In an address about black scientists that he delivered the year before his death, he quoted a sentence from Gunnar Myrdal's *American Dilemma*: "[The] Negro genius," Myrdal had written, "is imprisoned in the Negro problem."[73] Drew countered this assertion with his own: "While one must grant at once that extraordinary talent, great intellectual strength and unusual opportunity are necessary to break out of this prison of the Negro problem, we believe that the Negro in the field of physical sciences has not only opened a small passageway to the outside world, but is carving a road in many untrod areas, along which later generations will find it more easy to travel."[74]

But Drew added, "The breaching of these walls and the laying of this road has not been, and is not easy."[75] Drew went on to discuss the fate of Ernest Everett Just, the famous black marine biologist: "Even he, who was blessed with brains, insight, and great perseverance, found the walls here in America at times too thick to breach and too high to climb."[76] Drew explained his assertion by quoting Frank R. Lillie, Just's teacher and collaborator, on Just's career: "An element of tragedy ran through all of Just's scientific career due to limitations imposed by being a Negro in America, to which he could make no lasting psychological adjustment in spite of earnest efforts on his part. . . . That a man of his ability, scientific devotion, and of such strong personal loyalties as he gave and received, should have been warped in the land of his birth must remain a matter for regret."[77]

Drew clearly knew on some level that there was a cost in his own life, although he is not known to have ever discussed it. The cost was especially great for him, because his idealism, ambition, and humanitarianism were virtually unbounded. Drew always raced forward to the next obstacle, driving himself to his utmost, as if he personally could remove all the bricks from the wall. "He always seemed to possess a rational, organized plan," Asa Yancey said about him. "The isolated pious appeal was never present. Perhaps the best answer [to the power of his character] lies in the fact that his was a stainless and immaculate heart, and men would sense, see, feel, and stir themselves because of his logical, practical purity. . . . [He was] the only person . . . [I] had ever known who would be fully capable of fetching the Holy Grail—due to . . . [this] magnificent purity of heart."[78]

The problem with the solution Drew chose—as with Ernest Just's solution—was that the "wall" could never be removed in the logical way Drew sought to remove it, since its bricks were fashioned not from reason and truth but from fear, irrationality, and the distortion of truth. In hindsight, it seems clear that the prison of American racism shaped Drew and his life trajectory as surely as it shaped any black person born in the era of segregation. At a point in life that many individuals might have opted to live more comfortably or at a slower pace, Drew propelled himself to fulfill a mission that required unrelenting intensity of effort. Because Drew's life was cut off when he was still in his prime, and because the relentless pace at which he drove himself was clearly a factor in his death, it is hard not to discern a real thread of tragedy in Drew's own fate, tied up with his vision of the "solution." Jack White, one of the students and colleagues he was closest to, said of Drew, "He walked on his toes all the time [because his feet had been damaged], but he never gave in to physical discomfort—this surely contributed to his death."[79]

Similarly, Drew's wife and his brother both spoke with some pain when they recalled that he was a man who "never had enough time for anything."[80] And Robert Jason, dean of the Howard University Medical School, commented after Drew's death, "Perhaps it was because of the brilliant glare of . . . [the] vision in his mind's eye that he taxed his physical endurance too much and he closed his eyes."[81]

Ultimately, Drew emerges from the real historical evidence as a type of hero both quintessentially American and strikingly modern and universal. In some ways, Drew bore affinities with Martin Luther King Jr. Like Drew, King had a driving sense of mission from an early age and came to articulate a profoundly humanitarian vision that far transcended the limits of his time and place. King, of course, was born more than twenty years later than Drew: the tides of history swung him into a more turbulent turning point in American history and thus into a far more dramatic leadership role. But the pattern he played out was strikingly similar to the one Drew had followed in a relatively subdued and less public way.

Like Drew, King was born in a southern city — Atlanta, Georgia — in a relatively comfortable middle-class family, as the oldest son of a well-educated mother and a forceful father. Both men received their early education in excellent and sophisticated black institutions: King attended Atlanta's Booker T. Washington High School and graduated from Morehouse College in 1948, at the age of nineteen. Like Drew, King went on to complete high-level graduate training at two different northern, white institutions, and he too won fellowships because of his stellar academic performance. He received a bachelor of divinity degree from Crozer Theological Seminary in Chester, Pennsylvania, in 1951, finishing at the top of his class. And he was awarded a Ph.D. degree in systematic theology from the Graduate School of Theology of Boston University in 1955. In the same way that Drew recognized his partner for life after only one encounter with her at a party, King met and married Coretta Scott in whirlwind fashion in 1953; King apparently proposed to Coretta Scott on their first date, just as he was finishing his graduate work in preparation for his professional life as a Baptist minister at Dexter Avenue Baptist Church in Montgomery, Alabama. And King, like Drew, met the fate that transformed him into a historical figure almost immediately after completing his education. In 1954, the fateful year of the Supreme Court's *Brown v. Board of Education* decision, King took up the relatively uneventful life of a young pastor, husband, and father in Montgomery. But in December 1955, after Rosa Parks decided not to give up her bus seat to a white passenger, King was catapulted almost overnight into a leadership position, known worldwide as the president of the Montgomery Improvement Association and a Gandhian apostle of nonviolence. Sucked somewhat reluctantly into the maelstrom of history, King was never to live the relatively quiet, dedicated life of pastoring and teaching patterned after that of his mentor, Benjamin Mays, president of Morehouse College, that he had envisioned; neither was Drew able to carve out his own place in history exactly as he had anticipated. Both men died young, in traumatic ways that assured their enshrinement in myth. In April 1968, after thirteen swift and violent years as the major leader of America's civil rights movement, King met a hero's death, shot down in his prime at thirty-nine.

In strikingly different and yet hauntingly similar ways, both King and Drew played out the archetypal pattern of the Christlike hero, the one who in dying a tragic death gives life to the immortal and timeless[82] — what King variously described as "the truth of God . . . an overflowing love which seeks nothing in return . . . something in the universe that unfolds for justice . . . a creative force in this universe that works to bring the disconnected aspects of reality into a harmonious whole."[83] Like King, Drew was not only a black hero. He was also a universal hero in the classic sense Joseph Campbell described, the "man of self-achieved submission" who dredges up from his unconscious something forgotten by his whole generation and civilization and who thus deserves to be the culture hero of the day, a figure of world as well as local importance.[84]

Drew ultimately did transcend race, not only as an athlete and a scientist but also as a healer, teacher, and humanitarian of unusual vision. Thus he became a man "able to battle past his personal and local historical limitations to the generally valid, normally human forms . . . [his] visions, ideas and inspirations . . . pristine from the primary springs of human life and thought . . . eloquent, not of the present, disintegrating society and psyche, but of the unquenched source through which society is reborn."[85]

Drew's last published work, a historical article about black scientists that appeared the month he died, revealed his universal outlook, the final vision of teamship to which he had evolved but which was always in him: "a teamship which extends far beyond the realms of physical science." He admonished, "This team must include all of us who are interested in achieving goals higher than those of merely great scientific or technological achievement. There must always be the continuing struggle to make the increasing knowledge of the world bear some fruit in increased understanding and in the production of human happiness."[86]

Brotherhood, unity, understanding, human happiness: these noble concepts were absolutely real to Drew. Like many of his generation, he seemed to many of those who came later to have come from a simpler and gentler time. To many others who would hear and read about Charles Drew, he would seem almost too perfect, too good to be true —

even like a cardboard cutout figure. Drew was an unusually high-minded and driven man, even among his Dunbar and Amherst friends. One of his oldest friends, Ben Davis, said shortly after Drew died, "I can never forget him: his extraordinary nobleness of character, his honesty, his integrity and fearlessness."[87]

Drew's character was extraordinary, and in what seems an uncanny and yet absolutely fitting premonition of his own fate, Drew himself wrote a poem in his youth that foreshadowed his emergence as the hero-victim of the final Drew legend. Writing in response to a poem Mary Maxwell had written him, in which she says "the moon" probed her heart and discovered her love for him,[88] he declared,

> Your moon is horned and its points sink deep
> In my heart and let its life blood drip
> Drop by drop with a sad cadence,
> To the dark pool of comfortless doubt
> And longing in the depth of my being.
> Your moon crawls like an earthy thing
> In dark places. . . .
> My moon's points must be turned up towards
> The higher realms and not tipped down toward earth.[89]

With strange prescience Drew's poem suggests his ultimate fate. Drew's vision was so bright, and his pursuit of it so relentless, that one senses he was determined to deny the dark forces in American history, the shadow side of all life, although that shadow kept trying to snare him in its net. When he took the wheel of the big 1949 Buick Roadmaster and headed down the highway into North Carolina while his companions slept, Drew met the last requirement of Campbell's hero: "The last act in the biography of the hero is that of the death. . . . Here the whole sense of the life is epitomized. Needless to say, the hero would be no hero if death held for him any terror; the first condition is reconciliation with the grave."[90]

Drew took his fate upon himself: so bent was he on staying in motion toward the "higher realms," toward fulfilling his own vision, that the lower realms yawned wide and claimed him. His fate was not only that he was cut down in his prime in a small obscure spot in the American South but also that he came to play the role of the hero-victim in a classic black legend about bleeding to death. In a sense, the Drew legend was the shadow Drew spent his life battling and running from. Through it, he met his shadow — as he did in his own poem, projecting it onto a woman whose love he did not want. The moon-horns that bruised his heart in the poem probably represented the earth-bound, instinctual demands of a woman from whom his heart soared away. His fate inexorably drew him into an enduring historical encounter not only with the lofty realm of American science and its humanistic values but also with its underworld of white racism and its tragically destructive myths.

7

Dark
Myths
and
Wretched
Superstitions

Drew's work with blood, on the eve of World War II, put
him at the epicenter of several deeply rooted yet conflicting mythologies about the meaning of blood and race in
America. As in any war situation, emotions ran high: old
fears were activated and new hopes were born as soldiers
went to face the conflict and inevitable bloodshed. There
was the eons-old mythology surrounding the whole concept of blood, blood as symbolic of life itself and of the
power to give life.[1] Coexisting with this concept was another equally ancient mythology: blood as the vital substance that bound families, tribes, and even nations into a
biological and communal whole; blood as race; blood as
the link that passed on genetic inheritance and connected
members of a group to each other. During the war, Hitler

and other Nazi leaders sought to define the German nation as a kind of Aryan blood-brotherhood, ultimately justifying the mass genocide of European Jews and all others labeled "racially impure."[2] Though America was fighting to defeat this fascist outlook, during the war this country revealed itself as a nation similarly imprisoned by "blood" mythology, the centuries-old racist mythology that whites as a "race," united by "one blood," were superior and blacks inferior[3] — the peculiarly southern mythology that held that even a drop of black blood in one's genetic makeup was a kind of tragic curse, not only limiting one to a lifelong low-caste status, unless one could "pass" as white, but also condemning one to a somewhat less-than-human status.[4]

Vigorously competing with this white racist mythology was an equally powerful mythology, rooted in Christianity yet defined most fully through the institution of the black church, that held that blacks and whites in America, as children of God, were of "one blood," united in their humanity and in their hope for a better world.[5] Connected to these beliefs and the spiritual faith they embodied was a further mythology, deeply rooted in the African American community, that blacks, through the blood they had shed, had earned "blood brotherhood" with white Americans.[6] Through their sacrifice, according to this vision, blacks had won full equal rights in postwar America and thereby redeemed America as a nation.[7] This belief found widespread popular expression in the black press's Double V campaign: war victory to black citizens and soldiers meant defeat of the racist Axis forces in Europe and Asia *and* defeat of racial segregation and discrimination at home.[8]

In addition, a myth that united both whites and blacks in the war effort was the quintessentially American myth of America as a free, democratic nation with equal opportunity for all. The majority of white and black Americans had very different angles of vision on this myth's meaning. While to most black Americans the Double V campaign was necessary for the democratic struggle to have any validity, many white Americans rejected such a notion, as countless letters and statements of badly treated black soldiers vividly illustrated both at the time and in the postwar years.[9]

During the war years, especially, these myths collided, leading to social strife and interracial violence. Both white and black Americans were called on to spill their blood for their country, and each group felt that its sacrifices should advance its vision of a preserved or renewed America. As blacks continued to face segregation and discrimination throughout the war, many of them became angry and bitter. As whites were increasingly confronted by blacks' new sense of empowerment, many increasingly feared and resented them. Rumors spread, race riots erupted; brutal lynchings and unexplained murders occurred.[10]

In the midst of this tumult, part of the foundation for the widely known Charles Drew legend was laid. The rumor and the legend — as we have seen — largely stemmed from the irony inherent in the conjunction of Drew's pioneering work with blood and the American Red Cross's blood exclusion and segregation policies.[11] Newspaper articles about Drew's role in World War II throughout the 1940s highlighted this irony, setting the stage for this well-known legend of Drew as victim. But Drew's role on the eve of World War II launched his life and legacy into being the battleground of other legends as well.

There have been at least six distinct but interrelated legends about Drew. The first legend represents an inflation of his role as a blood scientist: it is stated sometimes that he was the "discoverer of blood plasma" and other times that he was the "father of the blood bank." A second legend, which might be termed the "angry prophet of truth" legend, depicts Drew holding a press conference and publicly resigning from the American Red Cross in furious protest of its blood segregation policy. The third legend is the victim legend, the widely known story of Drew's "bleeding to death."

The remaining legends we might call "counter-legends," because they essentially represent reactions to the first three legends — reactions shaped to a large degree by a white supremacist cultural perspective so deeply rooted as to be almost invisible. The fourth legend, or counter-legend, is that Drew was not a significant blood pioneer, that his role in plasma and blood bank work was relatively minor. This counter-legend is obviously rooted in traditional white supremacist mythology, which historically has inflated white achievements and minimized black ones. The fifth legend is that the American Red Cross has always been a humanitarian organization, committed to helping all people. While this counter-legend has its own kernel of truth, it served to blind Red Cross officials to their full responsibility in accepting and promulgating the blood segregation policy. The ironies multiply: this policy was deeply rooted in the irrational white racist mythology that viewed black people as inferior to white people and black blood as a pollutant of white blood. Finally, the sixth legend is that Charles Drew did not suffer mistreatment of any kind. Red Cross officials have been especially eager to correct the

"Drew as victim" legend, but in the process they have failed to include in their historical record Drew's objections to the blood segregation policy, which represented his and other black people's mistreatment at the hands of the American Red Cross.

To understand the mythological matrix surrounding Drew's life even before his death, it is necessary to briefly trace how these different mythologies were invoked during the war years and, at the same time, to look at some of their historical underpinnings.

A complex symbolism flows from blood. As Ashley Montagu noted, "Blood . . . is a word which, from the beginning of recorded history . . . has possessed a high emotional content." In a society confronting the reality of the AIDS epidemic, Americans of the late twentieth century are fully aware of the intense feelings and fears associated with blood.[12] The fear of receiving contaminated blood has probably never been greater; but even prior to the spread of AIDS, people throughout the world have long viewed blood as central to their conceptions of health and sickness. Blood is the most obviously important constituent of the human body, and its loss results in weakening or death: this accounts for the many powerful feelings attached to blood and explains the peculiar power of the Drew legend.[13]

In primitive folklores all over the world, blood continues to have a magical and sometimes mystical significance.[14] In American medical folklore, especially among rural black and white southerners, the concepts of "good" blood and "bad" blood have long been at the very center of a whole system of what constitutes good health and illness.[15] In his study of the Tuskegee syphilis experiment, James Jones noted that the black men who were treated in the study had no idea they were being treated for syphilis. The doctors and nurses only told them that they were being treated for "bad blood," a phrase that had multiple meanings to these rural folk and carried no special stigma.[16] In many rural cultures, blood imagery and symbolism are inextricably tied up with rituals of healing, initiation, and transformation.[17] The whole Christian tradition rests on the idea of a savior who redeemed the world by shedding his blood for others.[18] Both white hymns and black spirituals attest to the enduring emotional force of this concept. Some of the more primitive folk belief systems combine spiritual and physical beliefs about blood, as in the case of a southern black woman who testified to this vision of salvation: "a little white man chops open the breast with an ax, takes out the heart, pours out the black blood, washes it pure . . . and closes in the opening."[19] Another woman told of a similar vision: "I see'd myse'f laid out on a table. Dat same littl' w'ite man wid de lily-w'ite hands cut me plum' open, tu'k mah heart out, an' rinsed hit in drippin' blood ontil hit wuz w'ite ez snow."[20]

American Red Cross officials, in their publicity drives to enroll blood donors, understood the powerful symbolism tied up with blood and tapped into it in order to stir more people to give their blood. The Red Cross gathered "blood donor testimonials" from top-ranking military officers and used them as part of a special publicity campaign. In one of these testimonials, Commanding General Jacob L. Devers of the U.S. army ground forces was quoted as saying,

> When your blood flows into the veins of a wounded soldier, the soldier knows it is more than medicine for his body. It is a part of you that you are giving to help keep him alive. The psychological effect is tremendous.
>
> During the difficult campaign of last winter, I visited many hospitals in the 6th Army Group area. I talked to young American boys who were undergoing intense suffering. All of them wanted to live. The giving of your blood can make their chance for life a reality. Your frequent donation of blood will give them the right they so richly deserve — to live.[21]

The deeper one looks into the ancient and powerful mythology tied up with blood — even apart from Charles Drew's role with it — the more one realizes that blood is a symbol so fraught with meaning to all people that historical incidents involving blood are probably always good tinder for igniting mythic conflagrations.[22] The Red Cross was playing with fire when it asked people to become "saviors" by donating blood. Charles Drew himself emerged as a "Savior" par excellence, for in his role as plasma pioneer he made the giving of blood to others possible. Obviously, when race and racial injury were added to this potent brew of symbols — when the refusal to use black blood could so easily be viewed as the refusal to grant life to black soldiers — the mythology surrounding Drew was only a short step away.

In protesting the exclusionist and segregationist blood policies, black Americans (and white Americans who empathized with their plight) revealed the extreme potency of this life-giving blood symbolism. Ordinary American citizens, both black and white, and the leaders of many civil rights and humanitarian organizations wrote hundreds of letters to the American Red Cross, to President Franklin Roosevelt, to First Lady Eleanor Roosevelt, and to the surgeon generals of the army and navy from 1941 to 1945, expressing their outrage and dismay at the exclusion and segregation policies. These letters offer moving testimony to the pain these discriminatory blood policies caused throughout World War II and to the democratic values black citizens cherished.[23]

Sylvia Tucker, a black woman in Detroit, Michigan, was the first person officially to protest the exclusion policy of the American Red Cross. She wrote Eleanor Roosevelt about the impact on her as a mother of having her blood refused by the local Red Cross:

> I was shocked . . . and grieved to learn that the "eternal color question" was paramount to the grave war situation. After explaining . . . that both my loyalty to my country and to my young son, who will be eligible for Military Service in two months, prompted my offer, . . . [I] challenged . . . [the doctor] to accept my blood and place it in a container and label it "Negro Blood" and after due process make it available for some Negro mother's son, who, like his white American brothers-in-arms, must face shot and shell and death as these things know no "color line." I begged him to do this — I would have paid for the processing, if need be. . . . I fear that the time may come when all blood — white or black — may be needed — so many, many lives depend upon it! . . .
>
> This is not a letter of hate, despite the disappointment and bitterness and humiliation I suffered at the Red Cross on last Thursday — rather, it is an appeal for immediate mutual understanding and goodwill and the exercise of "the brotherhood of God and the fellow-ship of Man." The American Red Cross holds the destiny of thousands of human being[s], white and black, — make them understand that "We are Americans, too," and we want to make the blood sacrifice — we must make the blood sacrifice not only for the present "5%" but for the vast percentage of soldiers that must be called and must face the Hell of War before this conflict is over.[24]

Walter White, executive secretary of the NAACP, was a persistent spokesman against the policies. He wrote Norman Davis, chairman of the American Red Cross, this characteristic letter protesting the segregation policy soon after it was announced in January 1942:

> A more honorable position which the Red Cross could and should have taken, in our opinion, would have been for it to say frankly and

unequivocally to the Army and Navy that it would not be a party to the creation of an unscientific myth. . . .

The position the Red Cross, the Army and the Navy have taken is all the more inexplicable in view of the fact that we are informed that the blood of the Chinese, and even of Japanese, have been taken since Pearl Harbor and mixed with "white" blood. How ironic must be the laughter today in Berlin and Tokyo as they listen to American assertions that the war is being fought against the racial ideology of Aryanism and to wipe out totalitarianism based on racial bigotry! This proposal to jim-crow blood plasma is as unacceptable to any self-respecting Negro as was the refusal to accept Negro blood.[25]

What Walter White and many others pointed to again and again was the irony that an American war was allegedly being fought to end racism, yet the war effort involved a racist policy of blood segregation.[26] As Walter White and others who shared his views were well aware, the jim-crowing of blood both epitomized and resulted from the irrational symbolism at the heart of America's caste system — the white cultural mythology that labeled black people as inferior. This mythology also included the persistent belief that blood carried with it the hereditary qualities of the racial stock. Although science had demonstrated that genetic inheritance was passed not through the blood but rather through chromosomes, such beliefs persisted then and persist today as revealed by such popular concepts as "pureblooded," "halfblooded," or "fullblooded"; "good blood"; "blood tie" or "blood relationship," "blood brothers" or "blood sisters"; and "foreign blood."

Tied to these ancient beliefs about blood were specific fears about mixing black blood and white blood. The lynchpin of America's caste system, as with virtually all caste systems throughout the world, was the belief that the blood of the white race must be kept pure and must not be mixed with that of inferior races.[27] The fear of mixing black and white blood was deeply ingrained in popular American culture and folklore. Abraham Lincoln, the Great Liberator himself, once commented, "Judge Douglas is especially horrified at the thought of mixing the blood of the white and black races. Agreed for once — a thousand times agreed."[28]

Throughout the world, in societies where caste structures are intact, members of the dominant group or race fear "pollution" — from even the most minimal social contact, such as shaking hands, to the ultimate pollution of intermarriage. However, white Americans' fear of blacks' polluting qualities has historically had a special intensity due to the highly developed ideology of white superiority and black inferiority that reinforced slavery and, subsequently, segregation.[29] American doctors played an important role in creating, elaborating, and lending scientific respectability to this ideology. In medical journals in the nineteenth and early twentieth centuries, respected members of the medical profession advanced an array of pseudoscientific theories about the disastrous effects of black "blood" contaminating the white race through intermarriage. Having imbibed these widely prevalent yet often contradictory[30] racist fears from their earliest days, many white Americans feared far more than the mere loss of caste from mixing their blood with blacks: they feared somehow becoming the subhuman, uncivilized "thing" that blacks were reputed to be in the prevailing racist mythology. It in fact is highly fitting that in the "Drew as victim" legend, Drew suffers at the hands of white doctors, for in a larger sense, especially at this highly charged moment in his life, he did. White doctors gave the respectability of medical theory to what was essentially a primitive belief in inviolate caste distinctions between black and white Americans. Very often, doctors focused on "black blood" as being in some crucial way different from "white blood" — a medical viewpoint that had been shown to be false well before World War II.

During the antebellum era, a Louisiana physician with a wide following, Samuel Cartwright, published medical articles for the explicit purpose of justifying slavery.[31] Cartwright's views demonstrate that southern men of science were important mythographers of white racism. It is doubly and triply ironic that Charles Drew, a black man of science, came to effectively refute some of the false beliefs that this white "scientific" mythological thinking led to, and that Drew's life and death then became the vehicle for a historical legend that, though also a form of racial mythology, pointed the way to a still larger historical truth: the waste of black lives.

Cartwright repeatedly returned to different blood as a metaphor for black inferiority, depicting the gulf between the races as profound: "Even the negro's brain and nerves, the chyle and the humors, are tinctured with a shade of the pervading darkness. His bile is of a deeper color, and his blood is blacker than the white man's."[32] Cartwright contended that the black man not only had a smaller brain but also had smaller lungs, which failed to sufficiently oxygenate the blood. The result was "a deficiency of red blood in the pulmonary and arterial systems," leading to an indolent, sluggish temperament and ultimately a "debasement of mind" that, in Cartwright's view, "rendered the people of Africa unable to take care of themselves."[33] A direct product of this defect was a disease that Cartwright called "dysaesthesia aethiopica" or "hebetude of mind," an "obtuse sensibility of body" that overseers called "rascality."[34] Cartwright drew even larger conclusions about the effect of imperfect Negro physiology: "The black blood distributed to the brain chains the mind to ignorance, superstition and barbarism, and bolts the door against civilization, moral culture and religious truth."[35]

Josiah Clark Nott, a surgeon who practiced in Mobile, Alabama, was another well-known proslavery theorist. Nott argued his case from a different angle: he attacked conservative southern theology, believed in the polygenic origin of races, and held that blacks as a separate race were incapable of being civilized. In 1854, Nott and George Gliddon, another proslavery polygenist, published a massive eight-hundred-page study called *Types of Mankind* that was read widely. In an 1866 article titled "The Negro Race," Nott also focused on blood as the critical differentiating factor between the races: "It is certain that the white race is deteriorated by every drop of black blood infiltrated into it — just as surely as the blood of the greyhound or pointer is polluted by that of a cur."[36]

White medical men focused on the high black mortality rates between 1860 and 1900 as further proof of black inferiority. To black leaders such as W. E. B. Du Bois and Booker T. Washington, these rates pointed to the terrible social and economic conditions blacks were being forced to endure — bad housing, insufficient jobs and pay, inadequate food and medical care.[37] But to many white "scientists," the same data represented proof of black people's moral unfitness for physical survival as free people. The prevailing belief in this period of Darwinian logic, which celebrated the "survival of the fittest," was that blacks, whether "full-blooded" or mulatto, were genetically so inferior and backward that they would become extinct as a race. The medical science of the day was a crucial component in support of this belief, just as it had been a bulwark to moral complacency about slavery.[38]

In 1896, the American Economic Association published an influential study by Frederick L. Hoffman, a life insurance statistician, titled "Race Traits and Tendencies of the American Negro"; it pulled together the "scientific" conclusions of the previous thirty years and concluded that immorality and vice were built into the black man's very nature and would lead inexorably to disease, infertility, and ultimate racial extinction.[39] A crucial dimension of the "scientific" forces arrayed against blacks were still more medical articles written by southern physicians, most of whom argued vehemently that blacks were fundamentally different from and grossly inferior to whites. These doctors based their conclusions on the Civil War anthropometric statistics, on postwar black mortality rates, and on their own (less systematic) medical observations. They claimed to find, among postwar blacks, higher rates of insanity; a greater tendency to die from surgical operations; growing sexual license and the spread of venereal disease; increasing numbers of stillbirths and higher infant mortality rates; an increase in criminal violence; and, even, lower rates of suicide. Illogical as their interpretation may seem, the doctors derived the same meaning from all these phenomena: the strain of freedom was too great for the black man.[40]

In few areas of writing does one stumble across such extreme flights of phobic fantasy and political self-interest masquerading as "science." Doctors, perhaps more than any other group, considered themselves experts on black genital "peculiarities," and they did much to fan white fears of black sexuality, particularly the fear of black men raping white women. The horror whites have historically felt toward the idea of a black man raping a white woman, apart from their awareness of the suffering experienced by any woman so violated, stems from this threatened event's symbolic nature as the ultimate violation of the taboo against race-mixing. Lynching was felt to be justified as the appropriate punishment for violation of such a powerful social taboo. In fact, lynching — accompanied by burning of black men's bodies, their dismemberment, and the collection of black body parts as trophies — became a kind of social ritual that reinforced white supremacy and inculcated racist hatred of blacks in the young.[41] For these larger social purposes, physicians were powerfully motivated to depict black male sexual aggressiveness as an inherent trait and to exaggerate the dangers of whites' receiving blacks' blood.

Many physicians in the segregation era "depicted syphilis as the quintessential black disease."[42] A remedy for it that some people advocated as a means of dealing with "the animal passions of the Negro" was castration — a solution that would, argued the *Atlanta Journal-Record of Medicine* in 1906, produce Negroes who were "docile, quiet and inoffensive."[43]

In 1907 a U.S. army doctor named Robert Shufeldt published *The Negro: A Menace to American Civilization*, a book that epitomized the most extreme racist attitudes of many white doctors of his generation. In it he wrote, "Now does anyone for a moment suppose that even in the event of

emasculation rendering . . . [the] negro impotent, it would have a particle of influence in deterring thousands of other ignorant negroes . . . ?
With the surgeon's knife actually pressing upon his scrotum; with the
blazing fagots so near him that he could actually feel the heat of the
flames, he would nevertheless seize his victim and outrage her if it lay
within his power to do so."[44] Writing in a medical article about blacks
and syphilis, another doctor commented, "[Blacks] are just as devoid of
ethical sentiment or consciousness as the fly and the maggot."[45]

Given these attitudes, it is not hard to see the degree to which America's blacks have long been — and still are — the society's ultimate national scapegoat, forced to carry the painful burden of embodying all the
projected beasts and demons of the collective white American psyche.[46]
While the primary white fear of blood-mixing traditionally expressed
itself as an absolute taboo against intermarriage between the races, in
midcentury America white fear was so profound and the mythology of
black inferiority so powerful that for many whites, even the idea of receiving a blood transfusion from a black person carried the threat of loss of
white identity.

Many white Americans were the victims of ignorance, poor education,
and superstition — victims, in some sense, of their own culture's dominant mythology about race. White fears were real and profound, as demonstrated by the many letters white Americans wrote to the Red Cross, to
the White House and other governmental authorities, and even to Charles Drew himself. Typical of these letters is one by an unknown white
person that was sent to a U.S. congressman by an official of the National
Humane League:

> The families of several young men and women, now serving with
> our armed forces overseas, have heard rumors which, at first, seemed
> too fantastic even to warrant serious thought . . . that blood plasma
> taken from Whites, Asiatics and Negroes is being injected, without re-
> gard to its origin, into the bloodstreams of our wounded soldiers. . . .
>
> [T]his unproved, potentially dangerous stuff *to future generations* is
> now being put into the bloodstreams of our wounded heroes. . . .
>
> [T]he color of a child is directly influenced by the blood of the
> mother and of the father. In fact, in the final analysis, the embryonic
> baby is the direct result of the mixing of the blood of the parents.
>
> No one knows the starting point of the pigmentation responsible
> for this coloration. A glance through the medical books will confirm
> this. Therefore, like the germs of the common cold, the incipient

organisms of color may be too tiny for the most powerful microscope to detect. The color of one's skin may start in infinitesimal globules in the blood. These infinitesimal globules may be present in the plasma now being used — but they may be present in such a limited degree that two, three or more generations might go by before the foreign color taint will develop sufficiently to make itself manifest. . . .

As a layman, you probably know of instances where negroes have slowly turned white. No medical man can explain definitely the reason for this and nothing known to science will stop such transformation. . . . It is important to remember that far, far too many *medical certainties* have turned out to be horrible *wrong guesses.*

Are the babies, or grandchildren or great grandchildren of our wounded white soldiers to be white, brown, red, yellow or black? How many white men, having a choice, would rather die there on the battlefield without plasma rather than run the chance of coming back to be the father, grandfather or great grandfather of a brown, red, black or yellow child?[47]

In the early fall of 1941, different blood centers had a variety of policies toward black donors, depending largely on local custom and law. In the New York and Philadelphia blood centers, for example, black donors were accepted, but their blood, instead of being pooled with whites' blood for the national wartime stockpiling program, was donated to local hospitals. In Baltimore, Maryland, where the hospitals were segregated, a young black woman was turned away when she went to give blood with her fellow white employees in August 1941, triggering articles of protest in the local black press.[48] American Red Cross officials, realizing that local incidents were more likely to erupt elsewhere in the absence of a clear national policy, contacted their national headquarters to urge that such a policy be adopted.[49]

As the black press ignited national awareness of the blood mixing issue, a number of white southern politicians played on racist fears to win white political support. Typical was a May 1942 speech by Representative John Rankin of Mississippi. In this speech Rankin commented,

one of the most vicious movements that has yet been instituted by the crackpots, the Communists, and parlor pinks of this country is that of trying to browbeat the American Red Cross into taking the labels off the blood bank they are building up for our wounded boys in the service so that it will not show whether it is Negro blood or white blood.

That seems to be one of the schemes of these fellow travelers to try to mongrelize this Nation. . . .

Thank God, the Red Cross has stood its ground and refused to permit this outfit to have Negro blood pumped into the veins of our wounded white men on the various fronts. . . .

They seem to have some crackpot alien doctors advising them that it makes no difference what race this blood comes from.[50]

In the fall of 1941, American Red Cross chairman Norman H. Davis met with army surgeon general James C. Magee[51] and navy surgeon general Ross T. McIntyre, and together they agreed on the policy of black exclusion. Red Cross National Blood Program director G. Canby Robinson explained, "The reason for the policy is the opinion that there are so many people who would disapprove of having the plasma from colored blood used indiscriminately with that of white blood that it would jeopardize the project. It is certainly more of a 'white problem' than a 'colored problem.' "[52] When black protest erupted in the subsequent months, officials came up with the segregation policy as a "liberal" alternative. The Red Cross as a scientific and humanitarian organization officially took the position that there was no scientific basis to the policy. Some individual American Red Cross officials even fought the policy, because they felt that it was morally indefensible and an embarrassment to the organization. The chairman of the Princeton chapter of the American Red Cross sent the following statement to the national chairman: "While fully recognizing the superstitions and prejudices which the Red Cross is trying not to offend in this cautious policy [of segregation], I object to it so strongly on principle that I should resign from the Chapter rather than publish it as our policy. . . . It is surely . . . the height of unwisdom . . . to tell . . . [black] people that the nation, which asks their willingness to sacrifice their lifeblood, will not accept it as human blood in the general blood plasma."[53] Chairman Davis himself publicly admitted that the policy was based solely on emotion. But he and chairman Basil O'Connor, who replaced him in 1944, ultimately bowed to white public pressure, falling back on the morally ambiguous position that the prejudices of the white majority must prevail. Davis explained to a magazine editor in 1942,

It would of course have been easy for me to state at the very beginning that if the Army and Navy so desired and agreed the Red Cross would be quite willing to mix the blood but, since the Red Cross is an auxiliary of the Army and Navy in time of war, I did not feel that it would be wise or ethical to try to put the blame on the Army and Navy. . . .

The Red Cross has no prejudices. It extends its aid to those in need without regard to race or religion. But it is not the Red Cross job to settle racial controversies. The question really is whether or not the views of the majority of those for whom the blood is being procured . . . are to prevail or whether the views of the minority who wish to donate their blood shall prevail.[54]

From the moment Drew as a blood plasma pioneer was forced to encounter this white racist mythology about the dangers of black blood, he became legendary material. The central irony was that Charles Drew himself, who had worked in a color-blind effort to help create America's blood program, was barred from giving his own blood because he was black. A further irony was that Drew himself was a man of "mixed blood" whose very being refuted the lie of white superiority and the need for racial purity.[55] Eventually Drew not only suffered from racism but also challenged its very premises with scientific authority. In doing so, he symbolized the struggles of black Americans of his generation. During World War II, black men and women, entering the struggle in unprecedented numbers, were also confronting the paradox of American democracy as never before, as they faced segregation and racism not only at home but wherever their government sent them.[56]

Letters from black soldiers themselves, and from ordinary black people to the president of the United States protesting relatives' or friends' treatment, reveal much about the attitudes and feelings of blacks caught up in these paradoxes during the war. One black soldier who was denied the use of American Red Cross recreational facilities in Italy wrote to his wife about his disillusionment with both the Red Cross and the U.S. government:

Every day, you read in the papers about the war being fought for the liberation of subjugated people. Yet, the soldiers over here fighting for that purpose are subjugated. It's farce. . . .

I'm inclined to believe that there is a different interpretation of democracy for every race. . . . [O]urs is certainly different from that of the white man. To us, it means denial, subjugation, persecution. To him, it means freedom! and a right to live and enjoy life as he sees fit.

Someday . . . through the intervention of the Grace of God, there will be a change. Because, I know, and believe, that a just God will not continue to tolerate these things. I know that someday He will clear this world of the *stink* and *filth* of race hatred.[57]

Drew himself was caught up in this tide of historical change and feeling. His individual fate mirrored the violation of Christianity and democracy and the unnecessary humiliation that black Americans were being forced to endure on so many fronts during the war.[58] At the same time, his actions epitomized the kind of heroism other black Americans of his generation were demonstrating. Just as black soldiers were patriotically giving their lives — and their blood — for their country, Drew had risen above race to serve the Allies' cause as a blood savior par excellence. And just as black people protested the injustice of the situation, Drew himself publicly spoke out against the American Red Cross's blood segregation policy, calling it a humiliation to all black Americans.[59]

During the war, when Drew was known to have played a role in bestowing the life-giving power of blood and yet to have suffered a symbolic refusal of blood, his actual role was inflated. In the early 1940s, the first Drew legend was born: that Drew single-handedly, or almost single-handedly, discovered plasma, fathered the blood bank, and saved countless lives during World War II. The first articles inflating Drew's role appeared in black newspapers shortly after the American Red Cross had adopted its policy of segregating blood. One piece that appeared in the Chicago Defender in the fall of 1942 began, "No Negro blood accepted but . . . it was an American Negro surgeon to whom English medical men appealed to organize and send U.S. blood plasma overseas. . . . When the American Red Cross set up its first blood collection center in New York for our own armed forces, it was a Negro surgeon who was selected to supervise the entire project and expand the system to every city in the U.S. . . . When the Japanese bombed Pearl Harbor and maimed hundreds of American soldiers and sailors, it was blood collected by a Negro surgeon that saved their lives."[60] When Drew received the Spingarn Medal in 1944, more articles appeared, similarly dramatizing Drew's role. While the black press initiated most of the stories, some were reprinted in mainstream newspapers. One such article noted that blood was segregated, yet "the man who more than any other is responsible for the medical miracle which has saved the lives of tens of thousands of soldiers and civilians throughout the world is a Negro."[61]

The year 1944 also witnessed the appearance of the first article about Drew in what was regarded as a reputable, unbiased publication. It described John Scudder and Drew as a team, giving a fairly complete description of what they actually did; appropriately, Drew was given the leading role. This article was a follow-up to an article on the national blood collection program in the same magazine's September issue that had omitted any mention of Drew. A doctor at Meharry Medical College wrote the magazine pointing out Drew's contribution; the editors subsequently interviewed Drew and wrote the follow-up article detailing his role.[62]

The first legend, like the Drew victim legend, contained a larger truth: it came into being partly because Drew was an exceptional man who played a dramatic role in the development of the national blood program. But it also evolved because Drew was indirectly and symbolically mistreated due to his race in relation to the blood segregation policy. Drew himself insightfully connected his receiving the Spingarn Medal in 1944 with the ongoing larger mistreatment of blacks implicit in the blood segregation policy. In a letter he wrote to John Scudder after receiving the award, he commented,

> Not having been associated with anything that even closely pertains to blood or plasma since 1941, I was a little surprised . . . since the whole Negro race feels pretty badly about the Army attitude toward blood donors, I suppose there is some small satisfaction in the thought that at one time I was associated with this particular phase of activities connected with the war effort. There is a great deal of bitterness, not only about this particular phase but about opportunities and treatment of Negro troops as a whole, bitterness which makes me very unhappy for there are no suggestions which I can make which would have any effect in removing or relieving any of the situations which caused this bitterness and are a source of constant humiliation to anyone who would like to serve his country in a time such as this.[63]

Over the years, as public awareness about discrimination and about the historical neglect of black heroes grew, so did the Drew blood pioneer legend. While the legend reflected Drew's achievement, it also served as a kind of compensation for his mistreatment, and for the historical record's omissions of the achievements of other black heroes. American Red Cross historian Clyde Buckingham also concluded that the tendency to amplify Drew's role in blood bank research grew out of the Red Cross's blood segregation policy and the "question of interracial relationships." Buckingham too traced the rise of the first Drew legend to the early 1940s—to the claims that Drew was founder of the blood bank or the sole pioneer of blood plasma. Buckingham commented, "The introduction of the racial issue was to have a far-reaching effect on subsequent writers until by the mid-1960's in some textbooks, the Dr. Drew of legend would become the new symbol of his race's struggle for equality, and the historic Drew would be in danger of being lost—a casualty to the mythmaking process."[64]

This blood pioneer legend has frequently been incorporated into the major Drew legend, since it adds to the irony of Drew's mistreatment,[65] but it also frequently stands alone, either in newspaper articles and biographical entries about Drew or in more general pieces focusing on the need for more attention to black history's unsung heroes.[66]

The legend obviously represents a vast simplification of a very complex historical undertaking that involved many people. Drew clearly was not the sole founder of the blood bank or the discoverer of blood plasma, even though he can reasonably lay at least as much claim to these titles as any of the other scientists involved in blood research can. Drew himself, even though he had clearly felt the exhilaration of being on the cutting edge of an important undertaking, was always modest about what his own achievement had been, fully recognizing that scientific breakthroughs are largely the work of teams of scientists. In an address Drew made the year before he died, he commented, "Scientific data has increased at such a rapid pace that no one man can become a master . . . of all the knowledge of his time. Each man becomes a specialist in his field, but each problem, as a rule, requires the combined efforts of many specialists."[67]

A second legend about Drew emerged later, in the period when the major Drew legend had begun to circulate widely. This second legend has had many permutations, but like the first legend, it essentially serves to dramatize Drew's World War II experiences. Its basic idea is that Drew took decisive public action when he learned of the blood segregation policy. Drew's popular biographers may be credited with this legend, although newspaper writers have also contributed to its spread. In most versions, the legend goes that Drew was still working for the American Red Cross when he learned of the policy and that he hastily called a press conference and denounced the policy as unscientific. Emma Gelders Sterne was the first biographer to fabricate this scenario: she wrote that

ALMOST he had been able to surmount the extra obstacle of being a Negro in America. But the segregation of blood was not an affront to

himself alone, or to the Negro people alone, but to humanity's progress in conquest of nature's secrets. To permit outworn superstitions,
old prejudices, to enter the realm of science was to poison the well of
truth itself. . . . After trying in vain to get the order withdrawn, Drew
had his secretary call in a couple of newspaper reporters. . . . "Tell
them that the Medical Director of the National Blood Bank Program
will see them . . . ," Charley said. He wanted to make it perfectly clear
he was speaking in an official capacity. . . . "I have been asked my
opinion of the practice of separating the blood of Caucasian and
Negro donors," Charley said. "My OPINION is not important. The FACT
is that test by race does not stand up in the laboratory. That is all,
gentlemen."[68]

Other versions portray Drew not only speaking out against the policy
but also publicly resigning from the Red Cross in protest.[69] In most of
these versions Drew also resigned because, they report, he learned that
since he was black, he could not continue serving as medical director
when the blood program became national in scope. A popular biography by Richard Hardwick, somewhat more accurate and even-toned
than the others, also describes Drew calling a press conference. Hardwick adds an explanation for Drew's action: "There were . . . rumors to
the effect that when the blood program became a nationwide endeavor
Charles Drew might not be the proper man to head it up."[70]

With each succeeding version of this scenario, Drew's statement
of protest grows more lengthy and melodramatic, the moment more
charged with emotion. Robert Lichello has Drew calling the press conference to explain the reasons for his resignation from the Red Cross job
after he has learned not only that blood will be segregated but that he
will probably be replaced by a white man:

"Gentlemen . . . , you have asked for my opinion concerning the
policy of segregating the blood of Negroes from that of Caucasians,
and I tell you that I am adamantly, resolutely opposed to such a policy.
It is insulting, it is unscientific, and it is immoral. The disservice that
has been done has been done not only to the Negro people but to the
cause of Truth itself. How have we, in this age and in this hour, allowed
once again to creep into our hearts the dark myths and wretched superstitions of the past? Are we truly the heirs of those honored men of
science who sacrificed their lives in the greater service of humanity —
or are we the children of bigotry, blinded by yesterday's evil? In the

laboratory I have found that you and I share a common blood; but will we ever, ever share a common brotherhood? As repugnant as this scientific fact may appear to some, their quarrel is not with me, but with the Giver of Life whose wisdom made it so."[71]

In yet another version Drew publicly fought the segregation of blood and was fired from his Red Cross job because he refused to back down from his position.[72] A juvenile biography by Roland Bertol depicts Drew as very feisty. When the army insists on segregating blood, Drew instructs his assistants, " 'Tell them . . . that we are segregating blood. Then go ahead and mix it all up.' " Bertol goes on to present Drew as taking on the whole U.S. army against the advice of his friends, enraging "prejudiced white doctors" and others who were "jealous of his important position." Ultimately, in this version, Drew's enemies force him out of his Red Cross job. This second legend, which I term the Drew "angry prophet of truth" legend, presents such an irresistibly dramatic scenario — and a fitting one for writers who wanted to challenge the racist policy of segregating blood — that many magazine and newspaper writers have repeated it.

But this legend, like the victim and blood pioneer legends, is not literally true. Drew had left the employ of the Red Cross and had been working at Howard University Medical School for several months[73] by November 1941, when the American Red Cross announced that it would exclude black blood donors.[74] There is no evidence that Drew ever personally called a press conference, either while he was still in New York City or after he returned to Washington. Finally, there is no evidence to suggest that Drew left his American Red Cross job because he knew of the blood policy before it was publicly announced, or that he left in protest.[75]

Nonetheless, just as the other legends evolved because they represent larger truths, this legend contains its own kernel of truth and springs from the same ironic conjunction of historical events. The "prophet of truth" legend represents a telescoping of Drew's forthright defense of scientific truth and racial justice over a period of many years into a single highly dramatic moment. And although Drew did not leave his American Red Cross job in angry protest at blood segregation, he probably did leave, at least in part, because the organization had no place for a black man at its highest levels. There is some evidence to suggest that had Drew been white, he might have been asked to stay on to take charge of the technical aspects of the national blood program during the war, since he was probably the person best qualified to do the job.[76]

Since 1942 there have been scores of popular newspaper and magazine articles about Drew. Even in the many articles that do not contain the "Drew as victim" legend, the mythologizing of Drew proceeds apace. Frequently the "angry prophet of truth" legend is repeated as a kind of substitute to convey the mistreatment that the victim legend underscores. Typical in this regard was a 1980 article in the Burlington, North Carolina newspaper, which debunked the victim legend yet dramatized the angry prophet legend, in much the same way that the popular biographies of Drew have done:

> Then came a blow to Drew's professionalism and obvious humanitarianism.
> Blood—he learned from his government—was to be segregated. That precious life fluid that flows through every man, woman and child, was to be kept separate. Blood from blacks was not solicited. And finally, the doctor was told, through the rumor mill, that he had been hired to set up the massive program and would later be replaced by "a more acceptable" medical man—a white man.
> The feelings that coursed through Drew must have been terrible. He resigned his post and in a press conference, Drew decried the decision as unscientific, insulting and immoral.[77]

The mythologizing of Drew has been so intense that a variety of American Red Cross officials, especially since the 1960s, have been involved in debunking the various Drew legends. American Red Cross public relations officials and historians have attempted to set the record straight on Drew's scientific and organizational contribution to the national blood program, on the conditions of Drew's resignation from the Red Cross, and on the circumstances surrounding Drew's death. Red Cross officials have sent memos back and forth in great consternation whenever some new article, documentary, or memorial to Drew has been published that even slightly inflates his role, or that refers at all to the Red Cross's blood segregation policy, or that touches on anyone's possible mistreatment of Drew at the time of his death. Officials have written many letters to individuals who have asked the Red Cross about Drew's alleged fame or mistreatment.[78] And Red Cross officials have written their own histories of the national blood program. In the process, Red Cross personnel have both wittingly and unwittingly constructed—or at least attempted to construct—their own set of counter-legends.

A fourth Drew legend, the first of the Red Cross Drew counter-legends, is that Charles Drew played a relatively minor role in helping to initiate the national Red Cross blood collection program. In the first twenty-five years or so after Drew did his pioneering blood work, Red Cross officials contributed to this antimythic construction of Drew's life largely by ignoring him. He was not employed by the Red Cross for long, and after he left, a succession of white medical men were appointed to run the national blood collection program, so it was easy to let him slip into insignificance.[79] It was only when the black community, through various spokespeople, let it be known that they felt Drew had been neglected that Red Cross officials bestirred themselves to recognize Drew's contribution.

G. Canby Robinson, the white director of the Red Cross blood program, was awarded the organization's Medal of Merit in 1948. An article in the *Washington Afro-American* quoted Drew as saying Robinson was "worthy of such an award." The article added, "There are those, however, who are of the opinion that Dr. Drew, credited with being one of the pioneer workers in blood plasma, the basis on which the blood bank operates, should also be a recipient of the Red Cross's Medal of Merit."[80] No medal was forthcoming, but a Red Cross vice president named Howard Bonham sent a memo to another Red Cross official, noting, "it is apparent that Dr. Drew's followers as well as the leading Negro press . . . wonder why recognition has not been given to Dr. Drew." Bonham proposed that Drew be appointed to a Red Cross national committee on blood as a "fine public relations move," something that had been proposed a month earlier by another Red Cross official, who felt that it would be "accepted by Negro America as a significant recognition of Dr. Drew's contribution" and that it would "enhance our whole blood donor program among Negroes." According to Bonham's memo, Drew was "very enthusiastic" toward this proposal when approached.[81]

After Drew died, Claude A. Barnett, director of the Associated Negro Press, wrote Bonham from Chicago asking for help gathering material on Drew for an article in a major newspaper highlighting his contribution. Barnett noted, "His relationship to the development of blood-plasma, one of the largest of Red Cross programs, should have made him important to [the] Red Cross, it is believed by many persons." Bonham responded in a cordial, friendly tone, saying, "We are very conscious of Dr. Drew's stature as a scientist and as an American Citizen," noting that Drew's contribution was acknowledged in an official pamphlet titled " 'The American Red Cross Blood Donor Service during World War II.'"[82]

It was not until the mid- to late 1960s, after the Whitney Young article had been published, that the flood of letters requesting information about Drew poured down on the American Red Cross. In responding to these letters, Red Cross officials obviously viewed themselves as simply trying to correct what one official termed the "many extravagant claims"[83] about Drew—misconceptions that they came to label Myth No. 1, Myth No. 2, and Myth No. 3[84] and that essentially correspond with what I have termed the first, second, and third legends. The information they have sent out over a period of years to many inquirers has been for the most part accurate. Yet when reading over their polite, carefully worded missives, one can detect a growing strain of exasperation and bewilderment emerging in response to the torrent of requests and misconceptions. "Both the black community and the American Red Cross establishment operate under a gross misunderstanding of Dr. Drew's work and his death," commented one official in 1981.[85]

Rudy Clemen, who served as the American Red Cross's information research specialist at its national headquarters from 1963 to 1983, expressed frustration about his twenty-year struggle to set the record straight on Drew:

> Ever since the sixties, because the man was black, they've tried to put him on a pedestal. At our centennial in 1981, they tried to put him on a par with . . . [people like] Clara Barton, the founder. It's nonsense! It's like making a fourth-string guard an All-American. How can they take a black man and put him on a par with people who worked for the organization all these years, the Rockefellers, Mrs. Russell Sage . . . [and others]. He only worked for the New York chapter from February to April. They've wanted to make him a hero.[86]

While Clemen's desire to deflate Drew was obvious, Red Cross officials at other times revealed a more subtle, unconscious method of trimming Drew's actual role down to size. For example, in one instance, an official defined Drew's scientific contribution very narrowly: "Dr. Drew's major accomplishment . . . was his endorsement of a procedure known as the Sharp and Dohme method for drying plasma. . . . there seems to be no documentary support for the frequently repeated claims that Dr. Drew was responsible for the scientific discoveries which made possible this dried plasma program."[87] Another official stressed that Drew worked for the Red Cross "for a period of less than seven months."[88]

Red Cross officials have at times fostered this counter-legend—it might be called the "not a savior" legend—in a somewhat explicit way. The Red Cross was so inundated with queries about Drew during the 1960s that in 1967, a Red Cross executive vice president asked the organization's historian, Clyde E. Buckingham, to research Drew's life thoroughly and prepare a monograph that could be used in-house as the "official record."[89] The tone of Buckingham's monograph on Drew was reductionist and patronizing. He frequently referred to Drew as a "young Negro scientist," yet he did not mention the age or racial background of any of the other scientists or Red Cross organizers whose contributions he discussed. Even though he documented the fact that Drew did original research on blood preservation, he seemed to insist that Drew's primary contribution was merely organizing and synthesizing the research of other scientists, as if this were an inferior and not an absolutely vital scientific function—although it was, given the circumstances. In seeking to minimize Drew's role, Buckingham attacked various straw men: he wasted many paragraphs noting the committees Drew did not belong to and the various high-level meetings Drew did not attend and discussing technical features of the dried plasma apparatus that Drew did not personally invent. He unnecessarily discussed the fact that Drew had not done any significant blood research before coming to Columbia University—an argument tantamount to saying that before Einstein came up with the relativity formula, he had not discovered the relativity formula. "When Dr. Drew arrived at Columbia University," Buckingham wrote, "[he was] only thirty-four years of age. He was . . . unknown. Up to this point . . . , he had published no scientific articles or books, and his brief biographical sketches do not mention any prior specialization or particular interest in the study of blood." Buckingham described Drew as if his life were a blank slate before he arrived at Columbia, but facts stated elsewhere in the monograph belied this scenario. In the final analysis, Drew's achievement was all the more remarkable given how quickly he became an expert in blood preservation. Buckingham also seemed to consider it highly significant in proving Drew's relative unimportance that Drew was never on the national payroll of the American Red Cross but was instead hired by the New York City chapter. In short, Buckingham tried hard to trivialize Drew's role.[90]

Even the Red Cross's national director of public relations felt that Buckingham had gone too far. Commenting on Buckingham's monograph a year after it was completed, he noted, "We had hoped the material prepared by Mr. Buckingham . . . would be helpful in providing positive information. It turned out to be more or less negative and seemed to minimize the creditable accomplishments of Dr. Drew."[91]

Buckingham is not the only historian of the blood program to minimize Drew's role. Two other American Red Cross monographs and a book-length study by an army medical officer about the national blood program rather dramatically reveal the extent to which historians not even consciously attempting to combat black cultural mythology are susceptible to distortion of the historical record due to their own blind spots and biases.[92] To venture into the particular structure of fact and opinion surrounding Charles Drew's actual experience between September 1940 and April 1941 is to walk into a hall of mirrors, each reflecting a slightly different version of events. Ultimately, one sees that the whole subject of Drew's scientific contribution is as fraught with bias and emotion as the subject of his death is. To some extent, the history of any event partakes of this confusion, but the fact that Drew was black — and a great man by any standard in white America, thus defying the usual racist stereotypes — robs white and black storytellers of their poise and objectivity. Race is such a trauma for all Americans that to take sides is almost inescapable.

The sobering fact is that if one relied solely on the original American Red Cross historical accounts of the national blood collection program, one would probably be unable to appreciate Charles Drew's significance. For a variety of reasons, these accounts either explicitly underplayed his role or buried it by failing to give him personal credit for the success of the pilot program he supervised. It is quite clear that if the black press had not written about Drew's role in the 1940s and no legends about Drew had thereby surfaced in the popular media in the early 1940s and then grown dramatically in the 1960s, he might well be unknown to both black and white Americans today.[93] At the same time, these studies did not disagree on the basic facts: together they present a complete picture of the same complex set of historical events, which featured many different actors. It is simply a case of different historians giving very different emphases and meanings to the same facts.

Robert H. Fletcher, who completed a lengthy monograph in 1950, was one of the first to write a history of the American Red Cross World War II blood program.[94] Fletcher did describe the New York pilot program as marking the true beginning of the Blood Donor Service; however, he never mentioned Drew in connection with this program.

Brigadier General Douglas B. Kendrick, in charge of blood plasma research and procurement under the surgeon general of the U.S. army during the war, published an 810-page book on the national blood program in 1964. Like Fletcher, Kendrick neither mentioned Drew's name in connection with the New York pilot program nor discussed the program in detail. One of the reasons for Fletcher's and Kendrick's omissions, admittedly, was that for these men, the main hero was an entity other than Drew — the Red Cross and its complex internal workings, in Fletcher's case, and the army in Kendrick's. Also, Drew did depart the national scene months before this country entered the war and the Blood Donor Service grew to the massive proportions it later assumed. But, to the extent that these historians played up the role of individual heroes other than Drew,[95] one inevitably speculates about the degree to which some institutional bias, tinged with organizational racism, was a factor in their vision of events.

DeKleine, medical director of the American Red Cross from 1928 to 1941, wrote a 1950 monograph on the blood program. He is the author most suspect on the count of harboring some prejudice against Drew: DeKleine was in New York, in charge of setting up the blood donor aspects of the Blood for Britain project, while Drew served as medical director of the project. Yet his monograph was an unabashed attempt to demonstrate that John Elliott of Salisbury, North Carolina, was the major blood plasma pioneer. DeKleine mentioned Drew in passing in connection with the American Red Cross pilot program in New York City, but he minimized Drew's role by not giving his title or describing what he did; he merely said Drew was "in charge of the bleeding unit under the direction of Dr. C. P. Rhoads."[96]

In the monograph, DeKleine acknowledged that he had a close personal association with Elliott from 1938 on and that he had consistently tried to get national Red Cross and military authorities to take note of Elliott's pioneering plasma research. DeKleine revealed that when Elliott was not chosen to serve as medical supervisor of the Blood for Britain project, DeKleine argued against its being launched at all, because he was convinced that it would be a failure without Elliott at its helm.[97] DeKleine not only failed to discuss Drew's role in connection with the British project; he also asserted that the project was a failure, noting the contaminated plasma episode that occurred before Drew took charge. Since DeKleine had been in New York serving as the Red Cross official in a pivotal role, there is no way he could have been unaware of Drew's achievement, either in the fall of 1940 or in 1950. Furthermore, by the time he wrote his monograph, DeKleine probably was aware that Drew had received more public recognition than Elliott had, and thus he may have been moved to write the monograph to give Elliott the credit he felt Elliot deserved.

DeKleine included a number of unedited letters between him and Elliott as his evidence for Elliott's pioneering role. He commented, "I quote all this correspondence to call attention to Dr. Elliott's contribution to the development of blood plasma. . . . This preliminary maneuvering would be lost to view unless it were recorded, and Doctor Elliott's relation to the development of plasma would be entirely over-looked. He did more than anyone else to bring plasma to the attention of medical groups."[98] DeKleine included one of Elliott's letters from 1940 in which Elliott himself, in true "sour grapes" fashion, asserted, "As you know I have undoubtedly pioneered most of the work on plasma as a substitute for whole blood. . . . I am being entirely ignored. . . . It seems to me that if a study is to be made as to the relative merits of several procedures that those who have had the greatest experience should have some part in such a study."[99]

This whole Elliott-DeKleine episode might be regarded as one of the many humorous and insignificant subplots that inevitably emerges in the course of historical research, and as such it might be aptly titled "Will the Real Blood Plasma Pioneer Please Stand Up?" But like so much in the larger saga of Charles Drew and the epic of American racism, there is more here than meets the eye. One other bit of evidence that floated to the surface from Red Cross archives came tellingly from the pen of Dr. DeKleine, suggesting, albeit inconclusively, that race — and racism — might well have played a role in all this. In responding to a Red Cross official's inquiry[100] about Drew's role with the organization, DeKleine wrote in May 1944,

> There was some discussion about . . . [Drew's] employment with the Red Cross as director of the technical phases of the Army and Navy project, but because of the fact that he was a negro, it was thought best not to employ him. He then became associated with Howard University.
>
> Doctor Drew had no relationship whatever to the development of the blood plasma project for the military forces, which was started shortly after the London project was discontinued.[101]

DeKleine's second statement, of course, was inaccurate; but the attitude toward Drew that it reflects is strikingly consistent with the attitude revealed in DeKleine's monograph. This highly placed Red Cross official, who had every reason to know what Drew's actual accomplishments were, seems to have been, for some reason other than a lack of sufficient information, unwilling to give Drew credit for what he did for the Blood Donor Service. This letter is by no means conclusive, but DeKleine's reference to Drew's race as a causal factor in Drew's departure is strongly suggestive. The narrowest interpretation of this letter, given its inaccuracy, would be that DeKleine was simply misinformed. This interpretation seems unlikely, however. More probable is that DeKleine himself believed that Drew's being a Negro did indeed bar him, or should have barred him, from a significant role. The broadest interpretation of the letter allows for the possibility that it is a piece of real evidence for one of the scenarios that the popular biographers of Drew paint. At the least it suggests that, just as Drew's well-informed colleagues later asserted, Drew was not even considered for the job of national technical director of the national blood program, because he was black. Unfortunately, further evidence on this whole issue is unavailable or inconclusive.

An ironic footnote to the whole episode involving DeKleine, Drew, and Elliot is that when DeKleine died in 1957, the *New York Times* gave him sole credit for organizing and setting up the Red Cross blood bank during World War II. As medical director of the Red Cross at the time Drew actually set up the first Red Cross blood bank in New York, DeKleine did play a supervisory role. However, blood banking was not his area of expertise. Furthermore, like Drew, he left the employ of the American Red Cross some months before the wartime blood collection program got fully underway.[102]

The fifth legend — a second counter-legend that American Red Cross officials have explicitly tried to put forth over the years — is that the American Red Cross has always been entirely humanitarian and non-discriminatory in its treatment of American citizens and of other people around the world.[103] In particular, American Red Cross officials have often taken the position that the Red Cross itself should bear none of the responsibility for having adopted a policy of segregating blood.

Though they briefly discuss the segregated blood policy and blacks' responses to it, Red Cross historians play down the policy's significance and take the position that the Red Cross had no real choice but to adopt it. Foster Rhea Dulles, in the major scholarly study of the organization, begins by asserting the democratic nature of the blood program: "There were no distinctions of class, sex or occupation among the donors who crowded the blood centers." Farther on, he notes that "in spite of the generally democratic functioning of the blood donor centers, a highly controversial issue rose over the use of Negro blood. . . . It was hoped that by personal interviews with prospective Negro donors, justifying this policy as a practical expedient and expressing appreciation for their offer of blood, 'general statements or press publicity, with consequent misunderstanding, may be avoided.'" Dulles goes on to relate that Red Cross chairman Norman Davis upheld the policy on the grounds that the army and navy required it and that it was not the organization's job to "settle racial controversies"; he says Davis also raised the question of whether "'under a Democracy . . . the wishes or prejudices of those who are to receive blood should prevail or the wishes of a relatively small percentage of those who wish to give their blood?'"[104] Dulles concludes, "The major point remained . . . that the Red Cross and the military authorities were in agreement in following a course . . . essential for the success of the blood program. . . . The American people were responsible for the popular attitude that fostered discrimination, and the segregation of blood was a reflection of the prevailing mores of the country."[105]

Charles Hurd, another historian of the American Red Cross, deals with the blood segregation policy similarly, saying that "furious . . . Negro leaders . . . cited unanimous opinions among experts that there is no racial difference in blood." Hurd himself takes no position on this scientific issue. Instead he ducks it and concludes, "In retrospect it appears that the Red Cross could have taken no other course."[106]

In publicly claiming that military authorities required the segregation policy, and in suggesting that the prejudices of the majority of Americans had to be respected, Red Cross officials and historians essentially washed their hands of the whole issue, especially its moral implications. Red Cross archives, however, reveal a more complex truth than the established line: Red Cross officials were acutely aware of the scientific and moral issues involved, but they, like most other white Americans, regarded the segregation policy as desirable and deemed it necessary to the success of the blood donor program. The policy conflicted with the Red Cross's mythology about itself as a humanitarian organization and with the informed judgment of some of its officials about what was morally and scientifically right. Especially in later years, the policy caused Red Cross officials much embarrassment.

When the early Drew legends began to proliferate, the Red Cross as an organization was forced to confront this dark chapter in its own history.

Its response—as revealed in Red Cross files on Drew at the national headquarters—was either to try to hide this humiliating piece of its history or to minimize its importance. Throughout the late 1960s, 1970s, and early 1980s, the organization's national headquarters received so many queries referring to the first three Drew legends that officials put together new "fact sheets" specifically to debunk Myth No. 1, Myth No. 2, and Myth No. 3. In one such fact sheet, put together in 1981, a Red Cross official called the blood segregation policy the Red Cross's "black eye." He asserted—wrongly—that the U.S. armed forces required the Red Cross to adopt the segregation policy.[107] Whenever it was possible, the Red Cross sought to prevent public mention of blood segregation or at least to play down its impact. In 1971, when a portrait of Drew was to be hung at the National Portrait Gallery in Washington, Red Cross officials were disturbed that a short biography of Drew under the portrait referred to the blood segregation policy. They sought to have the mention of blood segregation deleted or at least to have the biography revised. In an interoffice memo, one official commented, "We may get started again on the whole subject of blood segregation. If that appears likely, it might be better to forget the whole thing."[108] The "angry prophet of truth" legend was also disturbing to Red Cross officials; they were quick to assert that Drew did not leave the Red Cross because of blood segregation.[109]

Similarly, the authors of Red Cross monographs on the blood program dealt with the whole trauma of blood segregation by largely leaving it out of their historical record, either making no reference to it at all or confining their discussion to a brief mention and a justification of the Red Cross policy. In its official pamphlets about Drew, the Red Cross has never mentioned or discussed its blood segregation policy. William De-Kleine does not discuss the issue of separating black and white blood, even though he notes that the first Red Cross donor program in this country was set up to procure blood for indigent patients, primarily black patients. DeKleine explains that the hospital had had trouble finding enough black donors: "Colored folks generally were, at that time, very superstitious about giving blood and perhaps they still are."[110]

In his 145-page administrative history of the national blood program, Robert Fletcher limits his discussion of "policies concerning blood of negro donors" to three pages. Although he acknowledges the "storm of protest" and the "flood of denunciation" that attended both the exclusion policy and the segregation policy, he concludes with a justification of the American Red Cross's position:

The replies sent to all who wrote were based upon the realistic tenets, first, that the Red Cross had never claimed that any difference existed in the blood of the two races; and that, regardless of the merits of the matter, most men of the white race objected to having blood of Negroes injected into their veins. . . . Problems in . . . administration were not complex. Their solution lay in patience in dealing with individuals; and indefatigability in replying to the many communications received over the years.[111]

And in his 810-page book on the blood program, which was published in 1964, at the height of the civil rights movement, Douglas Kendrick never mentions the segregation of blood or suggests that any racial issues emerged in the program, even though he does discuss the enduring problem of procuring sufficient donors and the persistent rumors that hurt the program.[112]

Clyde Buckingham, Drew's Red Cross biographer, does find an "apparent motive" for Drew's growing legendary status in the "question of interracial relationships and segregation of blood" and believes that the "racial issue" explained why the "Dr. Drew of legend" became "the new symbol of his race's struggle for equality." But Buckingham goes no further: he does not document the impact of the blood segregation policy on black Americans or explore the reasons that the Drew legend might have grown out of the whole historical situation.[113]

Finally, the sixth legend or counter-legend is that Charles Drew was not mistreated in any way. Though Red Cross officials appropriately corrected the "bleeding to death" story, they also left a great deal out when they allowed a flat denial of mistreatment to stand as the final word on Drew's life and the manner of his death. Not only did they attempt to suppress any mention of the blood exclusion and segregation policies; they also failed to adequately address the larger truth of Drew's situation — or that of black Americans as a group during World War II. Their omissions, their refusal to acknowledge their own role in fostering racist policies during the war and afterward, and their failure to address or comprehend how the Drew legends emerged should be understood as part of the larger framework that contributed to the many legends' birth and growth. The Red Cross's slowness and reluctance in acknowledging Drew's role, its assumption that silence about its blood policies would allow them to be forgotten, its inability to imagine or address the circumstances that led to the victim legend — all displayed the same spirit as its bowing to white social prejudice and racist mythology by accepting the blood policies in the first place. Though representatives of a self-professed "humanitarian" organization, Red Cross officials revealed themselves to be either unaware of or insensitive to how segregated medical care functioned — how frequently it led to inhumane treatment and avoidable tragedies.

In the final analysis, the Red Cross's relationship to Charles Drew is not unusual: it exhibited a cultural outlook characterized by a blindness and denial of black reality endemic to the white cultural viewpoint long dominant in American society. Red Cross officials over a period of years were stubborn and myopic in their refusal to see and acknowledge the painful realities that the Drew legends were pointing to: the discrimination Drew himself faced in the form of the Red Cross segregation policy, the impact of the policy on thousands of other black Americans, and the enduring impact of more than three centuries of institutionalized racism — a discriminatory system to which their organization made its own contribution. Ultimately, it was as much a form of mythmaking to assert Drew's insignificance, to deny the existence or impact of blood segregation, and to censor information that conflicted with the Red Cross's humanitarian mystique, as it was to proclaim Drew's heroism, to over-dramatize his attack on segregation, and to participate in the creation of a legend about his death. But it is harder to perceive the mythmaking process in mainstream white America than in minority America: white mythology so often and so thoroughly prevails that it is often not even recognized as mythology. America's dominant myths are almost invisible until they are challenged by a minority cultural outlook that has been largely silenced.

The Drew legends — all of them — do challenge the cultural status quo of America. If they are taken seriously, Americans are forced to see their history differently. Not only do the Drew legends challenge the minor role the American Red Cross would have Charles Drew play in the development of blood plasma and the insignificance of the protest against blood segregation; they also call into question myths at the heart of dominant white American culture. The "Drew as blood pioneer" legend challenges the myth of black inferiority and insignificance — the idea that American blacks individually or as a group have made few significant contributions to American society. In underscoring the reality and hurtfulness of blood segregation, the "Drew as angry prophet of truth" legend directly challenges the myth that all Americans compete fairly and rise in the world according to individual merit. Finally, the "Drew as victim" legend cuts like a scalpel right into the dark heart of American history: by dramatizing cultural and racial murder, waste, and desecration of individual human life and talent, the major Drew legend challenges America's deepest vision of itself as a land of hope and opportunity, a land of new life and promise for all who step on its shores.

Thus, much more than the myth of the humanitarian and scientific Red Cross was at stake, even for the Red Cross officials and historians. Historical and even scientific truth are shown to have a large cultural component indeed. By accomplishing what he did in blood plasma research, by speaking out against blood segregation, and simply by being who he was, Charles Drew dramatized not only the absurdity of America's white racist mythology but also a fundamental dishonesty at the heart of mainstream American culture. As an international scientist and humanitarian, Drew's whole life called into question the established American order, which for many of American's citizens was as undemocratic, as totalitarian and fascist, as the very forces America was fighting in World War II.

The Death of an Invisible Man

What did they ever think of us transitory ones . . . — birds of passage too obscure for learned classification, too silent for the most sensitive recorders of sound; of natures too ambiguous for the most ambiguous words, and too distant from the centers of historical decision to sign or even to applaud the signers of historical documents. . . . What about those . . . boys coming now along the platform. . . . They were men out of time. . . . But who knew . . . who knew but that they were the saviors, the true leaders, the bearers of something precious? What if history was a gambler, instead of a force in a laboratory experiment, and the boys his ace in the hole?

— Ralph Ellison, *Invisible Man*

8

Wasn't He Riding with Dr. Drew?

Behind a legend and its hero are the visceral experiences of individual men and women, the essential threads from which the legend is woven. Nowhere is the larger truth of the Charles Drew legend revealed more concretely than in the life and death of a young black man named Maltheus Reeves Avery, who actually met the fate that the victim legend describes.

Maltheus Avery's life and death make up only one thread of the historical fabric behind the Drew legend; there were others, of course, each one of which could conceivably offer a story as poignant as Avery's own. But in the same way that Charles Drew serves the Drew legend well as hero, Maltheus Avery makes a fitting Everyman. In his very ordinariness, he highlights an extraordinary truth. In his particularity, he mirrors a common humanity. And in a nation that historically has provided medical care in a discriminatory way, Avery — even more than Charles Drew — is emblematic of all Americans who have suffered unnecessarily.

On 1 December 1950, exactly eight months after Drew's fatal accident in Alamance County, Maltheus Avery had an automobile accident in the same county. Critically injured, Avery was taken to the same hospital to which Drew had been taken. After being diagnosed, however, Avery was sent on to Duke Hospital in Durham, North Carolina. There he was refused treatment because Duke's "black beds" were full. He died less than an hour later.

The largely unknown reality of Avery's death lives on in the repeated telling — in North Carolina — of the Drew legend. People who do not remember this obscure young black man's name tell versions of the Drew legend that quite obviously refer to Avery's experience, although they attach Drew's name to their stories. But the pain of Avery's death lives on, not only on this metaphorical level but also in the lives of his family and friends. His death and its aftermath are an enduring witness to the human cost of segregation.

Early in the evening of Friday, 1 December 1950, Maltheus Avery, a twenty-four-year-old student at A&T College in Greensboro, North Carolina, and a World War II veteran with a wife and small daughter, was driving by himself from Greensboro to Henderson, North Carolina, a trip of approximately one hundred miles. About 30 miles from Greensboro, on Route 70 east of a rural community named Mebane, Avery's car sideswiped a furniture truck going in the opposite direction, driven by Fred Eugene Pope, of High Point, North Carolina. The accident occurred between 6:30 and 7:00 P.M. on a straight stretch of road in front of the Craftique Company, a local business; according to the highway patrol report, no reason for it could be given. A patrolman named J. S. Howell noted after observing marks on the road and after interviewing the truck driver that the truck, going west, almost went into a ditch to avoid the collision but was struck by Avery's car. Damage to the truck was estimated at between five and six hundred dollars. Avery's car, a 1939 black Pontiac, was completely demolished, and Avery himself was initially pinned in the car. A Mebane ambulance took him, unconscious, to the Alamance General Hospital's emergency room.[1]

The closest hospital, Alamance General Hospital, was at that time the only hospital in Alamance County, and it was the same one at which

Charles Drew had been treated. Privately owned by white doctors, this segregated forty-eight-bed facility had five beds in the basement reserved for black patients. In this period, the hospital was often overcrowded, since the county's population had grown significantly in the postwar years. The hospital's new emergency room had been built in 1948, and both black and white patients were routinely treated there.[2]

When Maltheus Avery was brought in, the surgeon on call "realized right away he was seriously injured."[3] He examined Avery and found he had fractures of the skull-, cheek-, and jawbones, and of a leg and an arm. He told reporters at the time that he decided Avery should go on to Duke University Hospital for neurosurgery and "definitive treatment."[4] Harold Kernodle, one of the two young surgeons at Alamance General who regularly worked in the emergency room during those years, did not remember Maltheus Avery specifically. But he vividly recalled the problems he faced when a patient with a traumatic head injury was brought in: "We mainly transferred head injuries. . . . We tried to take care of most everything else. . . . We had no neurosurgeon, and if [a patient's] . . . head needed to be operated on, we transferred him to Duke . . . or Greensboro. . . . I found out in the war that if you have a head injury it's better to transport in the first hour, rather than let them sit an hour, because of the bleeding into the brain and the swelling."[5]

Avery was in Alamance General Hospital's emergency room for some thirty to forty-five minutes before being sent on to Duke. The same ambulance driver who brought Avery from Mebane also transported him from Alamance to Duke Hospital; by ambulance, this thirty-five-mile trip normally took thirty-five to forty minutes.[6] When the ambulance arrived at Duke, the doctor on emergency duty called in a neurosurgeon who examined Avery and gave him "supportive measures."[7]

Duke University president A. Hollis Edens, responding to a letter of protest about the incident several weeks after it occurred, said that Duke's surgeons had concluded that Avery would not benefit from a brain operation.[8] According to the ambulance driver, however, Avery had been in Duke's emergency room only about ten minutes when the doctors there instructed him to take Avery on to Lincoln Hospital, Durham's black hospital, because there was no bed space available for him at Duke Hospital.[9] Although a large number of black patients were treated daily in Duke's outpatient clinic,[10] in 1950 Duke had only fifteen beds for black patients, out of a total of 120.[11] These beds were often full; when they were, black patients were routinely shuttled on to Lincoln, a smaller hospital — it had only ninety-three beds — and less well equipped than Duke.[12]

According to Charles Watts, a prominent black surgeon in Durham who practiced at Lincoln, black patients who were sent on to Lincoln frequently were not in any condition to be transported, even if they did survive the trip.[13] However, it was a matter of pride to Lincoln's hospital superintendent that no patient had ever been turned away from Lincoln due to lack of money, or for any other reason.[14]

The ambulance driver asked the Duke doctors to call Lincoln Hospital authorities to inform them that a critically injured man was en route to their hospital. When Avery arrived at Lincoln, though, officials there said they had not received a call from Duke.[15] They reported later that he was in a "dying condition" when he arrived in Lincoln's emergency room.

Maltheus Avery never regained consciousness; he died minutes after arriving at Lincoln, before being placed in a ward.[16]

The fact that Maltheus Avery had received inhumane treatment, regardless of whether or not further care at Duke could have saved him, was not lost on black or white observers of the incident at the time. Both black and white newspapers carried detailed news stories about Avery's death and ran editorials expressing shock and outrage that such an episode had occurred. Both black and white observers noted that a system of medical care predicated on rules excluding a group of people because of their race inevitably resulted in brutality, especially in emergencies. Not surprisingly, however, even though white editorialists saw the moral flaw in such a system, they were far less explicit than black editorialists in painting the problem as a larger one involving segregation itself. The attitude that segregation itself, and the prevailing system of medical care under it, was inescapable — an almost God-given fact of life — is apparent in these stories by whites. The newspaper stories thus open another window onto the contrasting racial outlooks that characterized the segregation era and that to some degree still prevail.

The *Durham Morning Herald*, after running a front-page story on Avery's death on Tuesday,[17] ran an editorial the next day entitled "Some Questions That Should Be Answered."[18] The editorialist began by noting that this was "another case" in which a person in need of emergency medical treatment had died because of being shuffled from one hospital to another, implying that such situations had happened often enough before to warrant general concern. He or she essentially concluded that the "nice proper rules and regulations of a hospital" — though necessary for its smooth and orderly functioning — should never "carry precedent over a man's vital need for medical aid." The writer made no reference to segregation or to the fact that Avery was refused because of a lack of beds for black patients. Presumably the audience understood this, since the newspaper had given the facts of Avery's case the day before. The newspaper of North Carolina's state capital, the *Raleigh News and Observer*, ran a detailed Associated Press story about the incident on Tuesday[19] and carried a related editorial on Thursday. Its writer concluded, "There should always be room in a hospital for the desperately injured. . . . Every hospital must have rules. But emergencies are above rules and should be so regarded."[20]

Durham's black newspaper, the weekly *Carolina Times*, did not cover the story until Saturday, 9 December, more than a week after it happened. By this time the editorials in the white newspapers had been published and the full dimensions of Avery's tragedy were known. The *Carolina Times* ran a huge headline at the top of its front page: "HOSPITAL REFUSES DYING A&T STUDENT"; in similar fashion, eight months earlier, this newspaper had run a banner headline about Drew's death. It also ran a photograph of Avery on the front page, just as it had run a photograph of Drew. In the story that followed, the writer — almost certainly *Carolina Times* editor Louis Austin — made it clear in his opening line that Avery, a World War II veteran, had died after being refused at Duke Hospital because "the carefully guarded segregation law of North Carolina prohibited him from being placed in any other space than that allotted for his race."[21] Austin editorialized further: "Matthew Avery, student at A. and T. College, who had served his country on [a] foreign battlefield fighting for democracy that was denied him on his native soil, even in his hour of calamity, probably paid with his life Friday for not being born a member of the superior race. Or may be Avery was going to die anyway, and there isn't enough brotherly love in North Carolina to let a Negro die where white folks are supposed to gasp their last."[22]

Austin went on to point out the limited number of beds for black patients at both Alamance General Hospital and Duke Hospital, making it clear that the whole system of segregation was at fault, not merely "the rules" at one particular hospital. In the following week's issue of the *Carolina Times*, Austin wrote a full-scale editorial titled "No Room in the Hospital." In it he concluded,

As much as we sympathize with the bereaved family of Matthew Avery, our deepest sympathy goes to those critically wounded attachés of Duke Hospital who are victims of a society that prohibited them from ministering to a fellow human being who was near death. . . .

The incident ought to furnish a good lesson for Durham and the entire South. It ought to impress upon members of both races how ridiculous some of our customs are in a world that is sick almost unto death with the idea of white supremacy.[23]

Austin's outlook was fairly typical of the viewpoint of the black press as a whole. The national *Afro-American*, a newspaper based in Baltimore, Maryland, ran a story about Avery's death on 16 December with the headline "SEGREGATION RESPONSIBLE; Dying Auto Victim Sent to JC [Jim Crow] Center." It began, "The tragedy of racial segregation in this so-called 'liberal' State [North Carolina] underscored the funeral of Maltheus R. Avery."[24] On 23 December, the *Afro-American* ran a split cartoon that showed Mary and Joseph being turned away from the inn in Bethlehem next to a black man on a stretcher being turned away from Duke Hospital. Its cutline read "Still No Room in the Inn — in Some Places."[25]

A&T College students wrote about the incident in their school newspaper. Several of them published a letter they had written to Duke University president Hollis Edens that echoed some of the themes expressed by the black press. "We are in no position to pass [judgment] upon the efficiency of the medical staff at Duke Hospital," they wrote, "but in the light of this incident, we are forced to wonder if this staff has ever heard of the Hippocratic oath and the teaching of the Nazarene."[26] The students questioned Edens about Duke Hospital's "unchristian" treatment of Maltheus Avery.

Newspaper coverage of the Avery incident, though not as dramatic and widespread as that of Drew's death, nonetheless spread the story across the country. The striking difference in consciousness between the reactions in the black press and the white press reveals much about the matrix in which the Drew legend was born. While to most white observers Avery's death was a profoundly disturbing and unnecessary "accident" — a lapse from the usual orderly progression of events — to many black observers and some white ones it was the symptom of a systemic injustice. As we have already seen, the incident was equated with the symbolic Gospel story of how the Christ child had to be born in a lowly stable. There was unquestionably a form of moral justice in this equation. Black Americans *were* being refused their full humanity — and those refusing to see their humanity were to a large degree refusing the practical application of the Christian spirit in their lives.

After reading a newspaper report of the incident, Paul L. Garber, a Bible professor at Agnes Scott College, wrote Edens about Duke's treatment of Avery: "[This] is not the sort of report friends of Duke University like to see. . . . I bring this to your attention as one quite zealous for the name of Duke University and for its character as a Christian institution."[27] A white Methodist schoolteacher wrote from Bad Axe, Michigan, "We in my small town are shocked over the incident. . . . When so called intelligent people — university institutions will neglect the life of one as good as I am, and shunt him around because of color — then it's about time we stopped calling ourselves Christians. . . . Leave out the spirituals from all biased institutions — call it not worth saving or listening to — shunt it too."[28]

A New York literary agent wrote President Edens that he hoped the incident was "not true. I find it hard to believe this," he said, "since the University is founded on Christian principals [*sic*] and is closely allied with the church. . . . I hope there are equal facilities for Negro citizens in the Duke Hospital with those for whites."[29]

James A. Dombrowski, who was then director of the Southern Conference Educational Fund in New Orleans, asked the most searching questions of President Edens. He wanted to know if there were "no empty beds whatever in the hospital on the night that Avery was received in the emergency room" and whether an empty "white bed" would normally be utilized for a black person at Duke Hospital if no "black bed" were available. Not satisfied with Edens's first response, Dombrowski wrote a second time, asking for more specific information. Dombrowski explained that the organization he headed was then conducting research on "racial policies of hospitals" and "discrimination in health services."[30]

To all who wrote, President Edens sent the same statement, asserting that "no brain operation [would have] offered . . . [Avery] any improvement." Edens asserted that Duke's brain surgeons had determined that Avery stood the "best chance" of survival at Lincoln Hospital rather than in Duke's emergency room. Edens underscored this highly improbable claim by adding, "If we had been as cold-blooded as has been suggested, the easiest course would have been to just continue with treatment in the emergency room until the patient died. Instead the doctors tried to give him his best chance."[31]

Edens consistently refused to say more about the incident. What he knew about it was based word for word on a letter that Duke Hospital superintendent F. Ross Porter had prepared in December in response to an inquiry about Avery.[32] Porter sent this letter to Edens when Edens needed to make a reply to the A&T College students, and he cautioned Edens to avoid "mention of 'negro beds' " that were referred to in the " 'A and T' letter."[33] In response to Dombrowski's second letter, President Edens took a somewhat apologetic tone but still stonewalled him: "Your letters raise a series of unrelated questions. They are addressed to a complicated problem of tangled social relations. I wish I knew a quick and easy solution. However, a detailed report to you on Duke University's approach to the problem, I am convinced, would not help the situation."[34] Duke's position on the whole incident was not unusual: segregation was a deeply entrenched social norm, and President Edens simply was unwilling to open Duke's longstanding policy of segregation up to public scrutiny.[35]

Edens's stance of deflecting criticism by refusing to address the real questions and by focusing on a flattering version of Duke's actions was probably also adopted by many others connected with Duke.[36] For example, in 1950, the editor of Maltheus Avery's hometown newspaper, the *Henderson Daily Dispatch*, was a Duke graduate — Henry A. Dennis, who had graduated in 1913. This newspaper carried a story about Avery's accident and death on Monday, 4 December, but it did not report Duke's refusal to admit Avery. The story incorrectly stated that Avery "died en route to a Durham hospital," adding that he was "pronounced dead on arrival" there.[37] In the same issue the Henderson newspaper ran an editorial effusively praising the Duke Endowment, saying, "It is not possible to measure the good that has been done by the Duke benefactions. . . . [The fund has] relieved suffering and restored health to countless numbers of broken bodies where life has been prolonged and still continues where it might have ebbed completely but for the services thus made possible."[38]

Eugene Stead Jr., who in 1950 was physician in chief of Duke Hospital and chairman of the Department of Medicine, commented in 1983, "If there was no black bed available and if there were beds in the white service, he was sent somewhere else. Nobody sweated over it. It was just the era of segregated restaurants and toilets. . . . It happened every day, and some were bound to die."[39]

Avery died the same year Drew did, and some Durham residents fused the two incidents in their memories. But the Maltheus Avery story did not by itself spark the Charles Drew legend. The rumor of Drew's refusal was already circulating,[40] for a multitude of other historical events had already laid the foundations for this legend. But the Avery incident — and similar ones before and after — gave the Drew rumor additional credence. As the distinguished African American historian John Hope Franklin noted, there were a number of stories similar to Avery's, and just as factual, circulating at the time. Indeed, Franklin himself commented that he "wouldn't be surprised if the Drew story . . . [was] the exception — all the other cases pulled it back to the norm."[41] Franklin lived in Durham in this era and often drove through Burlington on his way to teach at Bennett College in Greensboro. "Burlington was not a place I wanted to stop," he recalled.[42]

Thus when Drew died, a familiar pattern — black man as victim of white mistreatment — fell into place. As black people related their own stories of mistreatment, local details were added to different versions of the Drew legend. Ultimately, the various Maltheus Averys were forgotten. Drew as hero subsumed them, and as he did, his stature as hero-victim grew larger.

In a striking and unforgettable way, this process of memory was revealed in my own purely serendipitous discovery of Maltheus Avery, which occurred while I was researching Charles Drew's death. In an interview, I asked the *Carolina Times* photographer who took a shot of Drew's wrecked car, "Do you recall anything about this incident, about Charles Drew's death?" The man replied,

> There was this item that came up. They took him one place and they didn't give him treatment. Then they took him [to a second place] and he died. The undertaker told us the story. He was refused treatment. . . . Louis Austin wrote a news story about it and lashed out in an editorial. He wasn't the type to miss a chance to write an acid story. Louis would talk about the incident years afterward. The man who developed the plasma technique was refused it in North Carolina. He was really moved by it. I don't know whether he magnified the truth or not, but he always had some basis for his biting editorials. . . . My opinion is that everything written afterward [about Drew] came out of the *Carolina Times* story.[43]

The *Carolina Times* photographer was not the only person to vividly — yet mistakenly — remember Louis Austin writing an editorial about

Drew's mistreatment. Austin's own daughter, who took over as publisher of the black newspaper after her father died, also asserted that Austin had written an editorial about Drew being refused treatment and then being taken to a second hospital. "The time delay was the cause of his demise," she said.[44] "Why didn't they do what they could do to get his vital signs going, first aid, you know—to prevent the loss of blood—to get the man ready for a trip down the road?" she demanded.[45] Like the photographer, this woman was undoubtedly remembering the story of Maltheus Avery. Her father had written the front-page stories about Drew and Avery and run editorial comments about both incidents in the same year.

In the early stage of my research, when the photographer and Austin's daughter insisted that Austin had written an editorial about Drew's mistreatment, I was puzzled. I had already studied the *Carolina Times* coverage of Drew's death and had found no such editorial. What *were* they both referring to? Had Austin written an editorial about Drew weeks or months later? If so, what had he found out that led him to do so? These two individuals' memories led me to make a systematic investigation of *Carolina Times* issues following the one about Drew's death. Soon I came upon the story of Maltheus Avery, "HOSPITAL REFUSES DYING A&T STUDENT," published eight months later. Thus, oral lore led me to dig up a buried historical event—Maltheus Avery's real tragedy. The whole chain of events demonstrated the degree to which the stories ordinary people tell and pass on contain historical truths—indeed, actual historical events.

The way in which Drew and Avery were indelibly fused in people's imaginations was also revealed by interviews I conducted in attempts to trace Maltheus Avery's real story. An A&T College infirmary nurse, Thelma Vine, when asked if she remembered the student who had been refused treatment after an auto accident, replied that she did not but that she did recall "the day of the accident with Dr. Drew. . . . Because of his being a black man he was not given the service he could have had."[46] Similarly, an A&T College dean from 1950, Warmoth Gibbs, was asked whether he remembered Maltheus Avery and his hospital refusal. At once he responded, "Wasn't he riding with Dr. Drew? As I recall, he was with Dr. Drew but Drew did not get treatment, not any. He did not get admission as a matter of fact. . . . He went to one or two hospitals, but he was turned away. He was going someplace South and he died on the way there."[47]

In telling Drew's story, these people were remembering not only Maltheus Avery's buried story but the whole system of segregated medical care and its impact on them personally. Each one also had his or her own story of medical mistreatment or fear to tell, albeit not so dramatic as that dramatized by the Drew legend. These individuals and the black press were right in seeing Avery's real refusal and Drew's legendary one as symptomatic of the whole system, not a regrettable lapse from some norm of better "separate but equal" care. Maltheus Avery's experience was no aberration either at Duke or in other any locale that allocated beds according to race. In many areas of the country — certainly in most of the South and in Washington — there were proportionally fewer beds for black patients than for white patients. While a disproportionate number of black beds was not a necessary precondition of a Maltheus Avery type of incident, it did greatly exacerbate the problem and make it more likely to happen.

Harold Kernodle Sr., the white surgeon at Alamance General Hospital, spoke at length about the difficulty of finding beds for black patients in this era and the distress it caused him.

> At times we couldn't get beds, especially with blacks. . . . We'd call up and they'd say, We don't have a bed. Then we had the patient. And I'd say, Well listen, someone's got to help us. . . . The trouble was, if they didn't have any beds, you were just lost. You could call all of them [all of the hospitals in the area, in Greensboro to the west and Durham to the east] . . . and now and then, there would be no beds. . . . It happened mostly on weekends, when they'd have more accidents and had been drinking. . . . Now the white as a rule, we were able to get them in. But there were not that many colored beds at the hospitals that admitted the coloreds. . . . You'd have some restless nights. At some point, they said stop sending patients. Call and check first [if there was a bed available]. You'd spend two or three hours calling around. It was a real problem.[48]

As an Alamance County physician, Kernodle was well aware of, and disturbed by, the Charles Drew legend. Since he had been one of the doctors who treated Drew, he knew it was not true and experienced it as a "slap" at him and the other hospital staff: "What upset me . . . [was] they said he died because we wouldn't admit him. . . . They said we let him lie there and die because he was black. . . . That was absolutely false. That was what hurt our feelings." As Kernodle saw it, the unavailability of black beds in 1950 — and the tragedies that inevitably arose from this situation — was a regrettable but inescapable fact of life under segregation: "The facilities simply weren't available," he commented. "There was nothing doctors could do about it."[49]

Eugene Stead Jr. said he did not remember the Maltheus Avery incident, but he, like Kernodle, knew that it could easily have happened: "Because there were fewer beds for black people in proportion to the [Durham] population, obviously we had a problem. If there were no beds in the black area and white beds were available, . . . [a black person] would be sent on to Lincoln or elsewhere. Lincoln had an emergency room. We really didn't have enough beds to serve all acutely ill black people. . . . Our greatest pressure was on black beds."[50]

In 1952 the Southern Conference Educational Fund published a study called *The Untouchables: The Meaning of Segregation in Hospitals*[51] that reported the bare facts of twelve different cases of black patients — Maltheus Avery among them — being refused hospital care over a twenty-year period. As part of the study, the fund conducted a poll to determine the relative availability of hospital beds to black patients throughout the South. The poll revealed that bed space seemingly followed census figures for the region, with 32 percent of the existing hospital beds made available to blacks. However, the report on the poll noted that "more than two-thirds of this space is fixed by quota, with no allowance made for degree of need or special contingencies. By virtue of segregation practices, then, the Negro, whose generally depressed economic status tends to increase his need for hospitalization, is often turned back by an inflexible, arbitrary barrier."[52]

For a number of reasons, the poll's statistics were not actually indicative of the lack of bed space for black patients. First, only 29 percent of the hospitals polled responded.[53] Second, the poll only revealed total figures; it did not look at the available bed space for blacks by locality, and other studies in this period revealed that different regions varied dramatically in the number of beds allocated to black patients. In some rural regions of the Deep South, there were almost no black beds, because there were no black hospitals. Finally, the poll statistics shed no light on the quality of care available to black patients. The study rightly concluded,

> But how does this approved order of things work out in practice?
> The administrative machinery of a segregated or "lily-white" hospital is always taxed by emergency cases. A prospective patient, lying

bleeding and unconscious on a stretcher, cannot be crisply told to go to an institution that serves "his own people." Yet, in essence, that has been done, is being done, and will be done—even though the rejected one dies as a result. Such brutality derives unthinkingly from the premise to which a Jim Crow hospital is dedicated. If routine medical and surgery cases are to be treated only on the basis of a person's skin color, the healing hand suffers atrophy and is fumbling at a time of undiscriminating crisis.[54]

Statistics never tell the whole story. Nor does the bare newspaper account of Avery's death reveal his or his family's specific tragedy. To see the full dimensions of segregated medical care's impact on human beings, it is necessary to examine who Maltheus Avery was and how his death affected his family. The Averys, a tightly knit family who trace their roots back a long way in rural North and South Carolina, have primarily lived their lives in small-town America. Like Drew's, their lives demonstrate the peculiar tragedies and triumphs of growing up black in America during the segregation era. Both caste and class were phenomena the Averys encountered daily, and Maltheus Avery's tragedy starkly revealed the near-immovable barriers that caste and class represented in their lives. When Maltheus Avery died and left behind a wife and fatherless young children, the whole family was severely traumatized. Living in a small southern town, virtually owned by a handful of white families, they were locked into the segregated system and were vulnerable to slipping into the underclass, into destitution and hopelessness—despite Maltheus Avery's parents' relative success and considerable determination to provide secure middle-class lives for their children.

Maltheus Avery's parents, Hazel Robena Bing and Napoleon Avery, were married on 28 May 1923 in the small community of Greystone, near Henderson, North Carolina.[55] Born in 1902, Hazel Avery traced her family—farming people with considerable land—back several generations in the Greystone area. After the Civil War, a white landowner by the name of Watkins[56] deeded hundreds of acres to Emma Watkins Hawkins, a female Bing ancestor who was one of his former slaves and also his daughter. The Bings and Averys today recognize a number of Watkins family descendants as relatives. And some of these white relatives attend Avery family reunions, held every two years in Henderson.[57]

To Hazel Bing's conservative family, Napoleon Avery seemed a somewhat shocking choice. Born in 1883, he was almost twenty years older

than she was, and he had already been married and fathered four children; thus he seemed to Hazel's family to be much too old. Hazel was
one of eleven children, and her sisters "were horrified she was fooling
around with an old man."[58] He was half-Indian, with fairer skin and high
cheekbones, and had met her at her aunt's boarding house for the men
at the quarry. He had been introduced as "Mr. 'Poleon, the boss of the
Negroes . . . the only Negro in the area with his own car."[59]

Avery was born in Rock Hill, South Carolina, and like Hazel Bing, he
traced his family back to rural black and white ancestors, including a
Presbyterian minister, as well as Native Americans. His father was a Ca-
tawba Indian, his mother half-black and half-white. In his youth, Avery
had gone to work on the Panama Canal, and though he witnessed the
"death and destruction" of many of the black workers there, he had
come back home as a skilled operator of heavy earth-moving machinery.
For a while Avery went back to school at Biddle University (now Johnson
C. Smith University) in Charlotte, North Carolina, and considered becoming a Presbyterian minister. He also worked in the Pittsburgh steel
mills during World War I. But he settled on construction and installation
of the steel derricks used to excavate rock quarries as his permanent
employment. Officially called a "prime assistant" by his employers, the
Raleigh Granite Company and the Superior Stone Company, he would
have been a supervisor had he been white, according to his sons. He was
known for his physical bravery. "On numerous occasions, he performed
the death-defying feat of traversing the supporting guy cables from the
top of the derricks in a canvas chair on a pulley, [going across] the
gaping hole [of a quarry] to personally determine the condition of those
all-important steel cables."[60] At the time he met Hazel Bing, his work
took him to quarries throughout the Carolinas, including the rock
quarry at Greystone. His sons remember him as a man of fierce temper.
"He could let loose a string of invective that would melt your teeth. His
nickname, among the men he worked with, was 'Uncle Snap.' "[61]

The couple's first son was born on 16 April 1926, two years after a
daughter had been born. At the time, the Averys were living in the small
rural community of Neverson, the site of a rock quarry where Napoleon
Avery worked, in eastern North Carolina's Wilson County. They named
the boy Maltheus Reeves Avery after the white country doctor who delivered him at their house, a general practitioner named Malthus R. Freeman,[62] but they soon gave him the nickname "Sonny."

Hazel Avery, whom one of her sons described as a "real first class old-fashioned southern matriarch," was ambitious for her children, and like many other black women of her generation, she hoped all of her sons — two more were born to the couple after Maltheus — would become doctors in order to escape the hard physical work and limited horizons that segregation typically imposed. This same son, Waddell Avery, noted, "She was determined we would break out of the rural mold, . . . and out of the yoke of segregation. . . . Sonny, Parnell, and I were all to be doctors. Doctor was 'it' — that was the top of Negro society. Evelyn was to be a schoolteacher."[63]

Soon after Maltheus was born, the couple again stirred comment from Hazel Avery's twelve siblings by buying a small house on Vaughan Street in downtown Henderson, instead of in rural Greystone, and situating their family there. Napoleon Avery's work, which was fairly steady, kept him away from his family most of the time at different rock quarries. He supported the family, but Hazel Avery essentially had to raise her children alone. She wanted them to get the best education possible. By living in town, in a black neighborhood that bordered US 1 and adjacent white neighborhoods, she could more easily send her children to the Henderson Institute, a black elementary and high school run by white Presbyterian missionaries that took boarding students from all over eastern North Carolina.[64] And although she herself continued to belong to a small Baptist church in Greystone, she shrewdly sent her children to the church of Henderson's black elite, the Cotton Memorial United Presbyterian Church, where she believed they would further enhance their education.[65]

By 1931, the family was complete. The Averys had four children — Evelyn, Maltheus ("Sonny,") Waddell, and Parnell. In addition to caring for her children, Hazel Avery worked five days a week in Henderson's tobacco factory, J. R. Taylor Company, and did laundry for white mill workers at night. Though Napoleon Avery's character as a skilled and steady worker and Hazel Avery's as a strict and dedicated mother brought some advantages to the situation, it was a tough life. Shaped by economic necessity and hemmed in by social constraints peculiar to the whole segregated era, the life they knew during their childhood was still exceedingly vivid to both Waddell and Parnell Avery, the two younger children, some fifty years later.

The Avery house, a one-story wood dwelling with a front porch, had no running water and was warmed only by a woodstove. The three Avery boys all slept in one bed. The children were expected to do chores in the afternoon after school, such as fetch water from the neighborhood well, chop kindling wood, haul in coal, or carry laundry back and forth from the mill workers' houses. There were many distractions and temptations for four children left to some degree to fend for themselves, especially since many of the families on Vaughan Street were not as stable as the Averys. "Only two families owned their own homes on the block, us and a dentist and his wife. Everyone in the block sort of had it in for Mother and Daddy," said Parnell Avery. "*Their* [our parents'] principles were more than drinking on the weekend, impregnating women, and never going to church. We got our principles through Mother and Daddy. It was because of them we became what we are."[66]

The Avery family had a steady but limited income. Both were too poor to go to the town's one black doctor — a Dr. Baxter, who had graduated from Leonard Medical College, at Shaw University in Raleigh — for anything but an emergency. "For all practical purposes, he was not there, as far as we were concerned. Every Friday night we got a dose of castor followed by black coffee. That was our medical care. That stuff would make an elephant sick," recalled Waddell Avery.[67]

Despite the family's limited resources — and partly because of them — both Napoleon and Hazel Avery were tough with their children and set definite goals for each one. While the families of other quarrymen would go live in the camps where the men worked and get their schooling "catch as catch can," the Avery children had to go to school all year long. They all took music lessons from an early age, though they had to drive twenty miles to get there. "All the grandparents and parents put the focus on the children," said Waddell Avery, adding,

> But Mother really kept at it. She managed the money and the children. Father didn't say a lot at home; he was a man of action. But he also taught us to get things in our heads so we wouldn't have to be under the heel and the thumb of the white man. All he wanted from us was no mistakes. Do it right and no excuses.[68]
>
> Mother and Father drummed it in. You've got to be twice as good as them crackers. . . .[69] It was the only way to break out from the oppression we were under. It *was* brutal and oppressive. I still remember those white and colored signs. . . . The main thing for blacks in the twenties was breaking the yoke of that horrible segregation. You aren't going to be in the white folks' kitchen, they told us. There was no objecting. If you did, you got knocked down, hit, whipped.[70]

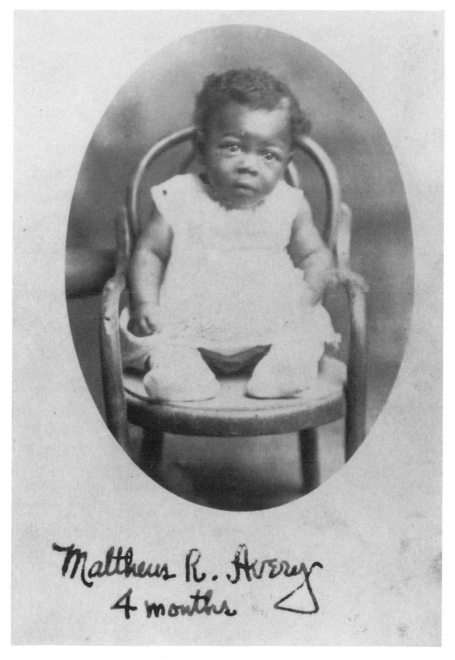

Maltheus R. "Sonny" Avery at the age of four months
(Courtesy of Waddell Avery)

Hazel and Napoleon Avery's
four children in the mid-1930s:
from left, standing, Evelyn and
Maltheus ("Sonny"); from left,
seated, Parnell and Waddell
(Courtesy of Malthaus Avery Blake)

Maltheus "Sonny" Avery and
his mother, Hazel Avery, in front
of their Charlottesville, Virginia,
home in 1940 *(Courtesy of Waddell
Avery)*

Corporal Maltheus R. Avery in a studio portrait done in 1945,
after Avery participated in the Allied invasion of Okinawa
(Courtesy of Waddell Avery)

Maltheus Avery in his high school graduation photo,
Charlottesville, Virginia, 1948 *(Courtesy of Waddell Avery)*

Nannie Bell Jackson, a fellow high school graduate
whom Maltheus Avery married in 1948 *(Courtesy of Malthaus
Avery Blake)*

Maltheus Avery running a crane and conveyor system at a rock quarry in Red Hill, Virginia, on a summer job in the late 1940s *(Courtesy of Waddell Avery)*

Napoleon Avery, the father of Maltheus Avery, ca. 1950. Sonny often worked with his father at rock quarries. *(Courtesy of Hilda Avery)*

Periodical Dept Duke Univ Library

The Carolina Times

THE TRUTH UNABRIDGED

Entered as Second Class Matter at the Post Office at Durham, North Carolina, under Act of March 3, 1879

FOR 28 YEARS THE OUTSTANDING NEGRO WEEKLY OF THE CAROLINAS

VOLUME 28—NUMBER 49   DURHAM, N. C., SATURDAY, DEC. 9th, 1950   PRICE: TEN CENTS

Hospital Refuses Dying A&T Student

Lack Of Bed Space Given As Reason

The tragic story of how a Negro World War II veteran and student of A. and T. College died within an hour here Friday night, after he had been refused admittance to Duke Hospital, because the carefully guarded segregation law of North Carolina prohibited him from being placed in any other space than that alloted for his race, came to light here this week to furnish more fodder for the highly geared communist mills of propaganda.

Matthew Avery, student at A. and T. College, who had served his country on foreign battlefield fighting for democracy that was denied him on his native soil, even in his hour of calamity, probably, paid with his life Friday for not being born a member of the superior race, Or may be Avery was going to die anyway, and there isn't enough brotherly love in North Carolina to let a Negro die where white folks are supposed to gasp their last.

Avery was injured in an automobile wreck near Mebane around seven o'clock Friday night and a Mebane ambulance took him to the Alamance General Hospital at Burlington where it was discovered that he had a fractured leg, a fractured arm, a fractured cheek and a fractured skull.

Doctors at the hospital in Burlington after an examination recommended that he taken to Duke where better facilities and more capable medical attention could be obtained. There are only five beds available for Negroes in the Burlington hospital.

(Please turn to Page Eight)

Hospital—

(Continued from Page One)
When Avery arrived at Duke he was refused admittance, hospital officials say, because there was no bed space available. They stated that only a small space is alloted Negroes.

Doctors at Duke claim that they examined Avery and gave him "suportive measures" before sending him to Lincoln Hospital, local Negro institution, where he died within an hour. Inquiry at Duke, Lincoln and the General Hospital in Burlington has not yet disclosed just what is meant by "suportive measure."

In a desperate effort to save Avery's life, if possible, the ambulance driver at the time he left Duke hospital with the seriously injured man requested Duke physicians to call Lincoln and inform them that he was on his way. Upon arrival he was told by Lincoln attaches that they had received no call from Duke.

Wreck Victim

Matthew Avery, A. and T. College student who died here last Friday night after being refused admittance at Duke Hospital because all of the space available for Negroes had been taken. Avery, who was a native of Henderson, sustained severe injuries in an automobile wreck near Mebane. He was finally taken to Lincoln Hospital here where he died about an hour after being admitted.

Carolina Times front page from December 1950: "Hospital Refuses Dying A&T Student" (*Courtesy of the* Carolina Times)

Maltheus and Nannie Avery's two children, Evelyn Regina and Malthaus. The younger daughter, Malthaus, was born several days after her father's death. *(Courtesy of Malthaus Avery Blake)*

Parnell Avery, second from the left, and Waddell Avery, fourth from the left, at a New Year's party in the early 1950s *(Courtesy of Parnell Avery)*

Hazel Avery *(Courtesy of Parnell Avery)*

Lieutenant Colonel
Waddell Avery
(Courtesy of Hilda Avery)

Parnell N. Avery, M.D.
(Courtesy of Parnell Avery)

Waddell Avery and his mother, Hazel Avery, in 1988,
close to the time she died *(Photo by the author)*

Waddell and Parnell Avery in front of Duke Hospital in March 1990,
near where their brother was refused treatment forty years earlier
(Courtesy of the News and Observer Publishing Company)

Both Waddell and Parnell Avery recalled many fistfights with white boys, since they lived in a neighborhood bordering a white area and they regularly went in and out of a nearby white mill village on errands for their mother. But there were also friendships and even childhood romances with white children — with the sons and daughters of the white men Napoleon Avery worked with, and with neighborhood children. "We had a segregated society in which whites were not supposed to be intimately linked with us. But it was different from what people think. Sonny was romantically interested in a white redhead at one point. We had integrated hayrides in high school," recalled Parnell Avery.[71] Clearly, in a small, mostly rural town, the daily reality of segregation was a complex affair: the social barriers between blacks and whites were more permeable among black and white children who grew up together, and between black and white adults who worked closely together and to some degree relied on and trusted each other.

As Evelyn and Sonny grew older, they increasingly acted as the deputy mother and father of the family when their mother and father were not there. While this meant greater responsibility for them, it also gave them wider license to do as they pleased. And Sonny, according to both his younger brothers, took full advantage of his freedom.

Sonny was a well-built, lithe, athletic boy, bigger-boned and physically stronger than either of his brothers. His features resembled his mother's, but he inherited not only his father's reddish skin and high cheekbones but also his strong will, his daring nature and adventurousness. "Sonny was a free-spirited guy. He didn't like boundaries. . . . He was always bouncing up against mother's restrictions. . . . It was his inborn personality," his brother Waddell said.[72]

Like his father, Sonny was an outdoor person, gifted in mechanical and athletic skills. His brothers called him "Mr. Fix-It" because he could handle tools so well, with either hand. At a very young age he became a wizard at fixing cars. He learned to drive a car when he was nine, and loved cars all his life. He was his father's favorite because he listened and learned well when Napoleon Avery took him to rock quarries. By the time he was thirteen, he could operate the quarry machinery. His father made him his deputy and put him in charge of groups of men. According to his brother Waddell, Sonny considered himself full-grown by the time he was thirteen. "That was Sonny's element, working in that rock quarry, or working on cars. Just like Daddy, he couldn't stand gloves. If he skinned a knuckle, he would just put gasoline on it."[73]

Both Avery brothers remember the time all three boys, chafing under their mother's authority, decided to run away from home. They hopped a freight train from Henderson to Raleigh, then got on a freight transfer truck. As the day wore on, the two younger boys decided to head home, but Sonny kept on going. He did not return until late that night. When he did, his mother, in total exasperation, tied a belt around his chest and hung him up in a dark closet to restrain him. This incident made a deep impression on the younger boys, who had to listen to him holler.

The family moved to Charlottesville, Virginia, for a couple of years when Sonny was a teenager, and he started high school there. As a teenager, he was more restless than ever, with the same sort of wild streak and desire to roam that his father had displayed. Girls loved him, and their mothers feared him. "He was a charmer and a kingpin," said his youngest brother, Parnell. "He was really the man of the house when Daddy was away, and he was my idol."[74]

The family soon moved back to Henderson, where the two younger Avery brothers were able to complete high school at the Henderson Institute. But in 1944, at eighteen years old, unable to bear the restrictions of home life any longer, Sonny quit high school and enlisted to fight in World War II. Parnell Avery pointed out that the family needed the money. Sonny's army stint provided that, and several years later it helped the two younger Avery boys pay for college. After basic training at Indiantown Gap, Pennsylvania, Sonny came home much sobered and told his younger brothers that the army wasn't what he thought it would be. He was soon sent to the Pacific as a combat engineer, first to Saipan and later to Okinawa. He participated in the invasion of Okinawa on Easter Sunday, 1945, and stayed on as part of the occupying force until late that year. He sent home letters describing his terror during combat. He said that the "machine and tank gun fire was so intense he took his helmet from his head and put it over his heart. He was afraid his heart would jump out of his body," said Parnell Avery.

Waddell Avery recalled that Sonny once wrote home, "If I don't get back, I love you all because I am in the middle of hell." His overseas experiences marked him for life: he not only saw fellow soldiers die in the invasion but also, some months later, had to fight off Japanese soldiers armed with bayonets tied to bamboo sticks in a surprise attack and witnessed the typhoon and tidal wave that hit Okinawa in September 1945. "He was outside in a foxhole and he couldn't believe the wind; it was whistling like a freight train. Many people were killed. He talked about Typhoon Betty the rest of his life. It scared him to death," said Waddell.

Sonny came home a changed man, ready to settle down. "He saw there was more to life than having a good time," said Waddell Avery.[75] Discharged from Fort Leavenworth, Kansas, in 1946 as a corporal, he decided to return to Charlottesville on his own to finish high school there. He got a job and played football, and during his senior year — in 1948 — he married Nannie Bell Jackson, a Charlottesville girl with a mountain accent who worked as a beautician. She was from a rural family much like his mother's family.

By this time, Sonny's brother Waddell was in his second year of college at Virginia State University. His youngest brother, Parnell, also had graduated from high school in 1948, at Henderson Institute, and planned to enter college at Virginia State University in the fall. Not wanting to be surpassed by his brothers, Sonny enrolled in college at Hampton Institute in Hampton, Virginia, in the fall of 1948, majoring in auto mechanics. "Sonny was determined," said Waddell, who was the first Avery to graduate from college. "Sonny felt he *had* to finish college — the younger ones were finishing first."[76] By this time Sonny and his wife had had a daughter, whom they named Regina.

Sonny got through the fall semester at Hampton Institute, just barely,[77] but in the spring of 1949, he was failing his courses: the stress was too much for him. He told his brother Waddell that one day when a veteran in his class jumped up and said, "God damn it, I can't get this shit," he felt exactly the same way. The tension between book knowledge and his own experiential knowledge was too great. He had a nervous breakdown and went to McGuire's Veterans Hospital in Richmond to recover. In the summer of 1949, after getting out, he worked in a rock quarry in McLeansville, North Carolina, with his father and Waddell.[78]

In the spring of 1950, Waddell Avery graduated from college. Sonny, more determined than ever, decided to make another attempt to go to college. He moved his family back to Henderson and, in the fall of 1950, enrolled in auto mechanics at A&T College in Greensboro. Living with his mother and commuting to school, Sonny had more support than he had had on his own in Virginia, and he was doing well. He had advanced freshman status, and as a veteran he was enrolled in ROTC, planning to be commissioned as a second lieutenant when he graduated.

When he set out from Greensboro toward Henderson on the afternoon of 1 December, he was going home for the Christmas holiday with money in his pocket; as a veteran he received regular checks through the GI bill. He was especially eager to be with his wife, since she was nine months pregnant, expecting their second child any day. He may have been drinking; Parnell Avery said that Sonny was a drinker and that he had often wondered, after his death, if Sonny had had some alcohol the evening of his accident.

Sonny's wife, his sister, and his parents learned of Sonny's death when a highway patrolman came to the house on Vaughan Street in Henderson late on the night of 1 December. That same night, totally distraught, Avery's parents and sister rode to Lincoln Hospital in the hearse of the undertaker from Henderson's black funeral home, Garnes and Williams, to claim Sonny's body. There they learned that he had been refused treatment at Duke Hospital.

Almost fifty years later, Hazel Avery, sitting on a hospital bed, eighty-six years old and near death herself, commented on her son's death and mistreatment:

> I went to Duke Hospital. I went to both hospitals. I talked to the head nurse and the doctors. I done everything but cuss them. I ought to have done that. Evelyn laid them out because she had a plenty of temper. . . . I hadn't heard of such incidents happening. . . . I told them they could put him on the floor and treat him. They said they had no room. His wife was expecting to have a baby any minute. He was on his way home. . . . Sonny loved to work on cars. He was mechanically minded. He was a very good-hearted child, not hard-headed. . . . I will never forget that night as long as the world stands.[79]

Hazel Avery and all the other members of the family were in a state of shock. The double crisis created by Sonny's death and the baby's imminent birth were the family's immediate focus of grief and concern, but Duke's brutal action added to the family's sense of powerlessness and loss, especially as their full awareness of it sank in. Hazel Avery had told her children about Bessie Smith being refused treatment at a hospital and bleeding to death during their childhood — "My mother loved Bessie Smith; she played her songs on an old Victrola and told us . . . [the story] in the 1930s," said Waddell Avery.[80] But she obviously had not believed that such a tragedy could happen to one of her own children. It was one thing to pass such a story on, another to experience it firsthand.

There was one black lawyer in Henderson, a man named Charles Williamson who regularly handled civil rights cases and who had won local distinction in 1933 by courageously defending — in the face of extreme hostility and intimidation from local white people — a black man from nearby Kittrell, North Carolina, who was accused of kidnapping a white woman.[81] Hazel Avery said that she consulted him to see if he could sue Duke Hospital and "make a case of it a little afterwards, but he couldn't."[82] There were no legal grounds for a lawsuit; the family had no recourse except to express their anger and frustration to Duke hospital authorities and contact the newspapers to make sure they covered the incident. Apparently a number of such incidents occurred without being reported, since not every family contacted the newspapers. Such incidents were sufficiently routine at Lincoln that its authorities did not report them, especially since they wanted to maintain a good working relationship with Duke. Of course, it was not in Duke Hospital's interest to have the incident publicized.

Sonny's funeral was held on Sunday, 3 December, at Brookston Baptist Church, his mother's rural church in Greystone. He was buried in the church cemetery, essentially a family cemetery going back several generations. The gently rolling farmland it occupied had been donated to the church by Hazel Avery's family in the late nineteenth century, and Sonny's maternal grandparents and great-grandparents were buried there.

Waddell Avery had hoped to go to medical school but had been drafted into the army as a result of the Korean War. In basic training at Fort Jackson, South Carolina, he was pulled off all-night guard duty by a first lieutenant early Saturday morning and told of his brother's death. He obtained a twenty-four-hour leave and arrived home by bus on Saturday night. Parnell Avery drove down from Virginia State College in Petersburg, Virginia, where he was a senior. Both brothers and their sister, Evelyn, went to the funeral home and looked at their brother's body while he was being embalmed and dressed. It was the first corpse they had ever seen. "There was a bruise on his cheek, on his shoulder, his arm and his left leg. His whole left side was broken. He had a fractured skull and his jawbone was swollen. Evelyn started crying, but Parnell and I accepted the fact his spirit was gone. We didn't cry," Waddell recalled.

Their father, in an adjacent room, commented, "Do you realize that's our boy in there?" Waddell Avery said he almost cried then, but he and Parnell, having seen how overwrought both their parents were, had resolved that they would contain their emotions. Each felt that in some way he would now be called on to be the father of the family. The day of the funeral was cold, with occasional snow flurries. As they prepared to go to the burial site, Waddell Avery said to the minister, "Close the casket up. I don't want a snowflake on his face."[83]

Waddell Avery soon had to go back to army duty. By Christmas he had been sent to Fort Sam Houston in San Antonio, Texas, where he spent a lonely and bitter Christmas day with another black soldier. The two of them had been excluded from a trip for their company to a nearby ranch; they were the only black soldiers in the company.

Within days after Sonny's death, Nannie Bell Jackson Avery gave birth to a second daughter, whom she named Malthaus, after her husband. Crushed by the tragedy and by her new responsibilities, she moved back to Charlottesville, Virginia, to live with her mother in her country home. She fought with alcoholism and depression for the rest of her life. Although she married again and had one more daughter, she died in 1967, when Regina was seventeen and Malthaus was sixteen.

Parnell Avery was close to home in the aftermath of the event, and he found himself in a new caretaking role toward his parents. "It almost disintegrated our family structure and our relations with most people. We were in an underclass area. Mother was trying to get us out from being the scum of the earth; it almost made them lose that touch." He recalled that his sister, who was unhappily married and had two young children, also started drinking for the first time soon after Sonny's death. A woman of high temper, like her father, Evelyn had been very close to Sonny. Her marriage soon broke up.

Hazel Avery, Parnell said, was "absolutely grief-stricken," yet she had to use all her energy to try to control her husband's rage. "Although my father had worked with white people a long time, and loved them very much, he was extraordinarily bitter," said Parnell Avery. "He was out to murder the truck driver or anyone connected with the incident at Duke. I spent a lot of time out of college trying to hold Daddy down. I had to grow up overnight, from being the youngest to the oldest." He recalled an occasion when their father set off with a gun, bent on killing anyone connected with Sonny's death, and Parnell and Evelyn, neither of whom had a driver's license, set off in a wild automobile chase into Durham and Guilford Counties to stop him and bring him home.

The family's initial turmoil in response to Sonny's death gradually faded, but a more profound reaction took root in the Averys' lives, as new events continued to remind them of Sonny's fate. Hazel Avery deepened her resolve to support and protect her remaining children. When her oldest grandson began commuting from Henderson to classes at A&T College for a master's degree some twenty years after Sonny's death, she insisted on riding back and forth with him in the car on the almost two-hour trip, along with Evelyn Avery, his mother. "As the first grandson in the Avery family, I was 'Sonny' to them. 'We don't want to lose another son,' they told me,"[84] said Lynn Michael Napoleon Henderson, now a school principal. As Evelyn's son, Henderson was keenly aware of Sonny's life and death. His mother, motivated by Sonny's refused treatment, had enrolled in Duke's Nursing School soon after the incident, but she did not complete the training.

Henderson said he had "paid more attention to the story [of Sonny's refusal] when he went to Henderson High School . . . as one of ten blacks out of 161 students" in 1965, when it was being racially integrated for the first time. During his senior year, in 1966, he elected to do an oral report on black history for a psychology class. He said he had stumbled across the story of Charles Drew in a library history book on black leaders. Around the same time, he said, he heard that Drew had died "because he didn't receive the necessary treatment and because he lost so much blood." Henderson noted,

> I made the connection. I said, "Well, my uncle was denied treatment too." The civil rights movement and the sit-ins also made me see that my family was part of history. [In my report,] I covered black history. First I talked about social changes since integration. Then I talked about Frederick Douglass and other black leaders. I told Drew's story too, after I talked about segregation, about how difficult it was to tell a young child he couldn't go to a park because of the color of his skin. . . . The other students were shocked I selected that topic. They got very quiet. Some asked questions: "How did I feel about segregation?"

Henderson found out later that the Drew legend was not true, but he had no trouble understanding why so many people still believed it. He said that since he grew up under segregation himself, he has never been able to "get over" Sonny's incident, although he was only two years old when it happened. "Here was a human life and nobody cared enough. . . . My uncle was not necessarily a great man, but to his family he was. . . . To us he was a hero. . . . He was a good soldier and a very proud young man because of enlisting and doing well and then coming back to finish high school and go to college."

Hazel Avery's determination that her sons be doctors took on new life in her two remaining sons after Sonny's death; over the years, they increasingly came to confront what had happened to their brother in Duke's emergency room. Both dedicated their lives to health care. Working in hospitals, they came to understand better exactly what had happened to their brother. "We can reconstruct and imagine what went on in that operating room," said Waddell Avery. " 'Just send them on down the road and stabilize them. Just do enough so they can make the trip.' "[85]

Waddell's first reaction to his brother's mistreatment and death, he said, was rage. "This was the culture that would allow a man bleed to death, to be sent from one hospital to another. I wanted to desert the army. I wanted to steal ammunition and dynamite from the army and go blow up Duke Hospital. I thought all kinds of crazy things. Duke was intimidating . . . an untouchable citadel. How could you go up against all that power and money? It was an injustice, but there was no way to fight it at the time."[86]

In 1949, when he was a college junior, Waddell Avery became a member of Omega Psi Phi, the fraternity Charles Drew had belonged to, and he learned about Drew when he joined. In the spring of 1950, when Drew died, he heard that "they had let [Drew] bleed to death, sent him from one hospital to another. Everybody heard about it real quick," he said, "because Drew was so damn prominent." It was a familiar story, given that Hazel Avery had told her children about Bessie Smith.[87]

But the story about Drew had new meaning to Waddell Avery in 1951. His brother had died by then. He believed the Drew legend then, though he learned in later years it was not literally true. "It didn't surprise us if they let Drew bleed to death, that they would allow anyone to bleed to death. Your whole life confirms it's true. [They refused Sonny and] we were a prominent family in Henderson. Those Avery boys were achievers. My mother made us different; she believed work would keep us out of trouble."[88]

Also, although Avery had been drafted into the army right out of college to go to Korea as an infantry rifleman, he passed tests that exempted him from the life of a "buck private" and received medical training instead. By 1951, he was working in an army base hospital in Colorado Springs, Colorado, and going to graduate school in premed courses. Doing hematology work in a laboratory, he was once again among people familiar with Charles Drew's story and was learning how the medical system operated.

In addition to doing clinical laboratory work, Waddell Avery trained as a medical helicopter evacuation pilot, an occupational role that he and his fellow soldiers commonly described as "battlefield surgeon." From 1955 to 1962, he flew in missions all over the world, serving in thirty-five countries, including Chile, Madagascar, and African nations. In Vietnam, Avery was the officer in charge of medical evacuation for all army personnel during 1965 and 1966, but because there were not enough pilots, he ended up flying many medical evacuation missions himself. Avery said it was a job in which one could witness firsthand "how many ways there are to die."[89] Sonny was never far from his mind. In 1962, Avery's family came to Germany on the same ship that Sonny had returned from Okinawa on.

After retiring from the job of battlefield surgeon, Avery went on to receive training and to work as a hospital administrator. "I wanted to run hospitals right so that no one would ever be denied care," he explained.[90] In 1972, when he ended his twenty-two-year army career as a colonel, he turned down offers to work as a private hospital administrator. Instead he opted to work for the Department of Health and Human Services, because he felt that there he could position himself to "make a difference [in health care] on a national scale."[91] As deputy director of the National Rural Health Program, in the division of Health Services Financing, Avery helped to foster the development of some three thousand to four thousand community health centers throughout the country and to teach many of the staffs how to make the centers financially independent. He thereby helped extend health care to minority peoples, including the rural poor, ghetto blacks, and American Indians.

Waddell Avery was admitted to the American College of Hospital Administrators in 1972. A number of times, during his years in health care, Avery heard his brother's case of refusal discussed at conferences and seminars. Through his health care career and its political ramifications and through his own deep interest in American history, Avery came over the years to see Sonny's tragedy and its meaning in an increasingly broad context. As the senior male member of the Avery family and as the family historian, Avery played a key role in making all the Averys aware of their own history, including the story of Sonny's death and its meaning.

Parnell Avery, Sonny's youngest brother, who witnessed close-up the impact of Sonny's death on the family, also ended up devoting his life to medical care. Like his brother, he adopted a strong paternal role in the

Avery family by maintaining a close involvement with Sonny's wife and two daughters through many ups and downs. "We have an unsurpassed alignment," he said of his relationship with Regina and Malthaus Avery. Parnell also has three daughters of his own. Like Waddell's, Parnell's first reaction to the tragedy was anger. "I tried to call the president of the United States after it happened," he said. "I was so hostile."

Parnell Avery had musical talent, and in his youth, after performing in several Harlem nightclubs, playing the piano, and singing, he thought he would enter the entertainment world. "I never thought I'd go into medicine because our family was so poor. Money was as scarce as hen's teeth. But after Sonny died," he said, "I knew there had to be more to do with my life, so that no person, whatever color or background, would be turned away from a hospital. . . . I'm still mad about this thing. It's not the point that he died, but no one gave him any attention at one of our greatest southeastern medical institutions."[92]

After graduating from Virginia State College in 1952, Avery served a tour of combat duty in Korea from 1952 to 1953. While in the army, he took a medical aptitude test and did so well that he went back to Virginia State College when he returned and completed a graduate degree in biology. He married and taught high school for a couple of years in Henderson. In the spring of 1958, he learned that he had been accepted at Meharry Medical College in Nashville, Tennessee. His mother lent him one hundred dollars to hold his place.

"That was the beginning of the culmination of what I wanted to do after Sonny got killed," said Avery. He graduated from medical school in 1962 and returned to Henderson once again to serve as a general practitioner for four years. He then went back to Meharry and did a residency in surgery, which he completed in 1970.[93] He passed specialty boards and became a fellow of the American Society of Abdominal Surgery in 1979, of the International Academy of Proctology in 1981, and of the International College of Surgeons in 1990.

Through his involvement in the medical profession, Parnell Avery, like his brother Waddell, witnessed over many years the attitudes and conditions that resulted in the kind of treatment Sonny had received. He too became an activist as well as a medical caregiver. He participated in civil rights marches in Nashville while he was in medical school, and as a member of a variety of professional groups, he has traveled all over the country lecturing on social injustice in American medicine. "I have taken care of many old women on Medicare and Medicaid. These federal programs aren't giveaways. I know what it is to be in their shoes."

Parnell and Waddell Avery, perhaps more than anyone else, have had to grapple with the meaning of Sonny's death and mistreatment. As his brothers, they undoubtedly felt that his fate could be their own, and they shaped their lives accordingly. But despite their many actions in response to Sonny's death, the whole incident remains in many ways an unfinished chapter in their lives. To a large degree, for those still living, history must always remain an unfinished chapter, since its impact continues. It must be left to historians to close chapters and extract their meaning. What, then, is the meaning of Sonny Avery's death?

Parnell and Waddell Avery's mother, Hazel Avery, died in 1989. Her funeral, held on 23 February 1989 in the same small Baptist church where Sonny's death was mourned, drew Averys from all over the country: not only Sonny's daughter Malthaus and Evelyn's, Waddell's, and Parnell's families, but many more distant relatives and friends. The small church was filled to capacity, testament to Hazel Avery's valued role within her family and within her small rural community.

Snow intermittently drifted down on the surrounding fields, as it had on the day when Sonny was buried, almost fifty years before. Hazel Avery's grave had been dug in the clay near where Sonny and her husband were buried side by side. By this time, a granite headstone had been placed at Sonny's grave. On it was carved "Maltheus R. Avery April 16, 1926 Dec. 1, 1950 His Memory is Blessed. Son." In front of it stood a faded wreath of red, white, and blue paper flowers, tribute to a veteran.

But at this funeral there was not the sense of numbing tragedy that had obviously prevailed at Sonny's funeral. Hazel Avery's was not an interrupted life; her death bore no sting of abuse. The long night of legal segregation had ended during her lifetime. She had successfully raised four children and had watched all four of them grow up to lead fruitful lives; two even fulfilled her dreams by becoming high-level medical professionals. Sonny's brothers, having had their hero cut down, had been compelled to find their own heroism. Tragedy had been transformed into triumph.

The brothers' happier memories of Sonny seemed to prevail at their mother's funeral:

> He was five feet ten; he was well built, and he liked to lift weights. . . . I used to like to watch him cut wood, or take a file and sharpen an ax. . . . He was ambidextrist.[94]
>
> He was a good athlete. He loved baseball, boxing and football. He had good vision and good reflexes. He liked . . . music too. I can still

hear him say, "Mother, can I have the car?" What a driver! That's one thing Sonny could do. Anytime the car was moving Sonny was driving. If anything was wrong he'd get right out and fix it. He loved to drive, and he was a safe driver. He never got tired of it.[95]

He was full of life and he enjoyed life.[96]

Girls always flocked all over him.[97]

He was meticulous about grooming and dress. He liked to be sharp and he was.[98]

He had a physique and a walk girls were crazy about. Oh, he was evermore outgoing.[99]

To observe Hazel Avery's funeral was to realize how different it must have been to stand at Sonny's casket on that December day in 1950. Sonny's family had watched him risk his life for his country in World War II and had gained him back, without a scratch, transformed into a hero — only to see him die in a uniquely hurtful fashion. They had fought hard all their lives to escape the worst effects of segregation, and to some degree they had tried to deny its painful reality. Thus for them the tragedy was not only to see the high-spirited and deft young man they loved gone forever. It was also to have a particular set of hopes, illusions, and dreams about America smashed overnight. And it was to encounter American history in a highly personal way.

Even though the Averys had lived with segregation all their lives, they had not believed America would let their son, a combat veteran of World War II, die in this particular way. It literally took years for them to absorb exactly how this could have happened. Understandably, they still refuse to fully accept Sonny's tragedy today. It is too painful; it leads to too much rage. Through its system of medical care, America told them that their son's and brother's life was not worth as much as a white person's. Their schooling and acculturation had not prepared them to receive this message; it had taught them to fight such a defeating perspective.

Parnell Avery was unable to cry about his brother's death until some thirty-five years later, when, recovering from alcoholism and being treated by a psychotherapist at a detoxification center, he relived the moments when he walked into Garnes Funeral Home and saw Sonny in the casket. When he did, he said he tried to kill his white roommate. "He was black and blue but he let me do it. Afterwards, he asked me if I felt better. Then I cried," Avery recalled. Still trying to close the chapter on his brother's death, Parnell Avery said in 1988, "He would have died anyway, but it was like the biblical story. There *was* 'no room in the inn.' That bled my heart."[100]

Too often historians describe the sweep of historical events as impersonal phenomena happening to anonymous masses of people—especially if they are poor or of minority group status. When one reads most history books, it is far too easy to dismiss the real human tragedies emanating from historical circumstances because those tragedies happened to some group of people that the reader can define as "other," as made up of people not precisely like him or her, and thus not fully real.

The Avery saga reveals in a most graphic way the powerful impact of history on each and every individual and family, regardless of class, race, or sex. It also discloses the ways in which ordinary people are the crucial transmitters of history and the makers of historical events. From Maltheus Avery's short and vibrant life and death, and from his family's grief, rage, and creativity in response to it, the true fabric of American history is woven.

Conclusion: A Dark Stone of Enlightenment

The journey to discover the origins of the Charles Drew legend has been a long one. It has led through almost four hundred years of America's interracial history to the legend's truest source — a young man named Sonny Avery, whose life and death were symbolic of many others. At one level, the journey can be seen as following a path laid down by long-held racial belief that has received historical definition through the institutions of slavery and segregation. At another level, the journey continues today, elusively but persistently, as the social habits shaped by a white supremacist cultural heritage, its complex strands woven from a myriad of white and African American experiences and perspectives.

This study has explored some of the dimensions of that

heritage. One level of exploration traced the dramatic unfolding of two individual lives, what the social historian Fernand Braudel called "traditional history . . . the history of events: surface disturbances, crests of foam that the tides of history carry on their strong backs." Another level of exploration has turned our attention to what Braudel termed "social history, the history of groups and groupings" distinguished by "slow but perceptible rhythms," particularly the history of black and white Americans. A final level of exploration has arrested our gaze on the almost imperceptible rhythms Braudel called the "history of man in his relationship to his environment, a history in which all change is slow, a history of constant repetition, ever-recurring cycles," which also might be termed cultural history.[1] With its slower rhythms, this last type of history has been especially critical to an understanding of the Drew legend, for as an archetypal story that continues to be believed, the legend partakes of that "silent, submerged history" that reflects slowly evolving psychic and cultural realities, deeply entwined with a particular environment—the American South. As we have explored both black and white cultural phenomena, the emphasis has sometimes been on some of the exaggerations that emerge from a heritage of racial tension. At other times, the focus has been on the enduring realities embedded in this heritage—even in some of the exaggerations. In the end, the reality of Maltheus Avery's fate underscores the relevance of the Charles Drew legend.

The journey has made clear that all history, even that which claims to be "scientific" and "objective," is subjective. Yet this should not cause dismay. As southern historian Paul Gaston has written, "Myths are not polite euphemisms for falsehoods, but are combinations of images and symbols that reflect a people's way of perceiving truth. Organically related to a fundamental reality of life, they fuse the real and the imaginary into a blend that becomes a reality itself, a force in history."[2] History is indeed a hall of different mirrors, some dazzling, some distorting the past beyond recognition. And as shapers of our past we each have the opportunity at any given point in time to fashion new mirrors that are a little better made and a little more serviceable than the ones we have been using. As we do so, we inevitably try to remove the mirrors we find to be cracked and misshapen. As psychologist Rollo May observed, "Unless we achieve authentic myths, our society will fill the vacuum with pseudo-myths and beliefs in magic."[3]

Charles Drew's untimely death on 1 April 1950 sparked a black histor-

ical tale that in itself constitutes a historical event with profound meaning. Drew did not, as the legend states, bleed to death, but he did suffer
throughout his life from the historical circumstance of being born black
in twentieth-century America. He was a quintessentially American hero
by any measure, but because he was black, he could not reap the benefits
similar efforts would have brought a white man. In retrospect, it seems
inevitable that he would try to dislodge the very cornerstone of the
structure that confined him — the powerful cultural myth of white superiority and white difference, symbolized by blood. In retrospect, one can
even reasonably trace Drew's death, in part, to the segregated system. If
Drew had not felt compelled to drive all night to reach a destination in
the Deep South — a common practice among blacks in his time, when
most motels were closed to them — he almost certainly would not have
died when he did. On its deepest level, as a parable of life in America, the
Drew legend is true.

But it was not primarily the circumstances of Drew's life or death that
sparked the Drew legend. His historic encounter with the policy of segregating blood and his tragic death merely brought his fate into a grand
intersection with the larger fate of all black Americans. The larger historical truth of being black in America is what the Drew legend is grounded
upon. The legend can be understood as a statement emanating from
American black culture about the price of being black in America. The
legend attests to a powerful ethnic experience: that blacks in this country are subject to being metaphorically bled to death. No one in the race
is exempt from this peril — not even Charles Drew.

Thus the legend confronts, directly and critically, yet another American legend or myth, the one centered on Horatio Alger. The underlying
message is both stark and clear: America is not the democratic meritocracy it purports to be. This is a perspective that many white Americans do not want to hold, and one that many black Americans insist must
be acknowledged before the long reach of white supremacy can be finally confronted.

This is an ironic situation indeed — that black folklore, which many
white commentators over the years have dismissed as mere superstition
or gossip, should not only provide a viable cultural hero for the late
twentieth century but should also reveal so much about the darkest
corners of the American experience. We conclude by absorbing on a
deeper level the truth of this quiet statement by Robert Penn Warren: "If
poetry is the little myth we make, then history is the big myth we live."

The Charles Drew legend is certainly part of a big myth black Americans have lived for many, many years, one closer to reality than the still-larger myth we know as American history itself. Nowhere does the tension and irony between these mythic structures become more strained than when an American hero is dragged down by being treated, deliberately yet inappropriately, to degradation or, worse, death. This is precisely what happens in the Charles Drew legend. A multifaceted mythic paradigm, the legend is a prism that sheds light in more than one way. For not only does it powerfully convey the core of the black experience. It also quietly and subtly expresses the extreme tension between two clashing cultural ideals: white supremacy and democratic meritocracy.

Far from being a bit of black gossip, then, the Drew legend has much to tell late-twentieth-century Americans about who they are and what their history has been. Yet as one thread in the fabric of America's black culture, it is hardly unique. As we have seen, black Americans have been trying to tell their part of the story for a long time. Many other folktales could shed the same light that the Drew legend does. Perhaps better than any other ethnic group in America, black Americans know that the history we live comes from actual historical experience as reproduced in a cultural heritage that is transmitted daily through stories, jokes, songs, rituals, ceremonies, and styles of living. At the end of this journey, it is all the more clear that the Drew legend did not pop up overnight because it was a "great story," as one white North Carolinian said,[4] or because the civil rights movement needed good propaganda. Rather, the Drew legend came into being and persists because it is built on a many-layered foundation of black beliefs, tales, and well-founded superstitions about the conditions of black survival in white-dominated America.

The fact that the Drew legend points the way to historical realities even more tragic than the one it specifically describes even provides some direction for future American historians. For the truth behind the legend reveals in a graphic and unmistakable way just how inadequate traditional southern history long was, built as it was on a unique historical mythology of its own, premised on black invisibility. It is partly because of this competing white mythology embedded in mainstream history and culture that the Drew legend, ironically, became necessary and relevant. After the war, the defeated South attempted to resurrect itself through the power of imagination by creating an entire tradition of southern history to glorify the losers—white southerners—and their "Lost Cause."[5] Southern historians and writers created a body of historical myths so compelling that they not only effectively put blinders on several generations of white southerners but also bewildered and oppressed several generations of black Americans, who to a large degree were cut off from the necessary resources to research and write their own history. John Hope Franklin has fittingly characterized this southern historiography and its impact:

> For a hundred years southern historians found the dream so warm, the truth so cold, that they were slow to construct for the South an image of itself that was true to the reality of the past or relevant to its changing circumstances. . . . These histories gave the white South the intellectual justification for its determination not to yield on many important points, especially in its treatment of the Negro, that set it apart from the rest of the nation. . . . The new southern historians even helped persuade many non-Southerners that through the years the South had been treated unjustly, that its own course of action had been substantially right, and that its racial attitudes should be condoned if not imitated.[6]

Northern historians and writers played a part in fashioning and embroidering on this mythology.[7] The southern way of viewing American history became the American way.[8] Among its centerpieces were the Cavalier legend, which portrayed white southerners as spirited aristocrats tracing their blood lineage back to English kings, defending a venerable, God-given way of life; the plantation legend, in which childlike servants lived in contentment under the benign care of white slaveowners and their virtuous lady-wives; the Reconstruction legend, in which the "better sort" of southerners united against carpetbaggers, scalawags, and black Radical politicians; the rape myth, which pictured an innocent white maiden threatened by a bestial black man; and the Redeemer myth, which depicted Democratic political leaders as the noble saviors of their people. An essential building block of all these legends was black people's presumed innate inferiority and, since they were viewed as either childlike or savage, their inherent incapacity to participate fully in American democracy.[9] Fiction writers, journalists, and politicians were not the only ones who fostered this mythology; several generations of southern and northern academic historians did so as well. James Baldwin summed up the black response to traditional "white" American history in this comment: "History with a capital H, which is the creation of those who think of themselves as white, is my challenge, it is my dilemma, it is my trap — but it is not my creation."[10]

Given the fundamental incompatibility of these historic strands, no one can expect the job of untangling the intricate web of mythological fantasies surrounding America's racial past to be easy or swift. Black and white historians, acutely aware of the South's divided cultural heritage and of the polarized mythologies it has produced, have been trying to do the job for a long time. The task so defies rational analysis and simple understanding that in describing it, many people have relied on metaphors. C. Vann Woodward aptly called the South's segregated past a "twilight zone."[11] Lawrence Goodwyn perceived the southern heritage as "a muddle of a forest" that was almost impenetrable because of its "dense underbrush."[12]

And Paul Gaston, surveying this vast southern "thicket" of historical myth and fantasy, has pointed out that even when old myths begin to fade, new variants rise up to replace them. Late-nineteenth-century and twentieth-century southern industrialization, for example, was ushered in via the New South myth, which pictured a prostrate South lifted to its feet by benevolent white businessmen concerned with social betterment and racial harmony. This myth served to cloak the capitalist exploitation of new generations of southern workers, both black and white, within social arrangements and systems of production as paternalistic and racist as slavery's had been.[13]

The weight of these competing cultural traditions hangs especially heavily on the lives of black Americans. They are heirs to a cultural outlook that includes a deep awareness of human tragedy. This awareness has been largely absent from traditional American history, which all too often celebrates American progress, power, and democracy in a myth-laden liturgy of nationalism. Black Americans, in fact, still have much to teach their fellow Americans, and that is perhaps the primary import of this study. The African American cultural heritage might rightly be viewed as a dark stone of enlightenment, a touchstone that all Americans must claim in a profound way if they are to realize their full potential as human beings and as citizens sharing a common culture, for from this stone they can fashion more accurate and meaningful mirrors of the American experience. In the early years of the civil rights movement, James Baldwin eloquently summed up what the claiming of this heritage might mean for white Americans: "The only way . . . [the white man] can be released from the Negro's tyrannical power over him is to consent, in effect, to become black himself, to become a part of that suffering and dancing country that he . . . watches from the heights of his lonely power."[14]

In a moving essay that he wrote in 1967, black historian Vincent Harding provided further insight into the legacy of the black heritage: he identified the "gift of blackness" as the multiple gifts of faith, prophecy, compassion, healing, and finally "the capacity to distinguish between false spirits and true." Like Baldwin, he saw African Americans as uniquely equipped to see through America's false myths about itself, to tell "the American story as it is, not as it is written in most of our textbooks on political science and history." Part of the "bitter medicinal truth" Americans will need to face, said Harding, is how destructive America has been, not only to African Americans but to the "poor and the weak and the powerless all over the world." Harding concluded, "If we could exercise the gift of our blackness . . . [we could] join hands with all those who are seeking to build a new kind of freedom and . . . a new kind of world. . . . Our blackness . . . might make it possible for us to be delivered from the madness of American power, to seek a power that grows neither out of the barrel of a gun nor from the heat of burning jelly. The power of the sons of God."[15]

Much of what America has been, is, and can be is inextricably tied up with its black citizens. Indeed, America cannot become America until the black experience is fully acknowledged, incorporated into American history, and allowed to transform it. Much that we have held as truth about ourselves will burn to ashes in the fire of this new vision. But from the ashes, a phoenix of rare beauty may arise, just as Charles Drew emerged as a hero from the ashes of African Americans' bitterness during World War II and the civil rights movement. If we courageously face and accept responsibility for the tragedy that American history has been and continues to be today for many Americans, our democratic myths may yet be reborn.

Rites and ceremonies based on Charles Drew's life and legacy offer all Americans access to the rich African American heritage, even as they affirm basic humanitarian values. By standing metaphorically at the graves of Charles Drew, Maltheus Avery, and the many other black Americans who have "bled to death," Americans of all backgrounds can embrace a much more inclusive array of American heroes and heroines. They can also finally face the tragedy that is an inescapable component of American history. As James Baldwin knew so well, Americans as a group historically have not wanted to face "reality—the fact that life is tragic"[16] and ends in death. But he also knew, and King, Malcolm X, and many ordinary black people demonstrated with their lives, that facing this reality brings true freedom and an "unshakeable authority."[17]

A man notably free of racial blinders, Ralph Ellison, set the proper tone for America's future:

> Whence all this passion toward conformity anyway?—diversity is the word. Let man keep his many parts and you'll have no tyrant states. Why, if they follow this conformity business, they'll end up forcing me, an invisible man, to become white, which is not a color but the lack of one. Must I strive toward colorlessness? But seriously, and without snobbery, think of what the world would lose if that should happen. America is woven of many strands: I would recognize them and let it so remain. . . . Our fate is to become one yet many—this is not prophecy but description.[18]

Perhaps because he had absorbed the meaning of America's black history, Ellison had a profound understanding of how freedom might truly ring here. Ellison suggested that America might best be viewed as a richly woven fabric, emblematic of its complex and diverse unity of peoples. As Ellison knew, as a new generation of social historians have shown us in the past thirty years, and as an increasing number of Americans are beginning to understand, cultural pluralism is not merely the ideal; in America it is the reality.

In acknowledging this reality at a symbolic level, we might draw inspiration from South Africa. As a nation newly committed to equality and cultural diversity, it has adopted two national anthems, one Afrikaner and one African; also, South Africans are flying a flag that combines the green, gold, and black of the freedom movement with the red, white, and blue of the old apartheid state. It is a grand experiment in cultural redefinition and democracy. In new political acts and symbolic affirmations, America might also ignite the hopes of the many people all over the globe now torn apart by ethnic strife and bloodshed. We could begin with a simple act: when we stand and sing the traditional national anthem, we might also sing our other national hymn, "Lift Ev'ry Voice and Sing," and thereby make the black experience a part of our common heritage: "We have come over a way that with tears has been watered, / We have come, treading our path through the blood of the slaughtered."[19]

"Oneness" is a meaningful and far-reaching concept if all Americans understand that it does not mean the sacrifice and loss of individual and cultural differences but rather the honoring of them. With this awareness, the truth embedded in Christianity, science, and our common humanity—the truth Charles Drew bore witness to—becomes a truly powerful one: that we all indeed are one blood. Race itself, as history and science reveal, is but another cultural myth.[20]

Notes

ABBREVIATIONS

CD-ARC-NH   Charles Drew File, American Red Cross,
             National Headquarters, Washington, D.C.

CRDP   Charles R. Drew Papers

JAMA   *Journal of the American Medical Association*

JNMA   *Journal of the National Medical Association*

INTRODUCTION

1. Whitney Young, "Bigotry and the Blood Bank," *Baltimore (Md.) Afro-American*, 17 October 1964, p. A5.
2. Sterne, *Blood Brothers*; Hardwick, *Charles Richard Drew*; Lichello, *Pioneer in Blood Plasma*; Haber, *Black Pioneers*; Bertol, *Charles Drew*; Klein, *Hidden Contributors*; Richardson and Fahey, *Great Black Americans*; Mahone-Lonesome, *Charles R. Drew*; Yount, *Black Scientists*; Talmadge, *Life of Charles Drew*.
3. Stan Swofford, "Witness Dispels Myth in Black Doctor's Death," *Greensboro (N.C.) Daily News*, 11 July 1982, pp. A1, A3.
4. In *Home Fires*, a sociological study about the life of a postwar American family, author Donald Katz refers to Drew's daughter, Sylvia, as a close friend of the daughter in this family. He mentions that Drew died "with no access to the blood plasma technology he'd pioneered," but he does not indicate whether Sylvia Drew believed this (pp. 166–67).
5. Stanback interview.
6. Nevins, *Gateway to History*, pp. 64–66. Nevins and folklorist Richard M. Dorson were important figures in pointing out the importance of the historical content embedded in oral testimony. See Dorson, "Oral Tradition and Written History"; Nevins, *Gateway to History*, pp. iv, 62–68; and Billington, *Allan Nevins on History*, pp. 288–93.
7. I was influenced at the outset by writers, anthropologists, and sociologists who worked in the South, describing its people and folkways in the 1930s: Couch's *These Are Our Lives* and Terrill's and Hirsch's *Such As Us*, both of which drew on interviews done by the Federal Writer's Project; Powdermaker's *After Freedom*; Johnson's *Backgrounds to Patterns of Negro Segregation*; Dollard's *Caste and Class in a Southern Town*; and Myrdal's *American Dilemma*.
8. Oral testimony from the era of the civil rights movement, recorded in a growing collection of books, films, and video documentaries, has powerfully demonstrated the importance of people's beliefs in inspiring history-mak-

ing action. Some good examples are Chafe, *Civilities and Civil Rights*; Couto, *Ain't Gonna Let Nobody Turn Me Round*; Evans, *Personal Politics*; Hampton and Fayer, *Voices of Freedom*; Kluger, *Simple Justice*; Morris, *Origins of the Civil Rights Movement*; Norrell, *Reaping the Whirlwind*; Powledge, *Free at Last?*; Raines, *My Soul Is Rested*; Smith, *Winner Names the Age* and *Now Is the Time*; and Williams, *Eyes on the Prize*. Lawrence Goodwyn, aware of the power of oral testimony through his own participation in the movement, extended oral history methodology into two new arenas in his impressive studies of movement cultures: *Democratic Promise*, on the Populist movement, and *Breaking the Barrier*, on the Solidarity movement in Poland.

9. An excellent discussion of the many viewpoints about the precise relationship between folk memory and history, along with references to others who have dealt with this subject, is found in the preface to Montell's *Saga of Coe Ridge*. Taking the view that folk memory can be a reliable guide to a group's past, Montell cites an article about the Southern Paiute Indians of southern Utah, whose oral folk traditions reflect ancient historical facts. The Paiutes tell stories about a prehistoric people, the Puebloids, that are consistent with eight-hundred-year-old archeological evidence (Pendergast and Meighan, "Folk Traditions as Historical Fact").

10. African historians are familiar with the challenge of gleaning historical facts from long-established oral traditions. Vansina's *Oral Tradition* offers sound guidance on the subject. See also Haley, "Black History, Oral History and Genealogy."

11. Paul Thompson, *Voice of the Past*, p. 27.

12. Regarding the idea that oral history effectively amplifies and enriches traditional history shaped by elites, the best detailed discussion I have read is Paul Thompson's *Voice of the Past*, especially chapters 1 and 3, 1–21 and 72–100. Thompson points out that oral history is not only more democratic but that it "should make for a more realistic construction of the past. Reality is complex and many-sided; and it is a primary merit of oral history that to a much greater degree than most sources it allows the original multiplicity of viewpoints to be recreated" (p. 5).

13. Good examples of recent African American history books that rely on oral testimony and folklore as important sources are Montell's *Saga of Coe Ridge*; Rosengarten's *All God's Dangers*; Levine's *Black Culture and Black Consciousness*; Genovese's *Roll, Jordan, Roll*; Fry's *Night Riders*; and Joyner's *Down by the Riverside*. These works all demonstrate the importance of folk memory as a vital historical source, as does Goodwyn's fine article "Populist Dreams and Negro Rights."

14. "Robert Penn Warren," *Vanity Fair*, April 1983, p. 45.

CHAPTER ONE

1. *Washington Post*, 31 March 1950, p. A1.
2. "Restaurant's Refusal to Serve 3 Negroes Weighed by Court," *Washington Post*, 1 April 1950, p. B1.
3. "Integrating D.C. Eating Places," *Washington Post*, 25 April 1985, District

Weekly, pp. 1 and 7. This retrospective article identifies Terrell, but the 1950 article, cited above, does not. This historic case (*District of Columbia v. John R. Thompson Co.*, 346 U.S. 100 [1953]) eventually made its way to the Supreme Court, which ruled on 8 June 1953 to uphold the "lost" anti-segregation laws—termed "lost" because they had never been enforced. Four days later, Terrell and her three companions went back to Thompson's Restaurant and were served by the manager himself.

4. "Restaurant's Refusal," *Washington Post*.
5. See Green, *Secret City*, for documentation of segregation in Washington, D.C.
6. Walter R. Johnson, "April 1, 1950" (typed manuscript), 15 November 1982, CD-ARC-NH. Johnson wrote this account of Drew's death in 1982 and sent it to the American Red Cross headquarters at the instigation of C. Mason Quick, the North Carolina doctor who came forth to debunk the Drew legend. Johnson's account was printed two years later within Sampson's article "Dispelling the Myth." All material not attributed to other sources comes from this account. In 1982, doctors Samuel Bullock and John Ford also reconstructed the events surrounding Drew's death. (See letters cited from Bullock and Ford to Quick below.) C. Mason Quick's debunking of the Drew legend in 1982 unleashed a controversy that made all three of Drew's companions feel compelled to set the record straight. Their accounts of the incident agree. Only a few pieces of primary written evidence from 1950 survive: Drew's death certificate; a letter from Lenore Drew to one of the white doctors on the scene; the hospital records of John Ford; and several newspaper articles.
7. "Drew's Wife Urged Him to Take Plane," *Durham (N.C.) Carolina Times*, 15 April 1950.
8. Nora Drew Gregory interview.
9. White interview.
10. Charles Drew to Edwin B. Henderson, 31 May 1940, Folder 6, Box 136-1, CRDP. What the eminent black medical activist W. Montague Cobb termed the black "medical ghetto" is outlined in his article "Integration in Medicine," p. 3. For discussion of inadequate black medical care under segregation, see also Morais, *History of the Afro-American in Medicine*, pp. 89–102, and three works by Beardsley: *History of Neglect*, pp. 35–41, 77–100, and 273–309; "Making Separate, Equal"; and "Goodbye to Jim Crow."
11. White interview. Wynes discusses Drew's modest income and financial generosity in *Charles Richard Drew*, pp. 116–17. An excellent concise summary of Drew's life with a reference to his modest salary is W. Montague Cobb, "Charles Richard Drew," p. 244.
12. Robert S. Jason, "Charles Richard Drew" (speech delivered in April 1960 at the dedication of the Charles R. Drew Elementary School), Folder 2, Box 136-1, CRDP. Jason had been Drew's chief in pathology at Howard University in 1935 and 1936 and was dean of the Howard University Medical School when he made this speech.
13. Watts interview, 25 January 1983.
14. Johnson, "April 1, 1950."
15. Watts interview, 25 January 1983.

16. Ibid.; Cook interview. See also Wynes, *Charles Richard Drew*, pp. 49–54, and Lenore Robbins Drew's own account of this incident, "Unforgettable Charlie Drew."

17. Cobb interview. See also W. Montague Cobb, *First Negro Medical Society*.

18. See Wynes, *Charles Richard Drew*, pp. 83–92.

19. Drew's life and character are discussed in depth in subsequent chapters of this book, based on the author's own primary research.

20. Johnson, "April 1, 1950."

21. Mitchell interview, 19 February 1990. Mitchell, a fair-skinned woman of mixed descent, said that her strong motivation to set the record straight about Drew stemmed from a tragic incident in her own family history: her brother, Charles Orin Jeffers, a county extension agent, died from exposure in January 1940 after being burned in a house fire that killed almost every member of his family. When he was taken from the rural site to a nearby hospital in Petersburg, Va., he was refused treatment and had to be transported some seventy-five miles, to the Medical College of Virginia in Richmond. Mitchell said she has tried hard to repress the whole incident but acknowledged that it hasn't gone away (Mitchell interview, 8 September 1995).

22. John Ford to C. Mason Quick, 26 August 1982, Quick Papers. This letter is Ford's account of the circumstances surrounding Drew's death.

23. All information about the accident, as noted earlier, is derived from Johnson's account, "April 1, 1950," unless otherwise indicated.

24. Bullock interview.

25. Corbett interview.

26. Morris interviews.

27. Dixon interview. Dixon said that "five ambulances went out there" [to the site of Drew's accident]. Exactly which ambulance transported Drew to the hospital — and, specifically, whether it was a white or black ambulance — is still ambiguous; in February of 1990 Dixon told Gilberta Mitchell that McClure's Funeral Home, which was white, transported Drew. Mitchell herself had always heard that Alvis Pennix, a black ambulance driver at Sharpe Funeral Home, claimed to have picked Drew up. Sharpe Funeral Home did pick Drew's body up after his death at Alamance General Hospital (Mitchell interview, 22 February 1990). But in the 1986 interview Dixon said he thought "Carl Crabtree got there first." Crabtree, a white man, said he did not pick Drew up; he believed that Hargett and Bryant Funeral Home, which was black, had sent the ambulance that got there first (Carl Crabtree interview, 4 February 1983).

28. Charles Richard Drew, Certificate of Death.

29. Yount interviews.

30. Yount interview, 19 January 1983; Shanks interviews. Shanks, one of three black doctors practicing in Alamance County in 1950, said that he could only enter Alamance General Hospital in a professional capacity to observe surgery. He could not treat one of his patients there even on an emergency basis.

31. Harold Kernodle, after hearing Johnson's description of the scene, said the doctor in the long white coat must have been Carrington, the senior doctor

on staff, since he was the only one who wore a long coat (Harold Kernodle interview).

32. Ibid.
33. Ford to Quick, Quick Papers.
34. Harold Kernodle interview.
35. Charles Kernodle interview.
36. Dixon interview.
37. Lucille Crabtree interview.
38. M. Lenore Drew to R. E. Brooks, 30 April 1950, Yount Papers.
39. White interview; McCown interviews; Syphax interview.
40. Lenore Drew interview.
41. Harold Kernodle interview.
42. Yount interview, 19 January 1983.
43. Charles Kernodle interview.
44. Quick interview.
45. Charles Richard Drew, Certificate of Death.
46. Marvin Yount, "Additional Information Regarding the Death of Dr. Charles R. Drew, April 1, 1950" (typed manuscript), Yount Papers.
47. Johnson, "April 1, 1950."
48. Samuel Bullock to C. Mason Quick, 28 July 1982, Quick Papers. This is Bullock's account of Drew's accident and death.
49. Yount interview, 19 September 1985.
50. All these records are in Marvin Yount's personal papers. Over the years, Yount collected a large file on Drew's death because so many people, stirred by the controversy, contacted him for information.
51. Ford to Quick, Quick Papers.
52. Ibid.
53. H. B. Kernodle Sr., "To Whom It May Concern Re: Dr. John Ford," 3 April 1950, Yount Papers.
54. Harold Kernodle interview.
55. Yount interviews.
56. Kernodle, "To Whom It May Concern."
57. Ford to Quick, Quick Papers.
58. Yount interview, 19 January 1983.
59. Quick interview.
60. Pennix and Gray interviews with author.
61. "Noted Physician Fatally Injured in Auto Wreck Near Burlington," *Durham (N.C) Carolina Times*, 8 April 1950, p. 1.
62. Stanback interview.
63. Pennix interview.
64. Morris interviews. Morris also recalled seeing the large red crossed circle on Highway 49 some weeks after the accident occurred, and she confirmed that it lasted for many years.
65. Nora Drew Gregory interview.
66. Joseph Drew interview, 12 June 1985.
67. Lenore Drew interview.
68. Price interview.

69. Lenore Drew interview.

70. Nora Drew Gregory interview. Drew's ancestors had been buried in Harmony Cemetery, located at Eighth and Rhode Island Avenue NE in the District of Columbia, and a few years later their graves were moved to the newer, less crowded Lincoln Cemetery (Wynes, *Charles Richard Drew*, p. 116).

71. W. Montague Cobb, "Charles Richard Drew," p. 245.

72. Joseph Drew interview, 12 June 1985.

73. Nora Drew Gregory interview.

74. Pennington interview.

75. Their careers are discussed in detail in Wade, *Black Men of Amherst*, pp. 42–47, 53–57, and 67–77.

76. Cook interview, 24 September 1985.

77. "Medical Leaders at Dr. Drew Rites," *New York Times*, 6 April 1950.

78. Gordon interview.

79. "Charles Drew," *Daily Bulletin* (of the John A. Andrew Clinical Society, Tuskegee Institute, Tuskegee, Ala.) 1, no. 1 (3 April 1950): 1.

80. Eleanor Roosevelt to Lenore Drew, Folder 2, Box 134-3, CRDP.

81. Wynes, *Charles Richard Drew*, p. 116.

82. Hon. Hubert H. Humphrey, "Dr. Charles R. Drew," Proceedings and Debates of the 81st Cong., 2d sess., *Congressional Record* (10 April 1950).

83. "Charles R. Drew," *Washington Post*, 6 April 1950, editorial page.

CHAPTER TWO

1. *Baltimore (Md.) Afro-American*, 17 October 1964, p. A5.

2. Woodward, *Strange Career*, p. xvi.

3. See Tonkin, "History and the Myth of Realism." Tonkin argues, "To believe in the natural veracity of any narrative form is a false faith. . . . Since realism is a predominant mode of historical writing, it is too easily accepted as the opposite of myth. . . . We should dissolve this dichotomy."

4. Other scholars who have attempted to trace rumors and legends have discussed this inherent difficulty. In *I Heard It through the Grapevine*, Turner comments, "Tracing a rumor, legend, or indeed any primarily oral genre back to its earliest manifestations is always problematic" (p. 3). I share with Turner the conviction that despite the difficulty it is meaningful to understand the persistence of certain rumors and legends in folk culture.

5. Ibid., pp. 3–5.

6. Quander interview.

7. Johnson interview.

8. Thomas interview.

9. Redhead interview.

10. Mair interview.

11. Cook interview. A real incident of refused care that fed into the Drew legend, discussed in Chapter 8, did occur at Duke University in 1950.

12. Franklin's works include *From Slavery to Freedom*; *Racial Equality in America*; *Color Line*; *Race and History*; *George Washington Williams*; *Militant South*; *Reconstruction after the Civil War*; and *Free Negro in North Carolina*.

13. Stan Swofford, "Witness Dispels Myth in Black Doctor's Death," *Greensboro (N.C.) Daily News*, 11 July 1982, p. A3.

14. Franklin interview, 29 September 1982.

15. Franklin's *From Slavery to Freedom* is widely recognized as the major scholarly text on African American history and has been reissued in six different editions, in 1956, 1967, 1974, 1980, 1987, and 1994.

16. Franklin interview, 21 January 1987.

17. Vine interview.

18. Gibbs interview.

19. Dixon interview.

20. Morris interview, 4 April 1990.

21. Mitchell interview, 10 September 1985.

22. McCown interview, 20 November 1985.

23. Ibid. Ira McCown asserted, "I got . . . [the Drew rumor] through the black press." McCown very likely did read a story about Drew's death in a 1950 black newspaper, but he undoubtedly read the story about Drew's mistreatment — the legend — some years later. Given that McCown thought he first heard the rumor a day after Drew's accident, his testimony reminds us that people's memories are often faulty.

24. Quick interview.

25. "Drew's Death Stuns Bullock: Changed Flying Plan to Take 2 Others," *Baltimore (Md.) Afro-American*, 8 April 1950, pp. 1 and 2.

26. "Noted Physician Fatally Injured in Auto Wreck Near Burlington," *Durham (N.C.) Carolina Times*, 8 April 1950, p. 1.

27. Walter White, *Rising Wind*, p. 11.

28. Shibutani, *Improvised News*, p. v.

29. Turner, *I Heard It through the Grapevine*, p. 3; see also her chapters on "Cannibalism," pp. 9–32; "Corporal Control," pp. 33–56; and "Contamination," pp. 137–64.

30. Allport and Postman, *Psychology of Rumor*, pp. 33, 180.

31. Corbett interview.

32. Dalfiume, *Desegregation of the U.S. Armed Forces*, pp. 105–47. See also Wynn, *Afro-American and the Second World War*, pp. 99–121.

33. Woodward, *Strange Career*, pp. 118–19.

34. Smith, *Killers of the Dream*, pp. 226–27.

35. Allport and Postman, *Psychology of Rumor*, pp. 38–39.

36. Ibid., p. 43.

37. Dalfiume, *Desegregation of the U.S. Armed Forces*, pp. 105–6.

38. Woodward, *Strange Career*, pp. 149–68. Woodward notes, "In the first three years after the Brown decision, 712 school districts were desegregated, but in the last three years of the Eisenhower administration the number fell to 13 in 1958, 19 in 1959, and 17 in 1960" (p. 167).

39. "Drew, Woodson Mourned," *Pittsburgh Courier*, 8 April 1950, p. 1.

40. "Dr. Drew Killed in Wreck," *Durham (N.C.) Carolina Times*, 8 April 1950, p. 1.

41. Nora Drew Gregory interview.

42. Pennington interview.

43. See Savitt, *Medicine and Slavery*; Manning, *Black Apollo of Science*; Haller, *Out-*

casts from Evolution; James H. Jones, *Bad Blood*; and Beardsley, *History of Neglect*. See also Gamble, *Black Community Hospital* and *Germs Have No Color Line*; Kiple and King, *Another Dimension to the Black Diaspora*; and Seham, *Blacks and American Medical Care*.

44. Haller's *Outcasts from Evolution* describes the studies done and the thinking of this period in great detail; see especially pp. 19–20, 29–39, 40–68, and 209–10. Du Bois edited a famous study in 1906, *Health and Physique of the Negro American*, documenting the urban environmental factors that were a major cause of high black mortality rates. In this work, he pointed out that the "matter of sickness is an indication of social and economic position (not of race)" (p. 90).

45. See Bordley and Harvey, *Two Centuries of American Medicine*, pp. 277–92, and Stevens, *American Medicine and the Public Interest*, p. 135.

46. The two best comprehensive overviews are Beardsley, *History of Neglect*, and Morais, *History of the Afro-American in Medicine*.

47. W. Montague Cobb, "Integration in Medicine," p. 3. There is a large body of literature on black health care; many titles are included in the bibliography. One important source is the collection of writings by Dr. W. Montague Cobb, Howard University professor of anatomy, former editor of the *Journal of the National Medical Association*, and leader of the NAACP during its struggle to desegregate hospitals. Especially useful are two pamphlets that summed up the black health-care situation at midcentury: "Medical Care and the Plight of the Negro" and "Progress and Portents."

48. See Holt, Smith-Parker, and Terborg-Penn, *Special Mission*.

49. See Roman, *Meharry Medical College*, and Summerville, *Educating Black Doctors*.

50. See Savitt, "Entering a White Profession," pp. 507–40, and Beardsley, *History of Neglect*, pp. 77–100, for a thorough discussion of the handicaps black southern physicians faced. See also Reitzes, *Negroes and Medicine*, on the black medical profession at midcentury.

51. "Health Status and Health Education of Negroes," p. 211. Homicide is listed as an additional cause of high black mortality rates.

52. Beardsley, *History of Neglect*, p. 8.

53. Ibid., pp. 93–94.

54. Embree and Waxman, *Investment in People*, pp. 119–20.

55. "Health Status and Health Education of Negroes," pp. 202–3.

56. Cornely, "Segregation and Discrimination in Medical Care," p. 1075.

57. Seham, "Discrimination against Negroes in Hospitals," pp. 940–43. Seham noted, "There is no question that if the same care were available to Negroes in Mississippi and other Southern states as in Minnesota and other Northern states, Negro morbidity and mortality rates could be sharply reduced. Factors responsible for this difference are poverty, lack of Negro doctors and of doctors for Negroes and the exclusion of Negroes from first class 'white' hospitals" (p. 940). See also Seham's *Blacks and American Medical Care*.

58. W. Montague Cobb, "Medical Care and the Plight of the Negro," p. 6. Cobb estimated that there were about ten thousand hospital beds available to blacks in the whole country. Many of these were located in the 112 black

hospitals then in existence, of which only twenty-five were accredited and only fourteen approved for the training of interns.

59. *Hospital Care in the United States*, p. 163. This report cites an article (Eugene H. Bradley, "Health, Hospitals, and the Negro," *Modern Hospital* 65 [August 1945]: 43–44) that states that there were 124 hospitals exclusively for blacks in 1944, providing a total of twenty thousand beds.

60. McFall, "Needs for Hospital Facilities and Physicians," pp. 235–36. This article also provides a table showing the number of hospital beds for white and nonwhite populations in 1950, broken down by state.

61. In the climate of oppression that segregation created, other black people's traumatic deaths, even when they did not involve explicit refusals of treatment, also contributed to the spread of rumors. In remembering Drew's death, a few people recalled that prizefighter Jack Johnson may have suffered some mistreatment. Johnson, the first black heavyweight world boxing champion, died after a car crash near Raleigh, North Carolina, on 10 June 1946. Johnson was notorious for driving at high speeds, and he lost control of his big Lincoln Zephyr while rounding a curve on US 1 thirty miles north of Raleigh, on the outskirts of Franklinton. Johnson was taken to Raleigh's black hospital, St. Agnes', and he died there from internal injuries at 6:10 P.M., less than an hour after the accident (Farr, *Black Champion*, pp. 235–36).

62. Sprigle, *In the Land of Jim Crow*, pp. 137, 143. Sprigle, a white man who had disguised himself as black for his 3,400-mile journey through the South, concluded, "Does anybody wonder that I found mightily little pleasure in that . . . tour . . . much of it at 70 miles an hour? Every time we had a close shave with another car, I could see myself riding around in a Jim Crow ambulance, hunting a Jim Crow hospital while I slowly bled to death." In Sprigle's book, a whole chapter, "White Hospitals and Black Deaths" (pp. 135–48), deals with the subject of hospital refusals, including this one: on 25 April 1947, two members of the Clark University track team were seriously injured. After a five-hour tour that covered more than a hundred miles, they were refused at three different hospitals and were finally admitted to a black hospital. Joseph Brown died shortly afterward; Jeffrey Jennings lay in a coma for three weeks and later recovered.

63. Morais, *History of the Afro-American in Medicine*, p. 1.

64. "Crisis in Negro Medicine: Racism and poverty still shackle the Negro, both doctor and patient," *Ebony*, November 1967, pp. 77–78. The article also reports on the frequent practice of "hospital-dumping" of black patients in a large northern city.

65. Zora Neale Hurston described an encounter with a white doctor who was reluctant to treat her in an article significantly titled "My Most Humiliating Jim Crow Experience."

66. Morais, *History of the Afro-American in Medicine*, p. 1.

67. Franklin interview, 9 February 1983.

68. "2 Killed, 2 Injured as Fiskites' Auto Wrecks," *Memphis (Tenn.) World*, 10 November 1931, p. 1; "Dr. T. E. Jones Submits Report of the Commission on Interracial Cooperation," *Fisk Herald*, 8 December 1931; W. E. B. Du Bois, "Dalton, Georgia," *Crisis* 39, no. 3 (March 1932): 85–87.

69. Davis interview.
70. Buckingham, "Dr. Charles Richard Drew," p. 32.
71. Rothe, *Current Biography*, p. 180; Joel Francis, "Negro Surgeon, World Plasma Expert, Derides Red Cross Blood Segregation," *Chicago Defender*, 26 September 1942; Charles R. Drew, "The Spingarn Medal," *NAACP Bulletin* (September 1944), p. 11; Buckingham, "Dr. Charles Richard Drew," p. 32; "The UFWA Stand for United of All" (UFWA Leaflet), 8 August 1944, Folder 34, Box 135-2, CRDP.
72. Eugene Gordon, "He Made a Science of Blood Plasma," *New York Daily Worker*, 4 July 1943.
73. "Men of All Colors Owe Life to Negro Medical Scientist," *Des Moines (Iowa) Tribune*, 22 November 1944.
74. Rothe, *Current Biography*, p. 179.
75. Albert Deutsch, "Dr. Charles Drew, Surgeon — A Study in Blood and Race," *New York PM Daily*, 30 March 1944.
76. Allport and Postman, *Psychology of Rumor*, p. 155.
77. Thomas interview.
78. Allport and Postman, *Psychology of Rumor*, pp. 75, 86, 100.
79. Quick interview.
80. Bullock interview.
81. Syphax interview; White interview.
82. Gordon interview.
83. Ibid.
84. Shanks interview, 8 February 1983.
85. My sense of the movement has been shaped by many history books (cited in the next chapter and the Bibliography), but especially by autobiographies such as Moody, *Coming of Age*; Forman, *Making of Black Revolutionaries*; King, *Freedom Song*; Peck, *Freedom Ride*; and by collections of oral testimonies from participants such as Raines, *My Soul Is Rested*; Hampton and Fayer, *Voices of Freedom*; and Carson et al., *Eyes on the Prize Reader*.
86. An excellent book documenting the origins and scope of African American culture is Levine's *Black Culture and Black Consciousness*.

CHAPTER THREE

1. Carson et al., *Eyes on the Prize Reader*, "Speech by Martin Luther King, Jr. at Holt Street Baptist Church," pp. 50–51.
2. See Harding, *Hope and History*, p. 6. Harding notes, "Indeed, when we look back now from the vantage point of Beijing and Prague, from Berlin and Soweto, we realize that the post–World War II African-American freedom movement was . . . [a] seminal contribution to the massive pro-democracy struggles that have set the globe spinning in these times."
3. Martin Luther King Jr., *Testament of Hope*. This is the best collection of King's writings. Washington's introduction, "Martyred Prophet for a Global Beloved Community of Justice, Faith, and Hope," and his extensive bibliography (pp. xi–xxvii and 681–88) offer support and documentation for the interpretation of King and the movement elucidated in this chapter. See

also Bennett, "When the Man and the Hour Are Met," pp. 23–31. Bennett argues that King, although aware of Gandhian thought, began the Montgomery struggle inspired instead by Jesus and by a tradition of practical nonviolence rooted in the black church. King was transformed by his participation in the Montgomery movement — by "the blood of experience," in which he had to face death threats and violence toward his family. Through his suffering, he became a new apostle of nonviolence. Before Montgomery, American blacks inspired by Gandhi had long hoped to launch a nonviolent movement. A. Philip Randolph was hailed as an "American Gandhi," and James Farmer, who started the Congress of Racial Equality (CORE) in 1942, was another important forerunner. Methodist minister James M. Lawson Jr. also served as a vital link between the Gandhian tradition and the black struggle. Lawson and King met in 1957 and remained close until King's death. See Thurman, *Jesus and the Disinherited*; Powell, *Marching Blacks*; Branch, *Parting the Waters*, pp. 203–4; Kapur, *Raising Up a Prophet*, pp. 155–56; and Carson, *Eyes on the Prize Reader*, pp. 130–32.

4. See Cone, *Black Theology and Black Power*, especially pp. 91–115, and Robertson, *American Myth* on "Black American Morality," pp. 103–6. See also Lincoln and Mamiya, *Black Church in the African American Experience*, and Sernett, *Afro-American Religious History*.

5. Gregory, *No More Lies*, pp. 261–62.

6. Gregory, *Shadow That Scares Me*, p. 207.

7. Dick Gregory interview.

8. Fry, *Night Riders*, pp. 16, 9, 6.

9. See Hurston, *Mules and Men*; Walker, *I Love Myself When I Am Laughing*; Hughes and Bontemps, *Book of Negro Folklore*; Dorson, *American Negro Folktales*; Stuckey, *Slave Culture* and "Twilight of Our Past"; Dance, *Shuckin' and Jivin'*; Turner, *I Heard It through the Grapevine*; Joyner, *Down by the Riverside*; Montell, *Saga of Coe Ridge*; Levine, *Black Culture and Black Consciousness*.

10. Levine, *Black Culture and Black Consciousness*, p. xi.

11. Ibid., p. 88.

12. Ibid.

13. Gavins, "North Carolina Black Folklore," p. 412.

14. Hemenway, *Zora Neale Hurston*, p. 51.

15. Turner, *I Heard It through the Grapevine*, p. 220.

16. Fanon, *Black Skin, White Masks*, p. 64.

17. In a passage in *Invisible Man* about the death of a young black man, Todd Clifton, shot down in the street by a white policeman, Ralph Ellison wrote, "He bled and he died. He fell in a heap like any man and his blood spilled out like any blood, wet as any blood and reflecting the sky and the buildings and birds and trees. . . . They spilled his blood and he bled. . . . It's an old story and there's been too much blood" (p. 445). This passage summons up the image of Rodney King being beaten, an image that a black scholar termed "the image of the late twentieth century. Rich, cynical white citizens and their henchmen are everywhere pounding the hell out 'the rest of us' average Americans" (Baker, *Black Studies, Rap and the Academy*, p. 102).

18. Harding, *Beyond Chaos*, p. 1.

19. Aptheker, *Autobiography of W. E. B. Du Bois*, p. 422.

20. Harding, *There Is a River*, p. 331.

21. See "Interview with Bernice Reagon" in Carson et al., *Eyes on the Prize Reader*, pp. 143–45. Reagon relates how after a march in Albany, she began to sing an old spiritual, "Over My Head I See Trouble in the Air," and how she spontaneously substituted the word "freedom" for "trouble." See also Du Bois, *Souls of Black Folk*, pp. 264–78.

22. In 1877, a writer named V. L. Cameron estimated that the annual outflow of Africans to Islam was some 500,000 people. He commented, "Africa is bleeding from every pore" (Braudel, *History of Civilizations*, p. 132).

23. Gates, *Classic Slave Narratives*, p. 296. Douglass concluded after fighting off his oppressor, "He only can understand the deep satisfaction which I experienced, who has himself repelled by force the bloody arm of slavery. . . . It was a glorious resurrection, from the tomb of slavery to the heaven of freedom. My long-crushed spirit rose, cowardice departed, bold defiance took its place; and I now resolved that, however long I might remain a slave in form, the day had passed forever when I could be a slave in fact. I did not hesitate to let it be known of me, that the white man who expected to succeed in whipping, must also succeed in killing me" (pp. 298–99).

24. See Sheridan, "Guinea Surgeons," p. 603. Sheridan quotes John Barbot writing in 1732: "The Bloody Flux is also common, and sweeps away multitudes of the Blacks after they have lost all their blood." Sheridan further notes that black men more often died from dysentery than did black women, because of their "confinement and melancholia." Black men were kept in shackles, but the women were not (p. 604). See also Mannix and Cowley, *Black Cargoes*, p. 129, and Rawley, *Transatlantic Slave Trade*, p. 291. Rawley discusses mortality rates on pp. 285–87 and 293. On mortality rates, see also Curtin, *Atlantic Slave Trade*, pp. 275–76.

25. See Stampp, *Peculiar Institution*, pp. 295–307, 315, 318–20. The chapter called "Maintenance, Morbidity and Mortality" (pp. 279–321) is a good summary of the health conditions slaves endured.

26. Genovese, *Roll, Jordan, Roll*, p. 226. See also Savitt, *Medicine and Slavery*, pp. 281–307, and Kiple and Kiple, "African Connection," p. 215.

27. Savitt, *Medicine and Slavery*, p. 12; see also pp. 11, 13–14, and Stampp, *Peculiar Institution*, pp. 310–11. Savitt's book is the single best source on the health status and medical care of slaves.

28. Levine, *Black Culture and Black Consciousness*, pp. 63–67; Joyner, *Down by the Riverside*, p. 148; Genovese, *Roll, Jordan, Roll*, pp. 224–26. Genovese offers the most complete explanation of why the slaves preferred their own healers, emphasizing their belief in the spiritual roots of disease.

29. Haller, *Outcasts from Evolution*, pp. 40–68.

30. Du Bois, *Health and Physique of the Negro American*, p. 90.

31. NAACP, *Thirty Years of Lynching*; Raper, *Tragedy of Lynching*; Walter White, *Rope and Faggot*; and Hall, *Revolt against Chivalry*. An interesting study of the persisting psychological impact of lynching on black men is Harris's *Exorcising Blackness*; see especially pp. ix–xiii, 184–95.

32. Fry, *Night Riders*, pp. 170–211.

33. Ibid., p. 200.

34. Humphrey, "Dissection and Discrimination," pp. 273–74.

35. Genovese, *Roll, Jordan, Roll*, p. 226. Genovese writes that the slaves' "hostility toward white physicians had roots not only in an awareness of widespread ignorance and incompetence in the medical profession, but in their awareness that too many physicians used slaves as guinea pigs for their pet theories and remedies." See also Savitt, "Blacks as Medical Specimens," in *Medicine and Slavery*, pp. 281–307.

36. See Kiple and Kiple, "African Connection," p. 215, and Savitt, *Medicine and Slavery*, pp. 282, 287–88. Savitt's study focuses on Virginia, but its findings apply to other southern states as well. See also Savitt's valuable article "Use of Blacks," pp. 331–48, which offers the most thorough and concise treatment of this subject.

37. Savitt reports that Thomas Jefferson conducted an experiment in 1801 that involved vaccinating some two hundred slaves with cowpox in order to prevent smallpox (*Medicine and Slavery*, pp. 296–97).

38. Ibid., p. 301.

39. Ibid., p. 299. Dr. Walter F. Jones of Petersburg, testing a remedy for typhoid pneumonia on an unnamed number of patients, described its application on a very sick, weak twenty-five-year-old male slave: "The patient was placed [naked] on the floor on his face, and about five gallons of water at a temperature so near the boiling point as barely to allow the immersion of the hand, was thrown immediately on the spinal column, which seemed to arouse his sensibilities somewhat, as shown by an effort to cry out."

40. Ibid., pp. 302–3.

41. Ibid., p. 283.

42. Fry's documentation in *Night Riders* of the prevalence of night doctor legends demonstrates black people's fear of hospitals. See also Savitt, *Medicine and Slavery*, pp. 239, 245, 281–83; Starr, *Social Transformation of American Medicine*. In the chapter titled "The Reconstitution of the Hospital," Starr discusses the transformation of hospitals from "places of dreaded human impurity and exiled human wreckage into awesome citadels of science and bureaucratic order" (p. 144). He notes that in the eighteenth and nineteenth centuries, "particularly distrustful were the sick poor, who feared they might be used for surgical experiments or, in the event of death, turned over to medical students for dissection" (p. 152).

43. Humphrey, "Dissection and Discrimination," pp. 270–74.

44. Ibid. See also Savitt, *Medicine and Slavery*, pp. 290–93. Savitt writes, "There is little doubt that most of Virginia's dissection subjects were procured from midnight graveyard expeditions, and that most of these cadavers were black" (p. 292).

45. See Savitt, *Medicine and Slavery*, pp. 7–8; Cartwright, "Diseases and Peculiarities of the Negro Race"; Guillory, "Pro-Slavery Arguments"; Haller, *Outcasts from Evolution*; Shufeldt, *The Negro*.

46. The introduction to Savitt's *Medicine and Slavery*, titled "Were Blacks Medically Different from Whites?" (pp. 7–47), covers this discussion. An excellent article on the subject is Kenneth and Virginia Kiple's "African Connec-

tion." They comment, "As disease immunities in blacks were twisted and turned back on them, so were their disease susceptibilities" (p. 213).

47. Savitt, *Medicine and Slavery*, pp. 7–8. See also Cartwright, "Diseases and Peculiarities of the Negro Race," pp. 26–43. The preface to this article states, "Numerous Southern physicians such as Cartwright used their medical experience as the basis for developing quasi-scientific explanations for Negro inferiority" (p. 26). See also Guillory, "Pro-Slavery Arguments," pp. 209–27. Guillory writes, "Louisiana medical men waged a relentless campaign to secure medical independence from the North by trying to convince young Southerners that they could receive proper medical training only by attending Southern schools. . . . [The criticism] directed at the Northern medical profession included charges that Northern teachers had incomplete knowledge of many Southern diseases, that Northern doctors were totally ignorant of a special variety of 'diseases' which afflicted only Negroes. . . . The states' doctors [also] labored to defend the Southern contention that Negro slavery was morally right" (pp. 209–10). American doctors in general argued that Americans had different constitutions than Europeans and required different kinds of treatment; white southern doctors were unique in asserting black inferiority as a basis for different treatment. See Warner, "Selective Transport of Medical Knowledge," pp. 213–31; Warner, "Southern Medical Reform"; and Warner, *Therapeutic Perspective*.

48. See Lee and Lee, "Health of Slaves and Freedmen"; Legan, "Disease and the Freedmen"; Hasson, "Health and Welfare of Freedmen"; Foster, "Limitations of Federal Health Care." Segregation studies are cited elsewhere.

49. See Haller, *Outcasts from Evolution*, and Gould, *Mismeasure of Man*. Gould comments, "I criticize the myth that science itself is an objective enterprise. . . . Rather, I believe that science must be understood as a social phenomenon, a gutsy, human enterprise, not the work of robots programmed to collect pure information. . . . Science, since people must do it, is a socially embedded activity. It progresses by hunch, vision, and intuition. Much of its change through time does not record a closer approach to absolute truth, but the alteration of cultural contexts. . . . Facts are not pure and unsullied bit of information; culture also influences what we see and how we see it" (pp. 21–22).

50. Black writer Ernest Gaines's novel *A Gathering of Old Men*, about a group of elderly black sharecroppers who decide to risk death and stand up for a fellow sharecropper who has been accused of murdering their white boss, has one of the old men explain his action to his wife thus: " 'Oliver, woman!' I screamed at her. 'Oliver, How they let him die in the hospital just 'cause he was black. No doctor to serve him, let him bleed to death, 'cause he was black. And you ask me what's the matter with me?' " (p. 38). See also Gaines's short story "The Sky Is Gray," about a black child forced to endure a terrible toothache because he has to wait a long time for treatment from a white doctor.

　　In 1973 June Jordan wrote a poem called "For Michael Angelo Thompson," about a black youth who died when a Brooklyn hospital turned him away after he was struck by a city bus:

It was the city took him off
the hospital
that turned him down the hospital
that turned away from so much beauty
bleeding
bleeding
in Black struggle
just to live . . . (Rich, *What Is Found There*, pp. 64–68)

And in Alice Walker's novel about a civil rights worker, *Meridian*, it is "rumored that . . . [a young black boy has been] stolen by the local hospital for use in experiments." The story's civil rights activists try to get arrested "in protest against the town's segregated hospital facilities" (p. 35). In one scene, an activist trying to enlist a poor black man in the movement asks him, "Do you want free medicines for your wife? A hospital that'll take black people through the front door?" (p. 83).

Toni Morrison's 1977 novel, *Song of Solomon*, begins with a scene outside a white hospital known to the black characters as "No Mercy Hospital." From its roof, a black man trying to fly leaps to his death. The black boy who is the novel's hero and who after many trials learns how to fly in a spiritual sense is the first black child actually born in the hospital in 1931 (pp. 3–9). See also Welty, "A Worn Path," in *Collected Stories*, pp. 142–49.

51. Ellison, *Invisible Man*, pp. 231–33.

52. Ibid., pp. 234–35.

53. Ibid., pp. 231–36.

54. Fry, *Night Riders*, p. 210. Fry demonstrates not only that historical circumstances gave rise to this oral tradition but also that the oral tradition, in turn, had historical consequences: "to the folk, it was a dreary, dreadful business in which the night doctors were supposedly engaged. Not only did one have to fear a mysterious kidnapping and sudden death, but the terrifying thought of having one's blood drained, drop by drop — only to wind up in dismembered parts carefully scrutinized by over eager medical students . . . — was enough to give the average man pause. And it did. At least until the 1930s a number of disadvantaged people chose to avoid certain cities altogether, certain parts of cities in the daytime (areas adjacent to hospitals), and many avoided traveling at all at night unless accompanied by small groups" (pp. 210–11).

55. The following discussion of the hospital is based primarily on Bordley and Harvey, *Two Centuries of American Medicine*, pp. 277–92. Bordley and Harvey use a study by Corwin (1946) to show the dramatic growth of hospitals in the twentieth century: in 1873 there were 178 institutions providing inpatient care for the sick in the United States; probably only 149 of these were actual hospitals. The total number of patients receiving hospital care in 1873 was 146,472. By 1943 there were 6,655 hospitals with 1,649,254 beds, and during that year 15,374,698 patients were treated in hospitals (p. 288).

56. Stevens, *American Medicine and the Public Interest*, p. 135. Many other books also document the enormous changes in the American medical profession during this period. Major scientific breakthroughs include Louis Pasteur's

and Robert Koch's development of bacteriology in the late nineteenth century, the subsequent development of endocrinology as a science, and the vast improvement of surgery as a medical intervention in the early twentieth century due to the development both of anesthetics and of antiseptic and aseptic procedures.

57. Blood loss is feared in primitive societies. See Titmuss, *Gift Relationship*, pp. 15–16, and Turnbull, *Forest People*, p. 185. Turnbull comments, "Blood of any kind is a terrible and powerful thing [to the villagers], associated with injury and sickness and death."

58. Miles interview; Clemen interview; Parker interview. Charlene Drew Jarvis, "Needed: Black Americans to Save Black American Lives," *Washington Post*, 13 February 1994; Lori Teresa Yearwood, "A Martyr No More: Racism didn't kill Drew, after all," *Miami Herald*, 6 February 1994, p. 1; Robert Siegel, "Story of Dr. Charles Drew's Death a Modern Myth," National Public Radio, "All Things Considered," 23 February 1994; Patrice Gaines, "Armed with the Truth in a Fight for Lives," *Washington Post*, 10 April 1994, p. B5. Richard Titmuss pointed out in his book about blood donors that South African apartheid and American segregation, accompanied by the practice of labeling donated blood, have undoubtedly affected the willingness of blacks to give blood. He also noted the ironic fact that captive populations in the United States, South Africa, and other developed Western nations — namely indigent people and prisoners, many of whom are black — have been the major "providers" of both blood and teaching and research material "needed to sustain the fabric of medical systems" (*Gift Relationship*, pp. 188–94 and 220).

59. Shick, "Race, Class, and Medicine," pp. 101–3.

60. Tellers of the Drew legend often pair Drew's mistreatment with Bessie Smith's mistreatment. A black nurse believed Drew and Smith had suffered exactly the same fate (Vine interview). A black doctor who knew the Drew legend was not true but believed the Smith legend termed the Drew story a "take-off on the old Bessie Smith story, [which] no one [had ever] denied" (Shanks interview, 8 February 1983). The author of the Whitney Young column about Drew's death, who believed the Drew legend at the time and later learned it wasn't true, speculated, "I wondered later if someone had confused Drew's story with Bessie Smith's" (Brooks interview). A friend of Drew's who reported hearing the Drew legend shortly after his death commented, "The same thing had happened to a black singer" (Cook interview).

61. The most reliable account of Bessie Smith's death is found in Chris Albertson's biography, *Bessie*, pp. 215–26. As with Drew, none of the newspapers that immediately reported her death created the legend about her. However, a month after her death, an activist-writer named John Hammond wrote an article in *downbeat* magazine based on hearsay, titled "Did Bessie Smith Bleed to Death While Waiting for Medical Aid?," that fueled the rumors already circulating. In response to angry protest from hospital authorities, *downbeat* soon afterward carried a follow-up article debunking the Smith legend, saying she had been taken directly to Clarksdale's black hospi-

tal, "where she had died due to loss of blood." Despite this article and another debunking article in *downbeat*'s 17 October 1957 issue and yet another debunking article in *Esquire*—"The True Death of Bessie Smith," published in 1969—the legend inevitably lived on (pp. 215–19).

62. Albee, *Death of Bessie Smith.*

63. Albertson, *Bessie*, p. 218.

64. Moore, *Somebody's Angel Child*, p. 109. In this juvenile biography Moore incorporated some of the facts about Smith's death but nonetheless repeated the legend: "One ambulance rushed off toward Clarksdale . . . [with Bessie] inside. When they arrived at the large hospital in Clarksdale, the officials at the emergency ward informed Richard [Smith's companion] that they would not treat Negroes but that they could be helped at the G. T. Thomas and Funeral Home in the same town. Time passed. Bessie was bleeding to death. . . . They arrived at the G. T. Thomas Hospital. Bessie . . . slipped away."

65. Martin Luther King Jr., *Testament of Hope*, p. xxi.

66. Frazier, *Afro-American History*, pp. 105–6.

67. Ibid., pp. 64–75, 67.

68. Ibid., pp. 117, 119.

69. Ibid., p. 143.

70. Du Bois, *Souls of Black Folk*, pp. 275–76.

71. Martin Luther King Jr., *Testament of Hope*, p. 18.

72. Martin Luther King Jr., "Eulogy for the Martyred Children," in ibid., pp. 221–22.

73. Bilbo referred to Leslie P. Hill, who was a friend of Charles Drew (see Chapter 6): "According to . . . Hill, colored President of State Teachers College, Cheyney, Pennsylvania: 'A thousand years was needed to document and verify the assurance of the most vigorous of all the saints that God has made of one blood all the nations of men. But the laboratories did in the end indubitably produce the proof.'" Bilbo commented, "With such statements as these, men are supposed to be led to believe that there is no difference in the blood of the white and black races and that it is in accordance with the teachings of Almighty God that the blood of these races should mix freely" (*Take Your Choice*, p. 108).

74. Warren, *Segregation*, p. 44; emphasis in the original.

75. Jacobs, *Incidents in the Life*, p. 45.

76. Bontemps, *Great Slave Narratives*, p. 270.

77. Martin Luther King Jr., "Ethical Demands for Integration," in *Testament of Hope*, pp. 121–22.

78. A number of sources inform this description of the movement, but the most important have been Chafe, *Unfinished Journey*; Sitkoff, *Struggle for Black Equality*; Martin Luther King Jr., *Testament of Hope*; Carson, *In Struggle*; Harding, *Hope and History*; Carson et al., *Eyes on the Prize Reader*, and the *Eyes on the Prize* television series.

79. Whitney Young, *To Be Equal.*

80. Sitkoff, *Struggle for Black Equality*, p. 135.

81. Weiss, *Whitney M. Young, Jr.*, p. 155.

82. *Baltimore (Md.) Afro-American*, 17 October 1964, p. A5.

83. Pennington interview.

84. Brooks interview.

85. See Morais, *History of the Afro-American in Medicine*, pp. 159–88, and Beardsley, *History of Neglect*, pp. 245–309, for overviews of segregated medical care in this era.

86. See Morais, *History of the Afro-American in Medicine*, pp. 181, 244.

87. Chafe, *Unfinished Journey*, pp. 365, 343.

88. Sitkoff, *Struggle for Black Equality*, pp. 134–54.

89. Ibid., pp. 161–65, especially p. 164.

90. Ibid., pp. 185–92.

91. Ibid., p. 196.

92. Ibid., pp. 208–9.

93. Martin Luther King Jr., "I See the Promised Land," in *Testament of Hope*, p. 286.

94. William Loren Katz, *Eyewitness*, p. 449 (1967 or 1968 edition).

95. William Loren Katz to Marvin E. Yount Jr., 1 May 1971, Yount Papers.

96. See Harding, *Beyond Chaos*; Williams and Harris, *Amistad 2*, especially Stuckey, "Twilight of Our Past: Reflections of the Origins of Black History," pp. 261–95; Wood, " 'I Did the Best I Could for My Day' "; Meier and Rudwick, "On the Dilemmas of Scholarship in Afro-American History," in *Black History and the Historical Profession*, pp. 277–308.

97. Fitzgerald, *America Revised*, pp. 178–79, 190–92, 201.

98. Sterling, *Tear Down the Walls*, p. 154.

99. "Races: Black Vacuum," *Time*, 29 March 1968, 26.

100. "Dr. Charles Drew: Blood Bank Pioneer Who Bled to Death," *Sepia* 17 (December 1968): 48–49.

101. *Webster's Biographical Dictionary*, p. 292.

102. Thirlee Smith, "For Ghetto Kids, A Widow Recalls Blood Researcher," *Miami Herald*, [1970] (photocopy located in Folder 19, Box 134-12, CRDP).

103. Louise Montgomery, "Kids Talk with History," *Miami Herald*, Broward News Section, 21 November 1970 (photocopy located in Folder 19, Box 134-12, CRDP).

104. Memo from John C. Wilson to Clyde Buckingham, 15 May 1967 (attachment to Buckingham, "Dr. Charles Richard Drew").

105. Wynes, *Charles Richard Drew*, p. 63.

106. "Kinsmen Seek Official Day for Noted Figure," *Willingboro (N.J.) News-Press*, 21 December 1967, p. 1 (photocopy from CD-ARC-NH).

107. Alexander J. Repke, executive director of the Burlington County (N.J.) chapter of the American Red Cross, to Janet Livingston, administrative director of the Philadelphia Regional Blood Program, 27 December 1967, CD-ARC-NH.

108. Memo from Jack Henry, administrative director, Blood Program, 9 January 1968, CD-ARC-NH.

109. Susan N. Greene of Cambridge, Mass., to American Red Cross, 12 September 1971, CD-ARC-NH.

110. Pete Upton, national director of public relations, American Red Cross, to Susan N. Greene, 16 September 1971, CD-ARC-NH. Upton noted, "There are several versions of the [Drew] story. One that it happened in Virginia, another that he was refused blood by a hospital in Atlanta, though Atlanta is 400 miles away from the scene of the accident."

111. Yount interview, 19 January 1983. The book was written by William Loren Katz and first published in 1967.

112. Marvin Yount to Pitman Publishing Company, 26 February 1971, Yount Papers.

113. Enclosure with letter from Joan B. Nagy to Marvin E. Yount Jr., 1 April 1971, Yount Papers.

114. Marvin Yount Jr. to Joan B. Nagy, 23 April 1971, Yount Papers.

115. Edward Wagner to Marvin E. Yount Jr., 10 May 1971, Yount Papers. This deletion may be observed by comparing the original 1967 edition of the William Loren Katz book, *Eyewitness*, with the 1971 edition.

116. O. B. Okon, "Charles Richard Drew and the Black Week-end Science Symposium," *Kujichagulia* (Self-Determination) Umoja Newsletter, 14 April 1972, p. 3 (found in Folder 4, Box 135-12, CRDP).

117. Okon, "Charles Richard Drew," p. 2.

118. Ernestine Venture Fleming to Mrs. Nora Drew, 10 April 1950, Folder 2, Box 134-1, CRDP.

119. Georgia Douglas Johnson, "To Charles R. Drew," typed sheet dated 1954–55, Folder 2, Box 135-2, CRDP.

120. Okon, "Charles Richard Drew," p. 8.

121. Chalmers, *Crooked Places Made Straight*, p. 78.

122. Chafe, *Unfinished Journey*, pp. 430–32.

123. Ibid., pp. 442, 437–45.

124. Hamilton Bims, "Charles Drew's 'Other' Medical Revolution," *Ebony*, February 1974, pp. 88–96.

125. Bims, "Drew's 'Other' Revolution," p. 88.

126. Tom Tiede, "One Myth We Can Do Without," *Reidsville (N.C.) Review*, 14 March 1975.

127. Jay Ashley, "Grim Reaper Claimed Him Here," *Burlington (N.C.) Times-News*, 1 April 1980.

128. Stan Swofford, "Witness Dispels Myth in Black Doctor's Death," *Greensboro (N.C.) Daily News*, 11 July 1982, pp. A1, A3.

129. Yancey, "U.S. Postage Stamp," pp. 561–65.

130. Sampson, "Dispelling the Myth," pp. 415–18.

131. Katherine Fulton, "Between the Races, the Past's Shadow," *Nation*, 18 May 1985, pp. 590–93.

132. McCown interview, 20 November 1985.

133. Quick interview.

134. "A Racial Myth," *Greensboro (N.C.) Daily News*, 16 July 1982.

135. See Organ and Kosiba, *Century of Black Surgeons*, pp. 197–249, for a thorough discussion of Homer G. Phillips Hospital and the man it was named after. Phillips, a lawyer rather than a doctor, apparently did not bleed to death from a hospital refusal but was assassinated in 1931 "for reasons

never clearly ascertained." However, a young black intern, Bernise A. Yancey, died on duty in 1930 in a scandalous and unnecessary accident in the old hospital that Phillips had campaigned to replace. Yancey was electrocuted making an X-ray of a patient's chest because he was forced to use a defective, outdated X-ray machine. Thus, the origins of the Phillips "legend" are obvious (pp. 213–14).

136. Mark C. Turner to the Editor, *Burlington (N.C.) Times-News*, 10 August 1982.
137. Videotape of *M*A*S*H* episode supplied by Matthew Rauchberg, July 1995, Los Angeles, Calif.
138. Phillip McGuire, *Carolina Comments* 28, no. 2 (March 1980): 47.
139. Samuel A. Tower, "He Pioneered the Preservation of Blood Plasma," *New York Times*, 14 June 1981, p. D40.
140. James A. Able, "What Color Blood," *Summerville (S.C.) Journal-Scene*, 30 December 1981; *Southern Pines (N.C.) Pilot*, 18 November 1981.
141. Observation by author, Pleasant Grove, N.C., 5 April 1986.
142. "Society Honors Black Surgeons," *Duke University Dialogue*, 14 April 1989, pp. 1, 5.
143. Akwari interview.
144. Wynes, *Charles Richard Drew*, p. 119.
145. Mitchell interview, 10 September 1985; Walker interview, Duke University student; Darlene Hine, historian, speech at University of North Carolina School of Social Work, Spring 1987, Chapel Hill, N.C. (reported by Susan Worley).
146. Robinson interview.
147. Young interview. Questioned further, Young commented that he didn't know what to believe about Drew. He knew that black people believed Drew had bled to death and that white people tended to believe he had been treated properly. He said that having grown up in eastern North Carolina himself, he could imagine that Drew had bled to death. "I remember how black people, during that period, ate in little restaurants, had to go to the back door, drove packed in cars, drove all night if they had to, and they used to get killed all the time."
148. Richards interview.
149. Interview with Miles, American Red Cross head recruiter, District of Columbia headquarters; interview with Clemen, American Red Cross information research specialist, national headquarters, Washington, D.C. A supervisor at Harlem Hospital's blood bank noted in 1985, "Neither blacks nor Puerto Ricans want to give blood. They feel they are losing a part of themselves" (Parker interview). This same woman believed a version of the Drew legend: "Isn't [Drew] the man who died in front of that hospital because they wouldn't give him a transfusion? Wasn't he a black man?"
150. Clemen interview.
151. Charlene Drew Jarvis, "Needed: Black Americans to Save Black American Lives," *Washington Post*, 13 February 1994; Lori Teresa Yearwood, "A Martyr No More: Racism didn't kill Drew, after all," *Miami Herald*, 6 February 1994, p. 1; Robert Siegel, "Story of Dr. Charles Drew's Death a Modern

Myth," National Public Radio, "All Things Considered," 23 February 1994; Patrice Gaines, "Armed With the Truth in a Fight for Lives," *Washington Post*, 10 April 1994, p. B5.

152. Grier and Cobbs, *Black Rage*, p. 31.

CHAPTER FOUR

1. Campbell, *Hero with a Thousand Faces*, pp. 16, 19–20.
2. One scholarly biography has been written about Drew: Wynes, *Charles Richard Drew*. This work offers an accurate, thorough, highly readable account of Drew's beginnings. However, popular biographies of Drew abound, spawning stereotypes. One juvenile biography opens with young Drew portrayed as a very dark-skinned boy fishing for catfish in the Potomac River, chatting with an old carpenter about his life as a slave (Bertol, *Charles Drew*, p. 3). Another more detailed juvenile biography opens with Drew at Amherst, facing a dean about his low grades and sobbing as he excuses himself for his failure by saying that his background in segregated schools made him unable to compete (Lichello, *Pioneer in Blood Plasma*, pp. 24–25). Lichello also describes Drew as wearing patched pants (p. 31), calls him "a poor colored boy" (p. 42), and refers to Drew's father as a peasant "ill at ease in a world foreign to him" when visiting his son at his college (p. 35). The first popular biography of Drew — Hardwick, *Charles Richard Drew* — was another highly fictionalized version of Drew's life aimed at a juvenile audience; it focused on him as a good boy determined to succeed despite the obstacles in his path.
3. Joseph Drew interview, 12 June 1985.
4. W. Montague Cobb, "Charles Richard Drew," p. 239.
5. Joseph Drew interview, 12 June 1985. Joseph Drew was Charles Drew's brother. This interview and two others, on 31 July 1985 and 25 September 1985, were the major sources for the material on Drew's childhood, unless otherwise noted.
6. Ibid.
7. Established by Congress in 1870 as the Preparatory High School for Negro Youth, it became known as the M Street High School in 1891, after a move to new quarters; it was transformed into the more famous Dunbar High School in 1916, when a new building was erected. The M Street High School deserves as much credit for excellence as its more famous offspring, according to its graduates. Two articles describe its curriculum, principals, and teachers in detail: Rayford W. Logan, "Growing Up in Washington," and Robinson, "M Street High School." Logan wrote, "M Street High School was one of the best high schools in the nation, colored or white, public or private" (p. 503).
8. Richard Drew wore a moustache to conceal the scar on his lip from a boxing match (Wynes, *Charles Richard Drew*, p. 7).
9. Pennington interview. Pennington is Charles Drew's youngest sister.
10. Joseph Drew interview, 12 June 1985.
11. Nora Gregory interview. Gregory is Drew's oldest surviving sister.

12. Joseph Drew interview, 12 June 1985.

13. See Rayford W. Logan, *Betrayal of the Negro*, and Kirby, *Darkness at the Dawning*.

14. For statistics on lynchings, see Hall, *Revolt against Chivalry*, pp. 133–35; see also NAACP, *Thirty Years of Lynching*, and Raper, *Tragedy of Lynching*.

15. See Kousser, *Shaping of Southern Politics*.

16. See Woodward, *Strange Career*; Pauli Murray, *States' Laws*; and Cell, *Highest Stage of White Supremacy*.

17. Lewis, *District of Columbia*, p. 71. Lewis's chapter on black Washington, "The Tale of the Second City," is a useful short summary based on Green, *Secret City*, the comprehensive work.

18. Green, *Secret City*, p. 171.

19. Chase, " 'Shelling the Citadel of Race Prejudice,' " p. 371.

20. Lewis, *District of Columbia*, p. 71.

21. Gatewood, *Aristocrats of Color*, p. 39. Gatewood's chapter titled "Washington: Capital of the Colored Aristocracy" captures the flavor of life for this group (pp. 39–68). See also Moldow, *Women Doctors in Gilded-Age Washington*.

22. Lewis, *District of Columbia*, p. 73.

23. Ibid., p. 74; Green, *Secret City*, pp. 141–42.

24. Gatewood, *Aristocrats of Color*, pp. 49–61.

25. Joseph Drew interview, 12 June 1985; Wynes, *Charles Richard Drew*, p. 7. Wynes traces Drew's ancestry as follows: "His father, Richard, born in 1878 in Washington, was the son of Richard Thomas, Sr. (1852–1915), and Martha (Taylor) Drew (1859–1908). Richard Thomas, Sr., Drew's grandfather, came to Washington sometime in the 1870s from Charlottesville, Virginia, while his grandmother, Martha Taylor, came from Winchester, Virginia. Drew's great-grandfather, Thomas Drew (1828–68 or 1870), was a barber and a free man in Charlottesville, while his great-grandmother, Elizabeth (last name unknown), reportedly was part Indian. . . . Drew's mother, Nora (1880–1962), was the daughter of Emma (Mann) Burrell (1859–1926), and the granddaughter of Robert and Margaret (Freeman) Mann (dates?) of Upperville, Virginia. Margaret was white. Nora's father, Joseph, was born in Georgetown, District of Columbia."

26. Eva Drew Pennington, Drew's sister, said that she and some other family members believed that their mother's father, their grandfather, was a white man. Drew's mother, Nora Rosella Burrell Drew, was born eight years before any of her other eight siblings, and before her mother—Emma Mann of Double Poplars, Virginia—married Joseph Burrell. Mrs. Pennington speculated that she had had a liaison with either a Catholic priest or Senator Mann of Virginia, whom the Drew children apparently strongly resemble (Pennington interview).

27. See Holt, Smith-Parker, and Terborg-Penn, *Special Mission*; Moldow, *Women Doctors in Gilded-Age Washington*, especially pp. 37–47; W. Montague Cobb, *First Negro Medical Society*; Morais, *History of the Afro-American in Medicine*, pp. 48–58.

28. Green, *Secret City*, pp. 50–51.

29. Ibid., p. 169.

30. Both Charles Drew and his brother, Joseph Drew, were later to belong to this

exclusive fraternity, as were many of their friends and colleagues. Their father was not a member.

31. Green, *Secret City,* p. 179.

32. Historian Rayford Logan described Brooks, who was his pastor, as "one of the best influences in my young life. . . . He was a mighty Baptist preacher, a graduate of Lincoln University in Pennsylvania . . . He preached hell, fire and blood. But he preached also the social gospel and temperance. He had his own daughter, Antoinette [a childhood friend of Charles Drew], put out of church for dancing" (Logan, "Growing Up in Washington," p. 505).

33. Joseph Drew interview, 31 July 1985; he said that Elsie Drew had also suffered from tuberculosis. The riot was "ignited by rumors of black men attacking white women. Blacks fought back, importing weapons from Baltimore, and mulatto veterans in offices' uniforms circulated in white areas to gain intelligence. Blacks were proud of their solidarity and whites were sobered by it" (Lewis, *District of Columbia,* p. 74).

34. Wynes, *Charles Richard Drew,* pp. 10–11; Lewis, *District of Columbia,* pp. 106–8; Sowell, *Black Education,* pp. 108, 283–86.

35. Rayford W. Logan, "Growing Up in Washington," pp. 500–507. Logan does, however, recall "the horror and fear of lynching" (p. 506), which was reported on regularly in the black newspapers of the period.

36. Nora Gregory interview.

37. Ulysses S. Wharton, M.D., speech about Charles Drew after his death, Pittsburgh, Pa., undated, Folder 2, Box 134-1, CRDP. In the speech, Wharton said that he talked with Drew's mother shortly after his death and she told him about his intense crying as an infant.

38. Charles Drew to Nora Drew, undated letter from period 1928–32, Folder 1, Box 135-2, CRDP.

39. Charles Drew to Lenore Robbins, 21 April 1939, Folder 4, Box 135-1, CRDP. Drew's mother wrote him a supportive letter in this same period after he told her he was worried about having enough money to get married: "We only come this way once so why not begin your family life while you are still young. . . . Now Son a little more hard work there and clear thinking and you will be on top" (Nora Drew to Charles Drew, 4 August 1939, Folder 13, Box 135-1, CRDP).

40. Quite a few of Drew's letters to both of his parents are preserved, and these letters amply reveal his devotion to them both. Just after arriving at Columbia University in 1938, Drew wrote his mother, "Each new step has marked growth in a thousand ways, yet through it all I have seemed to remain essentially the same; the people and things dear to me from a very long time ago retain, and probably always shall retain first place in my thinking and feeling, so much so that though separated from them, never estranged and the living force in this intangible bond which holds so tightly is you" (Charles Drew to Nora Drew, 18 June 1938, Folder 15, Box 134-3, CRDP).

41. Nora Gregory interview.

42. Pennington interview.

43. W. Montague Cobb, "Charles Richard Drew," p. 240.

44. Rayford W. Logan, "Growing Up in Washington," pp. 504–5.

45. Charles Drew to Edwin B. Henderson, 31 May 1940, Folder 6, Box 136-1, CRDP.
46. Joseph Drew interview, 12 June 1985.
47. Cobb interview.
48. *Saturae*, Dunbar High School Yearbook, Washington, D.C., 1922, Folder 15, Box 134-5, CRDP.
49. Charles Drew to Lenore Robbins, "Sunday morning" [Summer 1939], Folder 11, Box 135-1, CRDP.
50. Lenore Drew interview; Wade, *Black Men of Amherst*. Wade points out that Drew was one of a generation of blacks at Amherst who came across to later militant black writers as culturally white: these writers described several of this group as " 'black Afro-Saxons,' . . . because their demeanor or style appeared basically elitist and non-ghetto. It has been held against them that their style was such that when in the presence of white people it was possible for whites to temporarily lose consciousness of the fact that they were in the presence of black Americans" (p. 41).
51. Hamilton Bims, "Charles Drew's 'Other' Medical Revolution," *Ebony*, February 1974, p. 88; Wynes, *Charles Richard Drew*, pp. 15–16.
52. Cobb interview.
53. Newton F. McKeon, "Charles Richard Drew, '26," *Amherst Alumni News*, May 1950, p. 184.
54. McKeon, "Charles Richard Drew," p. 184.
55. D. O. "Tuss" McLaughry, "The Best Player I Ever Coached," *Saturday Evening Post*, December 1952.
56. W. Montague Cobb, "Charles Richard Drew," p. 241. Cobb notes that many of Drew's students, the alumni of his Morgan teams, went on to become well-known athletes and coaches.
57. Charles Drew, Athletic Director, Morgan College, Baltimore, Md., "College Athletics," *The Morganite*, undated, pp. 7–8, attachment to letter: J. O. Spencer, president of Morgan College, to Charles Drew, Amherst College, 14 June 1926, Joseph Drew Papers.
58. Nora Drew Gregory interview.
59. David Hepburn, "The Life of Dr. Charles R. Drew," *Our World*, July 1950, p. 25.
60. Charles R. Drew, application to McGill University Medical School, 1 July 1928, excerpt from memorandum prepared by Andrew Allen, information office director, for E. H. Bensley, 25 February 1975, McGill University Medical School, E. H. Bensley Papers, Montreal, Canada.
61. W. Montague Cobb, "Charles Richard Drew," p. 241.
62. Cobb interview.
63. Oliver Pilat, "A New Plateau of Life," *Amherst Alumni News*, undated (found in Folder 2, Box 135-7, CRDP). Pilat writes, "Drew . . . took the advice of Old Doc Newport, the trainer, to step aside tactfully for some worthy white boy" (p. 27).
64. W. Montague Cobb, "Charles Richard Drew," p. 240. Cobb writes,

It was customary for the outstanding third year man on any team to be elected captain for his senior year. Fraternity politics entered sometimes, but in cases where there was no question as to the best performer, the custom was regularly followed. Drew was unchallenged top man in two sports and thus would have been expected to have been chosen captain of both football and track teams. In the class ahead of him, however, the logical candidate in the case of both the cross country and track captaincies was also Negro, and passed over. There was campus discussion, and the racial problem recurred, for the next major team election was for football captain. Again the Negro, this time Charley, was passed over. The conscience of the College was aroused by these three successive reversals of custom and open criticism was heard. When track election was held the following spring, Drew, as the team's high scorer, was unanimously elected captain.... There was a student group called "Scarab" composed of ten or a dozen seniors who were recognized as the most outstanding men on campus from the standpoint of all-round achievement. Scarab tapped its own successors each year from the Junior Class. Charley was a logical choice, but again was passed over.

65. Cobb interview.
66. Ibid.
67. Wade, *Black Men of Amherst*, p. 41. Wade discusses the careers of several of Drew's famous classmates, among them William Hastie, the first black federal judge; W. Montague Cobb; Mercer Cook, a noted French and African literature scholar and a U.S. ambassador to Senegal; and Ben Davis, a civil rights lawyer and New York City councilman elected on a Communist Party ticket. Wade comments, "It was the black bourgeoisie which led the civil rights movement because it was they who found most bitter the role of Nigger, despite their erstwhile strivings and class" (p. 62).
68. Pilat, "New Plateau," p. 27.
69. Neither John Scudder, whom Drew and others credit with much of the research and organizational work that made the blood plasma program possible, nor Earle Taylor, who became the director of the New York City American Red Cross blood plasma program after Drew left, or G. Canby Robinson, who became the first national director of the American Red Cross blood program, are legendary figures today.
70. "Helen" of Amherst, Mass., to Charles Drew, 4 June 1928, Joseph Drew Papers. One can surmise that "Helen" is white from her statement that she is an "ardent admirer of your [Drew's] people."
71. The "Helen" letter and a number of others written to Drew at this period of his life, most of them from women friends and all contained in the Joseph Drew Papers, reveal Drew's impressive seriousness. To one important girlfriend of this period, Lee Waller, Drew at times was like a big brother and almost a godlike figure. In one letter she wrote, "I feel all alone and little and scared in the darkness—there's just one light place and it's you dear—please reach out your big strong hand and keep me from stumbling in the darkness and keep me from being afraid. Charlie, you're not merely a brother—a sweetheart or a friend to me—You're Everything!" (Lee Waller in Springfield, Mass., to Charles Drew at Morgan College, May). In another letter she wrote, "I know Charlie, that you are far, far too perfect for me, but I shall try to deserve it" (Lee Waller in Westerly, R.I., to Charles Drew in Rosslyn, Va., 20 July 1926).

72. Useful articles outlining the status of black physicians during the first half of the twentieth century include Beardsley, "Making Separate, Equal"; Savitt, "Entering a White Profession"; and Louis T. Wright, M.D., "The Negro Physician," *Crisis* 36:9 (September 1929): 305–6. Wright comments, "As to Postgraduate training, the opportunities are very meager indeed. . . . On the whole they [blacks] are not welcome nor desired in most postgraduate schools. This is especially true as far as clinical courses are concerned. . . . Many of these physicians, therefore, who desire to do postgraduate work of a sound character, have been forced to go to Europe to study. It is a serious indictment of American institutions that so many Negro physicians have been forced to go to Europe to receive adequate clinical training of a postgraduate nature" (p. 305). Dr. Wright was one of the first fully trained black surgeons, and like many other black specialists of his generation, he received it through "paternalistic means," according to Charles Watts (Watts interview, 6 July 1988). See also Walter White, *Fire in the Flint*, and Manning, *Black Apollo of Science.*

73. Manning, *Black Apollo of Science*, pp. 210, 329.

74. See Roman, *Meharry Medical College*; Summerville, *Educating Black Doctors*; and Holt, Smith-Parker, and Terborg-Penn, *Special Mission.*

75. The limitations imposed on black doctors and the consequences for black health care in the twentieth century has been studied in a number of books and articles: see Reitzes, *Negroes and Medicine*; Savitt, "Entering a White Profession"; Organ and Kosiba, *Century of Black Surgeons*; W. Montague Cobb, "Medical Care and the Plight of the Negro" and "Progress and Portents"; Morais, *History of the Afro-American in Medicine* (especially chapter 6, "Against Great Odds," pp. 89–110); and Beardsley, *History of Neglect* (especially chapter 4, "Black Physicians and the Health of Their People, 1900–1940," pp. 77–100). Beardsley notes,

> Before 1940 the fifty-five or so white schools that took black applicants produced altogether no more than twenty black physicians each year. By contrast Howard and Meharry annually graduated somewhere between 100 and 125. So Howard and Meharry offered the only real opportunities for the aspiring black student. But until the 1930s, when substantial foundation support . . . finally produced a general upgrading, the quality of the average Howard and Meharry graduate left something to be desired. Between 1920 and 1946 an average of 54 percent of Meharry's graduates and 26 percent of Howard's failed their medical boards. That fraction compared poorly with the average of 6 to 7 percent from Harvard and Washington universities—or the 13 percent from Southern white colleges—who had to re-sit their exams. (p. 78)

76. Wade, *Black Men of Amherst*, p. 49. A letter to Drew from a Harvard Medical School official indicates that he applied too late and that an earlier letter he had written the school was lost (Louisa C. Richardson to Charles R. Drew, 4 June 1928, Joseph Drew Papers).

77. W. Montague Cobb, "Charles Richard Drew," p. 242. Cobb notes, "Howard required eight hours of English and (Drew) . . . had had only six hours which met the standard requirement at all other medical schools" (pp. 241–42).

78. Ibid., p. 240.
79. Charles Drew to Richard Drew ("Pa"), undated, Folder 17, Box 134-3, CRDP.
80. W. Montague Cobb, "Charles Richard Drew," p. 242; memorandum on Drew prepared by Andrew Allen, information office director, for E. H. Bensley, 25 February 1975, McGill University Medical School, E. H. Bensley Papers, Montreal, Canada.
81. Wade, *Black Men of Amherst*, p. 49. Wade notes that the top student in Drew's class was a woman.
82. C. F. Martin on Drew, June 1935, excerpted in memorandum on Drew by Allen for Bensley.
83. Charles Drew to Richard Drew ("Pa"), undated, Folder 17, Box 134-3, CRDP.
84. Wynes, *Charles Richard Drew*, pp. 18–20; Charles R. Drew, "New Year's Day, 1930, Musings," CRDP.
85. Wade, *Black Men of Amherst*, p. 49; Embree and Waxman, *Investment in People*, pp. 132–34. The chapter titled "Fellowships" opens with Drew's biography as an example of the good impact of the Rosenwald Fellowships. "At twenty-six, needing only one more year to complete his work at McGill, . . . [Drew's] money ran out. It was a bitter thing, after getting so close to his goal, to give up the career to which he was dedicated or at best to delay it, perhaps for years. . . . It was at this critical period that Charles Drew received the Rosenwald fellowship which enabled him to complete his education" (p. 133).
86. Wynes, *Charles Richard Drew*, p. 21.
87. Drew was involved in the relationship with Mary Maxwell for several years. She even visited Drew's family in Arlington and Washington at one point, according to Drew's sister, Nora Drew Gregory (Gregory interview). See letters from Mary Maxwell to Charles Drew, Folders 17 and 18, Box 135-1, CRDP. One highly fictionalized account of Drew's life at this juncture lays out a scenario in which Drew is in love with a young white woman while at McGill. Her friendly, urbane father, a successful doctor, urges him to pursue a medical career in Canada by passing as a white man. Though tortured over love of the girl, Drew decides he cannot do such a dishonest thing with his life, and he sobbingly departs (Lichello, *Pioneer in Blood Plasma*, pp. 65–70). There is no evidence to suggest that this particular scene ever took place, or that it contains any truth at all (May Maxwell to Charles Drew, 1 February 1934, Folder 17, Box 135-1, CRDP). A few years after the relationship ended, Mary Maxwell married a man of the Baha'i faith. Maxwell's mother wrote Drew with this news, and her letter may indicate some regret that her daughter had not ended up with Drew: "I long to be able to write to Mary something vital about you, who have, and always will, play such an important part in her life."
88. May Maxwell to Charles Drew, 6 January 1938, Folder 17, Box 135-1, CRDP.
89. Charles Drew to Otto Glaser, 6 June 1949, Folder 6, Box 136-1, CRDP. Drew wrote Glaser, "Much of this interest [in blood research] undoubtedly stems from your early teaching and interest in the relationships of fluid distribution in the developing embryo as a factor in its differentiation and definitive

form. I still feel that my senior essay on 'Growth' was one of the best things I have done; and certainly, the preparation of this paper opened up more new fields to me than any similar exercise I have carried out since leaving Amherst." Glaser wrote Drew back a warm letter, commenting, "You were and are one of those who make a teacher's life worthwhile. . . . As my mind plays over the past, it is curious how vividly certain little things loom up. . . . There was the time when as I was walking by, you came tripping lightly down the stairs of Tertsy's emporium. I don't think you saw me—but the grace and beauty of your young movements have left an indelible impression" (Otto Glaser to Charles Drew, 21 September 1949, Folder 6, Box 136-1, CRDP). See also Charles Drew, biology class notes on "fertilization of sea urchins, growth in boys and girls, hybrids," Folder 19, Box 134-5, CRDP.

90. In England, Beattie later became director of the research laboratories of the Royal College of Surgeons. At the start of World War II, when he served as director of the British Blood Transfusion Service, he contacted Drew.

91. Joseph Drew interview, 12 June 1985. Drew's brother refers to the McGill years as the period when Charles Drew first became interested in blood work. Drew's popular biographers have greatly dramatized Drew's early encounters with blood transfusions and fashioned their own scenarios about them. There is possibly some truth in these fictionalized versions, such as the one in Sterne, *Blood Brothers*, p. 138. Sterne writes about Beattie and Drew's difficulty in finding blood donors and their response to the patients' violent reactions when blood types did not match: "Above all, they came to know the terrible sense of defeat when no blood was available, or in cases of accident, when an hour lost could mean death."

92. See "Blood against the Blitz," *Ebony*, January 1946, p. 33: "One night while Dr. Charles Drew was an interne at the Montreal General Hospital, a big fire broke out. Flames swept the building and all doctors were put on emergency duty treating victims. . . . Patient after patient that he treated was not suffering from burns as much as shock. Just 30 years old then, it set him to thinking and studying the way shock worked; . . . it was this puzzle indelibly seared into his mind by the flames in the Montreal Hospital that spurred him to search for the antidote to shock."

93. Joseph Drew interview, 12 June 1985.

94. Evelyn Tykulsky, "Six Howard University Professors," *Our World*, January 1950, p. 31.

95. Embree and Waxman, *Investment in People*, pp. 133–34.

96. Lichello, *Pioneer in Blood Plasma*, pp. 62–63. Wade obviously used this fictionalized dramatization as a primary source when he traced Drew's interest in blood research to an urgent incident of this sort: "[Drew] witnessed an old man bleeding to death in the emergency room while interns and nurses searched frantically for a matching blood type. Drew's blood type matched the old man's, a transfusion was made, and a life saved" (Wade, *Black Men of Amherst*, p. 50).

97. Envelope from the Mayo Foundation addressed to Charles Drew at Montreal General Hospital, 2300 Tupper Street, Montreal, Quebec, Canada, 8 December 1934, Folder 18, Box 135-1, CRDP.

98. W. Montague Cobb, "Charles Richard Drew," p. 242.

99. Robert S. Jason, "Charles Richard Drew," speech delivered in April of 1960 at the dedication of the Charles R. Drew Elementary School in Washington, D.C., Folder 2, Box 136-1, CRDP. An article with a comment on the Mayo refusal notes, "Charley . . . applied for a residency at the Mayo Clinic and was candidly advised that American medicine had enough white surgeons—so what did it need with black ones?" (Hamilton Bims, "Charles Drew's 'Other' Medical Revolution," *Ebony*, February 1974, p. 3.)

100. Cobb notes that in the late 1920s, at the time Adams began his rebuilding program, "strict application of standards would have closed both Howard [University Medical School] and Meharry [Medical College], but the vital area of service they were rendering and the prospect of philanthropic aid produced extensions of time [to allow them to improve their programs]" (W. Montague Cobb, "Numa P. G. Adams," p. 46). Earlier, Cobb had explained, "The late twenties was a period in which the reforms in medical education initiated by the famous Flexner Report in 1910 were coming to fruition in the great medical centers . . . around the country, chiefly through the aid of major philanthropies. But poor, struggling Howard and Meharry had not received any of this money, and though medical school standards were climbing steadily higher, the two Negro schools were falling further and further behind" (p. 45). Todd L. Savitt notes that Howard and Meharry, though ill-equipped, did receive some funds during this period; see Savitt, "Abraham Flexner and the Black Medical Schools," pp. 65–81.

101. Wynes, *Charles Richard Drew*, pp. 35–40.

102. Robert A. Lambert, "Special Tribute," in W. Montague Cobb, "Numa P. G. Adams," p. 54. Lambert notes, "Adams kept a watchful eye for . . . potentially valuable human material. My 1934 diary records the statement that Adams was interested in Dr. Drew, 'graduate of Amherst, M.D. from McGill, now serving an internship at Montreal General Hospital.'" Cobb's article on Adams is an excellent source providing the historical background to Howard University Medical School's rebuilding program.

103. Numa P. G. Adams, Howard University College of Medicine, teaching personnel evaluation of Charles Richard Drew, 15 January 1936, Folder 12, Box 136-1, CRDP.

104. W. Montague Cobb, "Charles Richard Drew," p. 242.

105. W. Montague Cobb, "Numa P. G. Adams," p. 46.

106. Ibid., pp. 46–47. Cobb discusses at length the bitter, conflict-ridden atmosphere in which Adams had to try to achieve his goals. Pay was low; black faculty morale was often bad, when young men who had just graduated from the medical school were making much more money in private practice. Many turned against Adams, and Cobb concludes, "[Adams] was a first wave that cleared the ground and sank the new installations. He was exposed to the heaviest fire and became a casualty" (p. 51). However, Adams provided the necessary foundation for the medical school's later successes.

107. Adams, teaching personnel evaluation of Charles Drew.

108. Charles Drew to Nora R. Drew, 18 June 1938, Folder 15, Box 134-3, CRDP.

Drew wrote his mother, "I've had a good fast start, a pleasant one too, and expect to enjoy it a lot. At the present time I am working all day (and a good part of the night) in the laboratory making determinations of the components of blood in very ill patients under Dr. John Scudder. . . . He gave me two days instruction in techniques and then left on a short vacation and I've been stewing ever since. This morning at 1 A.M. I was called in to interpret the blood findings on a very sick patient with reference to the best therapy. Four days and a consulting specialist already (but between you and me I haven't the slightest idea about what all these figures mean in terms of living or not living)."

109. Lamb, *Presbyterian Hospital*, pp. 168–70, 201–3. Writing about the surgical residency program in 1940, Whipple described it thus: "At the present time we take eight graduates who shall have had a basic internship of one year of medical and six months, or more, of surgical training, for a year as Assistant Residents. Four of these are chosen for a period of two years' further training, during which experience is provided in surgical pathology, surgical bacteriology, the surgical research laboratory, the O.P.D., the Harkness Pavilion, and the ward services of the three surgical divisions. . . . At the end of this three-year residency the graduate is qualified to take the examinations for certification by the American Board of Surgery" (pp. 361–62). See also Rothstein, *American Medical Schools*, p. 176, a recent study corroborating the fact that Columbia was a leader in clinical training.

110. Clark interview.

111. Lamb, *Presbyterian Hospital*, pp. 10–11. The legend contained a germ of truth: "Dr. Oliver White was once called to care for an old, colored servant of a prominent family in the neighborhood. He found her in urgent need of hospital care, but because of her race he could not secure a bed for her in any hospital of his choice. Hotly indignant, he told Mr. Lenox that he hoped some day there would be a hospital 'broad enough to admit patients without regard to color or creed.' Mr. Lenox immediately accepted the idea as a fundamental principle for Presbyterian Hospital." A tablet engraved with the principle was placed near the entrance of the hospital (p. 11).

112. Watts interview, 6 July 1988.

113. McCown interview, 18 November 1985.

114. Ibid. According to McCown, Whipple said that Drew was the best resident he ever had.

115. Lamb, *Presbyterian Hospital*, p. 361.

116. Clark interview. Margery Clark graduated from the Columbia-Presbyterian School of Nursing in 1938 and subsequently worked as a head instruments nurse in the operating room. In 1940 she married David Clark, a Presbyterian Hospital resident, and thus could no longer keep her nursing job. She and Clark were both personal friends of Drew during this period. Later, from February to April of 1941, she worked as head nurse under Drew in the American Red Cross pilot blood plasma program. One of Drew's colleagues referred to this same incident. He said that Drew initially did not take his meals with the other residents at Presbyterian Hospital. "A resi-

dent, one Octo Lee of Mississippi, formally requested a conference on behalf of the residents to discuss the matter of Dr. Drew. Dr. Whipple smiles when he recalls the parrying which resulted. . . . Dr. Lee was registering a protest that the residents were denied the pleasure of having their meals with Charlie. This oversight was promptly corrected" (Frank Jones, M.D., "Charles R. Drew" [speech], 18 February 1951, Folder 3, Box 134-12, CRDP).

117. Nora Drew to Charles Drew, 4 August 1939, Folder 13, Box 135-1, CRDP. In this letter Drew's mother wrote him mainly to cheer him up about his financial problems and to encourage him to marry even though money was tight. "Your last letter, like some of mine, didn't sound so bright. I am very sorry conditions aren't better for you and I can only say as I have before — drop things at home and think about Charlie. . . . Living is very high in N.Y. as well as Washington. That's the reason we've never been able to get ahead. Yet you should be able to care for a family after you . . . have finished at Columbia. By trying real hard you should be able to make it on $150. Of course that may only take care of the simple way of living yet if you really love each other you might venture forth." Mrs. Drew added, "Sorry I can't help in a substantial way but I'm afraid that's out."

118. Charles Drew to Lenore Robbins, 16 April 1939, Folder 4, Box 135-1, CRDP.

119. Lenore Robbins Drew, "Unforgettable Charlie Drew."

120. Charles Drew to Lenore Robbins, 3 May 1939, Folder 5, Box 135-1, CRDP.

121. Charles Drew to Lenore Drew, 16 June 1939, Folder 6, Box 135-1, CRDP.

122. Wynes, *Charles Richard Drew*, p. 54.

123. Charles Drew to Lenore Robbins, 16 April 1939, Folder 4, Box 135-1, CRDP.

124. Charles Drew to Lenore Drew, 19 July 1939, Folder 7, Box 135-1, CRDP.

125. Charles Drew to Lenore Robbins, undated (probably written late summer 1939), Folder 11, Box 135-1, CRDP.

126. Drew to Robbins, undated (late summer 1939). W. Montague Cobb also noted the "reluctance" of the General Education Board of the Rockefeller Foundation to grant the funding for two-year as opposed to one-year fellowships, which were necessary for the pursuit of doctorates ("Numa P. G. Adams," p. 49.)

127. Drew to Robbins, undated (late summer 1939).

128. Drew to Edwin B. Henderson, 31 May 1940, Folder 6, Box 136-1, CRDP.

CHAPTER FIVE

1. Fletcher, "Administrative History," p. 26. Fletcher refers to the American Red Cross's pilot blood collection program in New York City from January to April 1941 as the real beginning of the Blood Donor Service, which he terms "the greatest cooperative undertaking in all medical history." Drew was medical director of this pilot program, which grew out of the Blood for Britain Project.

2. In 1940, President Franklin D. Roosevelt appointed two prominent black

leaders to key positions in the War Department and Selective Service Administration, responding to pressure from the black press and eager to win black support during his reelection campaign. William Hastie, dean of the Howard University Law School, was made civilian aide on Negro affairs to the secretary of war; Campbell C. Johnson was appointed special adviser to the director of the Selective Service Administration. At the same time, the army promoted Colonel B. O. Davis Sr. to the rank of brigadier general (Finkle, *Forum for Protest*, pp. 154–55).

3. Buckingham, "Dr. Charles Richard Drew," p. 20.

4. In announcing its policy of exclusion, the American Red Cross took the position that the army and navy had instructed it to "supply only plasma from white donors. This position is taken because about ninety-five per cent of those serving in the armed forces are white men, who it is understood prefer plasma from white donors" ("Statements of Policy Regarding Negro Blood Donors," 5 November 1941 policy, undated fact sheet excerpt, CD-ARC-NH). According to this fact sheet, the Red Cross held to its policy of segregating blood until 1 December 1950, when "instructions were issued from national headquarters to block out the racial designation on Donor Registration Cards." It was not until 1963, however, that the official Red Cross records no longer bore the racial designation of the blood donor, even for potential use as data for scientific studies (Robert Walhay to Catherine Scheader, 11 November 1971, CD-ARC-NH).

5. "Blood of Negroes . . . [was] cheerfully accepted; but it was always marked 'A.A.' to distinguish it from that of white donors with whose donations it was never mixed" (Fletcher, "Administrative History," p. 135). As late as 1967 — and perhaps later — blood from black and white donors was still kept separate in hospitals in some parts of the Deep South ("Some Hospitals Still Keep Negro, White Blood Apart," *Wall Street Journal*, 1 March 1967).

6. See Finkle, *Forum for Protest*, pp. 105–6; Foner, *Blacks and the Military*, p. 140. Finkle writes, "Blacks were particularly incensed by the Red Cross policy because black physician Charles R. Drew . . . had played a leading role in developing the blood bank system. . . . Not satisfied with the Red Cross policy [of segregating blood], many blacks refused to give blood." Foner notes the "irony of the situation" and incorrectly states that Drew resigned from the Red Cross on learning that black donors were to be excluded.

7. Buckingham, "Dr. Charles Richard Drew," p. 20. Buckingham wrote that John Bush, president of the Blood Transfusion Betterment Association, cabled Drew within days after the association's Board of Medical Control decided to create the position of "full-time medical supervisor," the only paid position in the whole project. The project had already been underway for six weeks, and those in charge agreed that there needed to be tighter supervision of technical methods and stronger leadership, since some of the plasma sent to England had been contaminated. "Receiving a four-month leave of absence from Howard University, Dr. Drew reported to New York the last week in September 1940" (p. 20).

8. The first blood transfusions, which used animal blood, date back to the mid-seventeenth century. It was not until the twentieth century that significant advances were made (Wynes, *Charles Richard Drew*, pp. 43–44).

9. Person-to-person blood transfusions had been viewed as safe medical practice since World War I; the 1901 discovery of four different blood groups
and the 1914 discovery of sodium nitrate's effect in preventing transfused
blood from coagulating had cleared away the widespread fears of a fatal
reaction from transfusion. But person-to-person transfusions, though effective, were often difficult to arrange in emergencies, when they were most
needed: matching blood types and finding the right donor were time-con-
suming and problematic. The loss of soldiers' lives in World War I and in the
Spanish Civil War dramatically demonstrated the need for more effective
life-saving medical interventions. Although doctors on the front lines in
both these wars did effectively use very small, rudimentary blood banks,
it was not until the late 1930s that the modern technology of blood and
plasma banking began to be developed. (Unless otherwise noted, this brief
history of blood preservation research and programs is based on Buckingham, "Dr. Charles Richard Drew," pp. 4–9.)

10. Charles Richard Drew, "Role of Soviet Investigators," pp. 367–68.

11. Wynes, *Charles Richard Drew*, p. 57.

12. DeKleine, "Early History," p. 10. DeKleine cites Elliott's article as follows:
Dr. John Elliott, "A Preliminary Report of a New Method of Blood Transfusion," *Southern Medicine and Surgery* 98, no. 12 (December 1936).

13. Buckingham, "Dr. Charles Richard Drew," p. 13.

14. Scudder, "Practical Genetic Concepts," pp. 266–67, quoted in Buckingham, "Dr. Charles Richard Drew," p. 10.

15. DeKleine, "Early History," pp. 6–8. According to DeKleine, the Blood Donor Service was begun so that enough donors would be on hand for indigent
patients in emergencies; he noted that the "hospital had difficulty in obtain-
ing donors, particularly for negro patients. Colored folks generally were, at
that time, very superstitious about giving blood, and perhaps they still are"
(Buckingham, "Dr. Charles Richard Drew," p. 7). See also DeKleine, "Red
Cross Blood Transfusion Projects," p. 2101.

16. Buckingham, "Dr. Charles Richard Drew," pp. 5–6.

17. Ibid., p. 13.

18. In May 1940 the National Research Council established several committees
on blood in order to pull together the nation's blood research experts to
serve as consultants in the face of the growing war situation. Committees on
shock, blood transfusions, blood substitutes, and blood procurement were
established. Drew, a Columbia University graduate student at this time, was
not appointed to any of these committees; John Scudder served on the
committee on shock (Buckingham, "Dr. Charles Richard Drew," p. 13).

19. Drew told of this incident in his speech on receiving the Spingarn Medal,
saying that it "did give birth more or less to the idea well if you can ship it in
bottles, why can't you get a lot of plasma and ship. With this idea in mind Dr.
Scudder and I went down to see the chairman of the Blood Transfusion
Association. He didn't take too many of our ideas seriously, but this one did
seem to make some sense." Drew noted that the Rome plasma was never
actually used, because Taylor did not need it when Whipple arrived and
because it had jelled in transit (Dr. Charles Drew, "The Spingarn Medal,"
NAACP Bulletin, September 1944, p. 11).

20. John Beattie to Charles Drew, telegram, 11 September 1940, photocopy in "Prologue to Blood Plasma," *What's New*, December 1944, p. 27. This footnoted article incorrectly states that the Beattie telegram initiated the whole Plasma for Great Britain project, when in fact it was already underway (Buckingham, "Dr. Charles Richard Drew," pp. 37–39).

21. In a speech, Drew said, "It was not . . . until a wire was sent to this country asking that five thousand liters of plasma be shipped and that five thousand more be sent the next week [that I became involved]. He [Beattie] did this over the heads of the higher officials. With this telegram, the whole thing became mobilized" (Drew, "Spingarn Medal").

22. John Beattie to Charles Drew, 4 November 1940, Folder 7, Box 134-5, CRDP. Beattie wrote Drew, "I am glad to hear that you are now working on the blood plasma side of transfusion and I am sure it is the best way in which you people can help us. The plasma was wanted to form small depots for the use of the Royal Air Force at their several stations throughout England and the Near East." In response Drew sent a detailed report to Beattie in early December (Charles Drew to John Beattie, 7 December 1940, Folder 7, Box 134-5, CRDP).

23. Buckingham, "Dr. Charles Richard Drew," p. 22.

24. As noted earlier, it was Scudder who originally recommended that plasma be shipped to U.S. allies abroad. In the summer of 1941, Drew and Scudder helped draft procedures to be followed if a large blood collection program were launched (Buckingham, "Dr. Charles Richard Drew," p. 15). Drew's dissertation obviously laid the foundation for pulling together all that was known about blood preservation, but Drew continued to collect and incorporate in his own research widespread information about blood processing throughout the months he worked in the two New York City projects. The urgent necessity for a large-scale national program inspired his efforts and those of other scientists throughout this period, since all of them were aware of the impending war.

25. Drew contacted key individuals in twelve cities after a 9 December meeting of the New York Red Cross chapter and the Blood Transfusion Betterment Association; at this meeting, the researchers discussed the need for a national program, with New York City as its logical starting point (Buckingham, "Dr. Charles Richard Drew," p. 24). As early as May 1940, the U.S. military's preference for dried plasma had been discussed at high-level meetings. In the summer of 1940, a number of different projects to produce dried plasma on a limited basis got underway, some sponsored by U.S. military authorities. By the fall of 1940, there was much discussion in governmental and military circles of the need for a large stockpile of dried plasma should the U.S. enter the war, and New York City, which had experience in enrolling donors on a large scale, was already viewed as the logical site of a pilot dried plasma program, with Charles Drew as the best qualified to supervise it (pp. 23–25).

26. Ibid., pp. 25–27.

27. Ibid., p. 28. The original report Drew wrote was entitled *Report of the Blood Transfusion Association Concerning the Project for Supplying Blood Plasma to En-*

gland, Which has been Carried on Jointly with the American Red Cross from August 1940 to January 1941 and was published on 31 January 1941 in New York City by the Blood Transfusion Betterment Association. Three months later Drew wrote an expanded version called "Plasma for Great Britain," a copy of which has been retained in National American Red Cross Archives, Washington, D.C. (Buckingham, end page).

28. Ibid., p. 31.
29. DeKleine, "Early History," p. 37.
30. Fletcher, "Administrative History," pp. iv, 24–28.
31. Kendrick, *Blood Program in World War II*, p. 15.
32. Charles Drew to Howard Fast, 28 November 1945, Folder 6, Box 136-1, CRDP. Drew wrote a man organizing a New Masses Annual Cultural Awards dinner in his honor, "I feel . . . that while the honor of being the Medical Director of the British plasma project was granted me, as well as the assignment of setting up the first Red Cross Blood Bank, that all of the basic scientific work which made these assignments possible was done in collaboration with Dr. John Scudder; . . . if any award is to be made . . . Scudder should share in such an award."
33. Charles Drew to Edgar B. Carter, 6 November 1944, Folder 6, Box 136-1, CRDP. To this man, who had published an article about the projects that led up to the national blood program, Drew wrote, "I have not tried to evaluate too closely what my relative place is in this story or should be. No matter how you write the story, it will be unfair to many people."
34. Charles Drew to Nora Drew, 25 October 1940, Folder 15, Box 134-3, CRDP.
35. Charles Drew to Lenore Drew, undated, Folder 11, Box 135-1, CRDP. Drew writes, "To make this day very happy we just received a cable from England stating that since the standardization of technique (that's when I took over here) no more infected material has arrived in England."
36. Charles Drew to Lenore Drew, 9 January 1941, Folder 8, Box 135-1, CRDP. Drew writes, "You will be pleased to hear that the state department considered your husband too valuable a citizen to expose himself to the rigors and dangers of the European scene at this time. . . . From word we have received in this office today there is some evidence that the word has been passed down to have certain of our armed forces ready for war if need be by the first of April. To that end we have been asked to start collecting blood for plasma for the U.S. Navy by Monday week. . . . I do not know what the next step is at this time but what ever it is I am pretty sure, I believe, that your hubby will be in the middle of it."
37. Charles Drew to Lenore Drew, undated, Folder 11, Box 135-1, CRDP. Drew writes, "Just had a most interesting day. Tested out one of the 'Transfusion Trailers' destined for England this week by attaching it to a Red Cross ambulance and, with the whole crew of nurses, traveled out to the State Agricultural School in Farmingdale L.I. (about 35 miles) to take blood from the student body. We set up in the gymnasium and everything went extremely well."
38. Drew spent time with Scudder and his wife at their vacation retreat at Shelter Island, and the two men kept in touch in the years after Drew left. In a

letter describing a weekend Drew spent at Shelter Island, Drew depicts a scenario that may well have epitomized Scudder's and Drew's relationship. Scudder inadvertently started a forest fire when he decided to single-handedly burn some trash. Drew rushed out to help Scudder, and largely through Drew's vigorous efforts all day long — he personally dug a long ditch to stop the flames — the two men contained the fire (Charles Drew to Lenore Drew, 7 May 1939, Folder 5, Box 135-1, CRDP).

39. Charles Drew to Lenore Drew, 10 February 1941, Folder 5, Box 136-1, CRDP. Ira McCown, one of Drew's New York colleagues, recalled that Drew felt he had surpassed Scudder: "Drew soon found out he knew more about blood than Scudder. He'd never say anything about it. He felt it in his bones. 'Oh, Scudder's all right,' he'd say. They were close personal friends. But Scudder got a little jealous because Whipple was giving more attention to Drew" (McCown interview, 20 November 1985).

40. George Goodman Jr., "Dr. John Scudder, 76, a Pioneer in Establishing Blood Banks, Dies," *New York Times*, 8 December 1976. This journalist maintains that Scudder's views "were based on a lack of scientific information about blood . . . [and] did not reflect a racial bias." This claim is hard to uphold, given that as early as 1941 there was known to be no scientific basis for segregating blood and that in 1950 the American Red Cross officially changed its policy of segregating blood. Drew's brother Joseph said that Drew and Scudder were "at odds over the blood segregation issue" (Joseph Drew interview, 31 July 1985).

41. Clark interview.

42. Ken Olson of Trudeau, N.Y., to "Charley" Drew, 19 April 1940, Folder 17, Box 135-1, CRDP.

43. Charles Drew to Lenore Drew, 10 February 1941, Folder 5, Box 136-1, CRDP.

44. Charles Drew to Lenore Drew, 24 February 1941, Folder 8, Box 135-1, CRDP. This letter dramatically reveals the extent to which Drew felt misunderstood, unappreciated, and unsupported by his wife during this period. It is almost a classic statement of wounded male pride and at the same time a catalogue of fairly typical marital conflicts: "I look ahead for weeks at a time to seeing you, to letting down from affairs of the mind and 50% of the time I run into an argument on a purely masculine basis. I can not come back here and write eulogies about the power of pure reason my wife is gifted with. I may not be a great flatterer but I am not a liar. Affection which is not spontaneous is unworthy of the name. Well over half of the letters you have written have been in the form of complaints — the things I don't do, or do do which you ought to be allowed to do, the letters I don't write or the lack of fire in those I do write."

45. Charles Drew to Nora Drew, 19 March 1941, Folder 15, Box 135-3, CRDP.

46. Charles Drew to Lenore Drew, 24 March 1941, Folder 9, Box 135-1, CRDP.

47. C. R. Drew, transcript statement, American Human Serum Association Symposium, 2–3 June 1941, p. 2, Folder 22, Box 134-3, CRDP. Ironically, in this same statement, Drew comments, "The collection of blood is not only a scientific problem but also a complicated social matter too. . . . The problem

of the Red Cross to get donors for these large projects . . . day after day, is really quite a job. Any rumor which gets a start at all . . . will show an immediate drop in the numbers of donors who will come in." A writer doing a magazine story on Drew after his death undoubtedly confused these historical facts when he stated that "ironically enough, at a time when the Red Cross was reported to be refusing Negro donors," Drew told newspaper columnist Albert Deutsch, " 'Actually . . . we accepted all donors. We told the Red Cross that the blood was segregated but we mixed it all up' " (David Hepburn, "The Life of Dr. Charles Drew," *Our World*, July 1950, p. 26). In the Blood for Britain program and the pilot American Red Cross program, the somewhat meager evidence indicates that the blood was not segregated. The exclusion-of-black-donors policy evolved in the late summer and fall of 1941 when there were indications that donor turnout was affected by rumors of racially mixed blood.

48. Charles Drew to Lenore Drew, September 1940 through April 1941, CRDP, Box 135-1; see also Wynes, *Charles Richard Drew*, p. 70. Drew's close friend Burke Syphax noted, "He always planned on coming back home."

49. Clark interview. Clark, whom Drew hired to serve as head nurse of the New York pilot blood program, recalled, "When he was offered this position at Howard University, we all thought it was great, an honor. The feeling was he was going on to better things . . . [as] head of the surgical service down there."

50. Charles Drew to Lenore Drew, 9 December 1940, Folder 8, Box 135-1, CRDP.

51. W. Montague Cobb, "Charles Richard Drew," p. 243. Cobb wrote, "Drew was allowed to leave the program just as it was about to become nationalized. . . . It seems strange that his country could find no further use for the services of a citizen who had been of such vital expert assistance in the critical hour. One hears that it was thought that a Negro would not be acceptable in a high place in a national program. Dr. Drew is not known to have murmured." In an interview, Cobb asserted the same point: "[Drew] was left hanging. If he'd been white he would have been offered another job in the army" (Cobb interview).

52. McCown interviews. McCown believed that Drew was "demoted," refused a job with the armed forces, when the blood program was nationalized and top officials realized that Drew was black. McCown maintained that even Whipple expected Drew to receive an army job, and that when he did not, Whipple told Drew, "Don't be losing your talent. You don't need this pseudo-political thing," and then arranged for Drew to become the chief of Howard University's Department of Surgery, replacing Edward Howes. According to McCown, Howes had a "chip on his shoulder" about Drew, partly because he had decided he wanted to stay on as Howard's head of surgery. Although Whipple undoubtedly was one of Drew's crucial backers for the Howard University job, it is unlikely that he personally had the power to "arrange" Drew's transfer to it. Drew was hired as chief of Howard's surgery department by Howard medical school dean Joseph Johnson, who replaced Numa Adams after his death. He was hired largely because Adams, while serving as

dean of the school, was determined to have a black doctor in this important position and had laid the essential groundwork for it. When Howes took the job of chief of surgery in 1936, he had had an agreement with Adams that he would leave after five years when a black surgeon had been trained to replace him. Indeed, as McCown asserted, Howes did grow to like the job and did not want to leave (W. Montague Cobb, "Numa P. G. Adams," p. 49).

53. One of Drew's colleagues, commenting about how Drew would have handled discrimination during his New York sojourn, said, "Discrimination would fall off him like water off a duck's back. His whole attitude was so secure" (Syphax interview). Drew's wife, commenting on how he reacted to racial obstacles, noted, "He wasn't a man to grandstand . . . He didn't waste his time if he saw he was going nowhere. He was a man who moved and wanted to keep on moving. He kept his equilibrium and went right on" (Lenore Drew interview).

54. McCown interview, 18 November 1985.

55. Charles Drew to Lenore Drew, 1939–41, Folders 4–9 and 11, Box 135-1, CRDP. The letters Drew wrote his wife during this period are the most revealing collection of writings that survive about Charles Drew. Reading them allows one to witness Drew's thinking and his very soul at a very critical stage of his life. These letters also highlight the strengths and weaknesses of Drew's marriage.

56. See Organ and Kosiba, *Century of Black Surgeons*, pp. 78–80.

57. Hepburn, "Life of Dr. Charles Drew," p. 23.

58. Watts interview, 25 January 1983.

59. Charles Watts pointed out that Allen Whipple supported Drew's taking the American Board of Surgery examinations at this juncture, after only three and a half years of residency (Watts interview, 6 July 1988).

60. Dulles, *American Red Cross*, p. 420.

61. Finkle, *Forum for Protest*, p. 105. (Finkle cites the following: *Chicago Defender*, 27 December 1941, 7 February 1942; *Pittsburgh Courier*, 27 December 1941, 3 January 1942.)

62. *Current Biography*, p. 180. Most later newspaper articles about Drew say that he spoke out against the Red Cross policy in 1942.

63. Cook interview.

64. Joel Francis, "Negro Surgeon, World Plasma Expert, Derides Red Cross Blood Segregation," *Chicago Defender*, 26 September 1942.

65. Ibid.

66. Charles Drew to Jacob Billikopf, 15 April 1944, Folder 6, Box 136-1, CRDP.

67. Charles Drew, "The Negro Physician in the Present War Effort," speech delivered at Station KSD, St. Louis, Missouri, 27 April 1943, Folder 2, Box 135-5, CRDP.

68. Previous recipients of the Spingarn Medal included, among others, Ernest E. Just; Louis T. Wright; Marian Anderson; Paul Robeson; Mary McLeod Bethune; W. E. B. Du Bois; James Weldon Johnson; Richard Wright; William H. Hastie; Thurgood Marshall; and Walter White (Walter White, *Man Called White*, p. 174).

69. Theodore G. Bilbo, a U.S. senator from Mississippi and a fierce segregation-

ist, was objecting to a federal appropriation to Howard University; he asked his fellow senators if they knew what was "being done there." He briefly mentioned Drew and referred to a speech he had given: "Dr. Charles R. Drew, Spingarn Medal winner and the first director of the American Blood Bank, who in giving the story of blood and blood plasma said that there is no difference between colored and white peoples' blood." Bilbo also attacked Howard University professor of anthropology William Leo Hansberry for teaching "American Negro youth that the white man descended from the Negro" (*Congressional Record*, vol. 90, part 5, 78th Cong., 2d sess., 20 June 1944, p. 6249).

70. Charles R. Drew, "The Spingarn Medal," *NAACP Bulletin*, September 1944, p. 11. Harold Kernodle, the white Alamance County surgeon who tried to save Drew's life, served in World War II. In an interview, he commented, supporting Drew's viewpoint, "During the war we gave any blood we could get! I thought blood was segregated after the war" (Harold Kernodle interview).

71. Charles Drew to John Scudder, 15 April 1944, Folder 6, Box 136-1, CRDP. Drew wrote Scudder, "Not having been associated with anything that even closely pertains to blood or plasma since 1941, I was a little surprised [to receive the award]. Maybe . . . since the whole Negro race feels pretty badly about the Army attitude toward blood donors, I suppose there is some small satisfaction in the thought that at one time I was associated with this particular phase of activities connected with the war effort. There is a great deal of bitterness, not only about this particular phase but about opportunities and treatment of Negro troops as a whole."

72. Drew, "Spingarn Medal," p. 11. Drew referred to the many letters he had received earlier in his speech as well, saying he had had "sincere people, asking whether it is possible to transmit characteristics of race by blood transfusions to another race." Drew noted that some of the letters were "very bitter": "Some simply said that if the only way to save my son's life is to give the blood of a Negro, let him die."

73. "The UFWA Stands for United of All," UFWA Leaflet, 8 August 1941, Folder 34, Box 135-2, CRDP. This leaflet indicates that Rayford Logan, the black historian, also spoke at this meeting on "Interracial Unity in America Today."

74. "Talk by Dr. Drew at meeting of Local 10, UFWA," memo from Mary Pond to G. Stewart Brown, 9 August 1944, attachment to memo from DeWitt Smith to the Chairman (of the American Red Cross), 14 August 1944, CD-ARC-NH.

CHAPTER SIX

1. In his book *Take Your Choice*, Theodore G. Bilbo, U.S. senator from Mississippi, attacked Hill, then president of State Teachers College in Cheyney, Pa., for writing that science after many years had finally proved the "one blood" concept (p. 108).

2. Leslie Pinckney Hill, "Toussaint L'O[u]verture" (attachment to letter from Hill to Charles Drew), 13 June 1944, Folder 6, Box 136-1, CRDP.

3. See Green, *Secret City*, chap. 11, "A New Alignment, 1939–1945," and chap. 12, "The Legal Battle for Washington, 1946–1954." In these two chapters Green documents the ways in which Washington's conservative whites attempted to strengthen the city's system of segregation. Green notes, "The mounting racism which had alarmed anti-segregationists as early as 1943 looked formidable at the end of 1945. Destined to become the most fundamental problem confronting the city during the next eight years, the conflict anticipated by half a decade the turmoil that engulfed the rest of the country in the late 1950s" (p. 274). One notable event was the District of Columbia Board of Recreation's 1944 adoption of a bylaw that made segregation of all city playgrounds absolutely mandatory, rather than optional, as it had been before (p. 270). A special report on segregation in Washington in 1948 concluded, "When people are divided by a master-race theory, liberty and justice are impossible. Nowhere is this plainer than in the capital, where one-quarter of the population is segregated according to color. Here we have been building ghettoes of the mind, body, and spirit" (Landis, *Segregation in Washington*, p. 91).

4. The best history of Howard in the Johnson years is Rayford W. Logan's *Howard University*. Mordecai W. Johnson was president of Howard University for thirty-four years, from 1926 to 1960. Born in Paris, Tenn., on 12 January 1890, Johnson graduated from Atlanta Baptist College, later known as Morehouse College, in 1911. He received a second B.A. from the University of Chicago in 1913, a B.D. from Rochester Theological Seminary in 1921, and an S.T.M. from Harvard University in 1922. He was an ordained Baptist minister as well and was noted for his gift of oratory, his wit, his "Messianic complex," and his support of academic freedom. He built Howard up dramatically — both its physical plant and its faculty — during his years in office (pp. 247–51). "The first Negro and the most dynamic of Howard Presidents," Dr. Johnson was a "controversial figure throughout his entire administration. . . . [He] knew what he wanted for Howard, and he was stubbornly determined to have his own way. As a result, his years in office were years of great progress and of a great deal of dissension" (p. 251).

5. Jack White, one of Drew's former students, commented, "Mordecai Johnson was very fond of Drew. He was probably one of Drew's best promoters [at Howard]. Some of Drew's philosophy came from Mordecai; both men were always looking toward the future, wanting to do something creative and imaginative. Some people work entirely for their own careers. But Drew and Johnson became prominent because of their good works. Each had a personality that was attractive to a lot of people" (White interview).

6. David Hepburn, "The Life of Dr. Charles Drew," *Our World*, July 1950. Hepburn wrote, "Undoubtedly, he got his greatest satisfaction from creating Negro surgeons. Nothing else could compensate for the financial sacrifice he made by staying in '*this jimcrow shack*' as Mordecai Johnson has called Freedmen's. There is no doubt that in industrial work or private practice, he could have made five times the $7,000 he made there."

7. See Holt, Smith-Parker, and Terborg-Penn, *Special Mission*, for a full account of Freedmen's Hospital in this period and for a treatment of its early history.

According to these authors, Freedmen's by the mid-1950s had deteriorated to such an extent that the secretary of health, education, and welfare called it a "dump" (p. 63). Freedmen's history is also told in W. Montague Cobb, "Short History of Freedmen's Hospital."

8. At that time, Howard University as a whole was a little world unto itself. An article that captures Howard's strengths and weaknesses during this period is Henry F. and Katherine Pringle, "America's Leading Negro University," *Saturday Evening Post*, 19 February 1949. These journalists list the many stellar black scholars out of four hundred faculty members who taught at Howard, including John Hope Franklin, Rayford W. Logan, William Lee Hansberry, Sterling A. Brown, Alain F. Locke, Ralph Bunche, and somewhat earlier, Judge William Hastie. Drew is mentioned as well: "Other men who have served on Howard's faculty have carried its name to all corners of the earth. . . . Dr. Charles Drew, medical director of Howard's Freedmen's Hospital, is known and respected among surgeons everywhere" (p. 93). The journalists further noted, "The thoughtful men and women who teach . . . [at Howard] realize that their world is too removed, too deliberately sheltered. . . . They know that isolation does not broaden their scholarship. Yet facts are facts. . . . As long as other doors are closed to Negro scholars, Howard is needed" (p. 36). Black doctors had their own medical society, the Medico-Chirurgical Society of the District of Columbia, which dated from 1884 (see W. Montague Cobb, "Medico-Chi at Ninety," pp. 256–62).

9. W. Montague Cobb, "Numa P. G. Adams," p. 50. This article describes the many financial, bureaucratic, and political obstacles Adams faced in trying to upgrade Howard's medical school. Cobb noted, "As the country emerged from the depression, the full-time faculty began to see its students after but a few years' practice giving overt evidence of prosperity through possession of what had somehow lamentably come to be regarded as a symbol of Negro medical arrival, a Cadillac. There were . . . losses to the field of private practice."

10. For a description of the professional obstacles Washington's black physicians faced in this era, see Holt, Smith-Parker, and Terborg-Penn, *Special Mission*, pp. 59–62. These authors point out that black doctors were not only barred from all hospitals but Freedmen's; they were also blocked from membership in the AMA and in virtually all the specialized medical associations. The results were "profound. . . . Like many other black professionals, therefore, the doctors were often caught in a self-perpetuating cycle of lost opportunities, lost competence, and lost community respect. . . . Many black professionals developed what one participant-observer called 'embittered frustration complexes' " (pp. 60–61).

11. W. Montague Cobb, *Bulletin* (of the Medico-Chirurgical Society of the District of Columbia) 6, no. 8 (December 1950), pp. 2, 4.

12. W. Montague Cobb, "Charles Richard Drew," p. 244.

13. Watts interview, 6 July 1988.

14. Hamilton Bims, "Charles Drew's 'Other' Medical Revolution," *Ebony* (February 1974), p. 1. Jack White, another of Drew's colleagues, said that Drew probably had more contacts than anyone except possibly Howard president Mordecai Johnson (White interview).

15. Watts interview, 6 July 1988.
16. White interview.
17. Charles Wynes noted, "At the time of his death, Drew was earning only about $7,000 a year at Howard, while any income from private patients . . . and miscellaneous income did not bring the total to more than $10,000. For instance, according to Drew's surviving income tax records, for 1943, Drew reported a gross income of $5,548; for 1945, $7,303; and for 1947, $8,199. Reportedly, he had offers as high as $20,000 from pharmaceutical companies to head up research projects" (Wynes, *Charles Richard Drew*, p. 117).
18. Charles Watts commented, "Why, with a name like his after his work in blood, he could have named his future. He could have gone into practice, or been a highly paid consultant. There was no end to his alternatives. Instead, he came back to Howard as a teacher, and at great personal sacrifice" (Bims, "Drew's 'Other' Revolution," p. 1).
19. Lenore Drew interview.
20. Kathy Sawyer, "Honoring the Pioneer of Blood Banks," *Washington Post*, 14 October 1976, DC section, p. 2.
21. Thirlee Smith, "For Ghetto Kids, a Widow Recalls Blood Researcher," *Miami Herald*, November 1970 [?], Folder 19, Box 134-12, CRDP.
22. Lenore Drew interview.
23. Charles Drew to Charles W. Cole, president of Amherst College, 29 May 1947, Folder 6, Box 136-1, CRDP.
24. Lenore Drew interview.
25. Preserved in the Drew papers (Folder 13, Box 135-5, CRDP) is a poem that Drew probably liked, called "You Tell on Yourself." Its message, which Drew obviously acted on, was that we are models to other people in everything we do:

> You tell what you are by the way you walk
> By the things of which you delight to talk
> By the manner in which you bear defeat
> By so simple a thing as how you eat . . .

26. Syphax interview. Syphax added, "He was the fire that would put a light under another person. Yet he was gentle. . . . He would do it in a friendly playful way. Somehow he made his students ashamed of not performing well."
27. Organ and Kosiba, *Century of Black Surgeons*, p. 89.
28. White interview.
29. Ibid.
30. Ibid.
31. Bims, "Drew's 'Other' Revolution," p. 3.
32. Ibid., p. 1. Charles Watts noted that during this period blacks "were admitted to fewer than five or six medical schools, out of 80 or more across the country at large."
33. Overviews of the struggles of black doctors for professional training and recognition in the twentieth century are provided in Morais, *History of the Afro-American in Medicine*, and Beardsley, *History of Neglect*. See also Reitzes,

Negroes and Medicine; Savitt, "Entering a White Profession"; and Beardsley, "Making Separate, Equal."

34. Holt, Smith-Parker, and Terborg-Penn, *Special Mission*, pp. 59–60.
35. Charles Drew to Jack White, 31 October 1946, personal papers of Jack White, Washington, D.C.
36. Bims, "Drew's 'Other' Revolution," p. 1. A useful article explaining the larger organizational framework in which Drew was working is R. Frank Jones, "Surgical Resident Training Program," pp. 187–93.
37. Lenore Robbins Drew, "Unforgettable Charlie Drew," p. 6.
38. Organ and Kosiba, *Century of Black Surgeons*, pp. 86, 89.
39. W. Montague Cobb, "Charles Richard Drew," p. 244.
40. Charles Drew to Charles Scudder, 1 November 1945, Folder 6, Box 136-1, CRDP. Drew wrote Scudder, "I had applied for membership in the American College of Surgeons sometime previous to the announcement that applications from Negroes would be considered."
41. Charles Drew to Brian B. Blades, 18 January 1950, Folder 6, Box 136-1, CRDP.
42. Drew to John Scudder, 10 September 1945, Folder 6, Box 136-1, CRDP.
43. Letters from Charles Drew to a number of different doctors, 1945– 50, Folder 6, Box 136-1, CRDP; Organ and Kosiba, *Century of Black Surgeons*, p. 86.
44. Wynes, *Charles Richard Drew*, pp. 91–92. Wynes notes that Drew was issued a certificate of fellowship on 11 November 1951.
45. Ibid., pp. 83–92. Wynes lays out the history of black physicians' struggle with the AMA.
46. Charles Drew to the editor of *JAMA*, 13 January 1947, Folder 6, Box 136-1, CRDP.
47. Charles Drew to Morris Fishbein, 30 January 1947, Folder 6, Box 136-1, CRDP.
48. "U.S., Soviet Scientists Stress Post-War Ties," *New York Daily Worker*, 10 March 1944.
49. W. Montague Cobb, "Charles Richard Drew," p. 245.
50. Organ and Kosiba, *Century of Black Surgeons*, p. 86.
51. Drew was not the major leader in these local struggles. W. Montague Cobb, a Howard University anatomist and Drew's childhood friend, was probably the most important political organizer behind the effort to desegregate the field of medicine, both in Washington and in the nation as a whole. The story of the early efforts to desegregate Washington's medical institutions is best told in Reitzes, *Negroes and Medicine*. Drew had other responsibilities. He belonged to the board of trustees of the National Society for Crippled Children; the board of trustees of the District of Columbia branch of the National Poliomyemitis Foundation; the board of directors of the District of Columbia chapter of the American Cancer Society; and the executive board of the Twelfth Street branch of the YMCA (W. Montague Cobb, "Charles Richard Drew," p. 244).
52. Landis, *Segregation in Washington*, p. 50. Unless otherwise indicated, the facts here about Washington's segregated medical facilities are derived from this book.

53. Ibid., p. 49.

54. Drew to Blades, 18 January 1950; Charles Drew to Robert J. Coffee, professor of surgery at Georgetown University, 18 January 1950, Folder 6, Box 136-1, CRDP.

55. Morais, *History of the Afro-American in Medicine*, pp. 152–53.

56. Drew to Blades, 18 January 1950; Drew to Coffee, 18 January 1950.

57. Landis, *Segregation in Washington*, pp. 49–53.

58. Charles Drew to Asa G. Yancey Sr., 6 May 1947, in Organ and Kosiba, *Century of Black Surgeons*, pp. 92–93.

59. Drew wrote Lenore Robbins after seeing Joe Louis fight in 1939, "when he really got going . . . it was something to behold. He is certainly a grand athlete, beautiful in action and a terrific puncher. Galento, at the end, just sort of walked away in a daze and slid down the referees' legs, a badly beaten, cut up clumsy looking little fat man. When he came to he acted as one with no breeding either as a gentleman or athlete usually acts. Joe Louis, in spite of his reputedly low I.Q. has yet to act other than a true thoroughbred" (Charles Drew to Lenore Robbins, 3 July 1939, Folder 7, Box 135-1, CRDP). During the same year, Drew wrote to Lenore about hearing Marian Anderson sing to a great crowd at the Lincoln Memorial after the Daughters of the American Revolution had refused her the opportunity to perform at Constitution Hall:

    In all my life I have never seen such an impressive thing. With the soft rays of a pink sun gleaming against the white marble beauty of that magnificent structure and reflecting itself in the long still pool of water that stretches off towards the Washington monument she raised her exquisite voice in song and lifted with a sweep of melody a whole race to higher levels of thought, feeling and hope. Countless thousands paid her the tribute of almost reverent silence when she sang her songs of joy and sorrow. She held them beneath her magic sway, making them laugh or sigh at will and when she finished with "Nobody knows de trouble I've seen" many eyes were moist with unashamed tears and hearts too full for words. [I was] Filled with a strange pride and awed by the loveliness and significance of it all. (Charles Drew to Lenore Robbins, 13 April 1939, Folder 4, Box 135-1, CRDP)

    Many others felt as Drew did when Anderson sang at the Lincoln Memorial. "On Easter Sunday afternoon the concert took place at the feet of the 'Great Emancipator' before an audience of 75,000 people. No one present at that moving performance ever forgot it. It was the turning point, one man averred, in Washington Negroes' seventy-year-old fight against discrimination" (Green, *Secret City*, p. 249).

60. "Dr. Drew Attacks AMA Policies," *Call-Post*, 21 June 1947; also in "Correspondence: Negro Physicians," p. 222.

61. Landis, *Segregation in Washington*, p. 49.

62. Watts interview, 6 July 1988. Burke Syphax also recalled that Drew prided himself on his gentleness of manner and that for a large man, he had relatively small, gentle hands: "Once he was treating a crabby old lady who yelled at him, 'Dr. Drew, get your hands off me. You're rough!' and he turned so red" (Syphax interview).

63. Nora Gregory interview.
64. Asa G. Yancey Sr., quoted in Organ and Kosiba, *Century of Black Surgeons*, p. 90.
65. Charles Drew to Lenore Drew, 16 June 1939, Folder 6, Box 135-1, CRDP.
66. Hill, "Toussaint L'O[u]verture."
67. Charles Drew, speech for the Temple Israel Brotherhood, Boston, Mass., 21 March 1946, Folder 14, Box 136-1, CRDP.
68. Charles Drew to Mrs. J. F. Bates, 27 January 1947, Folder 6, Box 136-1, CRDP.
69. Organ and Kosiba, *Century of Black Surgeons*, pp. 91–92.
70. Du Bois, *Souls of Black Folk*, p. 45.
71. Wright, *Black Boy*, p. 284.
72. Redding, *On Being Negro*, pp. 15, 112–13.
73. Charles Richard Drew, "Negro Scholars," p. 135. The journal notes that Drew delivered an address based on this paper at the annual meeting of the Association for the Study of Negro Life and History, held in New York City on 30 October 1949.
74. Charles Richard Drew, "Negro Scholars," pp. 135–36.
75. Ibid., p. 136.
76. An excellent biography of Just is Manning's *Black Apollo of Science*.
77. Charles Richard Drew, "Negro Scholars," p. 138.
78. Organ and Kosiba, *Century of Black Surgeons*, pp. 90, 84. Another of Drew's students, Matthew Walker, made a similar comment about him: "He had the purest heart of anyone I have ever known" (p. 67).
79. White interview.
80. Lenore Drew interview; Joseph Drew interview, 31 July 1985.
81. Robert S. Jason, "Charles Richard Drew" (speech delivered 28 April 1960 at the dedication of the Drew Elementary School, Fifty-sixth and Eads Streets, Washington, D.C.), Folder 2, Box 136-1, CRDP.
82. Lincoln, *Martin Luther King, Jr.*, pp. xvii–xix; Bennett, *What Manner of Man*.
83. Martin Luther King Jr., *Testament of Hope*, pp. 8, 10, 14, 20.
84. Campbell, *Hero with a Thousand Faces*, pp. 16–17.
85. Ibid., pp. 19–20.
86. Charles Richard Drew, "Negro Scholars," pp. 148–49.
87. Hepburn, "Life of Dr. Charles Drew," p. 28.
88. Mary Maxwell, "The Horned Moon," 23 October 1932, Folder 3, Box 135-2, CRDP.
89. Charles Drew, poem in Drew's handwriting (untitled and unsigned), Folder 3, Box 135-2, CRDP.
90. Campbell, *Hero with a Thousand Faces*, p. 356.

CHAPTER SEVEN

1. Cooper, *Illustrated Encyclopedia*, p. 22: "Blood the life principle; the soul; strength; the rejuvenating force, hence blood sacrifice."
2. See Lifton, *Nazi Doctors*, especially pp. 12–18. In this book, which is based on interviews with German doctors, Lifton explores the important role doctors

played in the mass genocide of Jews during World War II, and in particular the psychological and ideological factors that allowed them, as medical healers, to kill and torture people on a vast scale.

3. See Foner, *Blacks and the Military*, p. 175. Foner concluded, "The experience of black servicemen and women during World War II — the segregation, discrimination, and mistreatment — gave evidence, even in the course of a struggle presumably fought to wipe out a monstrous racism overseas, of the racism that pervaded . . . [American] society. Responding to discrimination early in the war, a black college student angrily declared, 'The Army jim-crows us. The Navy lets us serve only as mess-men. The Red Cross refuses our blood. Employers and labor unions shut us out. We are disfranchised, jim-crowed, spat upon. What more could Hitler do than that?' " (p. 142).

4. See Myrdal, *American Dilemma*, p. 100: "The one who has got the smallest drop of 'Negro blood' is as one who is smitten by a hideous disease. It does not help if he is good and honest, educated and intelligent, a good worker, an excellent citizen and an agreeable fellow. Inside him are hidden some unknown and dangerous potentialities, something which will sooner or later crop up." See ibid., p. 114, for a discussion of the related "black baby myth" — the popular belief that the slightest amount of African ancestry could lead to an unexpected "throw-back," the birth of a black infant, to some future generation. See also Warren, *Segregation*, pp. 11, 43. A white cabdriver told Warren, "A black-type person and a white-type person, they ain't alike. Now the black-type person, all they think about is fighting and having a good time and you know what. Now the white-type person is more American-type, he don't mind fighting but he don't fight to kill for fun. It's that cannibal blood you cain't git out." Another white man showed him literature that read, "Negro blood destroyed the civilization of Egypt, India, Phoenicia, Carthage, Greece and it will destroy America!" In *Absalom, Absalom*, a fictional epic about miscegenation, William Faulkner explores the fears and traumas rooted in this theme through a sensitive exploration of one southern family that is racially mixed.

5. Adam Clayton Powell commented in 1945 that it was the "hypocrisy of the [white] Christian church" that kept America racially "split asunder." Christianity, he said, had "never been tried." Black people would need to "Christianize religion" in the postwar world and thereby help America give birth to true democracy (*Marching Blacks*, pp. 200, 202–3).

6. One of the *Pittsburgh Courier*'s war correspondents urged black soldiers to demand combat duty; he asked, "Is it not true that only those who spill their blood are in a position to demand rights?" (quoted in Wynn, *Afro-American and the Second World War*, pp. 101–2). A black soldier noted, "There were definite instances of segregation before combat and immediately afterwards but during combat it did not exist" (Motley, *Invisible Soldier*, p. 158).

7. See Powell, *Marching Blacks*, p. 205. "The black man is out to save America, to salvage its best, and to take his position in the vanguard of those building an international order of brotherhood. . . . One day when the colorless, colorful world of the future arrives, unborn generations will walk on the face of the earth and praise the hour when America's most persecuted minority took on its shoulders the burden of salvaging a people's society."

8. See Finkle, *Forum for Protest*, pp. 108–28, for the rationale behind the Double V campaign.

9. Collections of letters and interviews include McGuire, *Taps for a Jim Crow Army*; Ruth Danenhower Wilson, *Jim Crow Joins Up*; and Motley, *Invisible Soldier*.

10. See Odum, *Race and Rumors of Race*, on the spread of wartime rumors. See Lee, *Employment of Negro Troops*; Dalfiume, *Desegregation of the U.S. Armed Forces*; Wynn, *Afro-American and the Second World War*; Foner, *Blacks and the Military*; and Walter White, *Rising Wind*, for detailed accounts of wartime racial friction. A particularly brutal lynching occurred early in 1942, soon after the war broke out, and became a symbol of the struggle for democracy at home. Cleo Wright was arrested in Sikestown, Missouri, on charges of raping a white woman; a mob of six hundred seized him, tied him to the back of a car and dragged him at high speed, then poured gasoline on him and set him ablaze (Finkle, *Forum for Protest*, pp. 106–7).

11. Studies of blacks in World War II almost invariably tell about blacks' anger over the Red Cross blood policies and about how blacks were further incensed when they learned of Drew's pioneering blood plasma work. See Finkle, *Forum for Protest*, pp. 105–6; Foner, *Blacks and the Military*, p. 140; Dalfiume, *Desegregation of the U.S. Armed Forces*, p. 107; and Wynn, *Afro-American and the Second World War*, p. 85.

12. A book discussing in depth the dangers of receiving blood contaminated by the AIDS virus is Feldschuh's *Safe Blood*. See also Eckert and Wallace, *Securing a Safer Blood Supply*.

13. Montagu, *Man's Most Dangerous Myth*, pp. 280–82.

14. In his book about the social psychology involved in donating blood, Richard Titmuss noted, "The history of every people assigns to blood a unique importance. . . . For centuries . . . in all cultures and societies, blood has been regarded as a vital, and often magical, life-sustaining fluid, marking all important events in life, marriage, birth, initiation and death, and its loss has been associated with disgrace, disgust, impotence, sickness and tragedy" (*Gift Relationship*, pp. 15–16).

15. Holly Mathews, a medical anthropologist at East Carolina University in Greenville, N.C., has developed a taxonomy of folk illnesses and associated remedies. One of its key concepts held that bodily health can be determined by the flavor of the blood—e.g., "sweet" blood vs. "bitter" blood (Mathews interview).

16. James H. Jones, *Bad Blood*, pp. 71–73. " 'Bad blood' meant different things to different people among rural blacks, and usually more than one thing to all of them. It was a catchall phrase that referred to many different ailments" (p. 71). For further documentation of rural black folk beliefs about blood, see also Charles Johnson, *Shadow of the Plantation*, pp. 196, 201–2.

17. See Titmuss, *Gift Relationship*, pp. 15–18.

18. Ibid., p. 15: " 'The blood is the life' says Deuteronomy (xii, 23). 'For this is my blood of the New Testament which is shed for you' (Matthew xxvi, 28)."

19. Puckett, *Folk Beliefs of the Southern Negro*, p. 540. Puckett also documents a medical "panacea" in which "an old woman doctor whipped a girl's lap with

pawpaw switches to drive out the bad blood ('black blood') from her muscles" (p. 390).

20. Ibid., p. 541.

21. "Blood Donor Testimonials and How to Use Them" (fact sheet of the Blood Donor Service, National Headquarters, American Red Cross), 1 August 1945, File 505.09 ("Misc. Criticisms and Commendations"), Box No. 902, Records of the ARC 1935–46, National Archives Gift Collection, RG 200, National Archives, Washington, D.C.

22. See Dundes, *Blood Libel Legend*, a study of a nine-hundred-year-old anti-Semitic legend that alleged that Jews murdered Christian infants to obtain blood to make matzah.

23. Fletcher, "Administrative History," pp. 135–36. Fletcher notes that all of the Red Cross's attempts to lessen the hostility of black Americans failed: "The flood of denunciation continued, as is amply attested by hundreds of communications in the files not only of National Headquarters of the American Red Cross but by many in those of the White House and of the Office of the Surgeon General of the War Department" (p. 135). A great number of these letters to the American Red Cross are located in one place: Folders 1941–43 and 1944–46, File 505.09 ("Negro Blood"), Box 909, Records of the American Red Cross (1935–46), National Archives Gift Collection, RG 200, National Archives, Washington, D.C. (hereafter cited as Negro Blood file).

24. Sylvia M. Tucker to Mrs. Franklin D. Roosevelt, 14 December 1941, Folder 1941–43, Negro Blood file.

25. Walter White to Norman Davis, 27 January 1942, Folder 1941–43, Negro Blood file. White had a sense of humor as well as a capacity for outrage. Writing to Norman Davis on 15 May 1943 after visiting a blood donor center, he once again protested the practice of segregating blood: "I saw no Negroes there today, although I was followed by Wellington Koo, Jr. Whether he stipulated that his blood be given only to Chinese, I do not know. I intend, upon my next visit, to stipulate that my blood be given only to males of Scotch-Irish extraction, with Moustaches, and coming preferably from Bradford County in Pennsylvania" (Folder 1941–43, Negro Blood file).

26. A prominent black doctor representing the National Medical Association wrote President Roosevelt in 1944 and mentioned Charles Drew's work with blood: "To the enemy at least" the practice of blood segregation "would smack of a fascist practice of which they most assuredly would approve namely to divide and conquer" (T. M. Smith to the president, 29 December 1944, Folder 1944–45, Negro Blood file).

27. Sickels, *Race, Marriage and the Law*, p. 15. Sickels notes, "Of all the attributes of an inferior group, the most feared is its power to pollute. . . . the ultimate pollution and ultimate challenge to the dominance of the superior racial caste is intermarriage."

28. Ibid., p. 33.

29. Myrdal, *American Dilemma*, pp. 97–101. "In this magical sphere of the white man's mind, the Negro is inferior, totally independent of rational proofs and discourse. . . . He is 'the opposite race' — an inner enemy, 'antithesis of character and properties of the white man.' . . . As the color white is asso-

ciated with everything good, with Christ and the angels, with heaven, fairness, cleanliness, virtue, intelligence, courage, and progress, so black has, through the ages, carried associations with all that is bad and low: black stands for dirt, sin, and the devil. . . . [Thus] the Negro is believed to be . . . dangerous . . . and [thus he] is segregated, and one deep idea behind segregation is that of quarantining what is evil, shameful, and feared in society" (p. 100).

30. "Resolutions against Segregated Blood Banks," National Medical Association, office of chairman of War and Defense Committee, 17 August 1942, Folder 1941–43, Negro Blood file. In this resolution the authors point out that it is medically contradictory to oppose blood-mixing while endorsing the common southern practice of using black wet nurses for white babies: "It is quite certain that along with the nutritious elements in the milk of these colored women, the white infants ingested many of the same substances which were circulating in the blood stream of the women who suckled them. It is most unlikely that it did them any harm."

31. Guillory, "Pro-Slavery Arguments," pp. 210, 212–13. Guillory reports that the Louisiana State Medical Convention in 1849 appointed Cartwright chairman of a committee commissioned to study and prepare for the profession a report on the diseases peculiar to Negroes. Cartwright published his findings in several articles: "Report on the Diseases and Physical Peculiarities of the Negro Race" [Part 1], *NOM and SJ* 7 (1851): 692–713; ibid. [Part 2], *NOM and SJ* 8 (1851–52): 187–94; "Diseases and Peculiarities of the Negro Race," *DeBow's Review* 11 (July 1851): 64–69; and *DeBow's Review* 11 (September 1851): 331–36.

32. Cartwright, "Diseases and Peculiarities of the Negro Race," reprinted in Paskoff and Wilson, *Cause of the South*, p. 27. All of the following direct quotations from Cartwright appeared in this *Cause of the South* reprint, which combined the two *DeBow's Review* articles cited in note 31 above.

33. Cartwright, "Diseases and Peculiarities of the Negro Race," p. 29. See also Savitt, *Medicine and Slavery*. Savitt notes that blacks historically have "shown higher incidence and more severe manifestations of respiratory illness than have whites" and that "even today there is some confusion among medical authorities regarding [the reasons for] the susceptibility of Negroes to severe pulmonary infections" (p. 36). Savitt concludes that a variety of environmental factors probably accounted for the higher rate of respiratory illness among southern blacks (p. 37).

34. Savitt, *Medicine and Slavery*, p. 37.

35. Ibid., p. 41.

36. Gossett, *Race*, pp. 64–65. Nott also argued that the American Indian was incapable of civilization: "it is vain to talk of civilizing them. You might as well attempt to change the nature of the buffalo" (quoted in Gossett, *Race*, p. 65).

37. Du Bois edited a famous study in 1906, *Health and Physique of the Negro American*, documenting the urban environmental factors that were some of the causes of the high black mortality rates. In it, Du Bois pointed out that the "matter of sickness is an indication of social and economic position (not of race)" (p. 90).

38. Haller's *Outcasts from Evolution* describes the thinking of this period in great detail.
39. Ibid., p. 60.
40. Ibid., pp. 40–68.
41. Hall, *Revolt against Chivalry*, pp. 145–57. Hall refers to this constellation of attitudes that justified lynching as the " 'Southern rape complex.' " Hall recounts that "Strange Fruit," the famous song about lynching that was written for Billie Holiday by poet Lewis Allen ("Southern trees bear a strange fruit, / Blood on the leaves and blood at the root"), was inspired by the death of Holiday's father in Dallas, Texas: he was refused medical treatment by Dallas's white hospitals (p. 306, note 58. See also Holiday, *Lady Sings the Blues*, pp. 70–71, 86–88). See also Harris, *Exorcising Blackness*, pp. 1–28. Harris elucidates in depth the "psychology of myth-making" behind lynching, noting that it was premised on the myths of black sexual prowess and aggressiveness and of virtuous, innocent white womanhood. She notes, "Unfortunately, some myths, once established, acquire the power to destroy" (p. 18).
42. James H. Jones, *Bad Blood*, p. 24.
43. Haller, *Outcasts from Evolution*, p. 56.
44. Shufeldt, *The Negro*, p. 150.
45. Haller, *Outcasts from Evolution*, pp. 59–60.
46. A useful book that explores the psychological dynamics involved in this historical phenomenon of scapegoating is Kovel's *White Racism*.
47. Unsigned letter submitted to Rep. Pete Jarman by Caryl B. Abbott, 10 March 1945, Folder 1944–46, Negro Blood file.
48. Baltimore was a segregated southern city, and the refusal to accept the young black woman's blood was based on the local custom of segregated hospital care. She apparently was informed that she could give her blood at the local black hospital, but not with her fellow white employees at the whites-only blood center. See "The Separation of Negro Blood in the Processing of Plasma" (memo from DeWitt Smith to the chairman of the American Red Cross), 28 July 1944, Folder 1944–45, Negro Blood file.
49. "Visit to Baltimore, Md." (memo from Albert McCown to Mr. Fieser), 12 August 1941, Folder 1941–43, Negro Blood file.
50. Rep. Rankin of Mississippi, "The Gentleman from Mississippi" (speech delivered in Congress on 28 May 1942), reprint from *New York PM Daily*, Folder 1941–43, Negro Blood file.
51. Unlike either Davis or McIntyre, Magee was personally opposed to mixing black and white blood (James C. Magee to Norman H. Davis, 18 August 1941, Folder 1941–43, Negro Blood file).
52. G. Canby Robinson to A. J. Berres Jr., 17 December 1943, Folder 1941–43, Negro Blood file. Robinson also commented "off the record" that he could not guarantee that the designation of Negro blood was "strict."
53. Arthur Lee Kinsolving to Mrs. Leon, 4 April 1942, Folder 1941–43, Negro Blood file.
54. Norman Davis to William L. Chenery, 12 March 1942, Folder 1941–43, Negro Blood file. Davis further commented in this letter, "Frankly I have

never dealt with a problem more loaded with dynamite and more difficult of a solution that would be universally acceptable. . . . Strange as it may seem there is less prejudice and trouble over this question [of mixing blood] in the South than there is in the North but after all prejudices are more difficult to deal with than facts."

55. In an article attacking the blood segregation policy, newspaper columnist Albert Deutsch described Drew thus: "Handsome, modest, well-endowed both physically and mentally, he is a living refutation of the myth of white supremacy. He has fought his way up through the dense mass of discrimination that only a Negro knows. He is all American caliber, a man deserving homage from all, black and white" ("Dr. Charles Drew, Surgeon — A Study in Blood and Race," *New York PM Daily*, 30 March 1944).

56. Woodward, *Strange Career*, p. 131. Woodward notes, "American war propaganda stressed above all else the abhorrence of the West for Hitler's brand of racism and its utter incompatibility with the democratic faith for which we fought. The relevance of this deep stirring of the American conscience for the position of the Negro was not lost upon him and his champions. Awareness of the inconsistency between practice at home and propaganda abroad placed a powerful lever in their hands." An excellent source on the experience of black soldiers in World War II and in particular on the discrimination they faced and their subsequent morale problems is Ulysses Lee, *U.S. Army in World War II*. Discussing the results of a study on morale, Lee notes, "That many of the conditions which produced deep concern among Negro soldiers lay outside the purely military sphere was indicated in their questions. Over a quarter of Negro soldiers . . . asked questions about the racial pattern after the war: 'Will I as a Negro share this so-called democracy after the war? . . . Will colored people be continued [*sic*] subjected to the humiliating law of Jim Crow and segregation as before the war?' " (p. 327).

57. Letter from a soldier in Rome, Italy, to his wife . . . in the War Department, 17 September 1944, Subject File 1940–47 ("Blood Plasma — Red Cross"), Entry 91–Box 183, Records of the Office of the Secretary of War, RG 107, National Archives, Washington, D.C. Many other letters are contained in Folder AG 291.21, AG Decimal File 1940–45 ("Negroes and Negro Race"), Box 1071, Records of the Adjutant General's Office, Army, RG 407, National Archives.

58. Ulysses Lee, *U.S. Army in World War II*, pp. 331–32. Lee notes that symbols of the black soldiers' low status, and sources of particular resentment for them, included being forced to harvest cotton, to clean streets in southern cities, and to have their blood segregated by the American Red Cross. Lee then refers to Drew: "The irony of the situation was further heightened by the widely publicized fact that a pioneer researcher in blood preservation, medical supervisor of the emergency Blood for Britain project in 1940, and director of the first American Red Cross Blood Plasma Bank, a pilot unit for the armed services established in 1941, was Dr. Charles R. Drew of the Howard University School of Medicine. . . . News of this sort of action, once it got to troops, lowered general morale."

59. The actual statements and public appearances Drew made were discussed in Chapter 5.

60. Joel Frances, "Negro Surgeon, World Plasma Expert, Derides Red Cross Blood Segregation," *Chicago Defender*, 26 September 1942.

61. "Men of All Colors Owe Life to Negro Medical Scientist," *Des Moines Tribune*, 22 November 1944 (reprint from *Coronet* magazine).

62. "Prologue to Blood Plasma," *What's New* (publication of Abbott Laboratories, North Chicago, Ill.), December 1944. Edgar B. Carter of Abbott Laboratories to Charles R. Drew, 1 November 1944, Folder 6, Box 136-1, CRDP.

63. Charles Drew to John Scudder, 15 April 1944, Folder 6, Box 136-1, CRDP.

64. See Buckingham, "Dr. Charles Richard Drew," pp. 34, 35, 36–44.

65. Whitney Young's 1964 column, which featured the major Drew legend's first appearance in print, inflated Drew's role as a blood plasma pioneer, calling him "the man who developed the theory of blood plasma and pioneered the blood bank" ("Bigotry and the Blood Bank," *Baltimore Afro-American*, 17 October 1964). In many but by no means all versions of the major Drew legend, Drew's role in blood work is inflated to some extent; thus legend number one and legend number three are commonly paired, heightening the irony of the story, as in Young's version.

66. In 1964, the same year the Whitney Young column was published, *Time* magazine ran an article on "Desegregated History" that described Drew as the "plasma expert . . . who set up U.S. blood banks" (*Time*, 27 March 1964, 59). In 1967 and 1968, the Old Taylor Distillery Company ran a series of advertisements in *Ebony* magazine celebrating black heroes as "Ingenious Americans." The short feature on Drew began, "A Negro started the most important bank in the world." The story credited Drew with introducing "the revolutionary idea of a central depository for blood" (*Ebony*, December 1968, p. 8). A 1981 *New York Times* article on Drew opened with the statement, "The pioneering work of Dr. Charles R. Drew made possible the preservation of blood plasma and the establishment of the now familiar blood banks" (Samuel A. Tower, "He Pioneered the Preservation of Blood Plasma," *New York Times*, 14 June 1981, section D, p. 40). Even a number of the articles written as major attempts to debunk the third Drew legend have added to the credibility of the first legend about Drew. Typical in this regard is the opening sentence of a 1982 story in a North Carolina newspaper: "A black physician wants to stamp out the myth that Dr. Charles Drew, a black who developed the blood bank system, bled to death in 1950 because a whites-only Alamance County hospital refused to treat him" ("Doctor wants to put end to story hospital refused to treat black physician," *Raleigh News and Observer*, 12 July 1982).

67. Charles Richard Drew, "Negro Scholars," p. 148. Drew delivered this address on 30 October 1949 before the annual meeting of the Association for the Study of Negro Life and History in New York City.

68. Sterne, *Blood Brothers*, pp. 169–70.

69. Even Jack Foner, a reputable historian, writes that Drew "resigned from the Red Cross upon learning that the armed forces refused to accept blacks' blood" (*Blacks and the Military*, p. 140). A distinguished black leader, William Hastie, did resign in protest during the war. When he resigned in January 1943, Hastie, the secretary of war's civilian aide on Negro affairs, publicly

denounced the army's discriminatory policies toward black soldiers; he wrote a series of articles that appeared in black newspapers and were also published in a 1943 pamphlet called *On Clipped Wings* (Finkle, *Forum for Protest*, pp. 154–56).

70. Hardwick, *Charles Richard Drew*, pp. 131–32. Drew's words to the reporters are slightly different from those Sterne attributes to him, but they are similar in style: " 'I will not give you an opinion. I will give you the scientific facts in the matter. The blood of individual human beings may differ by blood groupings, but there is absolutely no scientific basis to indicate any difference according to race.' "

71. Lichello, *Pioneer in Blood Plasma*, pp. 149–50. The quotation above has been repeated as Drew's own in many subsequent publications. It appears in another book about Drew: Klein, *Hidden Contributors*, p. 165. It also appears in several newspaper articles, including one published in 1980 in the main Alamance County newspaper that debunked the major legend (Jay Ashley, "Grim Reaper Claimed Him Here," *Burlington Times-News*, 1 April 1980).

72. See Sterne, *Blood Brothers*, p. 170; Bertol, *Charles Drew*, pp. 28– 32.

73. Drew returned to Howard University in early April 1941, about a month before his leave was officially up (Charles Drew to M. Lenore Drew, 17 March 1941 and 24 March 1941, Folder 9, Box 135-1, CRDP).

74. The statement of policy excluding black blood donors was issued on 5 November 1941 ("Statements of Policy Regarding Negro Blood Donors" [information sheet], CD-ARC-NH).

75. Letters from Charles Drew to Lenore Drew, January 1941 through June 1941, Folders 8 and 9, Box 135-1, and Folder 5, Box 136-1, CRDP. See also W. Montague Cobb, "Charles Richard Drew," p. 243. Cobb notes that despite "national resentment created by the blood segregation policy of the Red Cross . . . Dr. Drew is not known to have murmured."

76. See note 101 in this chapter.

77. Ashley, "Grim Reaper," 1 April 1950. A similar debunking article in a black newspaper also repeated the second legend: Yvonne Anderson, "Dr. Charles Drew: Dispelling the Myth?," *Greensboro Carolina Peacemaker*, 23 April 1983.

78. See CD-ARC-NH. Arranged in chronological order, the entries in this file on Charles Drew provide a window onto the rise of all three Drew legends and the competing Red Cross counter-legends. By reading them, one witnesses how a number of different Red Cross public relations officials over a period of years struggled in vain to rein in Drew well-wishers and mythologizers. For the most part, the official statements the Red Cross has made about Drew are historically accurate; but in the organization's persistent attempts to trim Drew down to life-size proportions, his historical contribution has been stated too narrowly.

79. In a Red Cross memo reporting on Drew's speech at an August 1944 Labor Day demonstration that had been organized to protest the segregated blood policy, an official commented in an accompanying letter that he believed Drew had never been involved with the American Red Cross blood program (Mr. G. Stewart Brown to Mary Pond, 9 August 1944, "Talk by Dr. Drew at meeting of Local 10, UFWA"; Dewitt Smith to Ramone S. Eaton, 14 August 1944; Dewitt Smith to the chairman, 14 August 1944, all in CD-ARC-NH).

80. "Red Cross Award Policy Questioned," undated [1948], *Washington Afro-American.*

81. Bonham to Dr. McGinnes, 14 April 1948, and Jesse O. Thomas to Howard Bonham, 11 March 1948, CD-ARC-NH.

82. Barnett to Bonham, 25 May 1950, and Bonham to Barnett, 2 June 1950, CD-ARC-NH.

83. Jack Henry to Irene Haas, 9 January 1968, CD-ARC-NH.

84. "Rough Draft, cw, 9/14/81," 14 September 1981, and attachment to memo from Elbert Brown to Lewellys F. Barker, 13 January 1982, CD-ARC-NH.

85. Ibid.

86. Clemen interview.

87. Ibid.

88. Pete Upton (national director, Office of Public Relations) to Mary Jo Nimmons, 28 April 1969, CD-ARC-NH.

89. Memo from John C. Wilson to Clyde Buckingham, 15 May 1967 (attachment to Buckingham, "Dr. Charles Richard Drew"), CD-ARC-NH.

90. Buckingham, "Dr. Charles Richard Drew," pp. 1–2, 10, 13, 15, 18, 20–22, 28, 29. Buckingham is the author of three published historical works about the Red Cross: *Red Cross Disaster Relief, For Humanity's Sake,* and *Clara Barton.*

91. Memorandum from Pete Upton to John C. Wilson, 4 February 1969, CD-ARC-NH.

92. DeKleine, "Early History"; Fletcher, "Administrative History"; Kendrick, *Blood Program in World War II.*

93. The first scholarly article about the early blood program, published in the September 1944 issue of *What's New,* completely left Drew out. As I mentioned in note 61 of this chapter, it was only after a black physician — Ira A. St. Hill, of Meharry Medical College — wrote the magazine editor to request that Drew's contribution be included that the magazine published a follow-up article that told Drew's story: "Prologue to Blood Plasma," *What's New,* December 1944. This situation is revealed by four letters between Edgar B. Carter of Abbott Laboratories and Charles Drew, 1 November 1944 to 11 January 1945, Folder 6, Box 136-1, CRDP.

94. In 1950 the Red Cross initiated and supervised the in-house publication of forty-nine separate monographs, all of which served as the foundation for Dulles's *American Red Cross,* also published in 1950. Fletcher's and De-Kleine's monographs were part of this project (Gilbo interview, 29 June 1994).

95. Kendrick, *Blood Program in World War II.* Kendrick, for example, largely focuses instead on Earl S. Taylor, who essentially took Drew's job in May 1941 and thus became technical director of the entire Blood Donor Service when it expanded, as one of the key pioneers of the blood program (p. xviii). Drew worked closely with Taylor in the first half of 1941 and trained him for the job before he left. However, Kendrick does at least indirectly recognize the importance of Drew's pioneering work when he notes the value of the Blood for Britain project and Drew's role as medical supervisor in it (pp. 13–15).

96. DeKleine, "Early History," p. 35. DeKleine reveals here that he knew Drew

worked in the New York Red Cross pilot program. As we shall see farther on, in a 1944 letter, he denies that Drew had any connection with the Red Cross blood program.

97. Ibid., p. 27. DeKleine writes, "I argued vigorously against sending liquid plasma overseas, not because of lack of appreciation for this important therapeutic measure but because no one except Dr. John Elliott had sufficient experience to direct the technical phases of processing liquid blood plasma on such a large scale. It was planned to collect several thousand pints a month and I could foresee trouble. I proposed Dr. Elliott's name as director, but this was not approved by the Blood Transfusion Association. It was evident that under the circumstances the project was doomed to failure."

98. Ibid., p. 21.

99. Ibid., p. 25, excerpted from letter from John Elliott to William DeKleine, 22 June 1940.

100. Walter Davidson, the Red Cross official, was with the American Red Cross in a number of roles from 1917 until 1945. His job just before retiring was that of assistant administrator, general services. He wrote seven of the monographs that were used as background for Dulles's history of the Red Cross, vols. 35 through 41 (Gilbo interview, 29 June 1994).

101. William DeKleine to Walter Davidson, 1 May 1944, CD-ARC-NH. This letter is especially puzzling, because DeKleine notes Drew's involvement with the Blood for Britain project yet seems unaware he was employed by the New York chapter in the winter and spring of 1941. In marked contrast, DeKleine's "Early History" (1950) notes Drew's role with the New York chapter but fails to mention his involvement with the British project. Given that DeKleine was in New York in 1940 and 1941 and involved with both projects, his failure to recognize the consistent role Drew played is hard to understand (see DeKleine, "Early History," p. 35).

102. "Dr. William DeKleine Is Dead at 79; Set Up Red Cross Blood Bank in War," *New York Times*, 27 September 1957, page unknown. Drew returned to Howard University in April 1941; DeKleine returned to private medical practice in September 1941, three months before the United States officially entered the war.

103. Tracing the Red Cross's deep international appeal, a Red Cross historian noted, "So absolute and uncompromising is the demand that a suffering human being shall be succoured for his own sake only, without respect of class, condition, creed or race, and above all without discrimination as to whether he be friend or enemy, that it lifts the Red Cross far above the plane of opportunism . . . [in its] humanitarian domain. . . . The creation of the Red Cross [was] an epoch-making event" (Huber, *Red Cross*, p. 13). See also Barton, *Red Cross*, pp. 94–103.

104. In this statement, Davis explicitly overlooked the fact that many of those receiving blood were black and that many of them objected to the polices of exclusion and segregation; it was assumed that black soldiers did not object to receiving white blood.

105. Dulles, *American Red Cross*, pp. 419–21.

of exclusion and segregation; it was assumed that black soldiers did not object to receiving white blood.

105. Dulles, *American Red Cross*, pp. 419–21.
106. Hurd, *Compact History*, pp. 236–37.
107. "Rough Draft, cw, 9/14/1981."
108. "Commentary at National Portrait Gallery re Charles Richard Drew" (memo from Harold W. Starr to George Elsey), 28 April 1971, CD-ARC-NH.
109. "Rough Draft, cw, 9/14/81."
110. DeKleine, "Early History," p. 7.
111. Fletcher, "Administrative History," pp. 35–36. Fletcher discusses the fact that the barrage of criticism aimed at the segregation policy never let up. He notes that the Red Cross seriously considered changing the policy late in the spring of 1942. Also, in attempts to soften black hostility, the Red Cross tried two experiments that completely and quite understandably failed. In Baltimore, a blood donor center "exclusively for Negroes" was tried; and in New Orleans, the blood donor center tried setting aside one day a week for black donors (p. 135).
112. Kendrick, *Blood Program in World War II*, pp. 119–20, 129.
113. Buckingham, "Dr. Charles Richard Drew," pp. 34–35.

CHAPTER EIGHT

1. "Student Dies of Mishap Injuries," *Greensboro Daily News*, 3 December 1950, News section, p. 8.
2. Yount interview, 19 January 1983; Marvin Yount, "A History of Alamance General Hospital, Inc.," 1949, Yount personal papers.
3. William B. Whitley, "No Beds Reason for Duke Refusing Injured Student," *Durham Morning Herald*, 5 December 1950, p. 1. According to this story, the surgeon did not want to be identified publicly. He "requested his name be withheld."
4. As we have already seen, Charles Drew would have been sent on to Duke if the surgeons who worked on him had believed he could survive the trip.
5. Harold Kernodle interview.
6. Carl Crabtree interview, 4 February 1983. Crabtree, who had been an Alamance County ambulance driver in 1950, pointed out that since there were only two-lane roads between Burlington and Durham in 1950, rather than an interstate highway, the trip could sometimes take longer.
7. Whitley, "No Beds."
8. "Duke's Answer," *Register* (newspaper of A&T College, Greensboro, N.C.), January 1951, p. 2. Edens's statement about the incident was based verbatim on a statement Duke Hospital superintendent F. Ross Porter made about the incident in a letter to a man expressing concern about Avery's treatment: F. Ross Porter to J. W. Harrison, 10 December 1950, Folder ("Duke University Medical Center [2] [1951–1955]"), Box 27, A. Hollis Edens Papers, Duke University Archives, Perkins Library, Duke University, Durham, N.C. (hereafter cited as Avery folder, Edens Papers). During the

winter and spring of 1951, Edens wrote a number of different people who expressed concern about and protest of Duke's treatment of Avery; each time, he repeated the same statement. Edens's position will be discussed further later in the chapter.

9. Whitley, "No Beds."

10. Starting in 1930, Duke's Outpatient Clinic treated many poor patients who came from all over the state, charging roughly a dollar a visit. In 1950, the clinic consisted of 131 examining and treatment rooms and professional staff in twenty specialties. By July 1950, 104,408 visits had been made to the clinic in the previous year, bringing the total visits to 1,375,437 during the twenty years of its operation (Davison, *First Twenty Years*, pp. 58–59). See also Gifford, *Evolution of a Medical Center.*

11. Stead interview. Stead, who in 1950 was physician in chief of Duke Hospital and chairman of the Department of Medicine, said that at that time the hospital's public "general medical service" wards had sixty beds for white patients and fifteen beds for black patients. For white patients there were an additional sixty private beds (in medical service) available. There were no private beds for black patients. If a black person was admitted as a private patient at Duke, he or she was placed in the black public ward. There were, of course, no black doctors on Duke's staff in 1950.

12. Reynolds, "Hospital Expansion," p. 35. In 1947, when Clyde Munger did a study of Lincoln Hospital, he recommended that Lincoln expand its number of beds from 93 to 125. Munger estimated that there were only 11 other beds for black patients in the whole drawing area that Lincoln served. Watts Hospital had 124 beds in 1947 and needed more, but Watts was exclusively white (pp. 33–34). Lincoln was extremely overcrowded, and its equipment was limited. "Lincoln's nursery was taxed to such extremes that babies were placed in double-decked bassinets. The operating room hummed with activity to the point that doctors often found it difficult to obtain help. . . . Perhaps most revealing, bed-pans were being sterilized in a solution-filled bathtub because the hospital did not own one bed-pan sterilizer." Eugene Stead Jr. corroborated this portrait of Lincoln's situation (Stead interview).

13. Watts interview, 6 July 1988. On the Maltheus Avery incident, Watts commented, "They moved him because they didn't care. He is typical of a lot of patients sent on to Lincoln under the guise of no beds. Every afternoon we would get four to five patients whose object was to go to the Duke Outpatient Clinic. . . . Many were sent who should not have been. Proper medical care would have dictated that you not move a patient to a smaller, less well equipped hospital — except that they were black."

14. William Rich, Lincoln Hospital superintendent, stated, "We are proud of the fact that we have never turned away anyone in need of our services because he or she could not pay for them" (*Durham Morning Herald*, 26 October 1939). John Zaven Ayanian, who quoted Rich, pointed out that the Duke Endowment's financial support of Lincoln Hospital was what made it possible for Rich to make this claim. He further noted that in 1925 Lincoln had become the first North Carolina hospital to be supported by the Duke Endowment. While the Duke Endowment was indeed an important benefac-

17. Whitley, "No Beds."
18. *Durham Morning Herald*, 6 December 1950, editorial page.
19. "Man Refused at Hospital Later Dies," *Raleigh News and Observer*, 5 December 1950, p. 7.
20. "Above Rules," *Raleigh News and Observer*, 7 December 1950, editorial page.
21. "Hospital Refuses Dying A&T Student," *Durham Carolina Times*, 9 December 1950, p. 1.
22. "Hospital Refuses," *Durham Carolina Times*.
23. "No Room in the Hospital," *Durham Carolina Times*, 23 December 1950, editorial page.
24. "Segregation Responsible," *Baltimore Afro-American*, 16 December 1950, p. 12.
25. "Still No Room in the Inn . . . in Some Places," *Baltimore Afro-American*, 23 December 1950.
26. "Student Protest to Duke Authorities in Open Letter," *Register* (A&T College), January 1951, p. 2.
27. Paul L. Garber to President Hollis Edens, date unclear [1951?], Avery folder, Edens Papers. Edens replied to Garber, "Really, that incident has been used unfairly more than any incident that has happened since I have been at Duke. . . . The enclosed statement from the Superintendent of the Hospital sets forth the facts in the case, but the Southern Patriot and its supporters refuse to accept the statement." Edens noted that the Patriot escaped libel only by "stopping short of a direct charge." He concluded, "We have taken the attitude that nothing is to be gained by arguing with a propaganda sheet" (A. Hollis Edens to Dr. Garber, 8 October 1951, Avery folder, Edens Papers).
28. Thelma Allen to president of Duke University, 11 April 1951, Avery folder, Edens Papers.
29. John Schaffner to President Edens, 12 April 1951, Avery folder, Edens Papers.
30. James A. Dombrowski to A. Hollis Edens, 29 March 1951; James A. Dombrowski to A. Hollis Edens, 22 June 1951, Avery folder, Edens Papers. The research that the Southern Conference Education Fund was conducting provided the material for a book published the next year — Maund, *The Untouchables*, which discussed Avery's case and a number of other hospital refusals.
31. A. Hollis Edens to James A. Dombrowski, 6 April 1951, Avery folder, Edens Papers.
32. Porter to Harrison, 10 December 1950, Avery folder, Edens Papers.
33. Ross to Dr. Edens (memo), 13 January 1951, Avery folder, Edens Papers.
34. A. Hollis Edens to James A. Dombrowski, 25 June 1951, Avery folder, Edens Papers.
35. Duke historian Robert F. Durden, writing about the university's climate in the early 1950s, said that Duke faced "great challenges" with regard to African Americans, having "carefully observed the state's and the region's laws and customs concerning racial segregation." Durden closed his book with these comments: "In light of Trinity-Duke's history, the Duke family's

conspicuous fairness toward African Americans, and the cosmopolitan nature of the university's faculty and student body, Duke stood at a critical junction in the 1950s. One would think that Duke University might grasp the opportunity to demonstrate in a particularly difficult yet vital area 'the real leadership in the educational world' that J. B. Duke had called for in his indenture" (*Launching of Duke University*, p. 500).

36. In 1990, forty years after Avery's death, some Duke officials displayed a similar attitude, defending Duke when given the opportunity to confront this incident from the institution's segregated past. Waddell and Parnell Avery had been invited to speak at a Duke history research seminar on segregation. An in-house Duke publication carried a story about their visit, and for the story, a Duke reporter had asked Duke doctors to comment on Avery's refusal of treatment. Rather amazingly, they took the position, as officials had in 1950, that Duke had done no wrong. They maintained that "Duke physicians gave young Avery all appropriate medical care"; that President A. Hollis Edens had written a "sympathetic letter outlining the physicians' medical rationale" to those questioning his treatment; and, finally, that it was "not possible to know whether moving . . . [Avery] to another hospital accelerated his death." The Duke reporter, who preferred to remain anonymous, ultimately deleted these comments from the story before it ran (draft copy, "Duke Doctoral Candidate Takes Long Look at Segregation in the South," 15 March 1990, p. 3; "Grad student looks at segregation in South," *Duke Dialogue*, 23 March 1990, p. 3). Several articles were published about the Averys' visit to Duke: Durham's *Carolina Times* ran the *Duke Dialogue* article, retitled "Duke Doctoral Student Looks at Segregation in the South," 27 April 1990, p. 9, and the *Raleigh News and Observer* ran its own story: Lynn Haessly, "A Victim of the Times," 29 March 1990, pp. 1E and 3E. The *Alexandria (Va.) Mount Vernon Gazette* ran a story as well: Hilary Adams, "Professor debunks Charles Drew myth leaving a true story of segregation," 8 March 1990, p. 3.

37. "Henderson Student Is Fatally Injured," *Henderson Daily Dispatch*, 4 December 1950, p. 5. It is possible that Avery's treatment at Duke was not yet known, as the first story that reported his refusal ran on December 5 in the *Durham Morning Herald* (see note 3 in this chapter).

38. "For the Common Good," *Henderson Daily Dispatch*, 4 December 1950, p. 4. I was not able to determine whether or not the conjunction of the Avery story and the Duke Endowment editorial was accidental.

39. Stead interview. A black woman who had been a patient at Duke Hospital for a stay of twenty days in 1951 wrote the hospital superintendent to bring to his attention several features of the hospital she found troubling. Nott Ward, which was reserved for black patients, she said, had only one bathroom for both men and women. "Just as disturbing," she wrote, "and perhaps of far more dangerous portent" was the fact that "almost without exception" black patients were called by their first names, while white patients were addressed appropriately (Pansy E. Pendergrass to F. R. Porter, 10 August 1951, Avery folder, Edens Papers).

40. Maltheus Avery's brother, Waddell Avery, who was a senior at Virginia State

College in Petersburg, Va., in the spring of 1950, said that he had heard the story of Drew's "bleeding to death" while he was still in college, because he was a member of Omega Psi Phi, the fraternity Drew had also belonged to (Waddell Avery interview, 9 July 1988).

41. Franklin interview, 9 February 1983.

42. Ibid., 29 September 1982.

43. Stanback interview.

44. Edmonds interview, 7 January 1983.

45. Ibid., 21 January 1983.

46. Vine interview.

47. Gibbs interview.

48. Harold Kernodle interview. Kernodle further commented, "What worried us was they might die before they got there [to the next hospital]. You don't want that to happen." Kernodle said that "every now and then" he or his brother, the other surgeon on duty, would ride with a patient in the ambulance to keep the patient's breathing open and fluids going: "We didn't do that for everybody. But we did it for some of them."

49. Harold Kernodle interview.

50. Stead interview.

51. Maund, *The Untouchables*. For this publication, the famous artist Ben Shahn did lithograph drawings that depicted black men in dying postures being turned away from hospitals.

52. Ibid., pp. 2–3.

53. There were 711 replies out of 2,414 inquiries sent. The American Hospital Directory listed 2,414 medical institutions for eighteen southern and border states and the District of Columbia, the areas where strict segregation prevailed in this period. It was learned that 584 (82 percent) of the hospitals admitted black patients and that 33,451 (32 percent) of a total of 102,969 beds were available to them (ibid., p. 2).

54. Ibid., pp. 3–5.

55. The major primary source for Avery family history was Waddell Avery, Maltheus Avery's brother, a man with a keen interest in history and thus an avid collector of family documents and recorder of family events. In two lengthy interviews at his home in Alexandria, Va., on 9 and 10 July 1988, he provided much of the information for this section of the chapter on Sonny Avery. Information is based on these interviews with Avery, unless otherwise indicated. Avery's testimony was backed up by a number of family photographs, letters, transcribed tapes, and documents, and also by a county history book with sections on the Avery family and its members: *Heritage of Vance County*. Sections consulted on the Avery family include Jacob and Martha Bing Sr., pp. 119–20; Peter and Emma Hawkins, pp. 234–44; the Napoleon Avery family, pp. 113–14. Parnell Avery, Maltheus Avery's other brother, was another important primary source. I conducted an interview with him in Monroe, N.C., at an Avery family wedding, on 6 August 1988. Parnell Avery's comments come from this interview unless otherwise indicated.

56. *Heritage of Vance County*, p. 382. Under its entry for Samuel Watkins, the

county history reports that Watkins was born 9 September 1852 and died 4 December 1914. In 1875 he and his uncle Charles Watkins opened the S & C Watkins Company, a general hardware store in downtown Henderson. The store became the Samuel Watkins Department Store in 1895, when Charles Watkins died, and after Samuel's death in 1914, the store continued under Watkins family ownership and management. Waddell Avery recalled being sent to this store as a child and wondering why he never had to pay for anything (Waddell Avery interview, 9 July 1988).

57. Waddell Avery said that Emma Watkins Hawkins was the offspring of a male Watkins family member and that he gave the land to her. According to *Heritage of Vance County*, "She was born in 1856 and was purchased as a slave girl in Richmond, Virginia and brought to Henderson, N.C. by the Samuel M. Watkins family." The book goes on to report that during the early years of their marriage, Emma Watkins Hawkins and her husband, Peter Hawkins, an emigré from the Republic of Haiti who came to the Henderson area as a Raleigh and Gaston Railroad worker, acquired a tract of land in the Greystone community that was suitable for farming. On two occasions they donated land for church expansion to the Brookston Missionary Baptist Church — on 31 July 1876 for the church site itself, and on 2 June 1892 for the church cemetery (pp. 243–44). The county history does not indicate how the couple acquired the land but elsewhere notes that Vance County was an area where slave-holding had been extensive. The black population made up roughly 50 percent of the county population, and "by 1910, the percentage of Negro land ownership in several of the counties in this area equalled or exceeded that in any other county in the South" (p. 33).

58. Waddell Avery interview, 9 July 1988.

59. Ibid.

60. *Heritage of Vance County*, pp. 113–14. A large photograph of Napoleon Avery in this county history reveals him to have been a lean-faced, thin-lipped man with high cheekbones. In this photo he wears a coat and tie; he has close-cut hair and a small, neat moustache.

61. Waddell Avery interview, 9 July 1988.

62. Hazel Avery interview; Jones interview. Jones said that most of the birth certificates from Old Fields Township in the 1920s, where Neverson was located, were signed by M. R. Freeman. No birth certificate for Maltheus Avery could be located; however, an "unnamed male" was born to Hazel and Napoleon Avery in Neverson on 7 July 1924, with M. R. Freeman attending. According to Waddell Avery, this certificate must be Evelyn Avery's, since 7 July 1924 is her birthdate (Waddell Avery interview, 20 December 1989). Josephine Newell, a former resident of this area of eastern North Carolina, remembered Malthus Freeman of Bailey, N.C., as a prosperous general practitioner who monopolized medical care in the area and drove away competitors (Newell interview).

63. Waddell Avery interview, 9 July 1988.

64. The Henderson Normal Institute was founded in 1887 and operated by the Freedmen's Board of the United Presbyterian Church, headquartered in Pittsburgh, Pa. The Rev. John Adam Cotton took over as head of the institute

in 1903 and greatly improved and expanded it. In 1911, a small hospital called Jubilee Hospital was built. Jubilee was the area's only black hospital, and it had fifteen beds and one operating room (*Heritage of Vance County*, pp. 36–38).

65. Named after John Adam Cotton, the church was built in 1914 on Chestnut Street in downtown Henderson by the United Presbyterian Church. Cotton was its minister as well as the principal of Henderson Institute (*Heritage of Vance County*, p. 38). "The church was our contact with the black gentry. She forced us into that group," Waddell Avery said (Waddell Avery interview, 9 July 1988).

66. Parnell Avery interview, 6 August 1988.

67. Waddell Avery interview, 9 July 1988.

68. Ibid., 10 July 1988.

69. Ibid., 9 July 1988.

70. Ibid., 10 July 1988.

71. Parnell Avery interview, 6 August 1988.

72. Waddell Avery interview, 9 July 1988.

73. Ibid.

74. Parnell Avery interview, 6 August 1988.

75. Waddell Avery interview, 9 July 1988.

76. Ibid.

77. Collis H. Davis, dean of students, Hampton Institute, to Mrs. Hazel Avery, 22 December 1949, Waddell Avery personal papers. Collis wrote, "I regret to inform you that Maltheus R. Avery was not doing satisfactory work at mid-semester in the following courses: English 101-D; Math 111-D; Biology 103-E."

78. Waddell Avery interview, 9 July 1988.

79. Hazel Avery interview.

80. Waddell Avery interview, 9 July 1988.

81. Williamson was Vance County's first and only black lawyer during this period. Born in Durham, N.C., he graduated from Howard University Law School and practiced in Vance County for more than fifty years. His wife, Mamie Williamson, commenting on the famous 1933 case, said, "It was difficult. . . . You can't know the hatred that went on then. . . . They had the trial . . . late at night, people were out there shooting all around the street, trying to intimidate us." The Durham attorneys on the case, who were black, were forced to hide in the trunk of a white acquaintance's car to get out of town safely (*Heritage of Vance County*, p. 40).

82. Hazel Avery interview.

83. Waddell Avery interview, 9 July 1988.

84. Henderson interview. All the comments from Lynn Michael Napoleon Henderson derive from this interview.

85. Waddell Avery interview, 9 July 1988.

86. Ibid.

87. Ibid.

88. Ibid.

89. Waddell Avery interview, 10 July 1988.

90. Ibid.
91. Ibid.
92. Parnell Avery interview, 6 August 1988.
93. Avery trained as a surgeon under Matthew Walker, chairman of Meharry's Department of Surgery. Walker had been a protégé of Charles Drew. Drew successfully arranged for Walker to sit for the American Board of Surgery examination, and Walker's performance was "superior" (Organ and Kosiba, *Century of Black Surgeons*, pp. 84–85, 122).
94. Waddell Avery interview, 9 July 1988.
95. Ibid., 10 July 1988.
96. Henderson interview, 20 May 1988.
97. Parnell Avery interview, 6 August 1988.
98. Waddell Avery interview, 10 July 1988.
99. Parnell Avery interview, 6 August 1988.
100. Ibid.

CONCLUSION

1. Braudel, *Mediterranean World*, pp. 20–21. Braudel discussed the difficulty of trying to weave together these different strands:

   The basic problem . . . is the problem confronting every historical undertaking. Is it possible somehow to convey simultaneously both that conspicuous history which holds our attention by its continual and dramatic changes—and that other, submerged history, almost silent and always discreet, virtually unsuspected by its observers or its participants, which is little touched by the obstinate erosion of time? This fundamental contradiction, which must always lie at the centre of our thought, can be a vital tool of knowledge and research. . . . Historians have over the years grown accustomed to describing this contradiction in terms of structure and conjuncture, the former denoting long-term, the latter, short-term realities. (p. 16)

2. Gaston, *New South Creed*, p. 9.
3. May, *Cry for Myth*, p. 24.
4. Hackney interview. (Hackney was deputy press secretary to North Carolina governor James Hunt.)
5. See Osterweis, *Myth of the Lost Cause*, and Charles Reagan Wilson, *Baptized in Blood*.
6. Franklin, "As for Our History," p. 3.
7. Gerster and Cords, "Northern Origins of Southern Mythology," pp. 567–82, and William R. Taylor, *Cavalier and Yankee*.
8. See Woodward, "From the First Reconstruction to the Second," pp. 217–63.
9. See Woodward, "Search for Southern Identity," pp. 17–31.
10. Speech by James Baldwin, Chapel Hill, N.C., 12 November 1984. An article that provides insight into the state of African American historiography is Wood's " 'I Did the Best I Could for My Day,' " pp. 85–225.
11. Woodward, *Strange Career*, pp. xvi.

12. Goodwyn, "Hierarchy and Democracy," p. 227.
13. Gaston, *New South Creed*.
14. Baldwin, *Fire Next Time*, p. 129.
15. Harding, "Gift of Blackness," pp. 1–6.
16. Baldwin, *Fire Next Time*, pp. 123–24.
17. Ibid., p. 133.
18. Ellison, *Invisible Man*, pp. 563–64.
19. "Lift Ev'ry Voice and Sing," the Negro National Anthem, words by James Weldon Johnson and music by J. Rosamund Johnson, copyright by Edward Marks Music Corp. (quoted in Angelou, *I Know Why the Caged Bird Sings*, pp. 155–56).
20. See Montagu, *Man's Most Dangerous Myth*, especially pp. 63–132.

Bibliography

ARCHIVES, MANUSCRIPTS, AND PRIVATE PAPERS

Duke University Archives, Perkins Library, Duke University, Durham, North
    Carolina
    A. Hollis Edens Papers
Manuscript Division, Moorland-Spingarn Research Center, Howard University,
    Washington, D.C.
    Charles R. Drew Papers
National Archives and Records Administration, Washington, D.C.
    Gift Collection, Records of the American Red Cross, 1935–1946 (Record
      Group 200)
      Box 902, File 505.09 ("Miscellaneous Criticisms and Commendations")
      Box 909, File 505.09 ("Negro Blood")
    Records of the Office of the Secretary of War (Record Group 107)
      Entry 91-Box 183, Assistant Secretary of War, Civilian Aide to the
        Secretary, Subject File 1940–1947: "Blood Plasma — Red Cross"
    Records of the Adjutant General's Office, Army (Record Group 407)
      Box 1071, AG Decimal File: 1940–1945, Folder AG 291.21: "Negroes and
        Negro Race"
National Headquarters, American Red Cross, Washington, D.C.
    Charles Drew File

PRIVATE COLLECTIONS

Avery, Waddell. Personal papers. Alexandria, Va.
Bensley, E. H. Personal papers. Montreal, Canada.
Drew, Joseph. Personal papers. Arlington, Va.
Quick, C. Mason. Personal papers. Fayetteville, N.C.
White, Jack. Personal papers. Washington, D.C.
Yount, Marvin E., Jr. Personal papers. Burlington, N.C.

INTERVIEWS

Akwari, Onye E. Chapel Hill, N.C., April 1989.
Avery, Hazel. Alexandria, Va., 10 July 1988.
Avery, Parnell. Monroe, N.C., 6 August 1988, January 1990.
Avery, Waddell. Alexandria, Va., 9 July 1988, 10 July 1988, 20 December 1989.
Brooks, Lester. New York, N.Y., 21 November 1985.
Bullock, Samuel. Washington, D.C., 3 February 1983.
Clark, Margery Templeton. Albuquerque, N.M., 6 December 1988.

Clemen, Rudolf A., Jr. Washington, D.C., 13 June 1985.

Cobb, W. Montague. Washington, D.C., 30 July 1985.

Cook, Mercer. Washington, D.C., 24 September 1985.

Corbett, Plese. Green Level, N.C., 13 November 1985.

Crabtree, Carl. Mebane, N.C., 4 February 1983, 19 December 1989.

Crabtree, Lucille. Graham, N.C., 4 February 1983.

Davis, Edward. Washington, D.C., 14 March 1983.

Dixon, Otris J. A. Burlington, N.C., 13 January 1986.

Drew, Joseph. Arlington, Va., 12 June 1985, 31 July 1985, 25 September 1985.

Drew, Lenore Robbins. Columbia, Md., 1 August 1985.

Edmonds, Vivian Austin. Durham, N.C., 7 January 1983, 21 January 1983.

Franklin, John Hope. Durham, N.C., 29 September 1982, 9 February 1983, 21 January 1987.

Gibbs, Warmoth. Greensboro, N.C., 2 March 1983.

Gilbo, Patrick. Washington, D.C., 7 May 1985, 29 June 1994.

Gordon, Joe. Winston-Salem, N.C., 24 February 1987.

Gray, Willis. Burlington, N.C., 25 January 1983.

Gregory, Dick. Durham, N.C., 21 January 1987.

Gregory, Nora Drew. Washington, D.C., 31 July 1985.

Hackney, Brent. Raleigh, N.C., 12 April 1983.

Henderson, Lynn Michael Napoleon. Henderson, N.C., 20 May 1988.

Johnson, Delyour. Washington, D.C., 23 September 1985.

Jones, Lisa. Wilson, N.C., 14 July 1988.

Joyner, John W. ("Brett"). Henderson, N.C., 27 April 1988.

Kernodle, Charles. Burlington, N.C., 19 September 1985.

Kernodle, Harold. Burlington, N.C., 13 January 1986.

McCown, Ira. Harlem, N.Y., 18 November 1985, 20 November 1985.

Mair, Beatrice. Washington, D.C., 24 September 1985.

Mathews, Holly. Chapel Hill, N.C., 30 March 1985.

Miles, Thelma. Washington, D.C., 12 June 1985.

Mitchell, Gilberta. Pleasant Grove, N.C., 10 September 1985, 19 February 1990, 22 February 1990, 8 September 1995.

Morris, Viola Covington. Burlington, N.C., 25 February 1990; Pleasant Grove, N.C., 4 April 1990.

Newell, Josephine E. Raleigh, N.C., 18 July 1988.

Parker, Maryse. Harlem, N.Y., 18 November 1985.

Pennington, Eva Drew. New York, N.Y., 20 November 1985.

Pennix, John. Burlington, N.C., 25 January 1983.

Price, Bebe Drew. Columbia, Md., 1 August 1985.

Quander, Betty. Washington, D.C., 1 August 1985.

Quick, C. Mason. Fayetteville, N.C., 27 January 1983.

Redhead, Chester. New York, N.Y., 20 November 1985.

Richards, Helen. Harlem, N.Y., 18 November 1985.

Robinson, Bobby. Washington, D.C., 23 September 1985.

Shanks, W. C., Jr. Burlington, N.C., 2 February 1983, 8 February 1983, 30 January 1995.

Stanback, C. R. "Chip." Durham, N.C., 27 October 1982.

Stead, Eugene, Jr. Durham, N.C., 3 March 1983.
Syphax, Burke. Washington, D.C., 30 July 1985.
Thomas, Stephen. Burlington, N.C., 10 October 1985.
Vine, Thelma. Greensboro, N.C., 9 March 1983.
Walker, Steve. Durham, N.C., 7 May 1987.
Watts, Charles. Durham, N.C., 25 January 1983, 6 July 1988.
White, Jack. Washington, D.C., 23 September 1985.
Wilson, Jackie. Henderson, N.C., 27 April 1988.
Young, Fred. Burlington, N.C., 25 April 1985.
Yount, Marvin E., Jr. Burlington, N.C., 19 January 1983, 19 September 1985.
Zane, Edward. Greensboro, N.C., 10 March 1983.

NEWSPAPERS AND PERIODICALS

Amherst Alumni News (Amherst College, Amherst, Mass.)
Baltimore (Md.) Afro-American
Bulletin (Medico-Chirurgical Society of the District of Columbia)
Burlington (N.C.) Times-News
Carolina Comments
Chicago Defender
Coronet
Crisis
Daily Bulletin (John A. Andrew Clinical Society, Tuskegee Institute, Tuskegee, Ala.)
Des Moines (Iowa) Tribune
Dialogue (Duke University, Durham, N.C.)
downbeat
Durham (N.C.) Carolina Times
Durham (N.C.) Morning Herald
Ebony
Esquire
Fisk Herald (Fisk University, Nashville, Tenn.)
Greensboro (N.C.) Carolina Peacemaker
Greensboro (N.C.) Daily News
Henderson (N.C.) Daily Dispatch
Kujichagulia (Washington, D.C.)
Memphis (Tenn.) World
Message
Miami Herald
Morganite (Morgan University, Baltimore, Md.)
NAACP Bulletin
Nation
Newsletter of the Blood Banks Association of New York State
New York Daily Worker
New York PM Daily
New York Times
Our World

Pittsburgh Courier
Progressive
Raleigh (N.C.) News and Observer
Reader's Digest
Register (A&T College, Greensboro, N.C.)
Reidsville (N.C.) Review
Saturday Evening Post
Sepia
Southern Pines (N.C.) Pilot
Summerville (S.C.) Journal-Scene
Time
Vanity Fair
Wall Street Journal
Washington Call-Post
Washington Post
What's New
Willingboro (N.J.) News-Press

GOVERNMENT PUBLICATIONS

Congressional Record
Kendrick, Brig. Gen. Douglas B., MC, USA. *Blood Program in World War II.*
   Washington, D.C.: Office of the Surgeon General, Dept. of the Army, 1964.
Lee, Ulysses. *U.S. Army in World War II, Special Studies: The Employment of Negro
   Troops,* Washington, D.C.: Office of the Chief of Military History, U.S. Army,
   1966.

MISCELLANEOUS UNPUBLISHED SOURCES

Baldwin, James. Speech. Chapel Hill, N.C., 12 November 1984.
Buckingham, Clyde E. "Dr. Charles Richard Drew." Unpublished monograph
   dated 22 April 1968. CD-ARC-NH.
Burlington, N.C. City Directory. 1950.
DeKleine, William, M.D. "Early History of Red Cross Participation in Civilian
   Blood Donor Services and in the Blood Procurement Program for the Army
   and Navy." Unpublished bound monograph, vol. 33-B of "The History of the
   American National Red Cross." Washington, D.C.: American Red Cross,
   1950.
Drew, Charles Richard. Certificate of Death No. 7019. 2 May 1950, Bureau of
   Vital Statistics, North Carolina State Board of Health. (Photocopy obtained
   from Joseph Drew, personal papers, Washington, D.C.)
———. *Report of the Blood Transfusion Association Concerning the Project for Supplying
   Blood Plasma to England, Which has been Carried on Jointly with the American Red
   Cross from August 1940, to January 1941.* New York: Blood Transfusion
   Betterment Association, 1941.
Fletcher, Robert H. "An Administrative History of the Blood Donor Service,
   American Red Cross during the Second World War." Unpublished

monograph, vol. 33-A of "The History of the American Red Cross."
Washington, D.C.: The American Red Cross, 1950.

Henderson, N.C. City Directory. 1950.

Hine, Darlene. Speech at UNC School of Social Work. Spring 1987, Chapel
Hill, N.C. (from a report by Susan Worley).

Johnson, Walter R. "April 1, 1950." Typed manuscript, 15 November 1982,
CD-ARC-NH.

Munger, Claude W. "Report of a Study of the Lincoln Hospital, Durham, North
Carolina," 1947.

Murphy, Mary. "Burlington, N.C." Working Paper for the UNC Southern Oral
History Project: "Perspectives on Industrialization: The Piedmont Crescent
of Industry, 1900–1940." 1980.

BOOKS, ARTICLES, AND DISSERTATIONS

Abelove, Henry, Besty Blackman, Peter Dimock, and Jonathan Schneer, eds.
Visions of History. New York: Pantheon Books, 1983.

Agee, James, and Walker Evans. *Let Us Now Praise Famous Men.* 1939. New York:
Ballantine Books, 1966.

Albee, Edward. *The Death of Bessie Smith.* 1962. Reprint, New York: New
American Library, 1988.

Albert, Peter J., and Ronald Hoffman, eds. *We Shall Overcome: Martin Luther
King, Jr., and the Black Freedom Struggle.* New York: Pantheon, 1990.

Albertson, Chris. *Bessie 1898–1937.* New York: Stein and Day, 1972.

Allport, Gordon, and Leo Postman. *The Psychology of Rumor.* New York: Henry
Holt and Company, 1947.

Anderson, Eric. *Race and Politics in North Carolina, 1872–1901: The Black Second.*
Baton Rouge: Louisiana State University Press, 1981.

Anderson, Jean Bradley. *Durham County: A History of Durham, North Carolina.*
Durham: Duke University Press, 1990.

Angelou, Maya. *I Know Why the Caged Bird Sings.* New York: Random House,
1970. Reprint, New York: Bantam Books, 1977.

Anson, Robert Sam. *Best Intentions: The Education and Killing of Edmund Perry.*
New York: Random House, 1987.

Aptheker, Herbert, ed. *The Autobiography of W. E. B. Du Bois.* New York:
International Publishers, 1968.

Ashe, Geoffrey. *Gandhi.* New York: Stein and Day, 1968.

Ayanian, John Zaven. "Black Health in Segregated Durham, 1900–1940."
Senior thesis, Duke University, 1982.

Ayers, Edward L. *The Promise of the New South: Life after Reconstruction.* New York:
Oxford University Press, 1992.

Bailyn, Bernard. "The Challenge of Modern Historiography." *American
Historical Review* 87, no. 1 (February 1982): 1–24.

Baker, Houston A. *Black Studies, Rap, and the Academy.* Chicago: University of
Chicago Press, 1993.

———. *Long Black Song: Essays in Black American Literature and Culture.*
Charlottesville: University Press of Virginia, 1972.

Baldwin, James. *The Fire Next Time.* New York: Dial, 1963.

Baldwin, James, and Margaret Mead. *A Rap on Race.* New York: J. B. Lippincott, 1971. Reprint, New York: Dell, 1992.

Barbour, Floyd B., ed. *The Black Power Revolt: A Collection of Essays.* Boston, Mass.: Extending Horizons Books, 1968.

Bardolph, Richard. *The Negro Vanguard.* New York: Rinehart, 1959. Reprint, New York: Vintage, 1961.

Barton, Clara. *The Red Cross: A History of This Remarkable International Movement in the Interest of Humanity.* Washington, D.C.: American National Red Cross, 1898.

Beardsley, Edward H. "Goodbye to Jim Crow: The Desegregation of Southern Hospitals, 1945–1970." *Bulletin of the History of Medicine* 60 (1986): 367–86.

———. *A History of Neglect: Health Care for Blacks and Mill Workers in the Twentieth-Century South.* Knoxville: University of Tennessee Press, 1987.

———. "Making Separate, Equal: Black Physicians and the Problems of Medical Segregation in the Pre–World War II South." *Bulletin of the History of Medicine* 57 (1983): 382–96.

Bell, Derrick. *And We Are Not Saved: The Elusive Quest for Racial Justice.* New York: Basic Books, 1987.

———. *Faces at the Bottom of the Well: The Permanence of Racism.* New York: Basic Books, 1992.

Bender, Thomas. "Making History Whole Again." *New York Times Book Review,* 6 October 1985, pp. 1, 42–3.

Bennett, Lerone. *Before the Mayflower: A History of the Negro in America, 1619–1964.* Rev. ed. Clinton, Mass.: Colonial Press, 1964.

———. *The Negro Mood and Other Essays.* New York: Ballantine Books, 1964.

———. *What Manner of Man: A Biography of Martin Luther King, Jr.* Chicago: Johnson Publishing, 1976.

———. "When the Man and the Hour Are Met." In *Martin Luther King, Jr.: A Profile,* edited by C. Eric Lincoln. New York: Hill and Wang, 1970.

Benson, Susan P., Stephen Brier, and Roy Rosenzweig. *Presenting the Past: Essays on History and the Public.* Philadelphia: Temple University Press, 1986.

Bertol, Roland. *Charles Drew.* New York: Thomas Y. Crowell, 1970.

Bilbo, Theodore. *Take Your Choice: Separation or Mongrelization.* Popularville, Miss.: Dream Publishing, 1947.

Billington, Ray Allen, comp. *Allan Nevins on History.* New York: Scribner's, 1975.

Blauner, Bob. *Black Lives, White Lives: Three Decades of Race Relations in America.* Berkeley: University of California Press, 1989.

Blight, David W. " 'For Something beyond the Battlefield': Frederick Douglass and the Struggle for the Memory of the Civil War." *Journal of American History* 75, no. 4 (March 1989): 1156–78.

Bontemps, Arna, ed. *Great Slave Narratives.* Boston: Beacon Press, 1969.

Bordley, James II, and A. McGehee Harvey. *Two Centuries of American Medicine, 1776–1976.* Philadelphia: W. B. Saunders, 1976.

Boyd, Harold Kent. "Louis Austin and the Carolina Times." M.A. thesis, North Carolina Central University.

Bradley, Eugene H. "Health, Hospitals, and the Negro." *Modern Hospital* 65 (August 1945): 43–44.

Bradley, Michael R. "The Role of the Black Church in the Colonial Slave Society." *Louisiana Studies* 14 (Winter 1975): 413–21.

Branch, Taylor. *Parting the Waters: America in the King Years, 1954–63.* New York: Simon and Schuster, 1988.

Braudel, Fernand. *A History of Civilizations.* Trans. Richard Mayne. New York: Allen Lane, 1994.

———. *The Mediterranean and the Mediterranean World in the Age of Philip II,* vol. 1. 2 vols. New York: Harper and Row, 1966.

Broderick, Francis L., and August Meier. *Negro Protest Thought in the Twentieth Century.* Indianapolis: Bobbs-Merrill, 1966.

Brunvand, Jan Harold. *The Baby Train and Other Lusty Urban Legends.* New York: W. W. Norton, 1993.

———. *Curses, Broiled Again! The Hottest Urban Legends Going.* New York: W. W. Norton, 1989.

———. *The Study of American Folklore, An Introduction.* 3d ed. New York: W. W. Norton, 1986.

———. *The Vanishing Hitchhiker: American Urban Legends and Their Meaning.* New York: W. W. Norton, 1981.

———, ed. *The Choking Doberman and Other "New" Urban Legends.* New York: W. W. Norton, 1984.

Buckingham, Clyde E. *Clara Barton, A Broad Humanity: Philanthropic Efforts on Behalf of the Armed Forces and Disaster Victims, 1860–1900.* Washington, D.C.: Public Affairs Press, 1977. Reprint, n.l.: Buckingham, 1980.

———. *For Humanity's Sake: The Story of the Early Development of the League of Red Cross Societies.* Washington, D.C.: Public Affairs Press, 1964.

———. *Red Cross Disaster Relief: Its Origin and Development.* Washington, D.C.: Public Affairs Press, 1956.

Buckler, Helen. *Daniel Hale Williams: Negro Surgeon.* 2d ed. New York: Pitman Publishing Corporation, 1968.

Burns, August Merrimon II. "North Carolina and the Negro Dilemma, 1930–1950." Ph.D. diss., University of North Carolina, 1979.

Burrow, John G. *AMA: Voice of American Medicine.* Baltimore: Johns Hopkins University Press, 1963.

Byrd, W. Michael, and Linda A. Clayton. "An American Health Dilemma: A History of Blacks in the Health System." *Journal of the National Medical Association* 84 (1992): 189–200.

Cable, George W. *The Negro Question: A Selection of Writings on Civil Rights in the South.* Garden City, N.Y.: Doubleday, 1958.

Campbell, Joseph. *The Hero with a Thousand Faces.* 1949. Reprint, Princeton: Princeton University Press, 1972.

Carmichael, Stokely, and Charles V. Hamilton. *Black Power: The Politics of Liberation in America.* New York: Random House, 1967.

Carnegie, M. E. *The Path We Tread: Blacks in Nursing, 1854–1990.* 2d ed. Philadelphia: J. B. Lippincott, 1991.

Carson, Clayborne. *In Struggle: SNCC and the Black Awakening of the 1960s.* Cambridge: Harvard University Press, 1981.

Carson, Clayborne, David J. Garrow, Gerald Gill, Vincent Harding, and Darlene Clark Hine, eds. *The Eyes on the Prize Civil Rights Reader.* New York: Penguin, 1991.

Carter, Dan T. *Scottsboro: A Tragedy of the American South.* Rev. ed. Baton Rouge: Louisiana State University Press, 1979.

Cartwright, Samuel A. "Diseases and Peculiarities of the Negro Race." In *The Cause of the South: Selections from DeBow's Review, 1846–1867,* edited by Paul F. Paskoff and Daniel J. Wilson. Baton Rouge: Louisiana State University Press, 1982.

Cash, W. J. *The Mind of the South.* New York: Knopf, 1941. Reprint, New York: Vintage, 1991.

Cell, John W. *The Highest Stage of White Supremacy: The Origins of Segregation in South Africa and the American South.* Cambridge: Cambridge University Press, 1982.

Chafe, William H. *Civilities and Civil Rights: Greensboro, North Carolina, and the Black Struggle for Freedom.* New York: Oxford University Press, 1980.

———. *The Unfinished Journey: America since World War II.* New York: Oxford University Press, 1986.

Chafe, William H., and Harvard Sitkoff. *A History of Our Time: Readings on Postwar America.* 2d ed. New York: Oxford University Press, 1987.

Chalmers, David. *And the Crooked Places Made Straight: The Struggle for Social Change in the 1960s.* Baltimore: Johns Hopkins University Press, 1991.

Channing, David. "Slavery and Confederate Nationalism." In *From the Old South to the New: Essays on the Transitional South,* edited by Walter J. Fraser and Winfred B. Moore Jr. Westport, Conn.: Greenwood, 1981.

Chappell, Louis. *John Henry: A Folk-lore Study.* 1933. Reprint, Port Washington, N.Y.: Kennikat Press, 1968.

Chase, Hal S. " 'Shelling the Citadel of Race Prejudice': William Calvin Chase and the Washington *Bee,* 1882–1921." In *Records of the Columbia Historical Association of Washington, D.C., 1973–1974,* edited by Francis C. Rosenberger. Washington, D.C.: Columbia Historical Society, 1976.

Chesnutt, Charles W. *The Marrow of Tradition.* 1901. Reprint, Ann Arbor: University of Michigan Press, 1969.

Chestnut, J. L., Jr., and Julia Cass. *Black in Selma: The Uncommon Life of J. L. Chestnut, Jr.* New York: Farrar, Straus, and Giroux, 1990.

Clarke, John Henrik. "The Boy Who Painted Christ Black." In *American Short Stories,* edited by John Henrik Clarke. New York: Hill and Wang, 1966.

Cobb, James C. *The Selling of the South: The Southern Crusade for Industrial Development, 1936–1980.* Baton Rouge: Louisiana State University Press, 1982.

Cobb, W. Montague. "The Black American in Medicine." *JNMA* 73 (December 1981): supplement.

———. *Bulletin* [publication of the Medico-Chirurgical Society of the District of Columbia] 6, no. 8 (December 1950): 2, 4.

———. "Charles Richard Drew, M.D., 1904–1950." *JNMA* 42, no. 4 (July 1950): 238–46.

———. *The First Negro Medical Society: A History of the Medico-Chirurgical Society of* the District of Columbia, 1884–1939. Washington, D.C.: Associated Publishers, 1939.

———. "Integration in Medicine: A National Need." *JNMA* 49, no. 1 (January 1957): 1–7.

———. "Medical Care and the Plight of the Negro" (pamphlet). New York: NAACP, 1947.

———. "Medico-Chi at Ninety, 1884–1974." *JNMA* 66, no. 3 (May 1974): 256–62.

———. "Numa P. G. Adams, M.D., 1885–1940." *JNMA* 43, no. 1 (January 1951): 42–54.

———. "Progress and Portents for the Negro in Medicine" (pamphlet). New York: NAACP, 1948. Reprinted in *Crisis* 55 (April 1948): 107–26.

———. "St. Agnes Hospital, Raleigh, N.C." *JNMA* 53, no. 5 (September 1961): 439–46.

———. "A Short History of Freedmen's Hospital." *JNMA* 54, no. 3 (May 1962): 271–87.

Coles, Robert. *Children of Crisis: A Study of Courage and Fear.* Boston: Little, Brown, 1964.

Cone, James H. *Black Theology and Black Power.* New York: Seabury Press, 1969. Reprint, San Francisco: Harper and Row, 1989.

Cooper, J. C. *An Illustrated Encyclopedia of Traditional Symbols.* London: Thames and Hudson, 1978.

Cornely, Paul B. "Charles R. Drew (1904–1950), An Appreciation." *Phylon* 11, no. 2 (1950): 176–77.

———. "Segregation and Discrimination in Medical Care in the United States." *American Journal of Public Health* 46 (September 1956): 1074–81.

"Correspondence: Negro Physicians and the American Medical Association." *JNMA* 39, no. 5 (September 1947): 222–24.

Couch, W. T., ed. *These Are Our Lives.* Chapel Hill: University of North Carolina Press, 1939.

Couto, Richard A. *Ain't Gonna Let Nobody Turn Me Round: The Pursuit of Racial Justice in the Rural South.* Philadelphia: Temple University Press, 1991.

Cox, Earnest Sevier. *The South's Part in Mongrelizing the Nation.* Richmond, Va.: White America Society, 1926.

———. *White America.* Richmond, Va: White America Society, 1923.

Curtin, Philip D. *The Atlantic Slave Trade: A Census.* Madison: University of Wisconsin Press, 1969.

Curtis, James. *Blacks, Medical Schools and Society.* Ann Arbor: University of Michigan Press, 1971.

Dalfiume, Richard M. *Desegregation of the U.S. Armed Forces: Fighting on Two Fronts, 1939–1953.* Columbia: University of Missouri Press, 1969.

Dance, Daryl Cumber. *Shuckin' and Jivin': Folklore from Contemporary Black Americans.* Bloomington: Indiana University Press, 1978.

Daniel, Pete. *The Shadow of Slavery: Peonage in the South, 1901–1969.* Urbana: University of Illinois Press, 1972.

Davison, Wilburt. *The First Twenty Years: A History of the Duke University Schools of Medicine, Nursing and Health Services, and Duke Hospital, 1930–1950.* Durham: Duke University Press, 1952.

DeKleine, William. "Red Cross Blood Transfusion Projects." *JAMA* 111, no. 23 (3 December 1938): 2101–3.

Dexter, Pete. *Paris Trout.* New York: Penguin Books, 1988.

Dixon, Thomas, Jr. *The Clansman: An Historical Romance of the Ku Klux Klan.* New York: Doubleday, Page, 1905.

Dollard, John. *Caste and Class in a Southern Town.* 1937. Reprint. Garden City, N.Y.: Doubleday, 1957.

———. *The Leopard's Spots: A Romance of the White Man's Burden, 1865–1900.* New York: Doubleday, Page, 1902.

Donald, David Herbert. "A Generation of Defeat." In *From the Old South to the New: Essays on the Transitional South,* edited by Walter Fraser Jr. and Winfred Moore. Westport, Conn.: Greenwood, 1981.

Dorson, Richard M. *American Negro Folktales.* Greenwich, Conn.: Fawcett Publications, 1958.

———. *Folklore and Traditional History.* The Hague and Paris: Mouton, 1973.

———, ed. *Folklore and Folklife: An Introduction.* Chicago: University of Chicago Press, 1972.

Douglas, Mary. *Purity and Danger: An Analysis of Concepts of Pollution and Taboo.* London: Routledge and Kegan Paul, 1966. Reprint, New York: Praeger, 1970.

Douglass, Frederick. *Narrative of the Life of Frederick Douglass.* New York: New American Library, 1968.

Drake, Alvin W., Stan N. Finkelstein, and Harvey M. Sapolsky. *The American Blood Supply.* Cambridge: MIT Press, 1982.

Drew, Charles Richard. "Annual Report of the Surgical Section of the National Medical Association." *JNMA* 39 (1947): 263–65.

———. "Banked Blood: A Study in Blood Preservation." Ph.D. diss., Columbia University, 1940.

———. "Carl Glennis Roberts, M.D., 1886–1950." *JNMA* 42 (1950): 109–10.

———. "Editorial—The Frederick Douglass Stubbs Surgical Oration." *JNMA* 40 (1948): 256–57.

———. "Negro Scholars in Scientific Research." *Journal of Negro History* 35 (April 1950): 135–149.

———. "The Role of Soviet Investigators in the Development of the Blood Bank." *American Review of Soviet Medicine* 1 (April 1944): 360–69.

———. "World Health and the United Nations." *JNMA* 40, no. 3 (May 1948): 100–101.

Drew, Lenore Robbins. "The Unforgettable Charlie Drew." *Reader's Digest,* March 1978, 1–6. Reprinted in *The Oracle,* Spring 1979, 7–12.

Du Bois, W. E. B. *Black Reconstruction in America: An Essay Toward a History of the Part Which Black Folk Played in the Attempt to Reconstruct Democracy in America, 1860–1880.* New York: Atheneum, 1970.

———. *Dusk of Dawn: An Essay Toward an Autobiography of a Race Concept.* New York: Harcourt, Brace and World, 1940. Reprint, New York: Schocken Books, 1968.

———. *The Health and Physique of the Negro American.* Atlanta, Ga.: Atlanta University Press, 1906.

———. "On Being Crazy." In *American Negro Short Stories*, edited by John Henrik Clarke, 8–10. New York: Hill and Wang, 1966.

———. "Reconstruction and Its Benefits." *American Historical Review* 15 (July 1910): 781–99.

———. *The Souls of Black Folk.* 1903. New York: New American Library, 1969.

Dulles, Foster Rhea. *The American Red Cross: A History.* New York: Harper and Brothers, 1950.

Dummett, C. O., and L. D. Dummett. *Afro-Americans in Dentistry: Sequence and Consequence of Events.* Los Angeles: Dummett, 1978.

Dundes, Alan. *The Blood Libel Legend: A Casebook in Anti-Semitic Folklore.* Madison: University of Wisconsin Press, 1991.

———. *In Quest of the Hero.* Princeton: Princeton University Press, 1990.

———. *Mother Wit from the Laughing Barrel.* Englewood Cliffs, N.J.: Prentice-Hall, 1972.

Dunning, William A. *Reconstruction, Political and Economic: 1865–1877.* New York: Harper and Brothers, 1907.

Durden, Robert F. *The Launching of Duke University, 1924–1949.* Durham: Duke University Press, 1993.

Eaton, Hubert A. *"Every Man Should Try."* Wilmington, N.C.: Bonaparte Press, 1984.

Eckert, Ross D., and Edward L. Wallace. *Securing a Safer Blood Supply: Two Views.* Washington: American Enterprise Institute for Public Policy Research, 1985.

Edmonds, Helen G. *The Negro and Fusion Politics in North Carolina, 1894–1901.* Chapel Hill: University of North Carolina Press, 1951.

Ehle, John. *The Free Men.* New York: Harper and Row, 1965.

Elkins, Wilson. "L. Richardson Memorial Hospital, Greensboro, N.C." *JNMA* 61, no. 3 (May 1969): 205–12.

Ellison, Ralph. *Invisible Man.* New York: Random House, 1952. Reprint, New York: Vintage Books, 1972.

Ellsworth, Scott. *Death in a Promised Land: The Tulsa Race Riot of 1921.* Baton Rouge: Louisiana State University Press, 1982.

Embree, Edwin R., and Julia Waxman. *Investment in People: The Story of the Julius Rosenwald Fund.* New York: Harper and Brothers, 1949.

Evans, Sara. *Personal Politics: The Roots of Women's Liberation in the Civil Rights Movement and The New Left.* New York: Random House, 1979.

Fanon, Frantz. *Black Skin, White Masks.* New York: Grove, 1967.

Farr, Finis. *Black Champion: The Life and Times of Jack Johnson.* New York: Scribner's, 1964.

Faulkner, William. *Absalom, Absalom.* New York: Modern Library, 1936.

Feldschuh, Joseph, with Doron Weber. *Safe Blood: Purifying the Nation's Blood Supply in the Age of AIDS.* New York: Free Press, 1990.

Fields, Mamie Garvin, with Karen Fields. *Lemon Swamp and Other Places: A Carolina Memoir.* New York: Free Press, 1983.

Finkle, Lee. *Forum for Protest: The Black Press during World War II.* Cranbury, N.J.: Associated University Presses, 1975.

Fitzgerald, Frances. *America Revised: History Schoolbooks in the Twentieth Century.* Boston: Little, Brown, 1979.

Foner, Jack D. *Blacks and the Military in American History: A New Perspective.* New York: Praeger, 1974.

Forman, James. *The Making of Black Revolutionaries.* Washington, D.C.: Open Hand Publishing, 1985.

Foster, Gaines M. "The Limitations of Federal Health Care for Freedmen, 1862–1868." *Journal of Southern History* 48, no. 3 (1982): 349–72.

Franklin, John Hope. "As for Our History . . ." In *The Southerner as American,* edited by Charles Grier Sellers Jr. Chapel Hill: University of North Carolina Press, 1960.

———. *The Color Line: Legacy for the Twenty-First Century.* Columbia: University of Missouri Press, 1993.

———. *The Free Negro in North Carolina, 1790–1860.* Chapel Hill: University of North Carolina Press, 1943. Reprint, New York: Russell and Russell, 1971.

———. *From Slavery to Freedom: A History of Negro Americans.* 7th ed. New York: Knopf, 1994.

———. "The Future of Negro American History." Photocopy, Perkins Library, Duke University.

———. *George Washington Williams: A Biography.* Chicago: University of Chicago Press, 1985.

———. *An Illustrated History of Black Americans.* New York: Time-Life Books, 1973.

———. *The Militant South, 1800–1861.* Cambridge: Belknap Press of Harvard University Press, 1956. Reprint, Boston: Beacon Press, 1966.

———. "Pursuing Southern History: A Strange Career." In *Developing Dixie,* edited by Winfred B. Moore Jr. Westport, Conn.: Greenwood, 1988.

———. *Race and History: Selected Essays, 1938–1988.* Baton Rouge: Louisiana State University Press, 1989.

———. *Racial Equality in America.* Chicago: University of Chicago Press, 1976. Reprint, Columbia: University of Missouri Press, 1993.

———. *Reconstruction after the Civil War.* Chicago: University of Chicago Press, 1961.

———. "W. E. B. Du Bois: A Personal Memoir." *Massachusetts Review* 31, no. 3 (Autumn 1990): 409–28.

Franklin, John Hope, and August Meier, eds. *Black Leaders of the Twentieth Century.* Urbana: University of Illinois Press, 1982.

Frazier, Thomas R., ed. *Afro-American History: Primary Sources.* New York: Harcourt, Brace and World, 1970.

Frederickson, George M. *The Black Image in the White Mind: The Debate on Afro-American Character and Destiny, 1817–1914.* New York: Harper and Row, 1971.

———. "Masters and Mudsills: The Role of Race in the Planter Ideology of South Carolina." *Atlantic Urban Studies* 2 (1978): 34–47.

———. *White Supremacy: A Comparative Study in American and South African History.* New York: Oxford University Press, 1981.

Frish, Michael. "American History and the Structures of Collective Memory: A Modest Exercise in Empirical Iconography." *Journal of American History* 75, no. 4 (March 1989): 1130–55.

Fry, Gladys-Marie. *Night Riders in Black Folk History.* Knoxville: University of Tennessee Press, 1975.

———. *Stitched from the Soul: Slave Quilts from the Antebellum South*. New York: Dutton Studio Books in association with the Museum of Folk Art, 1990.

Gaines, Ernest. *The Autobiography of Miss Jane Pittman*. New York: Dial, 1971.

———. *A Gathering of Old Men*. New York: Random House, 1983.

———. "The Sky Is Gray." In *American Negro Short Stories*, edited by John Henrik Clarke. New York: Hill and Wang, 1966.

Gamble, Vanessa Northington. *The Black Community Hospital: Contemporary Dilemmas in Historical Perspective*. New York: Garland, 1989.

———, ed. *Germs Have No Color Line: Blacks and American Medicine, 1900–1940*. New York: Garland, 1989.

Garrow, David J. *Bearing the Cross: Martin Luther King, Jr., and the Southern Christian Leadership Conference*. New York: William Morrow, 1986.

Gaston, Paul. *The New South Creed: A Study in Southern Mythmaking*. New York: Knopf, 1970.

Gates, Henry Louis, Jr. *The Classic Slave Narratives*. New York: Mentor, 1987.

Gatewood, Willard B. *Aristocrats of Color: The Black Elite, 1880–1920*. Bloomington: Indiana University Press, 1990.

Gavins, Raymond. "North Carolina Black Folklore and Song in the Age of Segregation: Toward Another Meaning of Survival." *North Carolina Historical Review* 66, no. 4 (October 1989): 412–42.

———. *The Perils and Prospects of Southern Black Leadership: Gordon Blaine Hancock, 1884–1970*. Durham: Duke University Press, 1977.

———. "A 'Sin of Omission': Black Historiography in North Carolina." In *Black Americans in North Carolina and the South*, edited by Jeffrey J. Crow and Flora J. Hatley, 3–56. Chapel Hill: University of North Carolina Press, 1984.

Genovese, Eugene D. *Roll, Jordan, Roll: The World the Slaves Made*. New York: Random House, 1972.

Gerster, Patrick, and Nicholas Cords, eds. *Myth and Southern History*. 2d ed. 2 vols. Urbana: University of Illinois Press, 1989.

———, eds. *Myth and the American Experience*. 2 vols. New York: Glencoe Press, 1973. Reprint, New York: HarperCollins, 1991.

———, eds. "The Northern Origins of Southern Mythology." *Journal of Southern History* 43, no. 4 (November 1977): 567–82.

Gifford, James F. *The Evolution of a Medical Center: A History of Medicine at Duke University to 1941*. Durham: Duke University Press, 1972.

Gilbo, Patrick F. *The American Red Cross: The First Century*. New York: Harper and Row, 1981.

Gilmore, Al-Tony. *Bad Nigger!: The National Impact of Jack Johnson*. Port Washington, N.Y.: Kennikat Press, 1975.

Gladney, Margaret Rose, ed. *How Am I to Be Heard?: Letters of Lillian Smith*. Chapel Hill: University of North Carolina Press, 1993.

Goodwyn, Lawrence C. *Breaking the Barrier: The Rise of Solidarity in Poland*. New York: Oxford University Press, 1991.

———. *Democratic Promise: The Populist Moment in America*. New York: Oxford University Press, 1976.

———. "Hierarchy and Democracy: The Paradox of the Southern Experience." In *From the Old South to the New: Essays on the Transitional South*, edited by Walter Fraser Jr. and Winfred Moore Jr. Westport, Conn.: Greenwood, 1981.

———. "Populist Dreams and Negro Rights: East Texas as a Case Study." *American Historical Review* 76, no. 5 (December 1971): 1435–56.

Goss, Linda, and Marian E. Barnes, eds. *Talk That Talk: An Anthology of African-American Storytelling*. New York: Simon and Schuster, 1989.

Gossett, Thomas F. *Race: The History of an Idea in America*. New York: Schocken Books, 1965.

Gould, Stephen Jay. *The Mismeasure of Man*. New York: W. W. Norton, 1981.

Grantham, Dewey W. *The Democratic South*. Athens: University of Georgia Press, 1963. Reprint, New York: W. W. Norton, 1965.

Green, Constance M. *The Secret City: A History of Race Relations in the Nation's Capital*. Princeton: Princeton University Press, 1967.

Gregory, Dick. *Nigger*. New York: Pocket Books, 1964.

———. *No More Lies: The Myth and the Reality of American History*. New York: Harper and Row, 1971.

———. *The Shadow That Scares Me*. Garden City, N.Y.: Doubleday, 1968.

Grier, William H., and Price M. Cobbs. *Black Rage*. New York: Basic Books, 1969.

Griffin, John Howard. *Black Like Me*. New York: Houghton Mifflin Co., 1960. New York: New American Library, 1961.

Guillory, James Denny. "The Pro-Slavery Arguments of Dr. Samuel A. Cartwright." *Louisiana History* 9, no. 3 (Summer 1968): 209–27.

Gutman, Herbert. *The Black Family in Slavery and Freedom, 1750–1925*. New York: Pantheon, 1976.

Gwaltney, John Langston. *Drylongso: A Self-Portrait of Black America*. New York: Random House, 1980.

Haber, Louis. *Black Pioneers of Science and Invention*. Orlando, Fla.: Harcourt Brace Jovanovich, 1970.

Hacker, Andrew. *Two Nations: Black and White, Separate, Hostile, Unequal*. New York: Scribner's, 1992.

Hagen, Piet J. Blood: *Gift or Merchandise: Towards an International Blood Policy*. New York: Alan R. Liss, 1982.

Haley, Alex. "Black History, Oral History and Genealogy." *Oral History Review* 1973: 1–25.

———. *Roots*. Garden City, N.Y.: Doubleday, 1976.

Hall, Jacquelyn Dowd. *Revolt against Chivalry: Jessie Daniel Ames and the Women's Campaign against Lynching*. New York: Columbia University Press, 1979.

Hall, Jacquelyn Dowd, James Leloudis, Robert Korstad, Mary Murphy, LuAnn Jones, and Christopher Daly. *Like a Family: The Making of a Southern Cotton Mill World*. Chapel Hill: University of North Carolina Press, 1987.

Haller, John S., Jr. *Outcasts from Evolution: Scientific Attitudes of Racial Inferiority, 1859–1900*. Urbana: University of Illinois Press, 1971.

Hampton, Henry, and Steve Fayer. *Voices of Freedom: An Oral History of the Civil Rights Movement from the 1950s through the 1980s*. New York: Bantam Books, 1990.

Harding, Vincent. *Beyond Chaos: Black History and the Search for the New Land*. Institute of the Black World, Black Paper No. 2, 1970.

———. *Hope and History: Why We Must Share the Story of the Movement*. Maryknoll, N.Y.: Orbis Books, 1990.

———. "The Gift of Blackness." Committee of Southern Churchmen, 1967.

———. *There Is a River: The Black Struggle for Freedom in America.* New York: Harcourt Brace Jovanovich, 1981.

Hardwick, Richard. *Charles Richard Drew: Pioneer in Blood Research.* New York: Scribner's, 1967.

Harris, Trudier. *Exorcising Blackness: Historical and Literary Lynching and Burning Rituals.* Bloomington: Indiana University Press, 1984.

Hasson, Gail S. "Health and Welfare of Freedmen in Reconstruction." *Alabama Review* 35, no. 2 (1982): 94–110.

Hastie, William. *On Clipped Wings: The Story of Jim Crow in the Army Air Corps.* New York: The National Association for the Advancement of Colored People, 1943.

Haws, Robert, ed. *The Age of Segregation: Race Relations in the South, 1890–1945.* Jackson: University Press of Mississippi, 1978.

"Health Status and Health Education of Negroes in the United States." *Journal of Negro Education* 18, no. 3 (Summer 1949): 197–208.

Hemenway, Robert. *Zora Neale Hurston: A Literary Biography.* Urbana: University of Illinois Press, 1977.

Heritage of Vance County, Vol. 1. Winston-Salem, N.C.: Vance County Historical Society and Hunter Publishing, 1984.

Herskovits, Melville. *The Myth of the Negro Past.* New York: Harper and Brothers, 1941.

Hine, Darlene Clark. *Black Women in White: Racial Conflict and Cooperation in the Nursing Profession, 1890–1950.* Bloomington: Indiana University Press, 1989.

Hodgson, Godfrey. *America in Our Time: From World War II to Nixon, What Happened and Why.* Garden City, N.Y.: Doubleday, 1976.

Holiday, Billie, with William Dufty. *Lady Sings the Blues.* Garden City, N.Y.: Doubleday, 1956.

Holt, Thomas, Cassandra Smith-Parker, and Rosalyn Terborg-Penn. *A Special Mission: The Story of Freedmen's Hospital, 1862–1962.* Washington: Academic Affairs Division, Howard University, 1975.

Hospital Care in the United States. New York: The Commonwealth Fund, 1947.

Huber, Max. *The Red Cross: Principles and Problems.* Geneva, Switzerland: A. Kundig Press, 1942.

Huggins, Nathan Irvin. *Black Odyssey: The African-American Ordeal in Slavery.* New York: Vintage Books, 1990.

Hughes, Langston, and Arna Bontemps, eds. *The Book of Negro Folklore.* New York: Dodd, Mead, 1958.

Humphrey, David C. "Dissection and Discrimination: The Social Origins of Cadavers in America, 1760–1915." In *Essays on the History of Medicine*, edited by Saul Jarcho. New York: New York Academy of Medicine, 1976.

Hurd, Charles. *The Compact History of the American Red Cross.* New York: Hawthorn Books, 1959.

Hurston, Zora Neale. *Dust Tracks on a Road.* Philadelphia: J. B. Lippincott, 1942.

———. *Mules and Men.* 1935. New York: Harper and Row, 1970.

———. "My Most Humiliating Jim Crow Experience." In *I Love Myself When I Am*

Laughing . . ., edited by Alice Walker, 163–64. Old Westbury, N.Y.: Feminist Press, 1979.

———. *Their Eyes Were Watching God: A Novel.* Philadelphia: J. B. Lippincott, 1900.

Ives, Edward D. *The Tape-Recorded Interview: A Manual for Field Workers in Folklore and Oral History.* Knoxville: University of Tennessee Press, 1980.

Jacobs, Harriet A. *Incidents in the Life of a Slave Girl, Written by Herself.* Edited by L. Maria Child. Cambridge: Harvard University Press, 1987.

Johnson, Charles S. *Backgrounds to Patterns of Negro Segregation.* 1947. New York: Thomas Y. Crowell, 1970.

———. *Shadow of the Plantation.* Chicago: University of Chicago Press, 1934.

Johnson, David B., ed. *Blood Policy: Issues and Alternatives.* Washington, D.C.: American Enterprise Institute for Public Policy Research, 1977.

Johnson, Guy B. *John Henry: Tracking Down a Negro Legend.* 1929. Reprint, New York: AMS Press, 1969.

Jones, James H. *Bad Blood: The Tuskegee Syphilis Experiment — A Tragedy of Race and Medicine.* New York: Free Press, 1981.

Jones, Leroi, and Larry Neal. *Black Fire: An Anthology of Afro-American Writing.* New York: William Morrow, 1968.

Jones, R. Frank. "The Surgical Resident Training Program at Freedmen's Hospital." *JNMA* 52, no. 3 (May 1960): 187–93.

Jordan, Winthrop. *White over Black: American Attitudes toward the Negro, 1550–1812.* Chapel Hill: University of North Carolina Press, 1968.

Joyner, Charles. *Down by the Riverside: A South Carolina Slave Community.* Urbana: University of Illinois Press, 1984.

Kammen, Michael. *Mystic Chords of Memory: The Transformation of Tradition in American Culture.* New York: Knopf, 1991.

Kapur, Sudarshan. *Raising Up a Prophet: The African-American Encounter with Gandhi.* Boston: Beacon Press, 1992.

Katz, Donald R. *Home Fires: An Intimate Portrait of One Middle-Class Family in Postwar America.* New York: Aaron Asher Books, 1992.

Katz, William Loren. *Eyewitness: The Negro in American History.* Rev. ed. New York: Pitman Publishing, 1971.

Kaufman, Martin, Stuart Galishoff, and Todd L. Savitt, eds. *Dictionary of American Medical Biography.* Westport, Conn.: Greenwood, 1984.

Keneally, Thomas. *Schindler's List.* New York: Simon and Schuster, 1982. Reprint, New York: Touchstone, 1993.

Kennedy, Stetson. *Jim Crow Guide: The Way It Was.* 1959. Reprint, Boca Raton: Florida Atlantic University Press, 1990.

Key, V. O., Jr. *Southern Politics.* New York: Knopf, 1949.

King, Martin Luther, Jr. *The Strength to Love.* New York: Harper and Row, 1963.

———. *Stride toward Freedom: The Montgomery Story.* New York: Harper and Row, 1958.

———. *A Testament of Hope: The Essential Writings and Speeches of Martin Luther King, Jr.* Edited by James Melvin Washington. San Francisco: Harper and Row, 1986.

———. *The Trumpet of Conscience.* New York: Harper and Row, 1967.

——. *Where Do We Go from Here: Chaos or Community?* New York: Harper and Row, 1967.

——. *Why We Can't Wait.* New York: Harper and Row, 1963.

King, Mary. *Freedom Song: A Personal Story of the 1960s Civil Rights Movement.* New York: William Morrow, 1987.

Kiple, Kenneth F., ed. *The Cambridge World History of Human Disease.* New York: Cambridge University Press, 1993.

Kiple, Kenneth, and Virginia Kiple. "The African Connection: Slavery, Disease and Racism." *Atlanta University Review of Race and Culture* 41, no. 3 (Fall 1980): 211–22.

Kiple, Kenneth F., and Virginia Himmelsteib King. *Another Dimension to the Black Diaspora: Diet, Disease, and Racism.* Cambridge: Cambridge University Press, 1981.

Kirby, Jack Temple. *Darkness at the Dawning: Race and Reform in the Progressive South.* Philadelphia: J. B. Lippincott, 1972.

Klein, Aaron. *The Hidden Contributors: Black Scientists and Inventors in America.* Garden City, N.Y.: Doubleday, 1971.

Kluger, Richard. *Simple Justice: The History of Brown vs. Board of Education.* New York: Knopf, 1976.

Knight, Etheridge. *Belly Song and Other Poems.* Detroit: Broadside Press, 1973.

Kousser, J. Morgan. *The Shaping of Southern Politics: Suffrage Restriction and the Establishment of the One-Party South: 1880–1910.* New Haven: Yale University Press, 1974.

Kovel, Joel. *White Racism: A Psychohistory.* New York: Pantheon Books, 1970. Reprint, New York: Columbia University Press, 1984.

Kraus, Michael, and Davis D. Joyce. *The Writing of American History.* Rev. ed. Norman: University of Oklahoma Press, 1985.

Lamb, Albert R. *The Presbyterian Hospital and the Columbia-Presbyterian Medical Center, 1868–1943.* New York: Columbia University Press, 1955.

Landis, Kenesaw M. *Segregation in Washington.* Chicago: National Committee on Segregation in the Nation's Capital, 1948.

Larkins, John R. *The Negro Population of North Carolina, 1945–1955.* Raleigh: N.C. State Board of Public Welfare, 1957.

Lawson, Steven F. *Running for Freedom: Civil Rights and Black Politics in America since 1941.* Philadelphia: Temple University Press, 1991.

Lee, Anne S., and Everett S. Lee. "The Health of Slaves and the Health of Freedmen: A Savannah Study." *Phylon* 38, no. 2 (1977): 170–80.

Legan, Marshall Scott. "Disease and the Freedmen in Mississippi during Reconstruction." *Journal of the History of Medicine* 28 (July 1973): 257–67.

Lemann, Nicholas. *The Promised Land: The Great Black Migration and How It Changed America.* New York: Knopf, 1991.

Levine, Lawrence. *Black Culture and Black Consciousness: Afro-American Folk Thought from Slavery to Freedom.* New York: Oxford University Press, 1977.

Lewis, David L. *District of Columbia: A Bicentennial History.* New York: W. W. Norton, 1976.

——. *King: A Critical Biography.* New York: Praeger, 1970.

Lichello, Robert. *Pioneer in Blood Plasma: Dr. Charles Richard Drew.* New York: Julian Messner, 1968.

Lifton, Robert Jay. *The Nazi Doctors: Medical Killing and the Psychology of Genocide.* New York: Basic Books, 1986.

Lincoln, C. Eric, and Lawrence H. Mamiya. *The Black Church in the African American Experience.* Durham: Duke University Press, 1990.

Lincoln, C. Eric, ed. *Martin Luther King, Jr.: A Profile.* New York: Hill and Wang, 1970.

Link, Arthur, and Rembert Patrick, eds. *Writing Southern History: Essays in Historiography in Honor of Fletcher M. Green.* Baton Rouge: Louisiana State University Press, 1965.

Litwack, Leon F. *Been in the Storm So Long: The Aftermath of Slavery.* New York: Knopf, 1979.

———. *North of Slavery: The Negro in the Free States, 1790–1860.* Chicago: University of Chicago Press, 1961.

Litwack, Leon, and August Meier, eds. *Black Leaders of the Nineteenth Century.* Urbana: University of Illinois Press, 1988.

Logan, Frenise A. *The Negro in North Carolina, 1876–1894.* Chapel Hill: University of North Carolina Press, 1964.

Logan, Rayford W. *The Betrayal of the Negro: From Rutherford B. Hayes to Woodrow Wilson.* New enl. ed. London: Collier, 1965.

———. "Growing Up in Washington: The Lucky Generation." In *Records of the Columbia Historical Society of Washington, D.C.,* vol. 50. Charlottesville: University Press of Virginia, 1980.

———. *Howard University: The First Hundred Years, 1867–1967.* New York: New York University Press, 1969.

Long, Dorothy, ed. *Medicine in North Carolina.* 2 vols. Raleigh: N.C. Medical Society, 1972.

Loveland, Anne C. *Lillian Smith: A Southerner Confronting the South, a Biography.* Baton Rouge: Louisiana State University Press, 1986.

Lumpkin, Katherine Du Pre. *The Making of a Southerner.* New York: Knopf, 1946. Reprint, Athens: University of Georgia Press, 1991.

Lynd, Staughton, ed. *Nonviolence in America: A Documentary History.* Indianapolis: Bobbs-Merrill, 1966.

McBride, David. *From TB to AIDS: Epidemics among Urban Blacks since 1900.* Albany: State University of New York Press, 1991.

———. *Integrating the City of Medicine: Blacks in Philadelphia Health Care, 1910–1965.* Philadelphia: Temple University Press, 1989.

McFall, T. Carter. "Needs for Hospital Facilities and Physicians in Thirteen Southern States." *JNMA* 42, no. 4 (July 1950): 235–36.

McGlone, Robert E. "Rescripting a Troubled Past: John Brown's Family and the Harpers Ferry Conspiracy." *Journal of American History* 75, no. 4 (March 1989): 1179–1200.

McGuire, Phillip, ed. *Taps for a Jim Crow Army: Letters from Black Soldiers in World War II.* Lexington: University Press of Kentucky, 1983.

McKinney, John C., and Edgar T. Thompson, eds. *The South in Continuity and Change.* Durham: Duke University Press, 1965.

McLaurin, Melton A. *Separate Pasts: Growing Up White in the Segregated South.* Athens: University of Georgia Press, 1987.

McMillen, Neil R. *Dark Journey: Black Mississippians in the Age of Jim Crow.*
Urbana: University of Illinois Press, 1989.

McNeill, William H. "Mythistory, or Truth, Myth, History and Historians."
American Historical Review 91, no. 1 (February 1986): 1–10.

Mahone-Lonesome, Robyn. *Charles R. Drew: Physician.* New York: Chelsea
House, 1990.

Mandelbaum, David G. *Society in India.* 2 vols. Berkeley: University of California
Press, 1970.

Manning, Kenneth R. *Black Apollo of Science: The Life of Ernest Everett Just.* New
York: Oxford University Press, 1983.

Mannix, Daniel P., and Malcolm Cowley. *Black Cargoes: A History of the Atlantic
Slave Trade, 1518–1865.* New York: Viking, 1962.

Maund, Alfred. *The Untouchables: The Meaning of Segregation in Hospitals.* New
Orleans: Southern Conference Educational Fund, 1952.

May, Rollo. *The Cry for Myth.* New York: W. W. Norton, 1991.

Mayo, Selz C., and C. Horace Hamilton, eds. *Hospitals and Hospital Service in
North Carolina.* Raleigh: Department of Rural Sociology, North Carolina State
College, 1960.

Mays, Benjamin. *Born to Rebel: An Autobiography.* New York: Scribner's, 1971.

Mebane, Mary E. *Mary.* New York: Viking, 1981.

———. *Mary, Wayfarer.* 1976. Reprint, New York: Viking, 1983.

Medical Care Services in North Carolina: A Statistical and Graphic Summary.
Prepared for the North Carolina Commission on Hospital and Medical
Care. Raleigh: Department of Rural Sociology, North Carolina State College,
1945.

Meier, August. *Negro Thought in America, 1880–1915.* Ann Arbor: University of
Michigan Press, 1969.

Meier, August, and Elliott Rudwick. *Black History and the Historical Profession,
1915–1980.* Urbana: University of Illinois Press, 1986.

Meier, August, Elliott Rudwick, and John Bracey Jr. *Black Protest in the Sixties.*
New York: Markus Wiener, 1991.

Moldow, Gloria. *Women Doctors in Gilded-Age Washington: Race, Gender, and
Professionalization.* Urbana: University of Illinois Press, 1987.

Montagu, Ashley. *Man's Most Dangerous Myth: The Fallacy of Race.* 4th rev. ed.
Cleveland: World Publishing, 1964.

Montell, William Lynwood. *The Saga of Coe Ridge: A Study in Oral History.*
Knoxville: University of Tennessee Press, 1970.

Moody, Anne. *Coming of Age in Mississippi.* New York: Dell, 1968.

Moore, Carman. *Somebody's Angel Child: The Story of Bessie Smith.* New York:
Thomas Y. Crowell, 1969.

Morais, Herbert M. *The History of the Afro-American in Medicine.* Rev. ed.,
Cornwells Heights, Pa.: Publishers Agency, 1976.

Morris, Aldon. *The Origins of the Civil Rights Movement: Black Communities
Organizing for Change.* New York: Free Press, 1984.

Morrison, Toni. *Beloved.* New York: Knopf, 1987.

———. *Jazz.* New York: Knopf, 1992.

———. *Playing in the Dark: Whiteness and the Literary Imagination.* Cambridge: Harvard University Press, 1992. Reprint, New York: Vintage, 1993.

———. *Song of Solomon.* New York: Knopf, 1977.

Motley, Mary Penick, ed. *The Invisible Soldier: The Experience of the Black Soldier, World War II.* Detroit: Wayne State University Press, 1975.

Murray, Albert. *The Omni-Americans: Some Alternatives to the Folklore of White Supremacy.* New York: Random House, 1970. Reprint, New York: Vintage, 1983.

Murray, Pauli. *Proud Shoes: The Story of an American Family.* New York: Harper and Row, 1978.

———. *Song in a Weary Throat: An American Pilgrimage.* New York: Harper and Row, 1987.

———. *States' Laws on Race and Color.* 2 vols. Cincinnati: Women's Division of Christian Service, 1950, 1951.

Myrdal, Gunnar. *An American Dilemma: The Negro Problem and American Democracy.* 2 vols. New York: Harper and Brothers, 1944.

National Association for the Advancement of Colored People. *Thirty Years of Lynching in the United States, 1889–1918.* New York: NAACP, 1919.

Nelsen, Hart M., Raytha L. Yokley, and Anne K. Nelsen, eds. *The Black Church in America.* New York: Basic Books, 1971.

Nevins, Allan. *The Gateway to History.* Boston: D. C. Heath, 1938.

Newby, I. A. *Jim Crow's Defense: Anti-Negro Thought in America, 1900–1930.* Baton Rouge: Louisiana State University Press, 1965.

———, ed. *The Development of Segregationist Thought.* Homewood, Ill.: Dorsey Press, 1968.

Norrell, Robert J. *Reaping the Whirlwind: The Civil Rights Movement in Tuskegee.* New York: Random House, 1985.

Novick, Peter. *That Noble Dream: The "Objectivity Question" and the American Historical Profession.* Cambridge: Cambridge University Press, 1988.

Numbers, Ronald L., and Todd L. Savitt, eds. *Science and Medicine in the Old South.* Baton Rouge: Louisiana State University Press, 1989.

Oates, Stephen B. *The Fires of Jubilee: Nat Turner's Fierce Rebellion.* New York: New American Library, 1975.

———. *Let the Trumpet Sound: The Life of Martin Luther King, Jr.* New York: New American Library, 1983.

Odum, Howard W. *Race and Rumors of Race: Challenge to American Crisis.* Chapel Hill: University of North Carolina Press, 1943.

Organ, Claude H., Jr., and Margaret M. Kosiba, eds. *A Century of Black Surgeons: The U.S.A. Experience.* 2 vols. Norman, Okla.: Transcript Press, 1987.

Osterweis, Rollin G. *The Myth of the Lost Cause, 1865–1900.* Hamden, Conn.: Archon, 1973.

Painter, Nell Irwin. *The Narrative of Hosea Hudson: His Life as a Negro Communist in the South.* Cambridge: Harvard University Press, 1979.

Parris, Guichard, and Lester Brooks. *Blacks in the City: A History of the National Urban League.* Boston: Little, Brown, 1971.

Paskoff, Paul F., and Daniel J. Wilson. *The Cause of the South: Selections from DeBow's Review, 1846–1867.* Baton Rouge: Louisiana State University Press, 1982.

Peck, James. *Freedom Ride.* New York: Grove, 1962.

Pendergast, David M., and Clement M. Meighan. "Folk Traditions as Historical Fact: A Paiute Example." *Journal of American Folklore* 72 (April–June 1959).

Phillips, Ulrich Bonnell. *Life and Labor in the Old South.* Boston: Little, Brown, 1929.

Poe, Clarence, ed. *Hospital and Medical Care for All Our People.* Raleigh: North Carolina Hospital and Medical Care Commission, 1947.

Powdermaker, Hortense. *After Freedom: A Cultural Study in the Deep South.* New York: Atheneum, 1939. Reprint, New York: Russell and Russell, 1966.

Powell, Adam Clayton, Jr. *Marching Blacks.* New York: Dial, 1945.

Powledge, Fred. *Free at Last?: The Civil Rights Movement and the People Who Made It.* Boston: Little, Brown, 1991.

Puckett, Newbell Niles. *Folk Beliefs of the Southern Negro.* Chapel Hill: University of North Carolina Press, 1926.

Rabinowitz, Howard. *Race Relations in the Urban South.* New York: Oxford University Press, 1978.

Raines, Howell. *My Soul Is Rested: Movement Days in the Deep South Remembered.* New York: G. P. Putnam's Sons, 1977.

Randall, Dudley, ed. *The Black Poets.* New York: Bantam Books, 1972.

Raper, Arthur F. *The Tragedy of Lynching.* 1933. Reprint, New York: Dover, 1970.

Raper, Arthur F., and Ira De A. Reid. *Sharecroppers All.* Chapel Hill: University of North Carolina Press, 1941.

Rawley, James A. *The Transatlantic Slave Trade: A History.* New York: W. W. Norton, 1981.

Redding, J. Saunders. *On Being Negro in America.* Indianapolis: Bobbs Merrill, 1951. Reprint, New York: Bantam, 1964.

Reitzes, Dietrich C. *Negroes and Medicine.* Cambridge: Harvard University Press, 1958.

Reynolds, P. Preston. "Hospital Expansion in the Era of Ultimatums: Historic Origins of the 'City of Medicine': Watts and Lincoln Hospitals, 1895–1966." Ph.D. diss., Duke University, 1984.

Rice, Mitchell F., and Woodrow Jones Jr., comps. *Health of Black Americans from Post Reconstruction to Integration, 1871–1960: An Annotated Bibliography of Contemporary Sources.* New York: Greenwood, 1990.

Rich, Adrienne. *What Is Found There: Notebooks on Poetry and Politics.* New York: W. W. Norton, 1993.

Richardson, Ben Albert, and William Fahey. *Great Black Americans.* New York: Crowell, 1976.

Robertson, James Oliver. *American Myth, American Reality.* New York: Hill and Wang, 1980.

Robinson, Henry S. "The M Street High School, 1891–1916." In *Records of the Columbia Historical Society of Washington, D.C.*, vol. 51. Charlottesville: University Press of Virginia, 1984.

Roman, Charles Victor. *Meharry Medical College: A History.* Nashville: Sunday School Publishing Board of the National Baptist Convention, 1934.

Rosengarten, Theodore, comp. *All God's Dangers: The Life of Nate Shaw.* New York: Random House, 1974. Reprint, New York: Vintage Books, 1989.

Rothe, Anna, ed. *Current Biography Who's News and Why 1944*. New York: H. W. Wilson, 1945.

Rothstein, William G. *American Medical Schools and the Practice of Medicine: A History*. New York: Oxford University Press, 1987.

Sampson, Calvin C. "Dispelling the Myth Surrounding Drew's Death." *JNMA* 76, no. 4 (1984): 415–18.

Samuel, Raphael, and Paul Thompson. *The Myths We Live By*. London and New York: Routledge, 1990.

Sandage, Scott A. "A Marble House Divided: The Lincoln Memorial, the Civil Rights Movement, and the Politics of Memory, 1939–1963." *Journal of American History* 80, no. 1 (June 1993): 135–67.

Sanders, Ronald. *Lost Tribes and Promised Lands: The Origins of American Racism*. Boston: Little, Brown, 1978. Reprint, New York: HarperPerennial, 1992.

Savitt, Todd L. "Abraham Flexner and the Black Medical Schools." In *Beyond Flexner: Medical Education in the Twentieth Century*, edited by Barbara Barzansky and Norman Gevitz. New York: Greenwood, 1992.

———. "The Education of Physicians at Shaw University, 1882–1918: Problems of Quality and Quantity." In *Black Americans in North Carolina and the South*, edited by Jeffrey Crow and Flora Hatley. Chapel Hill: University of North Carolina Press, 1984.

———. "Entering a White Profession: Black Physicians in the New South, 1880–1920." *Bulletin of the History of Medicine* 61, no. 4 (Winter 1987): 507–40.

———. "Herrick's 1910 Case Report of Sickle Cell Anemia: The Rest of the Story." *Journal of the American Medical Association* 261, no. 2 (13 January 1989): 266–71.

———. "The Invisible Malady: Sickle Cell Anemia in America: 1910–1970." *Journal of the National Medical Association* 73, no. 8 (1981): 739–46.

———. "Lincoln University Medical Department: A Forgotten Black Medical School." *Journal of the History of Medicine and Allied Sciences* 40 (1985): 42–65.

———. *Medicine and Slavery: The Diseases and Health Care of Blacks in Antebellum Virginia*. Urbana: University of Illinois Press, 1978.

———. "The Use of Blacks for Medical Experimentation and Demonstration in the Old South." *Journal of Southern History* 48 (1982): 331–48.

Sayers, James Denson. *Can the White Race Survive?* Washington, D.C.: Independent Publishing, 1929.

Schlesinger, Arthur M., Jr. *The Disuniting of America: Reflections on a Multi-Cultural Society*. New York: W. W. Norton, 1992.

Seham, Max. *Blacks and American Medical Care*. Minneapolis: University of Minnesota Press, 1973.

———. "Discrimination against Negroes in Hospitals." *New England Journal of Medicine* 271 (29 October 1964): 940–43.

Sellers, Charles Grier, Jr., ed. *The Southerner as American*. Chapel Hill: University of North Carolina Press, 1960.

Sernett, Milton C. *Afro-American Religious History: A Documentary Witness*. Durham: Duke University Press, 1985.

Shenkman, Richard. *Legends, Lies, and Cherished Myths of American History*. New York: William Morrow, 1988.

Sheridan, Richard B. "The Guinea Surgeons on the Middle Passage: The Provision of Medical Services in the British Slave Trade." *International Journal of African Historical Studies* 14, no. 4 (1981): 601–25.

Shibutani, Tamotsu. *Improvised News: A Sociological Study of Rumor.* Indianapolis: Bobbs-Merrill, 1966.

Shick, Tom W. "Race, Class, and Medicine: 'Bad Blood' in Twentieth-Century America." *Journal of Ethnic Studies* 10, no. 2 (Summer 1982): 97–105.

Shufeldt, Robert. *The Negro: A Menace to American Civilization.* Boston: Gorham Press, 1907.

Sickels, Robert J. *Race, Marriage and the Law.* Albuquerque: University of New Mexico Press, 1972.

Sitkoff, Harvard. *The Struggle for Black Equality, 1954–1992.* Rev. ed. New York: Hill and Wang, 1993.

Smead, Howard. *Blood Justice: The Lynching of Mack Charles Parker.* New York: Oxford University Press, 1986.

Smith, John David. *An Old Creed for the New South: Proslavery Ideology and Historiography, 1865–1918.* Athens: University of Georgia Press, 1991.

Smith, Lillian. *Killers of the Dream.* 1949. Reprint, New York: W. W. Norton, 1978.

———. *Now Is the Time.* New York: Dell, 1955.

———. *Our Faces, Our Words.* New York: W. W. Norton, 1964.

———. *Strange Fruit.* New York: Reyal and Hitchcock, 1944. Reprint, Athens: University of Georgia Press, 1985.

———. *The Winner Names the Age.* New York: W. W. Norton, 1978.

Sobel, Mechal. *The World They Made Together: Black and White Values in Eighteenth-Century Virginia.* Princeton: Princeton University Press, 1987.

Sowell, Thomas. *Black Education: Myths and Tragedies.* New York: David McKay, 1972.

Sparks, Allister. *The Mind of South Africa.* New York: Knopf, 1990.

Sprigle, Ray. *In the Land of Jim Crow.* New York: Simon and Schuster, 1949.

Stack, Carol B. *All Our Kin: Strategies for Survival in a Black Community.* New York: Harper and Row, 1974.

Stampp, Kenneth M. *The Peculiar Institution: Slavery in the Antebellum South.* New York: Vintage, 1956.

Stanton, William R. *The Leopard's Spots: Scientific Attitudes toward Race in America, 1815–1859.* Chicago: University of Chicago Press, 1960.

Starr, Paul. *The Social Transformation of American Medicine.* New York: Basic Books, 1982.

Steele, Shelby. *The Content of Our Character: A New Vision of Race in America.* New York: St. Martin's, 1990.

Sterling, Dorothy. *Tear Down the Walls: A History of the Civil Rights Movement.* Garden City, N.Y.: Doubleday, 1968.

Sterne, Emma Gelders. *Blood Brothers: Four Men of Science.* New York: Knopf, 1961.

Stevens, Rosemary. *American Medicine and the Public Interest.* New Haven: Yale University Press, 1971.

Stocking, George W., Jr. *Race, Culture and Evolution: Essays in the History of Anthropology.* New York: Free Press, 1968.

Stoddard, Lothrop. *The Rising Tide of Color Against White World-Supremacy.* New York: Scribner's, 1920.

Stuckey, Sterling. *Going Through the Storm: The Influence of African American Art in History.* New York: Oxford University Press, 1994.

———. *Slave Culture: Nationalist Theory and the Foundations of Black America.* New York: Oxford University Press, 1987.

———. "The Twilight of Our Past: Reflections on the Origins of Black History." In *Amistad 2*, edited by John A. Williams and Charles F. Harris. New York: Random House, 1971.

Summerville, James. *Educating Black Doctors: A History of Meharry Medical College.* University: University of Alabama Press, 1983.

Takaki, Ronald. *A Different Mirror: A History of Multicultural America.* Boston: Little, Brown, 1993.

Talmadge, Katherine S. *The Life of Charles Drew.* Frederick, Md.: Twenty-First Century Books, 1992.

Taylor, Julius N., ed. *The Negro in Science.* Baltimore: Morgan State College Press, 1955.

Taylor, William R. *Cavalier and Yankee: The Old South and American National Character.* New York: George Braziller, 1951.

Terkel, Studs. *Race: How Blacks and Whites Think and Feel about the American Obsession.* New York: New Press, 1992.

Terrill, Tom E., and Jerrold Hirsch, eds. *Such As Us: Southern Voices of the Thirties.* Chapel Hill: University of North Carolina Press, 1978.

Thelen, David. "Memory and American History." *Journal of American History* 75, no. 4 (March 1989): 1117–29.

Thomas, Vivien T. *Pioneering Research in Surgical Shock and Cardiovascular Surgery: Vivien Thomas and His Work with Alfred Blalock: An Autobiography.* Philadelphia: University of Pennsylvania Press, 1985.

Thompson, E. P. *The Making of the English Working Class.* New York: Pantheon, 1963. Reprint, Harmondsworth: Penguin, 1968.

Thompson, Paul. *The Voice of the Past: Oral History.* 2d ed. New York: Oxford University Press, 1988.

Thompson, Robert Farris. *Flash of the Spirit: African and Afro-American Art and Philosophy.* New York: Random House, 1983.

Thurman, Howard. *Jesus and the Disinherited.* New York and Nashville: Abingdon-Cokesbury Press, 1949.

———. *The Luminous Darkness: A Personal Interpretation of the Anatomy of Segregation and the Ground of Hope.* Richmond, Ind.: Friends United Press, 1965.

Tindall, George B. *The Emergence of the New South, 1913–1945.* Baton Rouge: Louisiana State University Press, 1967.

———. "Mythology: A New Frontier in Southern History." In *The Idea of the South: Pursuit of a Central Theme*, edited by Frank E. Vandiver. Chicago: University of Chicago Press, 1964.

Titmuss, Richard M. *The Gift Relationship: From Human Blood to Social Policy.* New York: Pantheon, 1971.

Tonkin, Elizabeth. "History and the Myth of Realism." In *The Myths We Live By*, edited by Raphael Samuel and Paul Thompson. London and New York: Routledge, 1990.

Trelease, Allen W. *White Terror: The Ku Klux Klan Conspiracy and Southern Reconstruction*. New York: Harper and Row, 1971.

Turnbull, Colin M. *The Forest People*. New York: Simon and Schuster, 1961; Touchstone, 1968.

Turner, Patricia A. *I Heard It through the Grapevine: Rumor in African-American Culture*. Berkeley: University of California Press, 1993.

Van Deburg, William L. *New Day in Babylon: The Black Power Movement and American Culture, 1965–1975*. Chicago: University of Chicago Press, 1992.

Vansina, Jan. *Oral Tradition as History*. Madison: University of Wisconsin Press, 1985.

Ventura, Michael. *Shadow Dancing in the U.S.A.* Los Angeles: Jeremy P. Tarcher, 1985.

Wade, Harold, Jr. *Black Men of Amherst*. Amherst, Mass.: Amherst College Press, 1976.

Walker, Alice. "Elethia." In *You Can't Keep a Good Woman Down*, 27–30. New York: Harcourt Brace Jovanovich, 1981.

———. *Meridian*. New York: Washington Square Press, 1977.

———, ed. *I Love Myself When I Am Laughing . . . A Zora Neale Hurston Reader*. Old Westbury, N.Y.: Feminist Press, 1970.

Warner, John Harley. "The Selective Transport of Medical Knowledge: Antebellum American Physicians and Parisian Medical Therapeutics." *Bulletin of the History of Medicine* 59 (1985): 213–31.

———. "Southern Medical Reform." In *Science and Medicine in the Old South*, edited by Ronald L. Numbers and Todd L. Savitt. Baton Rouge: Louisiana State University Press, 1989.

———. *The Therapeutic Perspective: Medical Practice, Knowledge, and Identity in America, 1820–1885*. Cambridge: Harvard University Press, 1986.

Warren, Robert Penn. *Segregation: The Inner Conflict in the South*. New York: Random House, 1956.

Washington, Booker T. *Up from Slavery*. 1901. Reprint, New York: Penguin, 1986.

Watt, Charles D., and Frank W. Scott. "Lincoln Hospital, Durham, N.C." *JNMA* 57, no. 2 (March 1965): 177–83.

Waynick, Capus M., John C. Brooks, and Elsie W. Pitts, eds. *North Carolina and the Negro*. Raleigh: North Carolina Mayors' Co-operating Committee, 1964.

Weare, Walter B. *Black Business in the New South: A Social History of the North Carolina Mutual Life Insurance Company*. Urbana: University of Illinois Press, 1973.

Weinstein, Allen, and Frank Otto Gatell. *The Segregation Era, 1863–1954: A Modern Reader*. New York: Oxford University Press, 1970.

Weisbrot, Robert. *Freedom Bound: A History of America's Civil Rights Movement*. New York: W. W. Norton, 1990.

Weiss, Nancy J. *Farewell to the Party of Lincoln: Black Politics in the Age of FDR*. Princeton: Princeton University Press, 1983.

———. *Whitney M. Young, Jr., and the Struggle for Civil Rights*. Princeton: Princeton University Press, 1989.

Wells, Ida B. *On Lynchings: Southern Horrors; A Red Record; Mob Rule in New Orleans*. 3 vols. 1892, 1895, 1900. Reprint (3 vols. in 1), New York: Arno Press, 1969.

Welty, Eudora. *The Collected Stories of Eudora Welty.* New York: Harcourt Brace
   Jovanovich, 1980.
West, Cornell. *Race Matters.* Boston: Beacon Press, 1993.
Whitaker, Walter A. *Centennial History of Alamance County.* Burlington:
   Burlington Chamber of Commerce, 1949.
White, Frank Hollowell. "The Economic and Social Development of Negroes in
   North Carolina since 1900." Ph.D. diss., New York University, 1960.
White, Walter. *The Fire in the Flint.* New York: Knopf, 1924.
———. *A Man Called White.* New York: Viking, 1948.
———. *A Rising Wind.* Garden City, N.Y.: Doubleday, Doran, 1945.
———. *Rope and Faggot: A Biography of Judge Lynch.* New York: Knopf, 1929.
Williams, Brett. *John Henry: A Bio-Bibliography.* Westport, Conn.: Greenwood,
   1983.
Williams, George Washington. *History of the Negro in America from 1619 to 1880:
   Negroes as Slaves, as Soldiers, and as Citizens.* 2 vols. New York: G. P. Putnam's
   Sons, 1882, 1883.
Williams, John A., and Charles F. Harris, eds. *Amistad 1.* New York: Random
   House, 1970.
———. *Amistad 2.* New York: Random House, 1971.
Williamson, Joel. *The Crucible of Race: Black-White Relations in the American South
   since Emancipation.* New York: Oxford University Press, 1984.
———, ed. *The Origins of Segregation.* Boston: D. C. Heath, 1968.
Wilson, Charles Reagan. *Baptized in Blood: The Religion of the Lost Cause, 1865–
   1920.* Athens: University of Georgia Press, 1980.
Wilson, Emily Herring. *Hope and Dignity: Older Black Women of the South.*
   Philadelphia: Temple University Press, 1983.
Wilson, Ruth Danenhower. *Jim Crow Joins Up: A Study of Negroes in the Armed Forces
   of the United States.* New York: William J. Clark, 1944.
Wolseley, Roland E. *The Black Press, U.S.A.* Ames: Iowa State University Press,
   1971.
Wood, Peter H. *Black Majority: Negroes in Colonial South Carolina from 1670
   through the Stono Rebellion.* New York: W. W. Norton, 1974.
———. " 'I Did the Best I Could for My Day': The Study of Early Black History
   during the Second Reconstruction, 1960 to 1976." *William and Mary
   Quarterly,* 3d ser., 35, no. 2 (April 1978): 185–225.
Woodward, C. Vann. *American Counterpoint: Slavery and Racism in the North-South
   Dialogue.* Boston: Little, Brown, 1971.
———. "From the First Reconstruction to the Second." In *The South Today: 100
   Years after Appomattox,* edited by Willie Morris. New York: Harper and Row,
   1965.
———. *Origins of the New South, 1877–1913.* Enl. ed. Baton Rouge: Louisiana
   State University Press, 1971.
———. "The Search for Southern Identity." In *The Burden of Southern History.*
   Baton Rouge: Louisiana State University Press, 1968.
———. *The Strange Career of Jim Crow.* 3d rev. ed. New York: Oxford University
   Press, 1974.
Wright, Richard. *Black Boy.* New York: Harper and Row, 1945. Reprint, New
   York: HarperCollins, 1992.

———. "Bright and Morning Star." In *American Negro Short Stories*, edited by John Henrik Clarke, 75–108. New York: Hill and Wang, 1966.

Wynes, Charles. *Charles Richard Drew: The Man and the Myth*. Urbana: University of Illinois Press, 1988.

Wynn, Neil A. *The Afro-American and the Second World War*. New York: Holmes and Meier, 1975.

X, Malcolm, with the assistance of Alex Haley. *The Autobiography of Malcolm X*. New York: Grove, 1965.

Yancey, Asa, Sr. "U.S. Postage Stamp in Honor of Charles R. Drew, M.D., MDSc." *JNMA* 74, no. 6 (1982): 561–65.

Young, Whitney. "Civil Rights Action and the Urban League." In *Assuring Freedom to the Free*, edited by Arnold Rose. Detroit: Wayne State University Press, 1964.

———. *To Be Equal*. New York: McGraw Hill, 1964.

Yount, Lisa. *Black Scientists*. New York: Facts on File, 1991.

Zinn, Howard. "The South as a Mirror." In *The Southern Mystique*. New York: Knopf, 1964.

Index

childhood, 230, 231, 245–46; in
World War II, 246–47; marriage,
247; education, 247, 330 (n. 77);
funeral of, 249–50, 255
Avery, Nannie Bell Jackson, 247, 250
Avery, Napoleon, 229–30, 231, 232,
245, 250
Avery, Parnell: childhood, 231, 232,
245, 246; education, 247, 254; and
brother's death, 248, 249, 250,
253–54, 255, 256–57; as physician, 254
Avery, Regina, 247, 254
Avery, Waddell: childhood, 231, 232,
245, 246–47; education, 247, 327–
28 (n. 40); and brother's death,
248, 249, 250, 252, 253, 255; military service, 249, 250, 252–53; as
hospital administrator, 253

Baldwin, James, 42, 263–66
Baltimore, Md., segregation in, 194,
318 (n. 48)
Baltimore Afro-American, 38, 222
Barnett, Claude A., 203
Barton, Clara, 204
Beardsley, Edward, 46
Beattie, John, 115, 116, 145, 146
Bertol, Roland, 201
Bethel Literary and Historical Associ-
ation, 101
Bethune, Mary McLeod, 30
Bible, 72–73
Bilbo, Theodore G., 72, 158, 285
(n. 73), 306–7 (n. 69)
Bims, Hamilton, 86–87
Bing, Hazel Robena. *See* Avery, Hazel
Robena Bing
Birmingham, Ala., 71–72, 76
Black folklore and culture, 58–60;
Drew legend in, 5, 33, 34, 43,
55, 57, 60, 68, 69, 73, 83, 92,
261; rumors in, 33–34, 39–40,
60; victim archetype, 43, 68; and
American history, 59, 263–64;
Christianity and, 61, 62, 72; blood

symbolism in, 61–63, 68, 69–72,
186–87; and civil rights movement, 62, 73; slave narratives, 62–
63; "night doctors," 63, 64, 68, 283
(n. 54); mistrust of physicians and
hospitals, 64, 65, 67, 68
Black physicians: segregated hospitals
and, 16, 45, 47, 112, 121, 163; professional organizations and, 16,
163, 167, 169–71; education and
training of, 45, 112, 119–20, 121,
294 (nn. 72, 75); and medical care
for black patients, 47, 157, 172;
and Drew legend, 53–54, 82; in
armed forces, 157–58; Drew as
leader for, 161, 162, 167–68, 169,
170–72
Black Power movement, 82
Blacks: mistreatment by medical
system, 6, 44–45, 47–48, 67, 225,
227; segregated motels and, 15,
261; exclusion from blood programs, 16–17, 49, 140–41, 155–
56, 194, 195, 300 (n. 4), 304–5
(n. 47); segregated hospitals and,
25, 37, 46–49, 75, 88, 219–20,
221, 227–29; and social effects of
World War II, 39, 40, 41–42, 184–
85, 189, 196–97; soldiers in World
War II, 39, 196, 197, 314 (n. 3),
319 (n. 56); and Drew legend, 40,
42, 43, 44, 49, 51, 52–54, 82, 85–
86, 87, 88–89, 92, 262; middle
class, 40, 86, 87, 100–101; in racist
medical theories, 45, 64, 65–66,
190–93, 282 (n. 47), 314 (n. 4);
disease and mortality rates, 45–46,
63, 172–73, 191, 276 (n. 44), 317
(n. 33); lack of hospital beds for,
47, 173, 221, 227–29; and civil
rights movement, 54, 73, 76; and
American history, 60, 71, 78, 176–
77, 262, 263–65, 266; and Christianity, 61, 62, 72; soldiers in Civil
War, 63; mistrust of physicians and
hospitals, 64, 65–66, 67, 68, 281

(n. 35); medical experimentation
on, 64, 66, 68–69, 186, 281
(n. 35); and grave robbing, 64–65;
reluctance to donate blood, 68,
92–93, 211, 284 (n. 58); killed in
racial violence, 73, 76, 77, 185;
Washington D.C. community, 100–
102; at Amherst College, 111, 292
(n. 50); establishment of blood
donor program and, 144, 194, 211;
white supremacist mythology and,
185, 189–94, 196, 263; protests
against blood segregation, 187–89,
198, 210

Black surgeons, 15, 121, 125, 168,
169

Blood banks: Drew's doctoral dissertation on, 16, 125, 143; New York
pilot program, 16, 140–41, 142,
143–44, 148–49, 206, 207, 299
(n. 1); exclusion of blacks, 16–17,
49, 140–41, 155–56, 194, 195, 300
(n. 4), 304–5 (n. 47); Drew legend
and, 49–50, 197–99, 202–7;
blacks' reluctance to donate, 68,
92–93, 211, 284 (n. 58); white
fears of blood mixing, 89, 150,
156, 189–90, 193–94; Drew's
research on, 115–16, 124–25,
143–45, 147–48, 199, 205, 301
(n. 19), 302 (n. 24); initial development of, 141–43, 144, 301
(n. 9); plasma research and, 142,
143, 147, 148–49; recruitment of
donors, 187; white racism and,
194–96. *See also* Blood segregation

Blood for Britain project: Drew as
medical director, 16, 140, 141,
143–44, 146–47; establishment of,
144–46, 207; Drew's report on,
147–48, 151, 302–3 (n. 27)

Blood segregation: armed forces and,
16–17, 155, 157, 189, 195–96, 210,
211; Drew's leadership in blood
program and, 17, 49–50, 98, 139–
40, 198; Drew's objections to, 49,

150, 152, 155–56, 157, 158–59,
185–86, 197; Red Cross and, 49–
50, 98, 141, 155, 185–86, 188–89,
194–96, 197, 209–10, 211–12, 300
(n. 4), 324 (n. 111); and Drew
legend, 140, 152, 185–86, 196,
197, 199–201, 202, 209, 211, 213;
absence of scientific basis for,
156, 159, 189, 195; black protests
against, 187–89, 198, 210

Blood symbolism: Christianity and,
61, 62, 72–73, 184; Drew legend
and, 61, 89, 92–93, 186, 187, 190;
black folklore and, 61–63, 68,
69–72, 186–87; civil rights movement and, 62, 71–72, 73; and medical care, 63, 66, 68, 69, 186, 190;
white racism and, 156, 183–84,
185, 189–91, 193–94, 314 (n. 4);
World War II and, 183–84, 189;
Red Cross and, 187, 189

Blood Transfusion Betterment Association, 144–45, 146

Bonham, Howard, 203

Braudel, Fernand, 260

British Red Cross, 144, 146

Brooks, Lester, 75

Brooks, Ralph, 20, 21, 22, 82

Brooks, Walter, 102, 291 (n. 32)

Brown, Ivan, 21

Brown v. Board of Education, 42–43,
75

Buck, Pearl S., 30

Buckingham, Clyde E.: monograph
on Drew, 80, 81, 147, 148, 205–6;
on Drew legend, 198–99, 212

Bullock, Samuel, 14, 15, 25–26; in
automobile accident with Drew, 17,
18–19, 23; on Drew's hospital treatment, 24, 38, 86–87; and Drew
legend, 53, 271 (n. 6)

Burlington, N.C., 225

Burrell, Emma, 98

Burrell, Joseph, 98, 290 (n. 26)

Bush, John, 140, 145, 146

107–9, 113, 292–93 (n. 64); ambition and competitiveness, 104, 105, 165; personal magnetism and charm, 104, 106–7, 114, 123, 143, 154, 174, 178, 180–81; self-confidence, 105, 153–54; effects of racism on, 109–11, 178, 261; responses to racism, 111, 153, 156–57, 172, 175–76, 177–78, 196, 197, 214, 306 (n. 53); views on racial prejudice and progress, 111, 156–59, 174–76, 177–78; devotion to work, 164; family life, 164–65; teaching ability, 165
—legend of: origin as rumors, 1–2, 31, 34–39, 51; Drew biographies and, 2; Whitney Young's publication of, 2, 31, 38, 58, 73–75, 76, 78, 204, 320 (n. 65); persistence despite debunkings, 3, 31–32, 51–52, 81–82, 86–91, 92; reflection of historical truth, 4–5, 6–7, 32, 36, 37, 44, 49, 88, 93, 225, 251, 260–62; and white racism, 5, 6, 60, 68, 97, 196, 208, 213–14; and segregation, 5, 6–7, 32, 44, 47, 92, 251, 261; in black folk culture, 5, 33, 34, 43, 55, 57, 60, 68, 69, 73, 83, 92, 261; and segregated medical care, 6–7, 8, 44, 47, 49, 52, 60, 75, 227, 252; newspapers and, 7, 37–38, 43, 79–80, 197; Drew as archetypal hero and, 7, 43, 97–98; Maltheus Avery's role in, 8, 217–18, 224–27, 251, 259, 260, 265; Red Cross's efforts to refute, 31, 80–81, 141, 185–86, 202–6, 207, 208–13, 214, 321 (n. 78); spread of, 33, 52–53, 54, 58; psychology of rumors and, 39–41, 42, 43, 51–52, 54–55; blacks and, 40, 42, 43, 44, 49, 51, 52–54, 82, 85–86, 87, 88–89, 92, 262; black physicians and, 53–54, 82; civil rights movement and, 54, 60–61, 73, 76, 82; Dick Gregory on, 57–

58; in mainstream American history, 61, 77–79, 81–82, 89–90; blood symbolism and, 61, 89, 92–93, 186, 187, 190; Bessie Smith legend and, 69; assassination of Martin Luther King and, 77, 78–79; Buckingham monograph and, 80, 81, 205–6; Black Power movement and, 82–83; Duke Hospital in, 86–88; and black reluctance to donate blood, 92–93; six component legends in, 185, 186, 204, 211, 213–14; "Drew as victim" legend, 185, 190, 202, 213–14; "Drew as blood pioneer" legend, 185, 197, 198–99, 213, 320 (nn. 65, 66); "Drew as angry prophet of truth" legend, 185, 199–202, 211, 213; "not a savior" counter-legend, 185, 202–9; "Red Cross humanitarianism" counter-legend, 185, 209–12; "no mistreatment" counter-legend, 185–86, 212–13

Drew, Charles Richard, Jr. (son), 164
Drew, Elsie (sister), 102
Drew, Eva. *See* Pennington, Eva Drew
Drew, Joseph (brother), 27, 28, 98, 99, 105, 116
Drew, Lenore Robbins (wife), 15, 82; marriage to Charles Drew, 16, 122, 123; and Drew's death, 22, 27, 28; and Drew legend, 79; Drew's letters to, 103, 122, 123–24, 149, 150, 151–52, 153, 174, 304 (n. 44), 312 (n. 59); on Drew's personality, 106–7, 123, 165, 168; tensions in marriage, 123, 151, 152, 154, 304 (n. 44); children born to, 123, 164
Drew, Nora (sister). *See* Gregory, Nora Drew
Drew, Nora Rosella Burrell (mother), 98–100, 101, 102, 290 (n. 26); closeness to son, 103; Drew's correspondence with, 149, 152, 291 (n. 40), 297–98 (n. 108), 299 (n. 117)

Memorial Hospital of Alamance
County, 82
Miami Herald, 79–80
Middle-class blacks, 40, 86, 87,
100–101
Mississippi, segregation in, 69
Mitchell, Gilberta, 37, 90, 272
(nn. 21, 27)
Montagu, Ashley, 186
Montell, William, 58
Montgomery bus boycott, 43, 56
Morais, Herbert, 48
Morris, Viola Covington, 19, 27, 37
Morris, Washington Irving, 19, 37
Morrison, Toni, 282–83 (n. 50)
Mudd, Stuart, 142
Murray, Peter M., 29
Myrdal, Gunnar, 177
Myths: history and, 2, 8–9, 260, 261;
in white culture, 213, 261–63, 264,
265

Nation, 87
National Association for the Advance-
ment of Colored People (NAACP):
awards Spingarn Medal to Drew,
50, 158–59, 161, 197, 198, 307
(n. 71); Legal Defense Fund, 75;
Washington branch, 101; and Red
Cross blood segregation policy, 155
National Committee on Segregation
in the Nation's Capital, 173
National Humane League, 193
National Medical Association, 169
National Research Council, 145, 148,
301 (n. 18)
National Rural Health Program, 253
National Urban League, 74
Nevins, Allan, 4
Newhouser, Lloyd R., 145
New South myth, 264
Newspapers: and Drew legend, 7,
37–38, 43, 79–80, 197; and Drew's
death, 26, 30, 37, 38, 43–44, 221,
226; and Avery's death, 220–22
New York, N.Y.: Red Cross pilot pro-

gram, 16, 140–41, 142, 143–44,
148–49, 206, 207, 299 (n. 1);
grave robbing in, 65; blood trans-
fusion service, 144; blood segrega-
tion policy in, 194
New York Academy of Medicine, 145
New York Daily Worker, 49–50
New York PM Daily, 50
New York Red Cross, 146
New York Times, 90, 209, 320 (n. 66)
"Night doctors," 63, 64, 68, 283
(n. 54)
Nineteenth Street Baptist Church
(Washington), 102
Nixon, Richard M., 77
North Carolina: segregation in, 17,
88, 221, 222; State Highway Com-
mission, 26–27, 90
North Carolina A&T College, 222,
224
Nott, Josiah Clark, 191

O'Connor, Basil, 195
Odum, Howard W., 39
Omega Psi Phi, 89, 90, 91, 252, 328
(n. 40)
Oral history, 4, 5–6, 270 (n. 12)

Parker, Rainey, 20
Parks, Rosa, 179
Patterson, F. D., 155
Pennington, Eva Drew (sister), 29,
44, 75, 104
Pennix, Alvis, 272 (n. 27)
Pennix, Esther, 25
Pennix, John, 26–27
Philadelphia, Miss., 76
Philadelphia, Pa.: grave robbing in,
65; blood segregation policy in,
194
Phillips, Homer G., 89, 287–88
(n. 135)
Physicians: treatment of black
patients, 45, 64, 66, 192–93, 281
(n. 35), 282 (n. 47); in black folk-
lore, 63, 68; propagation of white

superiority myths, 65–66, 190,
191–92. *See also* Black physicians
Pittsburgh Courier, 43
Plantation legend, 263
Pleasant Grove, N.C., 17, 22, 41, 91,
272 (n. 21)
Plessy v. Ferguson (1896), 100
Pope, Fred Eugene, 218
Porter, F. Ross, 224
Postman, Leo, 40, 42, 51, 52, 55
Presbyterian Hospital (New York):
treatment of black patients, 120–
21, 298 (n. 111); Drew's residency
at, 121; experimental blood bank,
143, 146
Price, Bebe Roberta Drew (daugh-
ter), 28, 123, 164

Quander, Betty, 34–35
Quick, C. Mason: and Drew legend,
3, 38, 53, 88, 271 (n. 6); and
Drew's death, 23, 25–26; friendship with Drew, 23, 88

Racial violence, 76–77, 185
Racism: Drew legend and, 5, 6, 60,
68, 97, 196, 208, 213–14; in medical care system, 8, 44, 60; Drew's
encounters with, 44, 49–50, 98,
109–11, 118, 140–41, 292–93
(n. 64); Red Cross and, 49, 140–
41, 185, 194–96, 212–13; effects
on Drew, 109–11, 178, 261; Drew's
responses to, 111, 153, 156–57,
172, 175–76, 177–78, 196, 197,
214, 306 (n. 53); and blood symbolism, 183–84, 189–90, 193–94;
World War II and, 183–85, 189,
319 (n. 56); physicians and, 190–
91, 192–93
Raleigh News and Observer, 221
Randolph, A. Philip, 278–79 (n. 3)
Rankin, John, 50, 194–95
Rape, 192
Rape myth, 263
Reconstruction legend, 263

Rector, Bus, 27
Red Cross. *See* American Red Cross
Redding, J. Saunders, 176–77
Redeemer myth, 263
Redhead, Chester, 35
Reichel, John, 142
Rhoads, C. P., 148, 207
Robertson, O. H., 141
Robinson, G. Canby, 195, 203
Rockefeller Foundation, 118
Rodman, Stuart, 154
Roosevelt, Eleanor, 30, 188
Roosevelt, Franklin D., 188, 299–300
(n. 2)
Rosenwald Fund, 46, 116
Ross, Marshall, 29
Rumors: in black culture, 33–34,
39–40, 60; distinguished from leg-
ends, 33–34, 55; World War II and,
39, 40; psychology of, 39, 40, 41,
42, 52, 54, 55

St. Hill, Ira A., 322 (n. 93)
Saturday Evening Post, 107–8
School desegregation, 42–43, 275
(n. 38)
Scudder, John, 29; Drew's blood
research with, 120, 121, 124, 143,
147, 197–98, 297–98 (n. 108); on
Drew's talent, 143; in Blood for
Britain project, 144–45, 146, 150,
302 (n. 24); Drew's relations with,
149, 150, 151, 303–4 (n. 38), 304
(nn. 39, 40); and blood segregation policy, 150; Drew's letters to,
169, 198
Segregation, 232, 245, 256; Drew
legend and, 5, 6–7, 32, 44, 47, 92,
251, 261; Washington antidiscrimi-
nation laws, 13–14, 270–71 (n. 3);
in North Carolina, 17, 88, 221,
222; World War II and, 39, 41, 42;
school desegregation, 42–43, 275
(n. 38); Christianity and, 72; in
Washington, 99, 100, 162, 173,
308 (n. 3); in armed forces, 157–